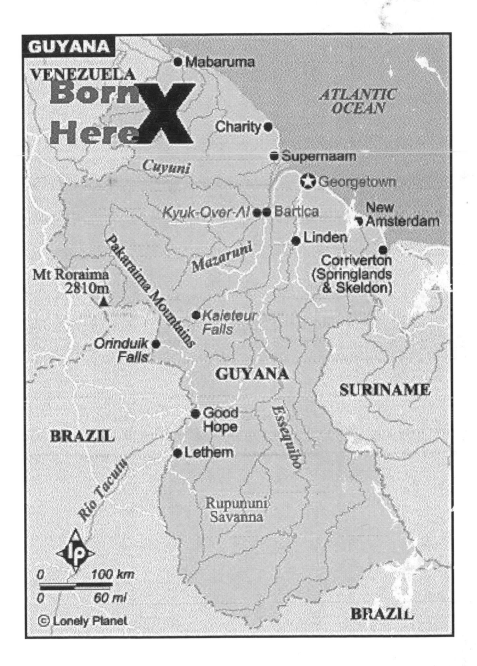

GUYANA

VENEZUELA

**Born Here** X

ATLANTIC OCEAN

● Mabaruma

Charity ●

● Supernaam

⊛ Georgetown

*Cuyuni*

Kyuk-Over-Al ●● Bartica

New Amsterdam

● Linden

Corriverton (Springlands & Skeldon)

*Mazaruni*

*Pakaraima Mountains*

Mt Roraima 2810m ▲

● Kaieteur Falls

Orinduik Falls ●

GUYANA

SURINAME

● Good Hope

*Essequibo*

BRAZIL

● Lethem

*Rio Tacutu*

Rupununi Savanna

0    100 km
0    60 ml

© Lonely Planet

BRAZIL

# WALK WIT' ME...

## All Ova Guyana

_To Ahalia_
_Many thanks for your support_
_hope you will enjoy the journey._
_Best wishes_
_Helena Martin_

_13th July 2014_

### HELENA MARTIN

**BALBOA.**
PRESS
A DIVISION OF HAY HOUSE

Balboa Press books may be ordered through booksellers or by contacting:

Balboa Press
A Division of Hay House
1663 Liberty Drive
Bloomington, IN 47403
www.balboapress.com.au
1-(877) 407-4847

ISBN: 978-1-4525-0309-7 (sc)
ISBN: 978-1-4525-0310-3 (e)

Printed in the United States of America

Balboa Press rev. date: 10/27/2011

*For*
*My late mother Carmen DaSilva,*
*my late mother-in-law Carmen Martin*
*And*
*My children Sabrina, Andrew, Tanya and Tracey*

# CONTENTS

ACKNOWLEDGEMENTS                                    xix

CHAPTER ONE

Walk Wit' Me—All Ova Guyana                            1

   1.  How It All Started                               2
   2.  Not Ghana, It Is Guyana                          2
   3.  A Proud Mud-head                                 3
   4.  My Brush with Fame                               4
   5.  Where Is Guyana?                                 5
   6.  The Pomeroon River                               6
   7.  My Parents' History                              6
   8.  My Father's Single Life                          7
   9.  My Mother's Single Life                          7
 10.  What Is Buck-Sick?                              10

CHAPTER TWO

1947 Jacklow, Pomeroon River                          13

   1.  Where It All Began                              13
   2.  My Earliest Memories                            15
   3.  My First Home                                   15
   4.  Primitive Plumbing                              18
   5.  A Baby Out Of the Blue                          19
   6.  The Backdam Crèche                              20
   7.  Visiting My Grandparents at Siriki              21
   8.  Action on the River                             22
   9.  The Boogie Men                                  23

| 10. | The Garrets | 23 |
| 11. | My First Funeral | 25 |
| 12. | My First East Indian Wedding | 26 |
| 13. | My First Dolly | 27 |
| 14. | My Grandfather Ol' Joe | 27 |
| 15. | The Unique Fowler Engine | 28 |
| 16. | Legal Trafficking | 29 |
| 17. | My Grandparents' Neighbours | 30 |
| 18. | Sunday-school On Saturday | 32 |
| 19. | Meeting My Great-grandmother Caroline | 32 |
| 20. | My Special Cousin | 34 |
| 21. | Farewell to Daphne and the Pomeroon | 35 |

## CHAPTER THREE

### 1952-55 Rupununi     37

| 1. | The Giant Silver Duck | 37 |
| 2. | Our Homestead | 39 |
| 3. | Living behind God's Back | 41 |
| 4. | Our Bizarre Playground and Zoo | 42 |
| 5. | Nature's Playstation | 43 |
| 6. | Pets We Acquired | 44 |
| 7. | Dangers We Encountered | 45 |
| 8. | The Faithful Dova | 46 |
| 9. | Mummy Cures 'Pip' | 48 |
| 10. | Branding the Cattle | 49 |
| 11. | Our Beautiful Horses | 50 |
| 12. | The Chigga (chigger) Plague | 51 |
| 13. | Another Embarrassing Experience | 51 |
| 14. | Bush Tucker | 53 |
| 15. | Buckman Food | 55 |
| 16. | The Ita Palm | 56 |
| 17. | Liquor Made By the Amerindians | 57 |
| 18. | Undiscovered Star | 58 |
| 19. | The Hart's And the Melville's | 60 |
| 20. | Growing Tobacco | 61 |
| 21. | Licks like Peas | 62 |
| 22. | Faddah C'ris'mus Is Dead | 63 |

23. Psychic Abilities ........................................ 64
24. School in the Savannah .............................. 64
25. Allergic To Kabaura Flies ........................... 65
26. Disaster Strikes Our Family ........................ 65
27. The Straw That Broke the Camel's back ........ 66

## CHAPTER FOUR

### 1955–99 La Penitence Street ........................ 69

1. Flying in a Morgue ................................... 69
2. A Year Lived In a Nightmare ...................... 71
3. De Black People School ............................ 71
4. Beauty and de Beast (a.k.a—Jekyll and Hyde) .. 72
5. Rescued By a Martin—Twice ...................... 73
6. De Coo-Coo Kid ..................................... 75
7. Absolute Stupidity ................................... 76
8. Teacher versus Vendor .............................. 77
9. Greed and Diarrhoea Goes Hand In Hand ...... 78
10. Mafia Censoring ..................................... 78
11. Memories of Uncle Deck and a Fudgicle ........ 79
12. The Secret Is Finally Out! .......................... 80

## CHAPTER FIVE

### 1956—Callendar Street ............................. 81

1. Living on Coconut Walk ............................ 81
2. A Corrupt Address ................................... 83
3. The Family Servant ................................... 84
4. Going To Old/Small School ....................... 86
5. Reunited At Last ..................................... 86
6. Donkeys Go To Heaven ............................. 87
7. Slates and Other Treasures ......................... 87
8. Rules and Embarrassment .......................... 89
9. Bata versus Yaatin' Boots .......................... 91
10. Picking Lice .......................................... 92
11. My African Coiffure ................................ 93
12. Homemade Coffins .................................. 94
13. Our Personal Dressmaker ......................... 95

| | | |
|---|---|---|
| 14. | A Mystery Cousin | 96 |
| 15. | Picked Up By the Police | 97 |
| 16. | Hidden Memories at X Durban Street | 98 |
| 17. | Corner Store Establishments | 99 |
| 18. | Cumfa Dancin' and Other Spirits | 102 |
| 19. | Anti-men on Punt Trench Dam | 104 |
| 20. | The Walking Telegram | 105 |
| 21. | My First Sexual Encounter | 105 |
| 22. | Cousins in St Ann's Orphanage | 106 |
| 23. | Watching the Punts | 107 |
| 24. | Charlie Has an Accident | 109 |
| 25. | Mercy Dash on Mota-bike | 109 |
| 26. | Haffa 'an' Charlie | 111 |
| 27. | Brown Betty and Window Shopping | 112 |
| 28. | Bezette the Belching King | 113 |
| 29. | Motor Racing at Atkinson Base | 114 |
| 30. | Churned Homemade Ice-cream | 114 |

## CHAPTER SIX

### 1957–58 Middle Road, La Penitence

| | 1957–58 Middle Road, La Penitence | 117 |
|---|---|---|
| 1. | Daddy Says Goodbye to Rupununi | 117 |
| 2. | The Goblin Landlord | 118 |
| 3. | No Plumbing Here | 119 |
| 4. | Our Adopted Uncle and Auntie | 120 |
| 5. | Frangipani Memories | 122 |
| 6. | Bowjie and Jumbie Spirit | 122 |
| 7. | Market Vendors | 123 |
| 8. | Making Pointa (pointer) Brooms | 125 |
| 9. | Pointa (pointer) Broom Commercial | 126 |
| 10. | The Ol' Higue Myth | 128 |
| 11. | Superstition and Ol' Wives Tales | 129 |
| 12. | Hitching a Ride on a Jackass Cyart | 131 |
| 13. | The Backdam Was Forbidden Territory | 133 |
| 14. | Roasted Spurwing | 134 |
| 15. | Keeping Cows in the Backyard | 135 |
| 16. | Kissing the Wicked Witch | 135 |
| 17. | The Calabash Cut | 136 |

| | | |
|---|---|---|
| 18. | Bottom-'ouse Activities | 137 |
| 19. | Money Making Scam | 139 |
| 20. | De T'eatah-'ouse was Popular | 139 |
| 21. | The Big Fight at Crossroad | 141 |
| 22. | Beuzin' Was Great Entertainment | 142 |
| 23. | The Window Was Our Cinema | 144 |
| 24. | Times Had Changed | 144 |

## CHAPTER SEVEN

### 1958 James Street, Albouystown — 147

| | | |
|---|---|---|
| 1. | Eavesdropping Heaven | 147 |
| 2. | Our Butcher Arthur | 148 |
| 3. | Live Chickens Equals Feather Pillow | 150 |
| 4. | Mummy Sets Up Shop | 150 |
| 5. | Ogling the Dead | 152 |
| 6. | Wedding Proposal from Lot 12 | 153 |
| 7. | The Nook | 154 |
| 8. | A Melting Pot | 154 |
| 9. | The Guyanese Vernacular | 156 |
| 10. | Incorrect Pronunciation | 157 |
| 11. | Understanding Our Patois | 157 |
| 12. | Emphasis and Double Meaning | 159 |
| 13. | Normal Guyanese Customs | 160 |
| 14. | Characteristics and Obversation of the Races | 161 |
| 15. | The Circus and Coney Island Comes To British Guiana | 167 |
| 16. | Visiting my Great Aunt Victorine | 168 |
| 17. | Ignorance in the Highest Degree | 169 |
| 18. | Titi Means Aunty and Mac-may Is More Complicated | 170 |
| 19. | Time to Shut Up Shop | 171 |

## CHAPTER EIGHT

### 1958–59 Sussex & Bel Air Streets — 173

| | | |
|---|---|---|
| 1. | Flapping My Sexual Wings | 173 |
| 2. | Going To the New/Big School | 175 |
| 3. | Learning Etiquette | 176 |
| 4. | My Practical Joke Backfires | 176 |

| | | |
|---|---|---|
| 5. | School Bullies | 177 |
| 6. | A Taunt for Each Race | 178 |
| 7. | The Putagee (Portuguese) | 178 |
| 8. | The Coolie (East Indian) | 178 |
| 9. | The Black-man (Africans) | 178 |
| 10. | The Games We Played | 178 |
| 11. | No Trophy for Me on School Sports Day | 181 |
| 12. | Pocket Money | 183 |
| 13. | The Phantom Flutee Vendor | 183 |
| 14. | School Curriculum and Frivolous Pastimes | 186 |
| 15. | Barbaric Teaching Tactics | 187 |
| 16. | My Best Friend | 187 |
| 17. | Hula Hoop Craze | 188 |
| 18. | Muddah Rat Goes Home | 188 |
| 19. | Puberty Blues | 191 |
| 20. | Sugah Bowl Catastrophe | 192 |
| 21. | Castor Oil and Cascara Agony | 192 |
| 22. | A Spoonful A'Sugah Works Magick | 193 |
| 23. | Guardian Angels in Abundance | 194 |
| 24. | Cures for Every Ailment | 196 |
| 25. | The Mystery of Nara | 198 |
| 26. | An Angel in the Nativity Play | 200 |
| 27. | Sex Education on the Streets | 202 |
| 28. | No Law and Order Here | 203 |
| 29. | Going To Pomeroon for School Holidays | 204 |
| 30. | The Big Day! | 205 |
| 31. | Flying Solo | 206 |
| 32. | The Slow Boat to China | 209 |
| 33. | Patsy Is a Man | 211 |
| 34. | We Meet Granfaddah | 214 |
| 35. | Granfaddah in Hospital | 214 |
| 36. | Gramuddah Philly Teaches Me to Tell Time | 215 |
| 37. | Granfaddah's New House | 216 |
| 38. | Market-day at Charity | 217 |
| 39. | Granfaddah Takes Us to Red Hill | 220 |

# CHAPTER NINE

**1959–60 Middle Road, La Penitence**                           221

| | | |
|---|---|---|
| 1. | A Sisyphean Move | 221 |
| 2. | Daddy Starts His Coffee Business | 223 |
| 3. | Mummy Throws 'Box-hand' for School Fees | 226 |
| 4. | Becoming a Carta-lick | 226 |
| 5. | A Proud St Joseph High School Student | 227 |
| 6. | Teenage Blues | 228 |
| 7. | Attacked By Hairy-worms | 229 |
| 8. | A Questionable Character | 229 |
| 9. | Schupid T'ings Mummy Told Me | 231 |
| 10. | Dead Men Walking | 234 |
| 11. | Guyana's Most Notorious Landmark | 235 |
| 12. | No Good Beaches in Guyana | 237 |
| 13. | Going To Shell Beach with Uncle Mike | 238 |
| 14 | Malaria Attacks Cousin Jim Struck At Santa Rosa | 239 |
| 15. | Religious Rigmarole at Easter | 240 |
| 16. | Flying Kites on de Seawall at Easter | 242 |
| 17. | Christmas and Flower Power | 244 |
| 18. | Muddah Sally and de Santapee Band | 246 |
| 19. | Visiting Over the Festive Season | 247 |
| 20. | Hindu Ceremonies | 248 |
| 21. | A True Legend | 249 |
| 22. | Elvis Is Alive and Well | 251 |
| 23. | Changing a Child's Name | 251 |
| 24. | My Darling Gramuddah Francesca | 253 |
| 25. | Gramuddah's Fashion Sense | 255 |
| 26. | Holidays at Gramuddah's Farm | 257 |
| 27. | Try-bes' was The Best | 258 |
| 28. | A Cheerful Place to Visit | 262 |
| 29. | Aunt Maud and Her Tribe | 263 |
| 30. | Visiting My Cousins at McKenzie | 265 |
| 31. | My Unforgettable Uncle Naysh | 266 |
| 32. | A Tiger Called Natius | 269 |
| 33. | Battles at Try-bes' | 270 |

34.  Lugga-Lugga                                                 271
35.  Birds of Prey                                               273
36.  My Tiger Died                                               274
37.  Holidays in Pomeroon–by Helena Martin (DaSilva)   274

CHAPTER TEN

**1961-63 Charles & Howes Streets**                              277

  1.   Another Cantankerous Landlord                   277
  2.   Confirmed By a Hypocrite                         278
  3.   A Big Bicycle Dilemma                            280
  4.   Mega Embarrassment                               281
  5.   Please Forgive Me Bruddah                        282
  6.   Kindness I Appreciated                           282
  7.   A Friend for Life                                283
  8.   Joel and I Joined the GUYS                       284
  9.   Black Friday                                     285
10.  Living in a Range                                           286
11.  Weird Religious Sects around Town                           287
12.  Smoking In the Botanical Garden                             288
13.  Monkey Business in the Botanical Garden                     289
14.  My Mother's Clothes                                         291
15.  I Became a 'Big Woman' Here                                 292
16.  Starching Cyan-Cyans (Can-Cans)                             293
17.  Flying Mother Nature's Flag                                 294
18.  Buying Unmentionables at Cendrecourt Drugstore             295
19.  My First Love and First Date                                296
20.  Bikini Disaster                                             297
21.  Chubby Checker Concert                                      298
22.  My Gambling Streak                                          299
23.  The End of the World                                        299
24.  Daddy Matchmaking with Chivalry                             300

CHAPTER ELEVEN

**1963–64 Drysdale Street**                                      303

  1.   Communal Living                                  303
  2.   Sweet Sixteen for Daphne and Me                  305

| 3. | Teaching at Stella Maris | 306 |
|---|---|---|
| 4. | Extra Duties without Pay | 309 |
| 5. | Getting a Telephone Call at Work | 311 |
| 6. | A Nun in Our Family | 311 |
| 7. | Pickcha Tekkin' with Phillippe | 312 |
| 8. | Mummy Had Major Surgery | 313 |
| 9. | How Could Mummy Be Pregnant? | 315 |
| 10. | Solex Envy | 316 |
| 11. | The Fashion Police | 318 |
| 12. | Attention Seeking | 318 |
| 13. | The Amazing Miss Thelma | 319 |
| 14. | Enduring Friendships | 320 |
| 15. | I Found a Second Name | 322 |
| 16. | Dr All-He-Saw Hospital | 323 |
| 17. | Infested With Vermin | 324 |
| 18. | Confessions for Stealing from de Safe | 325 |
| 19. | Lover Alert, Pickin' Fares and Cut-tail Lizard | 326 |
| 20. | Using Joel as a Decoy | 327 |
| 21. | Cinderella | 328 |
| 22. | Losing My Teeth at Seventeen | 329 |
| 23. | Party Animal | 330 |
| 24. | British Soldiers in Town | 331 |
| 25. | The Very Special Aunt We Called 'Boer' | 332 |
| 26. | Getting Too Big For My Boots | 333 |
| 27. | Visiting Uncle Sonny at Blankendal | 334 |
| 28. | Discovering Sex at Cousin Nita in Pomeroon | 334 |
| 29. | Near Drowning Experience | 337 |

## CHAPTER TWELVE

### 1964–65 Non Pareil Street 339

| 1. | Family Coming Out From the Woodwork | 339 |
|---|---|---|
| 2. | Daddy Expands His Coffee Business | 341 |
| 3. | A Trip to d'Riva for My 19th Birthday | 342 |
| 4. | Daddy Sings for My Birthday | 344 |
| 5. | Calypso in My Blood | 345 |
| 6. | Adopting Furrin Ideas | 347 |
| 7. | A Boyfriend Called 'Cow' | 348 |

8. My Favourite Joint (hang out spot) 349
9. Banks on de M.V. Malali 350
10. Related To Everyone in Pomeroon 353
11. If Yuh Cyan't Beat Dem Join Dem 353
12. A Search That Took Twenty Years 355
13. My Search Is Finally Over 356
14. Faith and Compassion Wins the Battle 356
15. Daddy Announces His Wedding Plans 358
16. Bicycle Tube to the Rescue 360
17. Christmas Eve Dramas 361
18. Frogs in My Bed 362
19. Christmas Day Struggles 363
20. Daddy's Wedding Day 364
21. Meeting My Husband 366
22. Carlos Plays Cupid 369
23. A Guest on Teenagers Choice with Bertie Chancellor 370
24. De Kissin' Bridge 374
25. Crossing a Metaphorical Bridge 374
26. Homesick for Try-bes'—by Helena (DaSilva) Martin 376

## CHAPTER THIRTEEN

### 1965–68—54 Albouys Street                                377

1. We Finally Own a Home 377
2. Living in Hell's Kitchen 378
3. Characters from the Neighbourhood 380
4. The Coffee Factory Is Built 382
5. Johnny Builds Me a Wardrobe 384
6. Daddy Buys a Cyar 385
7. How Could You Do That Mummy? 386
8. Nicknames for Daddy and Julian 387
9. A Shocked Kiskadee 389
10. Johnny Drops Migration Bombshell 390
11. Mummy Banned From Airport 392
12. The Airport Saga 393
13. Our Greatest Achievements 394
14. We Can Make Jell-O! 396
15. More Bicycle Drama 397

16.  No Goobye from Muddy                              397
17.  A Peeping Tom                                     398
18.  Guyana Gains Independence in 1966                 399
19.  Guyanese Idioms                                   401
20.  XM Sends Daddy to Hospital                        402
21.  My Father's Friends                               403
22.  Holiday in Trinidad and Barbados                  406
23.  My Overworked Guardian Angel                      406
24.  Buying Life Insurance from a Peacock              407
25.  The First Time I Saw Television                   409
26.  Joseph's House of Many Colours                    410
27.  A Four Dallah Buezin'                             412
28.  A Christmas Fright for Mummy                      412
29.  Fedna's Mota-bike                                 413
30.  Obeah Rituals in Our Home                         414
31.  Piercing Ears                                     415
32.  Good Ol' Bappo Buys Beer                          416
33.  Rescued By My Knight in Shining Armour            417
34.  Daddy Starts a Farm                               417
35.  A Very Special 21st Birthday                      418
36.  My Very Special In-laws                           419
37.  Tears To Sink the Titanic                         420
38.  Our Wooden Wedding Cake                           421
39.  Shameful Honeymoon Night                          425
40.  My Humble and Sincere Tribute                     425
41.  P.S: I Forgot To Tell You . . .                   425

GLOSSARY OF WORDS                                      429

CREOLE SAYINGS                                         446

AH REMEMBA                                             449

# ACKNOWLEDGEMENTS

Where do I begin? Without the help and encouragement beaming from an army of wonderful people I may not have had the inspiration and courage to complete this memoir. As everyone knows, *one hand cannot clap.*

Heartfelt thanks to my very 'Special' sister Cecelia; you have been my greatest source of help and encouragement throughout this process, thanks Sis.

To my amazing family and friends (you know who you are) who offered constructive advice, criticism, help and encouragement every step of the way. I would like to thank each one personally, but that would fill another book. Tanya and Mitzi you are both high on that list, thank-you.

The suggestion of a writing workshop by my long standing friend Joanne Moore led me to Trinity School for Seniors and inspiration, thank-you Jo.

Creative and Life Writing gurus Ruth Newman, Barbara Stapleton and Marie Mahoney, tutors at Trinity opened the door to enlightenment. Thanks also to fellow class members who have all contributed by sharing their inspirational stories especially Sue Levy for her input and enthusiasm. Helen Isles tutor and President for Society for Women Writers for valuable lessons learnt in her Novel Writing Class.

I am indebted to Kim Walters and Glennys Williams; two kind hearted women who dug deep into their busy schedule to dedicate countless hours of proof reading, words cannot express my gratitude.

Ian and Jacky Goddard willingly vacated their houseboat whenever I needed to escape. You are a true mate Jacky, thanks seems inadequate for the time you spent restoring my photographs to an acceptable standard.

My dear friend Norma Clarke has been my Guyanese research centre; the lines ran hot to Toronto. Thanks heaps, you can relax now *gyurl*. Judy Dyrting in Darwin for taking the time to send me information via post; it was very much appreciated. Thanks also to Margaret Robertson who has been my biggest fan; egging me on to finish.

Sincere thanks to cherished friends Dave and Les, proprietors of Jacobs Stock Photography for their generosity of the cover photo, blessings to you both. The picture of the *Grumman Goose* supplied by the late Henry (Harry) Irwin Hamilton (via his son) was a bonus, thank-you so much. You made my day Marco Farouk Basir when you gave me permission to use your picture of the M.V. Malali, very special indeed. Not forgetting Godfrey Chin whose e-mail inspired and gave me the 'kick start' I desperately needed.

A new friendship blossomed after I read Peter Halder's account of **"The Street Where I Lived."** Peter became another willing source who generously answered any query. Thanks for your time and patience Peter, we must meet someday.

Two people who contributed more than they know are Patrice and Sean Sawyer, total strangers who willingly loaned me their beach shack for eight glorious days, sheer magic. Thanks from the bottom of my heart.

Dashing Dr Kong Meng Liew thought he had encountered a new ailment when I broached the subject of '*Goadee*', he graciously answered my query then had the cheek to say he wanted his name on the bibliography. Well here it is doc thank-you!

Credit and thanks go to Balboa Press for making this dream a reality. A special thanks to Christine Paloma who promptly replied to my endless queries with patience. I am grateful for your understanding and calm approach throughout this process.

Last, but not least I would like to thank my husband, children and beautiful grandchildren for their patience and understanding. Grandma apologises for cuddling and spending so much time with the computer. Amber, Jessica, Sam, Michael, Kade, Kyle and Nina, I love you with all my heart!

# Walk Wit' Me – by Helena Martin (DaSilva)

My favourite pastime is taking a stroll down memory lane
Would you like to join me as I go there again?
Since this stroll will take an hour or two
It's only fair that I introduce myself to you
I can be every kind of woman as my mood varies
In case you are interested my star sign is Aries
Guyana in South America is the country of my birth
Immigrated at age twenty-one and now live in Perth
I have been shackled to the same man for forty-three years
We have four wonderful children and I know he still cares
Seven healthy grandchildren are my very best toys
Three beautiful girls and four adorable boys
Injustice of any kind I cannot tolerate
Or people who have no reason for always being late
Flowers I adore, roses, orchids, carnations or any other kind
But give me chocolate if you want to blow my mind
I love to gyrate to the beat of a calypso played on a steel drum
While indulging in a glass of potent Demerara rum
Patience is certainly not my best virtue
Right now it's my life experiences I'm dying to tell you
Come sit with me under the branches of my enormous family tree
I'll reminisce and you can laugh or cry with me
I am friendly, down to earth and love to talk
You will know everything else about me by the end of this walk

# Chapter One

*Small beginnings make great endings.—Proverb*

## WALK WIT' ME—ALL OVA GUYANA

"Johnny come."

"Go away!" I said, not wanting to be interrupted.

"Johnny come," my four-year-old sister insisted.

"Johnny in Australia, ah ritin' 'im a'letta, suh go an' play." CeCe persisted, so I decided to investigate after she said it for the third time. I heard voices coming from directly below the sitting room window and leaned over to take a look. My father and Johnny's sister were standing in front of the factory door chatting, but there was no sign of the man in question. CeCe pointed to the front door; I opened it, and there he was, bounding up the stairs. The moment that followed has been frozen in time because the unexpected surprise was too much of a shock. I did not know it in that instant, but his homecoming was going to mark the end of a very important and precious era of my life.

The yearning to document the tapestry of those poignant memories has been quelled many times in the last twenty years for one reason or another. No questioning; I know it was meant to be like that because I firmly believe nothing happens before its time.

## How It All Started

On an ordinary day in March 2008, I settled in front of the computer with a cup of tea to read my mail while listening to some music. Dr Hook was belting out, "Everybody is making it big but me," when I came across an e-mail sent by my sister-in-law, Mitzi. She had forwarded an article from a fellow Guyanese titled "The Street Where I Lived." This nostalgic piece left quite an impression. My impulsive nature led me to a chance meeting with the author of the article and more surprisingly, brought an end to the festering ambition I harboured for over twenty years.

Call it fate or whatever you may I still believe everything happens for a reason. I replied on impulse to congratulate the writer but never anticipated a reply, much less the request he proposed. Could I write a short story depicting life on the street where I lived? Did he say, "the street?" How absurd, I almost laughed out loud. The person in question might have been fortunate enough to have lived on a solitary street for the duration of his childhood; however, that was not my experience. I knew without doubt my story would have to be titled "All Ova de Place." Not only did we live on many streets, we also lived in different parts of the country. I honestly think my family holds the record for moving house; and for good reason. The new abode was always a few dollars cheaper or a few feet larger to accommodate our meagre budget and our ever increasing family. To this day, I despise moving. We have only moved once since our marriage. "Ah goin' out from 'ere in a box."

Guyanese say, "mout' open, story jump out," but I'm an Aussie now, so I thought I would "give it a go." One story turned into two, then another and that was how this memoir got started.

## Not Ghana, It Is Guyana

Every time I open my mouth, I have to explain where I am from. I say "Guyana" knowing full well the person asking would either say, "Oh, Ghana" or "Where is that?" I excuse them for thinking I said 'Ghana' because I still *kerry* (carry) a strong Guyanese accent after forty-three years of living in Australia. The answer to the "where is that" question has been simplified by Jim Jones. Sad as it was, I find mentioning Jonestown the quickest and most comprehensive way to tell someone where Guyana is located. A light bulb goes on and there is instant recognition. That human disaster put Guyana on the map, but I would like to tell you there is much more to my beautiful country. *Besize* (besides), Jim Jones was an American who used Guyana to conceal his dirty deeds. The mention of Jonestown urges me to quote the catch phrase made famous by a well known Australian radio and television personality who always said, "Shame! Shame! Shame!" after he presented an appalling story.

## A Proud Mud-head

Guyanese are famous for giving everyone a false-name, but how or why was the demeaning 'mud-head' tag bestowed upon us? It was the captain of the *Suffering Cross* (Southern Cross) who first brought this to my attention. On the journey to Australia, we were invited to the captain's cocktail party, which, in my opinion, should have been called "the captain's insulting party." Keep in mind I was very young and naïve, but did that give this ignorant man the right to insult one of his passengers? "And where are you from?" this stiffly starched captain smugly enquired. Pulling my five-foot-two stature to full measure and using my best English, I proudly replied, "I am from Guyana," only to be shot down in flames by his poison arrow. His jowls wobbled as he threw his head back and with a hearty laugh said, "Oh, a mud-head." I was so taken aback because until then I had no notion we were labelled with such a degrading name. I was lost for words and felt like kicking him when the other guests began snickering. I briefly weighed up my options and decided to retain my dignity. I smiled sweetly and moved on. The jackass obviously used me as a scapegoat to impress the other guests.

The captain's remark disturbed me and sent me on a mission to find the origin of the name. I can only conclude it is because Guyana is below sea level with numerous mudflats. Not that it matters, because I am proud to be a 'mud-head'. and if the captain had done some research, he too would have known that there are brilliant mud-heads holding down prestigious positions all over the globe. That old sea dog was lucky I was not an Australian or I would have called him a "dick-head."

## My Brush with Fame

There are many Guyanese who can lay claim to knowing or actually going to school with someone who became well known or even famous; celebrities like the author E. R. Braithwaite, who wrote 'To Sir with Love,' or the great cricketers Rohan Kanhai, Lance Gibbs and Clive Lloyd, to name a few. To my knowledge, no one I went to school with ever became famous. Then again, that boy that used to sit three seats behind me in fifth standard may have joined the circus and could be wowing the audience with his amazing ability to blow snot at a great distance. However, I did have a fleeting brush with fame. I once met Shakira Baksh, who became the wife of the famous actor Michael Caine. Shakira was born in Guyana the same year I was, but our paths never crossed until I met—saw her, actually, on the occasion I visited her home to have a costume fitting. Her mother, a prominent dressmaker in Georgetown, was commissioned to make the floral emblem costumes worn at the regatta on the Demerara River. I was one of the eight young women chosen to represent our national flora. The occasion was in honour of the Duchess of Kent, who visited Guyana for the 1966 Independence celebrations. I represented a beautiful golden hibiscus.

Miss Shakira Baksh was crowned Miss Guyana the following year and went on to become runner up in the Miss World pageant.

In 1968, the Miss World entourage arrived in Perth, Western Australia, to stage appearances at David Jones department store in the city. My immigration stamp was still wet when this event was announced. I had not encountered another Guyanese since arriving in Perth a few months earlier and was paralysed with homesickness. I naturally thought this was the perfect opportunity to bond with someone from home; I could not wait to meet Shakira!

I never envisioned sharing this embarrassing secret with the public after forty-three years, but I think the time has come to reveal all.

The appointed day arrived, and I could barely conceal my excitement as I made my way to the city. The designated area was packed to capacity, and I was overwhelmed. I picked my way through the crowd to secure a place closer to the stage, wondering how on earth I could possibly meet Shakira. It's not like we were bosom buddies back in Guyana. How will she recognise me? Quick thinking allowed me to scribble a note indentifying myself as a Guyanese and a mention of the flora costume her mother made. I shyly asked one of the sales assistants to kindly pass the note on to Shakira after the performance. Shakira sashayed onto the catwalk radiating a pure beauty compared to the other contestants. She had natural charm and carried herself with so much poise and elegance. It was indeed a very proud moment for the lone Guyanese standing in the crowd. My heart was pounding as the contestants vacated the stage, and I waited expectantly for Shakira to come out to meet me. What I did not expect was an announcement over the public address system summoning me to present myself. Where, I cannot remember because I was overcome with nerves and panic set in. Thankfully, my wobbly legs miraculously got me out of the building. To this day, I cringe whenever I remember the incident, but my mother would have laughed and said, "You were *yung an' schupid* (young and stupid)."

As you can see, I did not fit into the prestigious category of the rich and famous, but that does not mean I am short on knowledge or stories of my beloved homeland. I was born and raised in Guyana; my navel string is buried there. What makes me a true Guyanese? I *walk wid* (carry with me) hot peppersauce whenever I go out for a meal.

Don't worry; there is no need to ask, "Where is Guyana?" I will give you a briefing on the geography if you promise not to tell anyone I got the information from the internet!

## Where Is Guyana?

I must clarify one fact before I go on. Guyana was originally known as British Guiana, that name is recorded on my birth certificate. It was British Guiana for nineteen of the twenty-one years I lived there. The name was changed to 'Guyana' on the 26th May 1966 when the country gained independence, and it later became a Republic on the 23rd of February 1970. Not many people know this, but Guyana is the only English speaking country in South America. My birth added to the population of less than a million people. The capital Georgetown is known as the 'Garden City' and we call our flag the 'Arrowhead'.

This is the only geography lesson I am going to give you. Guyana is bordered by the Atlantic Ocean on the North; Brazil on the South; Suriname on the East and Venezuela on the West. Christopher Columbus first sighted the land and named it Guiana. Sir Walter Raleigh made two voyages to Guiana in search of El Dorado (the fabled city of gold), but he never found it. The name 'El Dorado' is synonymous with Guyana; especially in our folklore stories, song and rum. I endorse the names, 'de mudflat' and 'de mud-land' bestowed on Guyana in recent years by nostalgic Guyanese authors.

Guiana is an Amerindian word meaning, 'Land of Many Waters,' so it's not surprising I was born in a river district—in the Essequibo region to be exact.

## The Pomeroon River

Essiquibo, Demerara and Berbice are the three major rivers that divide our regions. The Essequibo is the largest of the three and consists of many tributaries and smaller rivers. One of these rivers is the Pomeroon, home to my ancestors and also the birth place of both my parents. The Pomeroon, commonly called 'd'Riva' is well known as a farming community. The river is divided into areas called 'grants', and named in the same way we name suburbs; some names are very unusual. Try Best was the name of my paternal grandparents grant but no one pronounced it that way; everyone said, "Try-bes'." My maternal grandparents lived at Siriki; then there is Verdon, Buxton, Martindale, Pickersgill and Grant Singapore to name a few more. I believe I have relatives living on almost every grant. Each grant is divided into smaller allotments and sold to potential farmers. Some identified their farm by giving it a unique name. My Great Uncle Kaiser named his place Zanzibar. Whenever my grandfather visited his brother, he would say, "Philly, a'goin' ova to Zanzibar." Zanzibar stood out in my memory because it had a certain magical ring to my childish ears. No other name sounded as exotic. Daddy said our farm was called, 'Rosalie', named after my mother . . . not as interesting . . . sorry Mummy.

## My Parents' History

I would like to tell you the little I know about my parents' history so you may understand them better. Both were born in the Pomeroon and hold the second child position in their large family. Their ancestors hail from Portugal; although there is some discrepancy as to whether it was

Madeira or the Azores . . . still to be determined. The blue eyes of my mother's aunts have been traced to a Flemish background, a well known link with the Azores. That is as much as I can divulge without concrete evidence. Bits of information were passed on here and there as I was growing up, but I never thought to ask for the more meaningful aspects of their lives. Most people never think of doing that until it is too late.

## My Father's Single Life

My grandfather Emanuel was married previously and had four children; Cyril, Rita, Carlos and Clothil. Emanuel then married my grandmother Francesca and they produced nine children. My father's siblings in order of birth are Mary, Joseph (Daddy), Philomena, Glerimena, Maudline, Michael, Rita, Claudia and Ignatius.

My grandfather passed away when my grandmother was pregnant with their last child, leaving her a reasonably young widow with nine mouths to feed. Farming was difficult so Daddy decided to try his luck as a *Pork-knocker* (prospector/miner) and headed for the goldfields at a very young age. He said times were hard with no gold in sight and very little to eat. Daddy said they ate a tiger once just to survive and he vomited the entire night. I also know daddy stopped eating corned-beef after his gold digging days because that was all they had to eat. He told us he got "buck-sick" (a term derived from Amerindian folklore) from eating it. Daddy also kept a souvenir from his pork-knocker days; a large shallow dish that he called a *batelle* (a pan used for prospecting). He would put gravel into the batelle to demonstrate the technique used to separate the gold from the debris. He also said mercury was used in that process. That is about all I know of my father's life before he married my mother.

## My Mother's Single Life

My mother was born to parents Jose and Philomena D'Agrella. She was christened Carmen Rosalie. Her siblings in order of birth are: Hermina, Carmen (Mummy), Olinda, Olga, Philomena, Annette, Desmond, Gleremina, Adele and Joseph. I believe I know a lot more about my mother because I spent a lot of time with her family and different things came to light from time to time.

My mother was good at suppressing her feelings . . . with good reasons, as it was too painful to divulge. My grandfather wanted boys because he needed labourers to work on his farm, but had to wait until his seventh child was born to realise that dream. That was very unfortunate for my mother and her sister Linda who were his second and third daughters. Aunty Hermina was their first born but grandfather allowed her to stay at home with my grandmother so she could learn to cook, sew and be *ladylike*.

With no sons on the horizon *granfaddah* (grandfather) could not wait until Carmen was old enough to hold a *cutlass* (machete). The same fate befell Aunty Linda who was a year younger. The girls worked in the farm whenever they were home or during school holidays. That was until their education was terminated in fourth standard. They began working from sun up to sun down on the farm. Many people have told me stories of the hardship my mother and her sister endured in their teenage years . . . two young women who worked harder than most men. Granfaddah promised the girls their wages. The sad part was, he always reneged on the deal. One time Mummy and Aunty Lin planned endlessly what they were going to spend the money on. However, *likka* always turned my grandfather into a demon and they made the mistake of asking him for their wages when he came back from Charity drunk. They got a good thrashing instead. My mother also endured tremendous trauma when her youngest sister, whom she idolised died in her care. She said it was common practice to take a bath at the waterside (no heating system there) and when the cold water was poured onto Adele, she jumped in shock. Subsequently caught pneumonia and died a few days later. She was five years old.

Mummy never forgave herself.

From what I was told the only source of joy my mother had was the pet she had in her teenage years. Someone had given her a Sakiwinki monkey she named 'Jacko'. Mummy said she made two outfits from some scraps of khaki and dressed the monkey like a doll. I wished she had a picture of Jacko.

My mother fled when she was eighteen to escape from her life of slavery. She went to live with her *Titi Shan* (Aunty Shandrina); one of grandmother's sisters who lived at Verdon. My father lived at Try-bes' which is very close to Verdon. It was here the romance blossomed and she married my father.

From what I understand her life was nothing but misery until she met my father. Daddy was a farmer but she was happy to work side by side with him in the farm because it was under much happier circumstances. She was *in love*.

My parents went to live in a place named 'Kwakwani' (somewhere in the Berbice) after they were married on the 14th August 1944. Daddy worked with a few of his cousins, and talked about cutting timber and herding cattle at a place called Tacama in that region. The venture did not work out so my parents packed up and left. They returned to the Pomeroon River in time for the birth of my eldest brother who was born on the 3rd February 1945.

You might be interested to know my parents are related. My maternal great-grandmother and my paternal grandfather are brother and sister.

My parents Joseph and Carmen DaSilva

## What Is Buck-Sick?

I told you earlier that Daddy got *buck-sick* (fed up) from eating corned-beef to excess. Let me explain the history of that phrase on behalf on the indigenous people of Guyana. I wish to advise the following information has been passed down and any inaccuracy is unintentional.

The term 'buck-sick' came about because the Amerindians had no way of preserving any food that was in abundance. For instance, if mangoes or crabs were in season they ate that at every meal so none of it would be wasted. They believed if they ate as much as they can, it will sustain them longer. As you can imagine they were sick of seeing and eating the item by the time the season was over and since we used the slang 'buck' to describe an Amerindian; we said "buck-sick." It somehow doesn't sound the same if you say "Amerindian sick," and I am not being disrespectful; it was the way we spoke back then. Whenever it was mango season Mummy used to say, *"Buckman mus' 'ave 'e pot turn dung."* [Amerindians won't be cooking while mangoes are in season.]

It was not only used in terms of food; for instance, if someone abandoned a *bat an' ball* (cricket) game after playing for hours on end, one of their friends would say, *"Wha' 'appen maan yuh buck-sick?"* [Have you had enough?] I was told the term relates to cricket, and since I do not wish to offend anyone, I would like to give you the spiel on that version.

This information came from a former Stella Maris student who I consulted. Colin still lives in Guyana and works for the indigenous community. I quote from Colin Klautky, "In Guyana, we used the term 'buck-stick' or 'buck-sick' in cricket. Buck-stick signifies a batsman attacking the bowling very badly, but when a batsman hits six repeatedly in one over, the bowler will be 'buck-sick' as is understandable. Of course the word comes from the Dutch BOK which means FAST-RUNNING WILD DEER, hence the name BOK in the brand-name Reebok and the name for some African antelopes such as Gemsbok, Steenbok and Springbok. A 'buck' is also a deer in the English language. Some indigenous Guyanese consider BOK an insult, but I personally have no problem with BOK since the Dutch were complimenting the swift, graceful way Aboriginal Guyanese ran through the forest (end of quote)."

And there you have it from another source. I like both versions; it all boils down to the same meaning, *fed up*.

I hope you are not buck-sick yet because we are only just beginning this walk. Just a minute, I need to warn you in advance about the vernacular. It might take you a while to get the hang of it. Yuh ready? Den come le'we guh.

# Chapter Two

*Home is where the heart is.—Proverb*

## 1947 JACKLOW, POMEROON RIVER

### Where It All Began

I invite you to walk with me on this nostalgic journey which began on the twenty-first of March 1947, in colonial British Guiana (best known as B.G to the locals).

Like most people, my curiosity led me in a search to see what great event took place the year I was born. It is documented that Chuck Yeager broke the sound barrier in August of that year. I was not impressed because I honestly thought I broke the record a few months earlier at my birth, but back to reality. I will humbly relinquish that crown for a more romantic visualisation of my birth. It is more than likely a blaze of screeching parrots hovering in mango trees heralded my birth on that eventful Friday morning I made my appearance. For the record, the time was 7 a.m. and the place was Jacklow in the Pomeroon River. The starring role went to my mother Carmen Rosalie DaSilva; a formidable woman with jet black hair (which she attributed to the religious use of Vaseline Hair Tonic), and a no nonsense approach to life. There was no hospital fan-fare; it was a simple home birth with a midwife in attendance. That was the trend in those days. Her dashing counterpart was a look-alike Clarke Gable called J.B—short for Joseph Basil. I imagine my father was most likely doing his part by boiling water, pacing the floor and anxiously waiting for the sound of my first wail. But that's just me thinking logically. He may have gone out working in the farm allowing the women some privacy to get on with the job of seeing me safely into the world. We are after all talking about events that took place over sixty years ago, and from what I understand, a man never meddled in *women's business*. From all the whisperings I have heard on the subject of childbirth, no man in his right mind would have attempted to be in the same room. Back then no one in their wildest dreams would have ever imagined a video camera being invented; much less taking it into a birthing suite to look down a woman's private part to record the event in detail. Perish the thought of showing it to all and sundry at a later date. That would be considered pornography and most likely a long jail sentence.

The 'no men allowed' tradition followed me to Australia. I gave birth to my children without a husband or camera present, mainly because the poor man fainted before he could get through the door of the delivery room.

It is only hearsay, but from all accounts I was a beautiful baby with everything intact. Since no one owned a camera, there is no proof of my beauty so I have to rely on my imagination. I am the second child for my parents; my brother Mervyn Joel was only thirteen months old when I arrived.

My parents decided on the name Helena for no apparent reason. I thought I was named after someone famous but that is just me having delusions of grandeur. I also noticed I was the only child in a family of seven who was not given a second name. What's up with that? Why were they so stingy? I never found out the reason for that *faux pas* so I console myself by saying they could not find another name good enough for their precious daughter. See, I told you I suffer from delusions of grandeur.

Wouldn't it be ideal if we could remember the event of our birth in detail and all that comes after? That is impossible for us mere mortals, although I consider myself fortunate to be blessed with quite a good memory. I can remember people, things, places and events from around the age of two or thereabouts.

I have no recollection of Joel being away from our home and from what I was told this happened in my infancy. Mummy said he was such a sickly baby they expected to lose him soon after birth. He was going downhill fast until a kind relative called Cousin Pullina rescued him. She took him away for a long period and must have worked magic. Mummy said she got a fright when she saw him again. Joel was so fat she thought he was swelling up to die. Thankfully, that was not the case. Excuse the pun but Joel pulled through because of Cousin Pullina's love and devotion. He thrived on a steady diet of *plantin pap* (plantain porridge), and was handed back as a healthy and robust specimen to my astonished parents.

## My Earliest Memories

I think it would be appropriate to begin with my earliest childhood memory. As I recall, it is without a doubt the picture of my father repeatedly throwing me high into the air then catching me. I always squealed with delight as much as fear. My head barely missed the rafters which I could almost touch, but I was always safe in Daddy's strong arms. Daddy must have gone over the boundary of safety one time because I remember my mother saying, "J.B watch sh' 'ead." The rafters must have been a bit higher between the sitting room and the kitchen because he always threw me up in that same spot. This is the only game I can remember ever playing with my father as a child.

## My First Home

Our home was more a hut, with just the bare essentials. But that was not important. To me, this tiny three room dwelling was the only true *home* I ever knew.

The thatched roof constructed from the fronds of the Troolie Palm made a comforting sound when it rained. Our Australian home has a tiled roof that can never reproduce that magical sound. In saying that, falling rain on any roof is still one of my favourite things.

We did not have the luxury of furniture bought from a store. The tiny sitting room was bare except for a long wooden bench roughly constructed onto one side of the wall; this served as a sofa.

No commercially bought carpets or rugs adorned the floors. Our homemade rugs made from a discarded *sugah bag* (burlap) and scraps of material gave a splash of colour to the floors Mummy kept scrupulously clean with water, soap and a metal scraper.

The entire family slept in the one bedroom which was long and narrow and not very spacious. This room was somewhat gloomy; always dark because the small timber window blocked out the sunlight. Two beds occupied this room. My parents slept in the big bed and I shared the smaller one with my brother; we slept head to tail. That *likkle* monkey wet the bed and me every night!

Mosquito nets suspended from the rafters were let down and tucked in tightly every evening before dusk to keep out the mosquitoes or we would be eaten alive. Bedtime routine was quickly mastered, no dilly-dallying when it was time to get into bed. Mummy pushed us in quickly through an entrance no bigger than a doggy door, and then tucked the loose end of the net in securely, making sure we were safe from those pesky insects. We sometimes slept too close to the net and woke with big red blotches that itched for hours.

The cosy atmosphere of the netting combined with the sweet aroma from our homemade mattress welcomed and lulled us into peaceful slumber. No *Dundapillah* (Dunder Pillow) mattress in our home, ours came straight from the farm complete with sound effects. The brittle dried leaves of the banana or plantain my parents used to fill the mattress sack made a rustling sound whenever we moved. The crackling became less noticeable as the leaves became compressed. When the mattress was no longer comfortable, Mummy undid the opening at one end of the sack; discarded the unwanted filling and replaced it with a new batch of fresh leaves. I remember jumping on the new mattress as if it were a trampoline just to hear the rustling sound. We were always quite comfortable because there was an abundance of dried leaves to refill the mattresses.

Our kitchen was just big enough to fit a small table and two narrow benches on either side. There were no fancy tablecloths on our table.

Mummy applied the same cleaning method she used for the floors. Our *wares* (dishes) were all enamel; chipped to the high heavens because of our carelessness.

Daddy drank his tea—coffee actually, we Guyanese call any hot beverage 'tea'. Mothers would say, "Is time fuh de baby tea" when in fact they meant milk. Confused yet? Wait, there is more!

Where was I? I was telling you about Daddy. He drank his tea from an enamel cup that was big enough to be a *posy* (chamber pot). A nasty thought just entered. I wonder if that was the same one used for the *posy* under the bed at night; I hope not.

A small enclosed alcove was built on the windowless wall of the kitchen to house our *fireside* (open fire place) where Mummy did the cooking. The fireside constructed from packed mud supported the heavy blackened saucepans my mother used to cook our meals. Since this was an open fire, we were often choked or blinded by smoke before she could get the raging fire under control. We were not allowed too close to the fire in case of falling embers. The dog got burnt once and the smell was awful. Daddy winked wickedly and said that was the smell of roast dog.

Mummy concocted a mud paste which she lovingly daubed on the ever increasing cracks of the fireside. It looked as smooth as a *calabash* (shell from a gourd) when she was finished.

A giant Breadnut tree stood guard outside the back door; the ripened fruit fell splattering the ground with mush. We helped to dislodge the big brown nuts trapped in the membrane. Mummy gave them a quick rinse then boiled them in salted water until they were tender. We all gathered on the back steps to peel and enjoy this delicious treat and always blamed the dog for the stinky atmosphere of breadnut farts the following day.

It was Daddy's job to have a steady supply of firewood; an old tree stump just outside the kitchen door was used as a chopping block. Daddy expertly split the wood into manageable sizes then got Joel and I to stack the smaller pieces in the corner of the kitchen. We were warned never to go in the yard while Daddy was wielding the axe; splinters, and sometimes bigger pieces were sent flying in every direction. The scar over my right eye lid bears witness to a flying splinter because I was 'ard *ears* (disobedient). My mother had no sympathy; she simple preached another lesson by saying, "If yuh doan 'ear, yuh will feel." And another valuable lesson learnt.

## Primitive Plumbing

There was no running water or sink in the kitchen for washing *wares*. A small platform was built on the opposite wall of the open kitchen for this purpose. The big wooden vat in the yard provided our drinking water and a big goblet kept it cool indoors. Water for the washing up was fetched up from *d'Riva* or the trench in front of our home. The dirty dish water ran directly into the yard when the *wares* were being washed. Scraps of food were thrown over the side for the chickens to peck at. Did I say scraps? As I recall there was never any; that was a luxury we could not afford. To tell the truth there wasn't much washing to be done after we finished licking our plates. I know what you are thinking and the answer is No! I have weaned myself from that disgusting habit.

My mother's favourite saying was, "Waste not; want not." That saying has always served as a yardstick in my life; to this day I cannot stand to see wastefulness of any sort.

We never played under the platform where the washing up was done. Experience had taught us an unexpected shower may come down at any given moment if Mummy was in the kitchen. This may all sound very unsanitary but it was the way of life. There were no Health or Sanitary inspectors upholding laws.

The plumbing left a lot to be desired . . . then again what plumbing? We had none.

A big enamel posy was kept under my parents' bed. Unfortunately this *posy* did not have the fresh smell of a bouquet of roses. It served as our lavatory during the night and was emptied each morning into the disgustingly smelly latrine on the dam. Our latrine had a large seat for the adults, and a small one for the children's *likkle bam-bam*. Looking down into the pit was quite interesting as long as you held your nose. It was fun watching the chain of tiny mud crabs as they came to enjoy the dinner we had so kindly provided. There were all sorts of other sea creatures competing for the smorgasbord.

If you think our washing up method was unsanitary, wait until I tell you how our latrine got flushed. Remember, pollution was not thought of back then; this was classed as 'normal' to the inhabitants.

It was common practice to build the latrine on the dam with the seats positioned over the mangrove and courida trees that grew alongside the river. This ingenious way of thinking allowed the waste to be flushed out daily with the ebb and flow of the tide. No one gave a thought as to where it all went. We drank heartily from the same river when we were rowing in the *corial*—yum!

I almost forgot the bathroom; it was insignificant, that's why. This sentry type wooden cubicle was built in the yard; not far from the house. It was not a very respectful bathroom in my opinion; especially since the fat *crappos* (crapaud/huge toad) took up residence. How I despised them. The quirky thatched roof resembled Hitler's moustache and the entrance boasted a curtain made from an old *sugah bag*. Buckets of water were transported from the river and a calabash was used to pour the water to *bade yuh skin* (bathe/wash). The bathroom was mostly used by my parents for privacy. We children preferred bathing at the *waterside* (edge of the river) where we could frolic and learn to swim and enjoy Mummy's *magick* trick. She scooped and clapped the water in a certain fashion to create a loud popping sound which could be heard from a great distance.

My mother was still able to mesmerise our children with this trick when she visited us in 1979. I never knew until recently that there was a story attached to this amazing feat. Uncle Deck explained its origin. He said my great-grandmother Charlotte was a strict disciplinarian and it was she who invented the sound for a specific purpose. She woke her employees up at *fo'day marnin'* (crack of dawn) and sent them down to the river to bathe and the ear splitting sound was the only evidence she had of the workers actually being in the water.

## A Baby Out Of the Blue

I must have been around two, when out of the blue a chubby baby arrived on the scene. There was none of this modern business explaining a pregnancy. To my knowledge, no Guyanese mother ever prepared the older siblings for the arrival of a new baby. I had no clue about my mother being pregnant. I don't think I even noticed she looked different, but then again she had big *bubbies* (breasts) so no one noticed the rest of her. That baby was my brother Arthur Charles. He is almost two years younger than me. Once he came along, Mummy did not have much time to play with me, because she was too busy giving him her *bubbie* or working in the fields. I don't remember too much about Charlie being a baby, he was just a major inconvenience in my opinion.

## The Backdam Crèche

There were no baby sitters; my two brothers and I spent a lot of time with our parents in the *backdam* (fields far from home). The ideal place was in between the suckers of a plantain or banana grove. It was well padded with the same familiar scent as our mattress. My parents tied the four ends of a bed sheet to the suckers to provide shade for our makeshift nursery. The three of us slept and played here for hours while our parents toiled in the fields to make their livelihood. Mummy took a break whenever Charlie cried to give him some bubbie; greedy little brat. Child Welfare would certainly frown today; they may even call it child abuse and take us into custody. We were very happy and always comfortable, except for *cop-cop* (ants) stinging us once in a while.

My parents often worked far from our home and navigating the trenches that separated each field was a bit tricky at times. The so called bridges across the trenches were fashioned from odd bits of timber or sometimes a strong spine from the coconut palm; it all depended on the width of the trench. The dog always ended up in the trench if he tried to cross with us. On occasion Daddy gave me a piggy back to the backdam. He was an expert at balancing on those narrow crossings; we never fell in once.

Mummy never went anywhere without her fishing rod; she took a break once in a while and caught fish in these trenches for dinner. She caught small flat fish called Patwa and others called Hourie, Sunfish and Yarrow. They were full of bones but very tasty, and if she fried those *crips* (crisp) enough, we were able to eat the bones as well. My brother and I were given short rods when we were a bit older so we could fish with them. Finding bait was easy, a little digging unearthed fat pink worms anywhere on the farm. An old tin or coconut shell filled with earth kept the wriggling bait fresh.

The backdam was a paradise; adorned with a prolific array of colourful birds such as, parrots, macaws, blue-sakis, hummingbirds and kiskadees. Those are the ones I remember with clarity. Parrots hung like Christmas ornaments from the trees behind our home when mangoes were in season. They competed with other birds for the fruit and made a hell of a racket.

Our home may have been very small but it was the happiest period of my childhood and my parents' marriage.

Many years later I sensed something was not right. Call it instinct, but that suspicion was confirmed when I was old enough to talk to Mummy about such matters. She told me the first ten years of her and my father's marriage were blissful. It was comforting to know I was born from a union of true love. Sadly, for one reason or other their marriage went downhill after that.

Let me tell you a bit more about my childhood days because you will hear more on the downfall of their marriage later on.

## Visiting My Grandparents at Siriki

I distinctly remember being in a small boat with my mother, brother Joel and the baby who had a nest in the bow. My mother issued a stern warning to sit very still as she strategically settled us on the narrow slats acting as seats in the *corial* (dugout canoe). The rim of the small corial was always perilously close to the lapping water and tipping over was imminent. A life jacket would have been beyond my parents' imagination in those days. We sat facing Mummy while she paddled furiously across the river. She stopped every so often to bale the water from the bottom of the leaking corial with a broken calabash.

I was always in awe of the *magick* trick my mother performed with her paddle. She dipped it into the river then did a quick flick which produced a loud popping sound. This was probably done to keep us amused or she was simply showing off. The unusual sound fascinated me, but I was never able to master the art when I was old enough to use a paddle.

These excursions were fun. I especially liked dangling my hand over the side to feel the rushing force of the water flowing in the opposite direction, but Mummy was a spoil sport. She always shouted at me to put a stop to this activity. I guess she was afraid I would lean over too far and topple out.

It seemed like an eternity before we arrived at my grandparents who lived at Siriki. We made so much noise rounding the last bend that *Gramuddah* (grandmother) and Aunty Glerie always came running onto the *stellin'* (jetty) to greet us. Aunty Glerie was my mother's youngest sister. She was very beautiful, unmarried and still living at home with my grandparents. She enjoyed playing with us, and since I was the only girl she spoilt me rotten. She and I shared a special ritual when mangoes were in season. We sat on the kitchen floor where she peeled them for my enjoyment. Many years later she reminded me that whenever she fed me green mangoes I ate faster than she could peel. She said I swallowed without chewing (still do) and repeatedly said the word "Maca-langa-mo" after each mouthful. I remember those times so well. I was learning to talk at the time. I was saying, "More mango." Mango is my favourite fruit to this day.

## Action on the River

Life in d'Riva was dictated by the rise and fall of the tide. Mummy always chose to travel in the direction the tide was flowing; it was a sure guarantee for a faster journey. Siriki was up river from our home at Jacklow; therefore, it was best to paddle up river when the tide was flowing in that direction. We always stayed until the tide turned before making the return journey home.

We had some hairy moments while travelling on d'Riva, especially when a big *mota-boat* passed and we were swamped with *swellin'* (a wake or swell). Even as a child I soon realised that a more powerful motor caused the swellin' to be bigger, this meant our boat rocked for a longer period. Thank goodness Mummy was an expert boatwoman; she knew how to steer the little corial in a certain angle over the huge waves to counteract the danger. Our suspended canoe rode the wave rocking back and forth until the swell subsided. I really enjoyed this motion and never gave a thought to the possibility of capsizing. To this day I still get a kick from swellin'; it transports me back to my childhood.

## The Boogie Men

As a child, I was admittedly very timid; always hiding behind my mother's skirt tails. One day I had real cause to hide. We arrived at Gramuddah to find a scary group of people waiting on the stellin'. A few of them were in strange attire and had black faces. This alarmed me as I had never seen these people before. They began dancing and making strange noises as our canoe drew close to the stellin'. These people had sticks and pretended to stage an attack on me. I was terrified. Mummy on the other hand, was not in the least bit startled. She went about tying up the corial while I screamed in fear and tried to push away from the stellin' to escape. Aunt Glerie and the other adults were laughing hysterically at the antics of the group, but I could not see anything remotely funny about the situation. No one took the slightest notice of my distress until I pissed my pants. That was when Mummy told the boys to take off the costumes so I could see who they were. They were laughing like hyenas at this stage but did as they were told. The hats and baggy coats were removed, and then they wiped the black coal off their faces to reveal their identity. Although badly shaken, I was relieved to see it was only Bonga and his *wutliss* (worthless) brothers who lived down the dam. They thought it was highly amusing to masquerade as boogie men. Fancy scaring a small child out of her wits and thinking it was funny. More stories about Bonga and his tribe later.

## The Garrets

I was very fond of Mrs Garret and her family who lived next door. To this day I can actually still conjure up their smell. Mr Garret died before I was born. Her son Harold was very kind and gentle; he played with us as kids. His sister was called an 'Ol' maid' because of her unmarried status. We seemed to spend a lot of time visiting the Garrets who only lived a short walk down the dam from our home. Their main source of income came from the cocoa they grew on their farm. At harvest time, thousands of colourful cocoa pods the size of footballs were plucked and transported from the farm in sugah bags then deposited in their front garden. I had the privilege to watch—not to mention eat, as soon as the family opened the cocoa pods to begin the chocolate making process.

A sharp cutlass was used to split the cocoa pod in two. The beans were scooped out then placed on the floor of the *drugley* (a platform with a roof used for drying purposes). This outhouse was operated by a pulley system in case you are wondering.

I enjoyed sucking the sweet fleshy pulp coating the beans and was allowed to indulge to my heart's content. There were huge mounds of discarded cocoa pods in their garden at the end of this operation. This part of the process went on forever; days, weeks, I couldn't say, time was irrelevant at my age. I know they kept a close eye on the weather while the beans were drying. The drugley roof was hastily pulled to cover the beans if anyone uttered the words "*It set up* (rain clouds forming)." To be honest, I was more interested on what went on indoors.

The Garrets' home had a certain aroma I associated with chocolate. They were very generous and I took full advantage of that. I followed them like a shadow knowing I was guaranteed some of the scraps as a treat. Damn the Garrets; I blame them for my chocolate addiction.

When the cocoa beans were sufficiently dried in the sun it was time to parch them. This was done at their fireside over a roaring fire. The beans were placed in a huge *canaree* and constantly stirred with a big wooden paddle to prevent burning. This may have been the most tedious part of the process; not to mention hot in that tropical climate. They constantly dabbed their red faces with a piece of old rag to stop the flow of perspiration that streamed down their tired faces. The beans were left to cool after they were parched to perfection.

Their kitchen was a hive of activity when it was time to make the delicate chocolate sticks. Everyone gathered around the table in their kitchen to tackle the grinding process. Harold secured the big cast-iron mill into place by screwing it onto one end of the long wooden table. An enormous white enamel basin was placed under the mouth of the mill and away they went. One person fed the mill while another turned the handle. The dark gooey substance slowly emerged from the jaws of the black gobbler. Without the aroma it could be mistaken for *doggy doo*, but damn it tasted good.

The next phase was the best! I was fascinated by the process of them moulding, rolling and cutting the chocolate into equal size sticks. These uniformed chocolate sticks were then placed on wooden trays and left to dry. Handling with care was necessary to prevent breakage. Packaging was simple back then. The hardened sticks were bundled up in various amounts then tied together with string and sold to the respective customer. Huge *sweetie* (confectionery) jars were used to store the remaining chocolate sticks. These were sold individually at the market or to private customers. Chocolate sticks were used to make the most delicious hot beverage which we naturally called 'tea'. Grated chocolate was stirred into hot water and milk then garnished with a dash of freshly grated nutmeg.

Those Garrets' were the causes of my childhood obesity...why take responsibility when you can blame someone else?

## My First Funeral

Most of the farms along the Pomeroon River had a stellin'. This allowed the residents to secure their boat before disembarking, in other words, this was their garage and driveway. Times were hard and we were not so fortunate. Two black logs lurking like alligators in front of our waterside did not make a stellin'; we had a *landin'*. Our small corial was moored between the logs and secured with a length of rope to a pole stuck at the edge of the river.

One day a *big-big boat* (a steamer) laden with people came alongside our landin'. Mummy came out of the house all dressed up. She was wearing the prettiest pink frock and carried her shoes in her hand. We all followed her to the waterside where she kissed us goodbye. She gingerly walked along the wobbly logs and a man grabbed her by the hand and dragged her aboard. On the top deck, right at the front of the boat sat a big box covered with flowers. Some of the people were crying and this frightened me. I thought they were taking my Mummy away for good and I began crying uncontrollably; begging my mother not to go, but she just waved until the boat was out of sight. Daddy reassured me that Mummy will soon be back and he was right. I later heard them talking about *Muddah* (mother) Lawson. I did not understand death at such an early age; but knew it was a sad thing just listening to them.

I must explain that Muddah Lawson was not a relative; we called her 'Muddah' as a mark of respect. I knew her very well because we lived between her and the Garrets. That old lady visited us often and may have even been present at my birth. She was an elderly lady of African descent with the whitest hair; a dear old soul who was always very kind to me.

## My First East Indian Wedding

This is another vivid memory. Mummy dressed me in my only good *dan-dan* (dress); the one with the collar, a big sash and tiny blue flowers, then she said, "We goin' to a'weddin'." It was my first. We arrived at the venue where my eyes became as big as saucers. I had never seen so many boats in one place; some were festooned with flowers and streamers of the brightest colours. I was overwhelmed before we got out of our corial. The atmosphere was electric with some sort of unusual music blaring. People were clamouring from one boat to another to get ashore; all this activity made me nervous. The women were dressed in brilliant colours, dripping in gold jewellery and talking in a language I could not quite make out. The bridal party is dim in my memory; I cannot remember seeing a bride, not one in white anyway. I remember the pungent aroma of exotic spices when I passed the women on the dam as we made our way to the house. The women were stirring big-big black pots that had legs; something I had never seen. I could feel the heat from the roaring fires, and had to wipe my eyes because the smoke had made them water. As we entered the muddy yard a group of men wearing bright turbans were banging on some drums under a huge mango tree; it didn't sound like real music. A mangy dog came to lick me and *a'buss cry* (burst out crying). I was so *fryken* (scared) I shot through the door and got separated from my mother. After what seemed like an eternity and a lot of confusion, everyone had to *siddung* (sit down) cross-legged on the floor and I followed suit. Someone handed me a big green leaf with food on it. The lady walked off without giving me a spoon and I burst out crying—again! No wonder my grandfather called me Suckie-Suckie. My mother was summoned. She explained the leaf was my plate and the meal was to be eaten with my fingers. I could not come to terms with that idea. A spoon was found and I settled down to enjoy the Indian cuisine. As I got older and became familiar with the custom of eating with fingers I actually enjoyed it. We mixed regularly with the East Indians who used a lot of hot peppers. Their curries were never cooked in a milder manner to accommodate children so I learnt to eat like the Indians in no time. My family and friends all say I have an asbestos mouth.

By the way, the leaves used as plates for Indian ceremonies were specially harvested from the Eddo and a certain waterlily plant.

I have the urge to tell you this joke. My brother Charlie known for his tall tales said an Englishman attended an Indian wedding and when asked what he thought of the cuisine, he said, "It was delicious, especially the lettuce leaf." Will someone please tell the man he ate the plate!

## My First Dolly

Oops! I just remembered I was telling you about my first memories but got side tracked thinking I was a comedian. I wanted to tell you about my first dolly. Not the shop bought one; she didn't last long because she was made of China. I tested her on a post under the house and she was smashed to bits. A sharp slap brought me to my senses, and since Mummy said, "Dollies didn't grow on trees" it was time to improvise. My motherly instinct led me to a piece of wood which I thought was the perfect size of a baby. It was round and heavy just like all babies are and it fitted perfectly in my arms. I lovingly wrapped that piece of wood in some old cloth and Dolly was ready to be nursed. I must have taken a lot of notice when my mother was giving Charlie her bubbie because I also pulled up my dress to put Dolly to mine; when no one was looking of course. Sad to say, my baby went hungry. I squeezed and squeezed but not one drop of that white stuff came out. I also sang and talked to Dolly just as if she were real. What's more she passed the test and did not break when I accidently dropped her. Daddy used her for fire-wood when I lost interest.

## My Grandfather Ol' Joe

Mention the name Jose D'Agrella in Pomeroon and you will hear a story. Those stories are not always complimentary but they were definitely fascinating. He was affectionately called 'Ol' Joe' by his peers. I feared yet still loved this rough diamond I called Granfaddah. He was of slight build but strong as an ox. His moustache gave him a slight resemblance to the dictator Adolph Hitler which is quite a coincidence since he too had the reputation of being a demon; someone to be feared. His thinning hair was always covered by his trademark, an old battered felt hat. I think it was the only hat he ever owned. We had one sure way to find Granfaddah in the crowd on Market-day. We just looked for *de 'at*. A nail on the kitchen wall was home to his prized possession and we kids knew better to leave it alone. That was one man who asked no questions, you got a hiding and then found out what you did wrong later. This khaki-clad old man was a formidable character you did not mess with.

My grandfather Jose D'Agrella

## The Unique Fowler Engine

Ol' Joe's boat was known for its unique Fowler engine; it had a distinct sound which could be heard for miles. This was a good thing, because as children, we all learnt to recognise the *putt-putt* sound long before the boat came into view. It gave us ample opportunity to either stop or hide any evidence of mischief.

There were many temptations on the farm and most things were taboo because *fun* was not a word in Granfaddah's vocabulary. Most things were out of bounds, especially the coffee mill when it was coffee picking season. This enticing two-storey building housed the pulping equipment. We were forbidden to play here. The freshly picked coffee was stacked on the top level after it was harvested. No ball pit today could match the fun we had playing in the mounds of coffee. Extra care had to be taken to ensure none of the fruit escaped into the huge hole in the middle of the floor. The coffee was only fed into this hole when Granfaddah was ready to do the pulping. A conveyer belt ran from the top storey to the bottom of the building and once the engine was started we kids had the task of feeding the coffee into the hole. We enjoyed watching the coffee being greedily gobbled up.

Granfaddah's rules were always obeyed; especially when he was around because we were all very scared of him. He used to say, "Ah goin' to tan yuh behine if yuh doan be'ave," and he certainly did when we stepped out of line.

## Legal Trafficking

Trafficking was another venture my parents tried; legally of course. The most dangerous drug my father ever meddled in was the *Cappadula* (local Viagra) and I only know that because his older nephews teased him about it mercilessly. Sorry Daddy.

Our little corial was traded in for a *balahoo* (big boat) when my parents decided to go into trafficking in d'Riva. I have to remind myself it was legal to traffic back then; they should have told me they owned a floating shop. The sold foodstuff and fresh produce. Daddy weighed the items while Mummy attended to the money matters. They conducted business without having to leave the safety of their boat.

We were nothing more than river gypsies; travelling to the mouth of the Pomeroon River and beyond. We stopped at little unknown settlements, mostly inhabited by the Amerindians. I only remember a few things from that period. The most vivid is of us pulling up close to a sand bank. We climbed out and stood on it in the middle of the vast river. My mother wanted to wash our *face an' 'an's* (freshen up) and change us into presentable clothing before we arrived at our next destination.

I can still see a boat laden with provisions and my two brothers and I wedged in between the sacks of food playing happily, not a Nintendo DS in sight!

My parents talked a lot about a place called Morawhanna. It is an Amerindian settlement in the Northwest. I asked Daddy to tell me about their trafficking period just months before he died. He said we ventured far and wide. They worked mostly in the Barama and Barima rivers which were arteries that linked the Northwest. These rivers were close to the mouth of the Waini River which is not that far from the Pomeroon River where we resided. I have heard those names over the years but Google has finally allowed me to have a good view of where they are on the map. An outboard motor would have been necessary to cover such long distances but I forgot to ask Daddy if we had such a luxury and my memory has deserted me.

## My Grandparents' Neighbours

Jose and Philomena D'Agrella were my maternal grandparents. Let me explain the origin of calling our grandmother 'Gramuddah'. Guyanese have a habit of talking very fast, and this is the very reason we did not grasp the word G-r-a-n-d-m-o-t-h-e-r. We said it the way it sounded. I had two grandmothers but I did not get to know Daddy's mother Francesca until I was much older. I adored this little dumpling of a woman who looked as if she was walking on her knees.

Visiting my grandparents was a joy. I loved the neighbours on the adjoining farms at Siriki. The Gomes family on the right were Portuguese and we are related in some way. Apparently Cousin Louis had *charangi* (lustful love) for Mummy and asked for her hand in marriage but she would not *voomps 'pon 'e* (show any interest). She told me she even hated the chicken he gave her as a gift. He ended up with a lovely Amerindian woman we called Cousin Alice. I enjoyed picking and eating Primrose and *Su-moo-too* (similar to kiwi fruit) as I walked around the dam to go and play with Doreen, Jenny and Oona.

The Ramdeens, a family of East Indian descent lived on the left. A connecting dam allowed the neighbours easy access to visit by foot. During the rainy season these dams flooded and the only option was by boat. The Ramdeens always came over whenever we visited our grandparents. They were a large family so there was no shortage of playmates. *Naabah* (neighbour) Christina, their mother, was a woman of ample proportions. She had a sunny disposition with a big smile permanently plastered on her beautiful face. She wore her shiny black hair in a fat plait that hung below her enticing backside. That woman fascinated me with her ability to call and get a child's attention from a mile away.

Within minutes of our arrival we could hear the children and see Naabah Christina waddling down the dam leading her brood like a mother duck. The fat baby secured to her hips always had a *Tikka/Bindi* (red dot on forehead) to ward off *bad-eye* (evil/envy). She had children of every size and age, and one permanently in the oven. On the odd occasion her long suffering husband Baboo; a tall quiet man with a huge *muff* (hair quiff) came along, but he was always mute. I just had a flash back to an incident that took place some years ago and feel it's my duty to share this joke with you.

I had a senior moment one day while driving to the casino with my Australian friends, Rod and Pauline. I was trying to recall the name of a television personality when all of a sudden I remembered his prominent hairstyle and innocently said, "Don't you remember the guy with the big muff?" Uncontrollable laughter broke out in the front seat. Rod was so shocked he almost lost the steering wheel. I was taken aback with their laughter and asked, "What the hell is so funny?" Trying to control his laughter Rod warned me to never use that word in the same context again. I was stunned to hear that 'muff' represented an entirely different part of the anatomy; if you get my drift. In Guyana it simply meant a bouffant hairstyle for men. You learn something new every day.

Let me get back to the Ramdeen family. The eldest son Reginald answered to multiple names; we called him Reggie or Bonga. You remember him? He is the *kangalang* (rascal/idiot) who masqueraded as the *boogie man*. Bonga ended up marrying the maid who worked next door to us in Drysdale Street, but he sadly passed away at a very young age leaving Raho with five children. [We still see the family whenever we go to Guyana].

I also have to explain the significance of the word 'naabah' in case you are not of Guyanese origin. It is our custom to respect anyone slightly older than oneself. You were *full-mout'* (disrespectful to elders) if you called that person by their Christian name. Taking the liberty to be full-mout' was considered rude and could extract a sharp slap or *dressin' dung* (reprimand) from your mother if she was within earshot. You addressed your elders as, Mr, Mrs, Aunty, Uncle, Cousin, Cumpay, Mac-may, Tea-cha or Naabah. That is how we came to have aunties, uncles and cousins of various colour and creed.

## Sunday-school On Saturday

Both of my parents were born into the Catholic faith, but they branched out and became Seventh Day Adventists after they were married. This faith begins their worships from sundown Friday to sundown on Saturday. We attended church every Saturday as a family. My brother and I were always taken to a different building on the same property. No one ever explained the reason and I was always very distressed after being separated from my parents. I cried a lot because I was too *likkle* to understand and thought they were deserting me. That would have been around ages two to five I figure. Many years later I found out we went to Sunday school, except we attended on Saturday. [No wonder I am so twisted]. Can't say I remember learning too much at that school.

## Meeting My Great-grandmother Caroline

Another vivid memory is that of my Great-grandmother Caroline. She was the one who came from Madeira or the Azores. I was taken into a bedroom with a *big-big* (a four poster) bed. The room was very dark and the bed was very high, I could barely reach to see the person lying in it.

A very old woman with alabaster skin, wearing a white bonnet and a white nightgown was lying perfectly still in the middle of the bed. She spoke to me very quietly (I don't remember what she said). Mummy lifted me up so the old lady could kiss me and she said, "Dis is yuh Great-gramuddah Caroline." We did not stay in the room too long because Mummy said she was very sick. That was the first and last time I ever saw my great-grandmother.

I visited Verdon many times when I was older because my grandmother's brothers and a sister still lived in that home. My Great Uncle Manling and Aunty Vergie never married. Aunt Vergie always smelled like cocoa and Uncle Manling was a hermit who picked up every leaf that dropped. He never talked to anyone. I was scared of him because he could not tolerate children and kept a stick to hit us. The bachelor and spinster moved to a *logee* (a thatched roof hut) on the property after another brother (Uncle Joe) took over the house. I was told Great Uncle Joe was married to an Amerindian woman but I cannot remember ever meeting her. She died and he was left to raise Thelma and David. When I met this gentle giant, he was living at Verdon with his second wife, an African woman we called Sister Eldica. Uncle Joe and his family attended the Seventh Day Adventist church with us and I got to know their three older children Sammy, Naomi and Esther.

Daphne and I had a picture taken with Sammy on our last visit to Guyana. He ran a stall in the market at Charity. It's eerie that Sammy sadly passed away last week as I was writing this bit of family history. R.I.P Sammy (August.09).

My Great-Grandmother Caroline Gonaslves (nee DaSilva) born 1st Jan 1872

Me, Sammy & Daphne in front of Charity Police Station

## My Special Cousin

It will be remiss of me to go on without telling you about Daphne. She was, and still is, my very *special* cousin. Not only were we both born at Jacklow; we almost shared the same birthday. But being the *fas'* (curious/inquisitive) person I am, I beat her to seeing the world by a whisker! We were inseparable as children and played for hours whenever we visited one another. Her beautiful little dog Tutu-Sac joined us when we played hide and seek in the big bamboo grove on their property. We especially enjoyed foraging under a gigantic *stinkin'-toe* (loquat) tree to find the fruit that had dropped. We broke the hard shell with a heavy object then extracted the fleshy flowery smelly fruit. We could not get it fast enough into our gobs! The unpleasant smell was no deterrent to us. This fruit got its name because of its foul odour . . . I am sure we were adorable *likkle* girls back then, but not too kissable after eating *stinkin'-toe*. I also remember picking and eating Primrose on their farm.

Daphne & Tu-tu Sac

## Farewell to Daphne and the Pomeroon

Another baby came along after Charlie, and that was my sister Cheryl; we called her Cher. Mummy fussed over her a lot because she was delicate. I can't remember my parents ever leaving her with us under the tent in the backdam. I was told Mummy took her to Georgetown at three months old to seek medical advice but I have to recollection of that.

My parents decided to leave Pomeroon for greener pastures. I was too young to grasp the importance of a major move, and I was not impressed with this grand idea of theirs. My one and only concern was leaving Daphne. They had no idea of the devastation it caused me emotionally. Saying *goodbye* to my dearest friend was the saddest day of my life. It is etched in my memory for all eternity. Many years would pass before I saw Pet again.

I was only five years old when we moved from Pomeroon and Aunty Linda had three children at that time. Her fourth child was a girl and Pet (Daphne) missed me so much she insisted the baby was named Helena after me. From that time onwards Daphne's sister and I were called 'Big Helen' and 'Lil' Helen'. Whenever I visit the family in Toronto they revert to using those titles. Only three members of my extended family ever called me Helena. Guyanese are notorious for dropping their H so it is no surprise that Ol' Francesca and a few aunts called me Ellen.

# Chapter Three

*The straw that broke the camel's back.*—*Proverb*

# 1952-55 RUPUNUNI

## The Giant Silver Duck

The transition from the Pomeroon to the Rupununi is dim in my memory. We may have spent some time with relatives in Georgetown before continuing the journey to the Rupununi, but a blanket of sadness was cast over my emotions and I have no recollection of that.

Daddy said I was as white as a ghost when we landed at Lethem and lucky that I was still alive! My ghostly appearance was due to the horrendous plane ride. I was terrified!

The term, 'sitting duck' could have been applied twice on that fateful day. I had no concept of what to expect when my parents said we were going on a plane. I was certainly not prepared to see a *big silver duck* sitting in the river when we arrived at the water ramp at Ruimveldt. Fear set in, because I could not grasp the concept that this lump of steel was capable of taking to the air and staying there . . . I just wanted to run away. My mother did not know, or believed in the art of gentle persuasion, and child psychology was not heard of in those days. Admittedly, the poor woman would have been stressed enough with the upheaval of moving home, without having to listen to me blabbering like a baboon. She grabbed my arm in a commando style position to get me up the steps, and I literally sailed into the aircraft. I think I still have the bruises.

You may be interested to know this aircraft was not custom built for passengers but was a 'Grumman Goose' geared for transporting cargo. The captain, a kind man by the name of Art Williams welcomed us aboard by saying, "Yu'al sit weh yuh cyan fine a'space." Two Negro men were still stacking cargo. Dis time (now) de place stinkin' like hell. "Wha' dead in 'ere?" I nervously wondered, as I pinched my nostrils and manoeuvred my way around the crates on the floor. Mummy said it was the *salfish* (salt-fish/salted cod). Why does it smell so bad when it tasted so good I wondered; salfish eaten with fried *green plantin* (plantain) was my favoutite food.

We were losing hope of finding a seat when Mr Williams showed us how to drop the seat that was propped up against the wall, and then he hastily pointed out our improvised seatbelts, which was really a loop on a strap suspended from the roof of the aircraft. Before long, Captain William's voice boomed from the cockpit, "We ready to tek off now, suh 'old on tite." The roar of the engines was deafening, the aircraft shuddered under the weight of the cargo as it took to the air. Maan, ah was suh fryken a'vomit. You bet I was howling! I cannot tell you how long that flight took, but I held on for dear life believing the aircraft would drop out of the sky at any given time; those air pockets were relentless.

The landing was a mystery, we had taken off from the middle of the Demerara River, but to my utter surprise we landed on an airstrip in Lethem. The maiden flight in the giant silver bird left me with a phobia for flying, but it didn't end there.

The Grumman Goose refuelling at Lethem airstrip.
Captain Art Williams standing under the wing

## Our Homestead

Arriving at the homestead is somewhat sketchy. I was probably still in shock. What I have not forgotten, is the unusual mode of the transport that awaited our arrival. This was my first experience of having to sit on a cart pulled by oxen.

The open panorama of the Savannah was a bit unnerving. I was overwhelmed by the dry barren landscape after living in a river district. The twelve mile journey to our new home seemed endless on the rough bush track—not a tree in sight for shade. I had never seen a mountain and I tell you, this was a big-big mountain. The majestic Kanuku mountain range which separates the North and South Rupununi provided a magnificent panoramic back drop for our home. The silent giant watched over us and looked as if it was within walking distance, but I soon discovered it was just an illusion.

The huge house that sat smack in the middle of the wide expanse of the savannah made a big impression on my deprived senses. The homestead stood in the middle of a large circle cleared of all vegetation and looked like a fairytale castle. My father said the clearing was compulsory; it was a deterrent for the wild creatures that might be looking for free lodging. For this reason the yard was always immaculately swept.

The house was built low with only three steps to climb. A few logees could be seen just beyond the boundary of our home, it was where the employees lived. The stockmen Daddy employed were mostly Amerindians who came from outlying villages in the Savannahs. They were mainly from the *Wapishana* (Amerindian) tribe and most of them disappeared without notice. Quitting work as soon as they have acquired enough funds to support their basic needs was a well known trait of the Amerindians. Extras and luxuries were not important to them . . . today many of us can learn valuable lessons from them.

*Did I remember to tell you the reason my parents settled in this region? Of course I haven't.*

This venture boasted a small cattle ranch with a by-line to cultivate and sell tobacco and timber. It was brought to light not long before my father's death that this was a joint venture between he and his brother-in-law who actually put up the capital. [More on that subject later; right now I would like to give you a tour of my new home].

To begin with, this home was very large compared to our humble dwelling in the Pomeroon, still only three rooms but as a child, I thought it was grand! It consisted of a long spacious kitchen; a huge sitting room and an enormous bedroom, which the entire family occupied. Hammocks were slung in the sitting room for any unexpected and sometimes unwelcome visitors who shall remain nameless.

No plumbing—again; the bathroom and latrine were outdoors.

The long narrow table in our kitchen accommodated not only our family, but the workers with senior ranking who dined with us daily. That sounds grand so I think it's only fair to tell you senior ranking meant the foreman and overseers, and they weren't too far above the ones shovelling the cow manure.

The table was always immaculately scrubbed for everyday use, but a red oilskin tablecloth graced the table for *high-fa-lootin* guests like Dr Glasgow who came to check on Cheryl but always ended up staying for a meal.

This move did not allow us the luxury of graduating to fancy crockery; we were still faithful to the chipped enamel. Come on, we weren't that common; we had two *good plates* (china) for guests, as I recall they even boasted a few pink roses around the rim. We were lucky we never had more than two guests at a time or they would have had to wait their turn. We only ever used spoons to eat, I was never taught to use a knife and fork. Etiquette was mastered much later in life with a few very awkward moments. Mummy only used a spoon when she cooked soup as she preferred to eat with her fingers, especially when she cooked Indian cuisine (this practice was done in private). She was after all, *de Mistress* of the homestead and had to act like a lady when we had company. We have a saying, "Monkey see, monkey do" and therefore, I imitated my mother.

I will let you in on a little secret if you promise not to tell. To this day, I still indulge in this practice on occasion; in private of course . . . It evokes wonderful childhood memories.

## Living behind God's Back

We lived twelve miles from Lethem in a remote village called Moco-Moco. Our mode of transport was a cart; the wheels made from timber assimilated the movement of a sea-saw. I thought the journey took a long time to Lethem because of the slow oxen and wonky wheels, but Mummy said it was because we lived behind god's back. This journey was undertaken once a month to coincide with the cargo plane, *de duck* faithfully delivered food rations, mail, medical supplies and farming equipment, but more importantly, *likka* for the *rum-shops* (drinking establishments).

As you will see from the picture provided, our cart was not very spacious. Daddy always walked, but I think that was necessary to lead the oxen along the sparse dirt track. The ride was very bumpy, but as children we thought it was great fun. We travelled to Boa Vista on occasion, when all the supplies weren't available in Lethem. This shopping post was a little further; close to the Brazilian border.

Going to Lethem once a month was a highlight. We were allowed a rare treat and I couldn't wait to get the *fowl-cock sweetie* I always chose. I slowly licked the colourful rooster perched on the stick to make it last longer. If we were lucky we snagged a cool drink, most times it was only a two cents bottle of lemonade but it was heaven.

Our cart was also used to transport water for use in the home and in the fields. Everything was watered manually, a mammoth task in that sun ravished savannah. The water came from a beautiful little creek some distance from our home, but looking back, it could not have been that far if my brothers and I walked there. The forty four gallon drums always returned half empty because of the bumpy terrain. We also had a massive vat behind the kitchen that was filled to overflowing proportions in the rainy season . . . the overrun was as powerful as a waterfall. My brothers and I stripped naked when it was raining then ran all over the yard and under the vat to enjoy the prickling sensation of the gushing water. That was one of our favourite things to do while living in the Savannah.

The vat water was for drinking purposes only, so we had to use it sparingly in the dry season. Big rats sometimes drowned in the vat stinking up our water but we still had to drink it!

## Our Bizarre Playground and Zoo

The sheep we reared were allowed to roam free during the day. In the lambing season the ewes often gave birth out in the savannah, and since the savannah was our playground, it was inevitable to come across newborn lambs concealed in the long grass. We picked one up thinking it had been abandoned and played with it for ages. *Ow meh goi* (an echo of pity), the ewe refused to feed her *likkle* baby when we reunited them. My parents said the mother had rejected it because she recognised our human scent and didn't think it belonged to her. We were warned not to touch the lambs and I have never forgotten that lesson. On the bright side . . . we were delighted to hear the lamb had to be bottle fed, and took turns and enjoyed every moment. At times there was more than one lamb to feed because a few had become sickly. They were returned to the flock when they were old enough to be weaned.

We were also privileged to attend the birthing of calves. It was always a delight to watch those adorable creatures climb out from their slimy sack, then try to stand on their wobbly legs while their mothers licked them sparkling clean. Those calves had the sweetest breath.

Another favourite pastime was watching the rams lock horns when they were fighting. We alerted one another by shouting, "Come quick-quick, de rams buttin' again!" I guess that is where Guyanese got the term 'butt-up' from. Here is an example. If we ran into someone unexpectedly, we would relate the incident to someone by saying, "Yuh wood not believe who *a'butt-up wid* (met up with) today." Georgetown was a small place so we were forever *buttin'-up* with someone.

The only pet we did not have was a snake. We saw dead ones on a regular basis, and on occasion a *Water Camoodi* (Anaconda . . . it swallows its prey whole). The rivers were infested with *Caiman* (overgrown alligator) so it was quite dangerous to swim. Not only is the *Bushmaster* (snake) long, it is deadly. Be careful ladies if you go to Guyana . . . the *sweet men* (lovers) like to make reference to this snake to brag about their sexual prowess.

Another big danger were the *Perai* (Piranah) and Electric Eels. These were prevalent in many of our rivers. A Perai could devour a small animal in seconds and the eels administered shocks that could be fatal.

Tigers and jaguars were a major threat in the Rupununi, the stockmen kept guard at night to chase away the ones who roamed too close to the homestead. However they still managed to help themselves to the cattle from time to time. We heard them growling many nights; it was very unnerving.

### Nature's Playstation

Nature was at its best here. We were fortunate to have the most beautiful little creek within walking distance of our home. The same one we got our water supply from. My brothers and I played in the crystal clear water for hours. One end was deeper than the other but we were old enough to look out for one another. We swam, caught fish and tiny crabs, and amused ourselves without adult supervision. That was our nature's own *playstation,* and far more enjoyable than the modern day invention.

We also had access to the largest guava bush—an acre at least, which we explored daily. The trees bore different varieties of guavas so we had a lot to choose from. My brothers and I made claims on our favourite trees, and no one was allowed to pick the fruit; we made the tree our personal possession. *Big-'ead* (Joel) was a big bully so fighting broke out if we were caught in *'is tree*—he was such a big bully!

When the guavas were in season my mother made the most beautiful guava jelly and *we eat till we belly buss* (to our heart's content). The chickens roosted under the guava bushes and laid their eggs and it was our job as children to seek out their nests to collect the eggs each day. They were creatures of habit so we knew where every nest was. It was a most enjoyable task; not to mention having fresh eggs for breakfast.

How many children can say they had anteaters in their backyard? We saw them ambling regularly on the horizon of the great savannahs. Seeing one of these giant monsters with their long snout always thrilled me. We roamed the savannah inspecting their dinner, and one day witnessed them devouring the giant ant hills . . . Daddy was with us of course.

Cashew trees also grew in abundance. In the cashew season the over ripe fruit made mushy custard on the ground. We picked our way along the gooey mess to collect the nuts which had fallen off the rotting fruit. When we had a decent amount Daddy made a big fire in the yard and roasted them for a treat. Cashew nuts are another addiction of mine.

## Pets We Acquired

We acquired an unusual pet after a hunting expedition. It was a bird with pencil thin legs, boasting an iridescent plume, and a rump resembling a shortened version of a guinea hen. Daddy said it was called a 'Warakabra', but I am not sure if that is the proper name. This bird walked around in a *cloaked-up* (huddled up) position looking like a lost soul. It followed us around like a dog. If you visit an Amerindian settlement you will see one of these birds roaming the yard or compound. Daddy told me the Amerindians revere this bird. They believe it is a reincarnation of their ancestors and I can see why. This stork like bird has the persona of a very wise old man contemplating something meaningful. The astute Warakabra lets out a screeching sound to announce reptiles approaching and that could be the true reason for its prominence in Amerindian villages. Toucans are also a big favourite of the Amerindians.

We had a parrot, and like all parrots in Guyana, she too was named Laura. Mummy clipped her wings periodically so she roamed freely, but could not fly away . . . I had a lot of fun with that parrot. I tested Laura's balancing skills by putting her on the end of a long stick, and then with arms outstretched, I twirled around and around as fast as I could go. She squawked and opened her wings wide to keep her balance as she swayed from side to side like a drunken sailor. That was one of my favourite games. Laura only ever occupied her cage at night and Mummy always covered it with a piece of black material. She said that was so Laura could know it was night and that left me wondering who threw a cloth over the poor parrots out in the wild.

The first thing our grandchildren do when they get up in the morning is turn the television on, in contrast my first chore was to remove the black cloth and let Laura out of her cage so she could become part of the family. She followed us around and we cleaned up after her.

Our monkey was a *Sakiwinki* (squirrel monkey) called Jacko, like all the other pet monkeys in Guyana (we were too lazy to find original names). Jacko was a terror, and very sexually charged; his *lolee* was always standing to attention. We never let him off the chain because he bites; I lost a chunk of my index finger one day when I ventured too close. I was inconsolable when Jacko was found dead one morning entangled in his chain. Daddy dug a hole out by the guava bush and we buried him.

## Dangers We Encountered

There were many dangers in this region which resulted in a few unpleasant experiences . . . I had a narrow escape one day. The huge outhouse where the chickens, turkeys, ducks and guinea fowl roosted at night was also used for storing grain. This was a very interesting building. It had nesting compartments along the walls; little nooks and crannies, and a loft. It was just right for hiding when we played our favourite game of 'hide and seek'. While going through the door one day to find a hiding place, I heard a strange noise and instinctively stopped dead in my tracks to investigate. A big snake was looking back at me about a foot or so away on my left. I noticed a small section at the end of its tail moving and it emitted a rattling noise. I immediately ran to the house to tell Mummy. She was visibly shaken because she knew right away it was a rattlesnake. It was the first time one was sighted on our property. One of the stockmen killed it and kept the rattle as a souvenir, most likely to entertain his children. Mummy warned us to run if we ever came across another one after explaining the danger, but that was the first and last time I ever saw a rattlesnake.

Dangerous snakes called 'Labaria' came into our home frequently, mainly in the evenings while Mummy was telling us *Nancy Stories* (fairytales). Daddy said they came to listen because she told the most interesting stories without ever opening a book. She kept us enthralled for hours and transported us to magical places. These stories were told many times over until we grew out of them, some I still remember.

*My walk is getting a bit wobbly here; I told you I get side tracked easily, my apology.*

I was telling you about the Labaria. We were never alarmed when one came slithering down the wall because no one showed any real concern. Daddy quietly got up, chopped its head off with a cutlass, and went back to doing whatever it was he was doing, which was usually *ketchin' flies* (he slept with his mouth open). We thought killing a snake was the most normal thing in the world, although we were warned of the deadly nature of the snakes and knew well enough not to touch them. To this day I am more scared of a *crappo*. Another danger we had to watch out for was the *Marabuntas* (type of wasp). They built their nest in the eves of our home, and surprised us in trees. The wasps usually minded their own business, but we always tempted fate by trying to see who could knock their nests down without being stung. You had to run like hell because the slightest disturbance would set them flying, giving them an opportunity to sting you. These little suckers packed a mean sting which hurt and left swelling for hours. My features were changed more than once when a Marabunta sting made me look as if I had Chinese ancestors. What a pity we did not have a camera. At certain times of the year there was an abundance of these nests but Daddy had a simple way to eradicate them . . . he wrapped a piece of cloth around the end of a long pole, doused it with kerosene; set it alight, then burnt their nests. We were told to stay indoors whenever this operation was performed because the Marabuntas went ballistic trying to escape the inferno.

## The Faithful Dova

Most people, especially the natives, used a fireside to do their cooking. We were fortunate and had the luxury of a huge *Dova* (Dover wood stove). Mummy fired that stove up first thing each morning. The oven worked overtime to feed the family and the workers . . . my mother was a wonderful cook. She baked the best bread I have ever eaten, not to mention her scrumptious *Pine* (pineapple) and Coconut tarts. There is nothing that excites me more than the smell of freshly baked bread. Just the *odda day* I walked past a bakery and was overcome with nostalgia.

And what about that huge cast-iron pot we used to scald the milk? Bluebell and Daisy produced a gallon or two each morning, and while milking them daddy sometimes squirted the warm *fraffy* (frothy) milk from their udders straight into our mouths. Milk never tasted better!

I was sometimes asked to stand and keep watch over the milk while it was being scalded in case it boiled over. I got *boxed* (slapped) around the ears a few times for not calling Mummy soon enough. She hated cleaning up the mess. The milk was left to cool to allow the cream to rise to the top, and I swear that cream was two or three inches thick. Mummy mixed the cream in with the butter to make the most delicious spread, and we used lashings of it on our bread. What the hell was cholesterol? I never heard anyone complaining about being fat either, we ate to our heart's content and enjoyed life.

I just remembered Puss-Puss; she was the only cat we ever owned. Mummy used to transfer the big pot of milk from the stove to a little stool in the corner because she needed all the top burners. We caught Puss-Puss learning over the brim of the pot helping herself to a drink while the milk was cooling. She got some good *licks* (lashes) for that mischief.

Talking about Puss-Puss stealing the milk reminds me of one of Daddy's lessons. Someone Daddy knew jeopardised his job when he was caught with his hands in the till, and charges were laid. Daddy already knew this person was not trustworthy so he was not surprised and said, "Yuh cyan't put cyat to watch milk."

Television cannot compare to the entertainment Puss-Puss and the rats provided. By the way I hope you are not planning on stealing our unique pet names? And don't get any idea about her being a pet, she was a working cat!

The homes in Guyana back then were bare of ceilings, there was nothing to disguise the ugly rafters, but we would not have had so much fun if they weren't exposed. Let me tell you how we spent our evenings. There was no electricity so as soon as it got dark my father lit the *gas lamp* (Tilly lamp fuelled by kerosene). Great care had to be taken; the slightest touch disintegrated the delicate mantle. Whenever we heard Daddy shout "caramba"; we knew he had destroyed yet another one.

You already know about Mummy and her beautiful Nancy Stories, but I forgot to tell you about the other bit of entertainment. We were distracted most nights by a commotion above us in the rafters. We sat very still and waited for the rats to commence their ballet performance as they traversed the beams. A long stick was kept handy specially for the purpose of knocking them down. They never stood a chance because Puss-Puss stood guard to grab and kill the felled victims. Yes, I know you are thinking that was mean, they were only mice . . . but no, I am telling you, they were rats; some of them were as big as a Chihuahua. Puss-Puss behaved like a child at times toying with their food. She boxed the rat around for a while to stun it, and then she sat on her haunches waiting to pounce whenever it was revived.

We also enjoyed watching the *Gangga-sackies* (Geckos) that competed with the rats for rafter space, those we left alone. I lived in fear, because sometimes they fell off when they ventured too close to the gas lamp that hung from the rafter. Have you ever heard about those creatures never letting go of a person until it heard thunder . . . well I believed it!

## Mummy Cures 'Pip'

Raising poultry was Mummy's forte. She sold some here and there, but they were mostly for our consumption. The turkeys did not fare too well, we lost most of the babies, until Mummy decided to feed them herself. Bread was soaked in warm water to make a soft mushy consistency before we gently pushed it down into their craw. They thrived, and I was quite happy to help with the feeding. We kept the baby chicks in cartons in the kitchen, and the faithful Dova doubled as an incubator.

Dickens 'Great Expectations' featured a character called 'Pip', but did you know that chickens suffered from an affliction called Pip? This disease affected their eating, but Mummy knew the symptoms well, and brought the ash out immediately! She opened their beaks then rubbed the ash on or around their tongue to remove the offending object. The chicken picked-up in no time and resumed eating normally again. I have no idea where my mother learnt all these remedies! An outbreak of *yaws* (sores) also plagued the chickens, and yet again my mother painted the offending appendages with a special ointment and they were gone.

Oh! How could I forget the quails? We lost a lot of those, but I believe it was the snakes helping themselves. Looking back I realised we were the *hoi-polloi*... eating gourmet cuisine. We devoured the tiny carcasses even though we had to pick the sparse meat off their puny frame. Mummy had some difficulty cooking the tiny birds, and some were charred on occasion. She also served up their eggs, tiny with a bluish tinge when peeled. What do you think they tasted like? Egg of course! We didn't keep the guinea fowls because they were pretty, and it certainly wasn't to listen to that dreadful cackling noise they made each evening at roosting time.

Another t'ing we had the privilege of enjoying was the Heart of Palm. Daddy and I took little excursions to the jungle where he cut down the tall palm. It was the only means of getting to the heart of the palm which grew at the very top. The heart was concealed in a very small section of foliage that had to be painstakingly removed before it could be dislodged from its secret hiding place. Time and patience were required but it was worth the effort if you wanted to savour this soft and juicy delicacy.

Venison is now considered a gourmet item but we just thought of it as 'deer' when it was on our menu. These things were all very ordinary to me back then, but in hindsight I realise I had a peek into the future of gourmet foods.

## Branding the Cattle

The corral on the perimeter of the yard was solely used for branding the cattle, and we were allowed to witness this barbaric procedure. The unsuspecting beasts were herded in one at a time for this painful experience. The makeshift gate was slotted into place as soon as the animal entered. Once it was secured, a stockman wrestled the animal into position while another one applied the red hot branding iron to its rump. The suffering animal let out a loud mournful bellow, and the smell of burning hide and flesh permeated the air. A handful of ash, combined with fresh cow manure was roughly applied to soothe the raw wound and it was time for the next victim.

Castrations took place somewhere else. The testicles were eaten as a delicacy by the Amerindians. Daddy tasted it but it was never on our menu, then again, it could have been without my knowledge.

## Our Beautiful Horses

We owned three beautiful horses, each a different colour and temperament. As you will see our imagination had no limits; the white one was called White Mare; the brown one was Brown Betty and the black stallion was Blackie; how unique is that? Brown Betty was the only one we were allowed to ride because of her quiet nature. The workmen rode White Mare and Blackie to round up cattle.

A crowd gathered one day out by the corral to watch one of the stockmen ride White Mare bareback. Mannie who had only been employed the day before was obviously unaware of the mare's unpredictable nature, and no one was going to warn him. You have to remember, we were short on entertainment in the Savannahs. Those gauchos were accustomed to riding bareback so all he needed was a lasso. For all I know, the other guys could have challenged him knowing the consequences. However we all gathered to watch this spectacle. White Mare bolted before Mannie was properly mounted. In a split second the bucking mare threw him. Loud laughter erupted as he tried in vain to stop the horse. He slid off and was left dangling on the horse's flank; almost touching the ground, but he could not dismount. The lasso was tightly wrapped around his wrist, and it was attached to White Mare's neck. We watched helplessly as he tried to undo the lasso without success. What horror! Mannie was dragged for quite a distance before White Mare ran out of steam and let him off, then Mannie returned with his tail between his legs. The severe laceration to his wrists was not a pretty sight, but no one had any sympathy; his fellow workmates thought it was hilarious.

## The Chigga (chigger) Plague

When I was little, I thought *chigga* (chigger) was a word my mother invented just so she could torture us. How I hated having chigga. We contracted this parasite from walking barefoot in the sand and bush. Chigga is a miniscule ball of larvae secreted deep in the soles of the feet. The symptom is severe itching, but that was not as bad as the excruciating pain Mummy inflicted while administering the cure. My mother was not the gentlest person on earth, but we had no choice if we wanted to alleviate the problem. She *prouged* (probed) and poked the inflamed area with a sharp needle until she located the chigga. If you think that was bad, wait for the next step . . . she then applied the dripping *soft greuse* (medicinal) directly into the gaping hole. Anticipating the pain for this procedure made it impossible to keep my foot still, and this used to vex Mummy when she missed the target. The soft grease was said to kill any residue.

[I still wonder if there is any truth in that cure].

We were only ever permitted to walk barefoot around the yard because my mother had a strict policy about wearing shoes. She said going barefoot gave people the impression you were poor, and god forbid that anyone should know our secret. To this day I cringe when I see anyone barefoot in public.

My mother also judged a decent man according to the state of his shoes.

Someone recently told me of a simple cure for chigger. Paint the affected spot with nail polish; the larvae will suffocate.

## Another Embarrassing Experience

While we are on the subject of pests, I might as well tell you about *betrushe* (Bete-rouge). This parasite attaches itself to your body, and only becomes a visible red speck after it has sucked its fill of your blood. This reminds me of a very embarrassing experience. It happened the time Daddy took my brother Joel and I on a hunting expedition.

I might as well tell you the whole story because I know *yuh fas'* and want to hear what happened.

Daddy had been promising to take us hunting *wan day*, and that day finally arrived. He said we had to leave when it was still dark because it was a long way to the jungle, then he asked if we still wanted to go. Of course we still wanted to go! We had to go by horseback. Daddy sat me in front of him on White Mare; Joel rode Brown Betty, and one of the stockmen rode Blackie. I was not prepared for the semi-darkness of the jungle when we arrived and I was *fryken*. We were only going to be there for a few hours, so the horses were tethered under a clump of trees at the edge of the jungle. There was a clearing through the trees that almost looked like a doorway. My father said that is where they always entered. The clearing disappeared in no time, and the vegetation became dense; leaving a feeling of vulnerability. Daddy hacked at the vines with his cutlass to clear a path while I kept as close as I could to him. The *rice-eaters* (mongrel dogs) had gone ahead to do their sniffing with the stockman in tow. We were told to watch where we were walking, and to avoid stepping on any dry twigs because silence was very important when you were hunting. Daddy had his rifle slung over his shoulder, but took it off when he thought he spotted a *Maam* (bird). These birds are easy prey because of their bright hue. We ate Maam, so Daddy was hoping to shoot one. He cocked his rifle thinking one had come into range, but it was a false alarm. The forest canopy echoed with all sorts of unusual noises and this unnerved me. Before long a group of howler monkeys were jumping from branch to branch right above our heads. That was the most exciting part of the expedition. The sloth Daddy pointed out was pretty cool too; he was curled up at the very top of a tall tree. Woodpeckers sounding like woodcutters were busy at work but we were not able to pinpoint their location. The dogs flushed out a *bush hog* (wild boar) from its hiding place; it came charging right in front of our path; screeching at the top of his lungs. I was *fryken BAD* (really scared) and nearly *dirty* myself, I think the animal was more scared of us! We were grateful it diverted because we could have been badly hurt . . . I wanted to go home after that.

We came across a nice little stream, and stopped to drink and cool off. There was a Kokerit Palm nearby with a big *truss* (a bunch of fruit) but it was still green and we couldn't take it home. A huge iguana lazing on a branch startled me with its evil eye. I am not very fond of those creatures; they look too much like a crappo.

A shot rang out in the distance and in record time we saw the stockman coming towards us with a dead *Labba* (large rodent). Joel and I were getting fidgety so Daddy said it was time to go home.

We were not in that environment for more than a few hours, but I came home covered in leeches and betrushe. The leeches were revolting; they hung on for dear life, and we had to pull hard to get them off. My entire body was covered in tiny red specks; betrushe had invaded every orifice you can imagine and it had to be removed. To say it was embarrassing is putting it mildly. That was the first and last time I went hunting with Daddy.

## Bush Tucker

Australian Aborigines call the food they forage for in the outback 'bush tucker', and I would like you to know we also have bush tucker in Guyana; although there are no *witchetty grubs*.

Hunting in the jungle was a regular occurrence for the Amerindians, and my father sometimes participated. However, I never associated hunting with being a sport while I was young; it was just another means of providing food. Until now, I never saw my father as being blood thirsty, but he must have been to be going hunting. Even though he didn't hunt often, I wonder why he felt the need when we were running a cattle ranch. I would like to believe it was just another means of providing other varieties of meat, and we did enjoy it very much. Labba, *Acuri* (Agouti), Deer and *Bush-hog* (Tapir) were abundant in the jungle. My father also talked about a 'Manicow', but I believe he was referring to the Bush Cow which we also ate. Animals were not the only things they hunted; they also brought back an assortment of birds. The most popular were the Marudi and Powis. The Powis is the biggest bird in the jungle; it looks like a turkey except for its bright yellow bill and colourful plume.

The jungle was teeming with wild life; no hunting expedition ever returned empty handed. The unlucky game was strung and hung by its feet from a pole, and two men transported the dangling carcass out of the jungle. There was no refrigeration, so to preserve the meat it had to be smoked. Skinning, gutting and preparing the meat were all done by the ranch hands under one of the logees. *Dem people* did not throw

53

out a morsel; every part of the animal was used. When it was cattle, they used the intestines and blood to make *black puddin'*; a delicacy most Guyanese enjoy. I said "most" because not everyone indulged; my mother was one person who refused to eat it. We also never ate tripe and *souse* (pickled pig face) in our household.

Smoking meat is a skill well known to the Amerindians. I will tell you what I remember but please don't take my word as gospel because it may not be one hundred percent accurate. A platform or structure was erected in preparation for the smoking; the prepared meat was wrapped in foliage of a certain variety for flavour enhancement, then a fire was lit under the structure . . . I can't remember if this was done before or after the meat was placed on the platform. Anyway the raging fire was brought under control and kept to a smouldering level for many hours. The smoke penetrated the meat slowly, and if my memory serves me right, the smoked meat was then wrapped in muslin bags and hung in a cool spot where it was left to be *cured*. This meat provided delicious meals for many weeks.

Labba was my favourite meat. I say "was", because that came to an end on one of my visits to Guyana. While visiting my cousin Nita in the d'Riva, a boat announced its arrival with the blowing of a horn . . . Cousin Nita grabbed a basin and ran to the waterside. She signalled her interest and the occupants pulled into the stellin'. Selling *bush meat* (wild game) is a regular occurrence in the river. I don't know why, but I was utterly disgusted that they were selling fresh labba and bush hog. The sight of the dead carcasses in the bottom of the boat oozing with blood made my stomach churn. A long sharp cutlass, a wooden block and a scale was all at hand to dole out the amount required. That would not have fazed me one bit when I was growing up in Guyana, but times had changed and I found the practice nauseating. I walked away before she could make the purchase. Cousin Nita was delighted to have a butcher on her stellin'. Why not? She couldn't get meat any fresher than that!

My husband and I had occasion to visit her two days later, and being a hospitable Guyanese, she offered us some of her *pepperpot* (local stew made with meat and cassareep). This is one of my favourite dishes, but I declined knowing it was made with the labba. Forgive me cuz; I lied when I said I had already eaten. The truth is, I had *kinna* (scorn/aversion) and had to find an excuse. Mummy always said, "Wha' de eye doan see, de mine doan know." How true, had I not seen her buy that meat I would have eaten the pepperpot heartily and more than likely asked for more.

I was going to tell you about our dogs when I got side tracked with that last story. Our dogs with the not so original names of Bonzo, Rover and Rex were vital on those hunting trips. They were trained not to return to the hunting party until they were on the trail of an animal. A high pitched cry from a dog was the cue for the hunters to take over the chase. A bush hog retaliated once; attacking and severely injuring one of the dogs. It was Rex and daddy had to take special care of the maggot infested wound; he survived, but unfortunately he was left with a limp.

Another gross memory is the blood filled ticks those dogs always had, and what's more we had to pick them off. As a child I did this without a thought; it was so natural and actually fun. You couldn't pay me to do that now!

## Buckman Food

Food like Farina and *Tasso* (cured meat), eaten by the Amerindians in the Rupununi were not things we were accustomed to in the Pomeroon. Mummy was not impressed; she said the Tasso was "Buckman food." There weren't too many things that were different, and we were not compelled to adapt to the Amerindian diet completely. We got food supplies from Lethem, so Mummy could still cook all her regular dishes. The staple diets of the Amerindians were Farina, Tasso and Cassava Bread. Fish and wild meat also featured prominently on their menu. The Amerindians showed Daddy how to prepare meat to make the Tasso. The meat was evenly sliced, then salted before it was put in the sun. When the meat was cured it became very dry. It looked like leather and was just as tough, but the unsavoury looks belied the taste; especially when it was roasted over an open fire. I ate it at every opportunity . . . don't forget I was a child and had my own choppers back then!

The Tasso was mostly eaten with farina, and was the staple diet of the stockmen. They took this non-perishable food on long journeys when rounding up cattle for days on end. They also always carried a canteen of drinking water because it was a well known fact you could easily perish in the Savannah. Farina is made from the cassava, although I never had the privilege of witnessing the process. We bought our supply from the Amerindians. It has a sourish taste, and resembles coarse pellets. Farina mixed with sugar and water made a very nice snack. A small quantity of farina satisfied your hunger because it expands in your stomach after it is consumed.

Two types of cassava were grown, each for a different purpose. The sweet cassava could be consumed but the bitter cassava had to have the poisonous juice removed before it was edible. The extracted juice was used to make *cassareep* (boiled for hours to get rid of the poison), and a delicious dish we called *Atchee* (fish stew). Atchee is a very simple dish consisting of fresh fish, a whole lot of very hot peppers and fresh thyme. The pot simmered on the fireside for days with the most divine aroma until it was all consumed. Cassava bread was eaten with the Atchee, and my aunts in Pomeroon knew how to make both of these typical Amerindian dishes which was most enjoyable.

A Wapishana sometimes arrived out of the blue with a *warishee* (woven backpack supported by a band across the forehead) on her back brimming with fresh fish. Mummy was always delighted, especially since she was accustomed to eating a lot of fish in the Pomeroon. Did I tell you she was an expert fisherwoman? And who said we did not know about caviar? I ate fish roe from the time I could walk. Mummy was most excited when gutting a fish and found roe. I detest the rank smell and removed myself whenever she was scaling and gutting fish, but she always called me when she found this treasure. Removing the roe intact is a delicate procedure, so it fascinated me to see the expert way Mummy removed it with one clean cut. This delicacy was gently put into the pot to cook for a short time before serving . . . it was delicious! If we only knew about putting it in brine, we could have made a fortune. However I never acquired a taste for caviar.

## The Ita Palm

*Ita* (E-taa) Palm found in the jungle produced fruit we enjoyed. The fruit could be mistaken for being ripe when it turned red on the tree, but that was an illusion. There was a special process to hasten the ripening of the fruit. The *truss* (bunch) of Ita was placed in a burlap bag, and then it was submerged in a creek. We checked every few days until it ripened. The fruit was ready to be eaten when the scale like appearance of the outer skin scale was soft enough to be removed without effort. The flesh was scraped off the seed and was mixed with sugar for a treat. We quickly acquired a taste for the unusual flavour. The decomposing matter in the creek water apparently contributed to the distinctive flavour. These were all things we learnt from the indigenous tribes. The Ita palm fronds were used by the Amerindians to make the thatched roofs on their huts. Another palm called the Turu, produced an elongated black fruit which we used to make a nice brew we called Turu *tea*.

## Liquor Made By the Amerindians

The Amerindians make alcohol beverages called 'Piwari' and 'Cassiri'. Double baked (almost burnt) Cassava bread, broken into small bits mixed with water forms the base of the Piwari. The women remove bigger bits from the mixture to chew, and then return the chewed bits into a jug. You may not believe this, but the saliva sterilises any bacteria that may remain in the cassava. A full jug is given a stir, boiled and emptied into a huge trough. This process is repeated until the trough is full. The brew is then left to ferment for a few days. This is a social drink and anyone, including babies can partake.

*Cassiri* on the other hand is more potent. It is made from sweet potatoes, sugar-cane juice and sometimes cassava could be added. All ingredients are boiled and the sugar content of the cane aids the fermentation process turning the liquid slightly pink. When I was a teenager, I happened to be at a gathering where we all sat in a circle and each person drank from a calabash that was being passed around. I had heard the nasty details of how one of these beverages were made, but could not remember which was which. I assumed they were drinking the one made with spit, but since it is considered disrespectful to refuse, I had to take a sip. I have no idea whether I drank Piwari or Cassiri. It was quite pleasant, and had a sourish taste similar to cider from what I could remember.

## Undiscovered Star

An English couple named Bert and Helen came to the Rupununi and stayed as our house guests. They brought a funny looking contraption I had never seen before. No one took the time to explain why or what they were doing in our home.

The couple took me out into the savannah one day, and Bert carried the contraption under his arm. We walked until we came across a track full of *putta-putta* (slushy mud) . . . I seem to remember my brother Joel being with us. Bert opened up the pole that stood like legs on the ground, fitted a black box draped with black fabric onto the top, and then told his wife he was ready. Helen walked alongside the track and directed me as I walked on the muddy path. She offered me a small comb and a mirror, and I was encouraged to smile. Bert in the meantime was peering into the object projected on the stand while he wound the handle. I was puzzled as to why I had to return these gifts to Helen time and time again. No one explained what it was all about. The same sequence was repeated over and over until Bert was satisfied. I never once thought of opening my mouth to ask what they were doing.

Those people left like ghosts in the night and their names were never mentioned again in my presence. The memory of that day stayed with me as I was growing up, but it wasn't until I came to Australia and saw television that it finally dawned on me they were most likely making a documentary. The subject was probably about the Amerindians living in a remote area. I looked very much like an Amerindian child, so it was possible they used me to portray one. I have this thought because I can see the resemblance in the two pictures that were taken of me in the Rupununi around that period (I bet they took those pictures). Mummy always had my arrow straight haircut with a *linsey* (fringe); the same as the Amerindian children. Quite believable because my great-grandmother was half Amerindian and several of my relatives have made reference regarding my *buck* appearance, especially when I gain weight. On a visit to Guyana, Cousin Nita whom I hadn't seen in years came out on the stellin' to greet me and laughingly said, "Oh, gawd Helen, de buck in yuh showin'." Yeah, I had gained a few pounds—I rest my case. Anyway I am still wondering whatever happened to that film. I have no doubt it was a documentary because I've since seen them made in remote places and little gifts are always offered as an incentive.

My sister Cheryl & I in Rupununi, our latrine is in the background

Charlie, Joel, Cheryl & me. The corral & cart in background

## The Hart's And the Melville's

My parents never socialised outside of our home to my knowledge. However, we heard rumours of the well-to-do people like the Hart's and Melville's who owned large cattle ranches in Lethem, Dadanawa to be precise. They were called 'big-shots' because of their wealth. Their homes were pointed out to me, but I could not tell you what they looked like on the inside because we were never once invited while we lived in the Rupununi. I bet you are wondering why I'm so *fas'* (curious). I felt we were snubbed, and for very good reason. You see, we are related to the two sisters who married those men. Olive and Verna's grandfather and my father's grandfather were brothers; something like that. I am too lazy to climb that branch of the family tree, but we were still family. Their mother was Aunt Vergie who lived just across the river from my grandmother Francesca. Olive and Verna were long married when I started spending school holidays with Gramuddah at Try-bes'. They sometimes came to visit their mother, and I met them once or twice. I used to associate their names with their complexions; one was as dark as one was fair. I think Cousin Verna was a school teacher. Aunty Vergie was a darling little woman who wore an apron permanently. She spoiled us rotten. Her two sons Tony and Vincent lived with her and ran the farm because their father died when they were very young. I suppose my family did not fit into the same prestigious category as the Hart's and Melville's, but I remember Mummy saying something about *rubbin' shoulders* with them. I was too young to understand what that meant and I thought they had sore shoulders. Olaf and Teddy are now both dead. I heard Cousin Olive passed away recently but Cousin Verna is still alive and going strong as I write this.

A big shooting scandal called the 'Rupununi Uprisings' rocked the empire in the late sixties and the family fled to Venezuela, but that is enough gossip for the time being. It's not a secret; you can read about it on the internet.

We had no immediate neighbours at Moca-Moca so playmates were scarce, not that we needed any, we amused ourselves by making up our own games. My eldest brother paid too much attention to what the cattle got up to, because he wanted me to play 'cows' with him. I went down on all fours then he jumped on my back; fully clothed of course and I went along with it. As a child I had no idea what it all meant but I know now. My brother is no longer with us, but I wonder if he ever remembered playing that game when he became an adult—*likkle* pervert.

## Growing Tobacco

I promised to tell you what I discovered about an uncle putting up the capital for the venture in the Rupununi. Aunty Rita and I were talking about my father's life and adventures after he passed away and I asked a question more out of curiosity. I wanted to know how my father ever afforded to own a ranch. Imagine my surprise when she said it was her husband who went into partnership with my father. But judging from what she told me, my father went there solely to manage the project. She said Daddy was responsible for the demise of the ranch because he went on drinking binges that lasted for days once he collected the proceeds from the sale of the cattle and tobacco. Implications suggested some of the money may have even been deposited into the *hairy bank* (loose women), but only Daddy can account or admit to that.

Growing tobacco was no easy task; clearing the forest was a laborious task without the aid of modern machinery. The felled trees were piled high and left to dry, and then they were burnt . . . this was known as the 'slash an' burn' method. The ground was then raked over and prepared for planting. I used to watch Daddy carefully tending the tobacco seeds in a huge shed until they became seedlings. Planting was a tedious and back breaking job since it had to be done manually. The seedlings were planted into neat rows, and soon grew into healthy looking plants that produced a plume of beautiful white flowers. However, deflowering was necessary to encourage more growth. I can still remember how rich and beautiful a healthy crop of tobacco looked. The tobacco went through several stages of processing until it was ready for the market. The mature leaves were plucked and tied together in bundles then hung upside down from the rafters and left to change colour. Separating the leaves and spreading them individually over the rungs of a large rack came next. Over a period of time the leaves looked as if they were decomposing. These fragile leaves were tightly packed in layers in a tobacco press which looked like a big wooden box to me. Daddy regularly turned the handle of some contraption to compress the tobacco. A dark liquid trickled constantly from a tube inserted in the bottom of the press while the tobacco was being cured. The end product was a bale of tobacco which was shipped to Georgetown to be sold. Many years later I discovered my grandfather also smoked this type of tobacco.

Daddy enlisted our help to tend the tobacco plants. Our job was to remove the green caterpillars from the leaves, not an easy task when the leaf was the same colour. Some of those suckers grew to a great size, but those were easier to see. We squashed the tiny ones between our fingers, and the fatter ones were put on the ground and stomped to death. The smell of tobacco lingered on our fingers forever! That alone should have deterred us from smoking, but curiosity got the better of us.

## Licks like Peas

This is not my most favourite story so please forgive me for not going into the gory details. The memory of this day is ingrained forever.

Before I go any further I should tell you that we had a new addition to our family. Another girl who was supposed to be named 'Annette' after Mummy's sister but the registrar made a blunder; he misspelt the name and wrote Anetta.

It was customary for Mummy to retire to her bedroom after lunch for a siesta. My brothers and I were left to our own devices. Boredom got the better of us one day and we decided to collect all the *sigrit* (cigarette) butts left lying around by the workmen. A *sigrit* was carefully fashioned using a piece of newspaper. Matches were easily found by the side of the trusted Dova and we proceeded to smoke. We were spluttering, coughing and almost choking when we heard her voice. Mummy needed one of her *likkle* slaves and had shouted, "Joel, bring meh a'cup a'watah"—glasses were reserved for visitors. No one kept Mummy waiting so Joel barely had time to give his mouth a quick rinse before taking her the water. It obviously didn't do the trick. He did not return and I was summoned. I instinctively knew from the tone of her voice that I was in deep shit. She asked me to bend down so she could smell my breath. I was ordered to stand next to Joel, and then she called Charlie into the room and smelt his breath. The evidence confirmed her suspicion. I began to wail . . . dreading the licks to come, but to our utter surprise she let us off with a stern warning after promising to at least maim us if we were ever caught again. Then she asked us to spy on one another, and said we were to report any attempts right away. It wasn't long before our spy 'Sly Fox', told Mummy that he saw Joel rolling a *sigrit*. Joel of course denied the accusation, but Mummy believed Charlie. The punishment my mother forced my father to inflict on my big brother will stay with me forever . . . AND—we had to watch so we too could learn the lesson. It is too barbaric for words, but I will say a lasso, a horse whip and a bucket of water were used. The saying *licks like peas* (a severe beating) certainly applied in this case. Unfortunately it did not deter my brother because he started smoking as soon as he could afford to buy the cigarettes.

## Faddah C'ris'mus Is Dead

A crashing end came to my fantasy of *Faddah C'ris'mus* (Santa Claus) the Christmas before my seventh birthday. The long shelf built for storage just below our bedroom ceiling gave the secret away. I could never see what was on the shelf and being a fas' child I was always snooping. No amount of craning my neck revealed anything, but I knew my parents hid things that were special up there. In the weeks leading up to Christmas Mummy went to Lethem on a shopping expedition. We were not allowed to go and this heightened my curiosity. Super sleuth kept a sharp eye on anything that looked suspicious. Bingo! I looked up and spotted the leg of a doll, just a few inches but it was enough. I said nothing, but made a mental note of the blue trousers and waited for Christmas morning. It was customary to put our pillow case at the end of the bed on Christmas Eve. We were always eager to go to bed knowing we would get a present or two if we were lucky. Boy was I surprised! It's a wonder I didn't get an academy award for my performance. I never said a word fearing I would never receive another present.

It was ironic because that doll was the best present I ever got when I was a child. I called her Baby, and she was extra special because she could open and shut her eyes. I was a bit careless one day and her eyes dropped into her head. Mummy did some manoeuvring with a table knife to put them back into position so I ran for the knife every time her eyes fell in, but they never stayed fixed for long. After awhile I gave up, still loving her in spite of her blindness.

My one wish was for a doll that walked and talked and on one of my visits to Toronto I discovered my grandmother Philly also had the same wish. My wish still hasn't been granted but Gramuddah got hers fulfilled when she went to live in Canada. She would have been over seventy years of age so there is still hope for me!

We only ever got presents from Faddah C'ris'mus. Our parents were not as indulgent (could not afford it actually) as the modern day generation. My grandchildren's gifts could fill a truck, but don't ask them a week later what they got because they wouldn't remember. I could tell you what gifts I received six years in a row. Flying saucers, marbles and water pistols were popular for a long time from what I can remember. I sometimes got a few tiny dollies, either dressed or naked. I wish I still had one of them; it would probably be an antique today.

## Psychic Abilities

What I am going to say next may sound bizarre. I was only around seven when this happened. My favourite spot was the kitchen steps where I sat most days when Mummy had her siesta because she did not want me to venture too far. One beautiful sunny day I sat there daydreaming, with not another soul around; Mummy was having her afternoon siesta and my brothers were out in the paddocks. Something caught my attention and I looked up to see a very tall man of hefty proportion wearing white from head to toe, he was also wearing a white cork hat (I saw one many years later and recognised it). He was walking across the yard coming towards me. I immediately got up and ran to the bedroom to tell Mummy we had a visitor, but when I returned there was no sign of that man. Not one single soul believed me. Mummy was actually cross because I had disturbed her. It was probably an apparition of one of my ancestors . . . it was so vivid. I realised as I got older how superstitious our culture was, and some of the stories my family told me were bizarre. Many I simply did not believe, but I know without doubt I saw that man in our yard. Maybe it was Faddah C'ris'mus!

## School in the Savannah

We were all at the age where we should have been going to school, but there were no schools in the Savannah. This problem was solved when a Negro family arrived in the Savannah to take up residence not far from us. I was about seven years old when their daughter, a beautiful young woman named Jackie came to teach us. The small hut behind our home was converted into a classroom, but felt more like a furnace. A blackboard, slates and pencils were bought and we were sent off each day to our lessons—only half-day. This venture did not last too long; the Primus family were disenchanted with the Rupununi and left before the sun could set.

We were sent to board with relatives in Georgetown not long after that—I preferred the furnace.

## Allergic To Kabaura Flies

In the rainy season the savannah produced an outbreak of insects called 'Kabaura'. These almost invisible insects came in great swarms wreaking havoc on my body. I was covered in sores from head to toe, earning me the name 'Sorey-sorey'. To make matters worse, I enjoyed picking at them, and this made healing difficult. Mummy was so frustrated until she finally solved the problem. She sewed me two pairs of long sleeved tops with matching trousers. I can clearly remember the colours of those outfits. One was maroon and the other was bottle green. How I hated wearing those restricting clothes.

## Disaster Strikes Our Family

Life in the Rupununi proved a difficult mission for my parents, in more ways than one. A labourer was also killed while in their employ while felling timber. Our many species of timber included, Mora, Cedar, Mahogany, Wallaba (obtained from the Purpleheart tree) Greenheart, Crabwood, Bulletwood and Silverballi. Those are not official names but they are identified as such by the locals.

Uncle Leonard (no relation) was the labourer who met his fate while felling trees in the jungle. Daddy said all safety precautions were in place when the customary shout of "timber" went out. Everyone knew where to stand when that happened, and Uncle Leonard was at a safe distance from the tree. Apparently parts of the tree were entangled in some vines, and a length of dead branch snapped off, crushing his skull. He just happened to be standing in the wrong place at the wrong time. The evidence was propped up against the wall in our sitting room—it looked so harmless. Uncle Leonard was not only an employee; he became a very close family friend who lived in our home. I was especially very fond of him and cried a lot when he died. His family held my father responsible for his death. A court case was held and my father was made to pay compensation to that family for a number of years. This caused major financial difficulties for our family until the amount was paid in full. I found out many years later that the amount was a pitiful twelve dollars a month. To my parents it might have been a million. I believe the *monthly curse* was nothing compared to my mother's; how she despised that family.

## The Straw That Broke the Camel's back

Whenever I think of the Rupununi my thoughts go to my sister Cheryl. As you know Cher was the last child born to my parents in the Pomeroon. She was only one year old when we left d'Riva. Cher was born with a hole in her heart and needed constant medical attention. I clearly remember the little jar of medicine Mummy had for her condition; the contents were pink. Mummy warned us to be gentle when playing with Cher after telling us she had a "weak heart"—whatever that meant? Sometimes when we were playing with her she would *loss away* (faint). I recall being really *fryken* one time because her eyes were rolling around. I searched frantically to find Mummy and shouted, "Mummy, come quick-quick, Cher loss away." Mummy dropped what she was doing and got a cup of water. She slapped Cher with one hand while she sprinkled the water on her face with the other hand. Cher woke up and Mummy cried while she hugged her tight. I went back to playing because this was a common occurrence. Mummy never let Cher out of her sight if she could help it. She went to the latrine one day, and that was a little distance from the house. Cher passed out while she was gone and I threw a whole cup of water in her face. She jumped and stretched her hands out and looked as if she was trying to *ketch sh' self* (regain consciousness); just like when Mummy did it, so I knew she was going to be alright. I told Mummy what happened when she got back and she gave me a sweetie for saving my sister's life. Mummy said she was having "fits," but I had no idea what that meant.

The night Cher died is etched into my memory. We all went to bed as usual, but I was awakened by a lot of commotion in the bedroom. I heard my mother saying something about fits. I was always las', so I got out of bed to see what was happening. Mummy said Cher was sick and ordered me back to bed. Our mosquito netting was not transparent so I could not see what was going on and I finally went to sleep. I was sharing a bed with my cousin Olive because de Snail (Uncle Carlos) and his young daughter were staying with us again. I guess that was a big fit she couldn't come out of because she died that night. In the small hours of the morning Mummy lifted up the netting, shook me awake and said, "Cher just died, come an' kiss sh' goodbye." I got out of bed and walked over to the bed where my sister lay dead. She looked as if she was sleeping. I kissed Cher on her cheek; walked back over to my bed, climbed under the mosquito net and went back to sleep. I was wearing my ugly black night gown that night. My gorgeous little sister was only four years old

Someone was sent off in the evening to fetch the doctor, but he never arrived on time. Mummy said she thought it was the hearty meal of curry and rice Cher ate the night before that brought on her heart attack; we will never know.

We buried Cher under a big tree in the middle of that damn ugly savannah. I was seven and a half years old when Cher died, but I remember circling the grave on my *likkle* bicycle as the ceremony was being performed. Mummy held Anetta in her arms as she wept.

There were only a handful of people at her funeral; no one came because we lived behind god's back!

I only weep now.

# Chapter Four

*Children should be seen and not heard.—Proverb*

# 1955-99 LA PENITENCE STREET

### Flying in a Morgue

Our education was a major dilemma. My brothers and I were of school age, but there were no schools in Moca-Moca. There was a school at Lethem, but it would have taken an entire day just to get there. The solution to that problem was finally solved, but in true Guyanese custom no one ever bothered to consult us. Children were 'seen an' not heard'; that was the golden rule. We were simply bundled up and literally led to the slaughter.

As much as I prayed this was just a dream, reality hit hard when I was told I had to enter the bowels of the *silver duck* once again. We had to return to *town* (city) to attend school and should have been there in September when the new school term commenced, but my parents opted for January so we could celebrate Christmas with them. This saved them the expense of another plane ride.

Anticipating the flight was bad enough without having to contemplate the notion of living with strangers. I say strangers because I never remembered ever meeting these relatives. At least I already knew what to expect in the Grumman Goose . . . just thinking of it sent shivers down my spine. Since we had no choice, that dreaded day finally arrived. We had to leave at *fo'day* (before dawn) *marnin'*, to make sure we did not miss the flight. When we got to Lethem with our meagre belongings, *de duck* was landing. It was the first time I had seen a plane land. Maan I was so fryken I put my fingers in my ears to drown out the noise as the Grumman came thundering down. Dat t'ing looked as if it was going to miss the runway and *mash we up* (smash us). Did I say runway? There wasn't one; not a custom built one anyway . . . it was more like a make believe cricket pitch. The *duck* pulled up sharp, and came to a screeching halt. A slit opened in the side of the aircraft and a step dropped down. Captain Williams came out shading his eyes from the brilliant sunshine. An army of men came from nowhere; some began unloading the cargo while others brought out a huge drum for the refuelling. We had to wait a long time because the men also had to load the cargo for the return flight to Georgetown. We waited in the outpost building and Mummy took the opportunity to feed us. After eating, she led us behind the building to wash our *face an' 'an's* and to change us into our *good clothes*. I was now dressed to impress and before long someone came to tell us it was time to leave. Daddy hugged me and I started to bawl. He was not going to Georgetown with us and nothing could console me. I think I saw Daddy wiping his eyes quickly before he gave me a push up the steps. I was in the throes of one of those ugly hiccup cries as I trudged up the steps; Mummy was behind pushing and urging me to hurry. Mr Williams was already in the aircraft and welcomed us warmly. I was so *shame* he saw me crying like a baby, but he didn't seem to take any notice. He patted me kindly on the head as I entered and said, "Yuh know wha' to do, guh dung de back." Why was it so dark I wondered? It soon became clear to my horror; dead carcasses occupied most of the cabin. I hoped it wasn't Bluebell or Daisy. Jostling my way through the hanging beasts I couldn't help but wonder if I was going to join them. I found a seat and tried not to look but there was no where to hide.

We took to the air after a few frog leaps . . . my lunch did not stand a chance!

Mummy tried to point out the famous Kaieteur Falls not long after we were airborne, but I was not interested. In hindsight, I regret not looking at the mighty Kaieteur. Apart from being overcome with the fright of flying, I was also panic stricken as to whether we were all going to drown when the plane landed in the river.

Kaieteur Falls is the world's largest single drop water fall. At 741 feet it is spectacular and I was not able to appreciate it once. My furtive glance only gave me a glimpse of what appeared to look like an ordinary white sheet hanging in the distance.

## A Year Lived In a Nightmare

It was a sugar-coated story from the beginning. All lies when Mummy said, "Yu'al goin' to live in town wit' a'nice aunty an' uncle in a'nice big-big 'ouse." For beginners, it was not Georgetown; it was Albouystown, and everyone knew it was a slum. This supposedly 'nice family' lived in La Penitence Street; obliquely opposite the Rio cinema. She especially lied about the aunty and uncle. I would have said, "Beauty an' de Beast." This aunt was Mummy's sister and certainly beautiful; I will give her that! Beast is actually too good a name to call that uncle. I preferred, de Jackass, Asshole or Son-of-a-bitch to name a few.

Nice house my ass; it was old and *frukudy* (dilapidated) and crowded with relatives. We barely had a corner to sleep in, but I will tell you about that later because I want to tell you about the *crosses* (difficulty/woes) Mummy had to bear to find us a school.

## De Black People School

Finding a suitable school proved to be a bigger challenge than Mummy anticipated. For a start, there weren't many to choose from; not from Mummy's point of view. She wanted us to attend a school where all the *Putagee* (Portuguese) children went because we were fair skinned. There were three choices, but we had to discount St Pius because that school was behind god's back. St Mary's in Brickdam or Carmel in Charlestown would have been suitable for us. We qualified as Portuguese without a doubt, but my mother overlooked one important factor . . . Catholic families had first preference, and since we were not of that faith we were rejected on that basis. It did not matter how *white* we were, because their policy about being a Catholic stood fast. The biased nuns suggested we joined the faith and promised us a place if a vacancy became available later in the school term. What a dilemma; Mummy could not hang around in town for that long. I was fed up of following her all over town looking for a school, and although she did not say anything, I got the message as to why she wanted us to attend that sort of school.

In desperation Mummy put on her best manners and went to see the headmaster of St Stephen's Church of Scotland School. The students at this school were predominantly noted for being African and East Indian descent. Mr C.B. Giddings, the headmaster who was Negro, listened sympathetically but was very sceptical. My mother made a solemn promise to Mr Giddings never to remove us if we were enrolled. He had dealt with mothers who had made promises on that pretext so he naturally assumed Mummy would renege on the deal. He had only just met Mummy and did not know her true character. It took a bit of convincing, but her charm must have won him over, because he agreed to take us onboard. True to her word we stayed at St Stephen's throughout our primary school days.

Mr Giddings was very impressed with Mummy for honouring her promise. He eventually became a close friend to our family until his death. I was jeered for attending 'de Black People School'; but I learnt to live with the stigma attached.

My mother declined when the nuns finally offered us a place. I was not angry because a wonderful turn of events had taken place by then and I was very happy at St Stephen's. I will tell you what happened a little later.

## Beauty and de Beast (a.k.a—Jekyll and Hyde)

Mummy frantically looked for a dressmaker after we were accepted at St Stephen's. She told the lady it was urgent because uniforms were compulsory in Guyana; another golden rule. A tailor took care of the boys.

We were handed over to Jekyll and Hyde after being kitted out for school; Mummy returned to the Savannah and our hell began.

On top of our guardians and their two children, we also shared this small cottage with Aunt Olga and her daughter Donna who was just a toddler at the time. I guess this was just another 'rite of passage' but all I can remember of that period is the *licks* we got from my aunt and her barbaric husband who was a policeman.

Anyone knows a policeman is supposed to uphold the law, but *de jackass* we lived with was inhumane. I always thought nurses were supposed to be caring, but nothing could be further from the truth in my aunt's case. A right pair of hypocrites they were. 'Children should be seen and not heard' was the creed highest on their priority list. We could barely breathe without being chastised while being in their care. Nothing my brothers and I did ever pleased them. We were given a severe beating one afternoon after school. Why? Because we ran noisily up the stairs; things normal children do. *De jackass* justified the beating by saying we ran up the stairs like a pack of wild race horses.

### Rescued By a Martin—Twice

Mrs Mena (Hermina) Martin and her family lived next door. Mena was our landlady; she also owned the *laang range* (a row of one room housing units) behind her home. Louis, her eldest son knew of our predicament. He took pity on us and compensated by sneaking us little treats whenever we visited them.

Like most homes in Georgetown, these two were also built an arm's length apart. The close proximity of homes allowed neighbours to conduct conversations when standing at their windows. I visited the Martins one day and was in heaven enjoying some *Max* (brand name) chewing gum when I heard Louis chatting to my uncle. You may have guessed by now that I was a *fas'* (nosey) child who never missed an opportunity to eavesdrop. I casually sidled over to Louis and that Son-of-a-bitch he was talking to immediately spotted me chewing my cud and bellowed, "Where did you get that gum; spit it out right now, you are chewing like a pig!" I SPAT! I was *vex-vex* because the t'ing still had *tas'e* (flavour). I hope you noticed his perfect English. He was one educated *Coolie*.

The Martins were my saving grace when we lived here, so I was happy the two families were on friendly terms. From what I heard, it was Mrs Martin who befriended my aunt. She had nursed the late Mr Martin at Mercy Hospital and this earned her the privilege of becoming a tenant. As much as I enjoyed visiting the Martins, it was a rare treat because aunty always had a chore waiting for me.

Playing with Agnes was what I looked forward to most. She was my age and had a beautiful *dolly-'ouse* with miniature furniture; it was sheer bliss rearranging the furniture and pretending it was my own home. The miniature China tea set still lingers in my memory; the cups and saucers were so dainty, and so very special to play with. Agnes also had clothes for her dollies. How rich were these people I wondered! Agnes had three older sisters, Zena who was closest to our age, sometimes sneaked to play with us when Mrs Martin was not looking. That lady was very strict and always had chores for Zena. Stanley was a *small bhai* (little boy); the last child in their family. He gave us *tizzick* (grief/annoyance) every time we played; interfering with everything and pestering us to allow him to play. Agnes and I were always chasing him but he was so *own-way* (stubborn/determined). Many years later I had a secret crush on him, but don't let him know I told you.

The late Gerry Martin owned a soap factory in Chappel Street. The family kept the business going after his death. They sold soap called Winson and Lily; those names were no longer around when I became older. I think that factory was later owned by the Weithers who sold the popular Zex soap.

Mena's nephew Boysie (Antonia) Gomes ran a *cake-shop* (patisserie) located under the front section of our home, probably rented to him by Mena whom I believed owned the entire block. Boysie lived in a tiny room at the back of the shop with his son Claudie (Claude) who was a very naughty boy. He had a *likkle* surprise waiting for me one day when I went down to our latrine in the yard. He took out his *soti* (penis) to show me. I was so fryken I ran back upstairs shaking in fear. I avoided him from that day onwards.

Apart from running the cake-shop, Boysie also made boxes for Banks/DIH (D'Aguair's Imperial House). This establishment was, and still is, one of the biggest and most known, and I hasten to add, the most revered by the men of the Guyanese community. There is enough rum at that place to sink the Titanic.

Mena's *bottom-'ouse* (vacant space below the house) became the workshop where Boysie made the boxes; his cousin Rika (Veronica) helped him with the task.

The coffee and curry aroma wafting through the neighbourhood came from the run down building on the left of our home. This factory was owned by Mr Rodrigues, but everyone called him by his trading name which was 'Ricks'. He rose to fame in no time and was mostly known for his 'Sari' brand curry powder which was very popular then and up to this day. Ricks became a household name and I believe he could have been the first entrepreneur to invent out sourcing all those years ago. He invited the public to bring their parched coffee beans to have it ground by him for a small fee. We were regular customers for a while.

Oh, the other Martin who rescued me many years later happens to be a cousin of the above Martins. I only found that out after we were married.

## De Coo-Coo Kid

My aunts were discussing making 'Coo-Coo' one day and my ears pricked up. Food was limited in this household so I didn't miss the opportunity to pipe up. Sounding like a parrot, I said, "Ah like Coo-Coo." I did not have a clue what it was made from, but the name sounded exotic. You can imagine my dismay when it was presented. The main ingredient of Coo-Coo is okra which is slimy and to me is not very palatable. How was I to know that this exotic sounding dish was made with slimy okra and nasty cornmeal? The first mouthful repulsed me and I refused to eat the rest. Instant anger welled in my aunt and she bellowed, "Yuh said yuh liked it, suh yuh gonna eat every bit." It was an impossible task because I just could not stomach it. My refusal to comply earned me a severe beating. They say that every experience teaches you a lesson. Well this one certainly taught me never to say I liked anything again unless I knew what it was made from. It is a wonder they did not give me the *false-name* (nickname) 'Coo-Coo'. Those are the sort of scenarios that could easily earn you a false-name and I knew it was only a matter of time before I got one. No one in Guyana escaped that tag!!! Suckie-Suckie was still a secret; only my immediate family jeered me about my crying.

It was just that sort of situation that earned my Uncle Cecil his false-name. This incident happened after I got married and immigrated to Australia. Charlie told me this hilarious story many years later when I visited Guyana. The story goes like this . . . Charlie and a few other relatives including Uncle Cecil (he married Aunty Glerie, my mango peeler) gathered to have a drinking spree. The cocky young men began by mocking Uncle Cee's age. They advised him to go easy on the *XM* (potent local rum) and pointed out the danger of him becoming intoxicated too quickly. Uncle Cee was incensed and was going to make the upstarts eat their words. He confidently said, "Dat is wha' yuh t'ink, but it wood neva 'appen to meh because a'know de secret to stayin' soba." He promptly dispatched one of the children to buy a huge loaf of bread. He scooped out the contents of the loaf and ate the lot. He was now ready to show them how clever he was, and the drinking began in earnest. According to Charlie it wasn't long before his six foot frame folded up like a deck chair and he collapsed in a corner; out like a light! They named him 'Bread Guts' when he surfaced the following day and he never lived that one down. Now you know how easy it is to get a nickname in Guyana. I love that story!

Let me tell you how one of my aunts got her name. My grandfather was supposed to register her birth when he got to Charity. Celebrations got out of hand and he ended up blind drunk and could not remember the name Gramuddah told him so he gave the registrar my grandmother's name instead. It's a *truh truh* story . . . my aunt's name became 'Ena' to differentiate from Philomena.

## Absolute Stupidity

I received some good licks from *de jackass* the day I took the liberty of using his coloured pencils. The big desk that occupied most of the postage stamp size sitting room had many items to tempt a young child. That ugly faceless Westclox clock was just begging to be prettied up so I obliged. I used the pretty crayons to duplicate every number three times. It looked so beautiful but the mischief was discovered as soon as the master got home from work. He summoned us with a loud bellow of, "You children come here!" We presented ourselves before he could blink. There was NO lying in this home and *besize*, I expected him to praise me for my artistic ability and proudly confessed before Uncle could finish saying, "I want to know who . . . I was smiling and waiting expectantly for the praise. My brothers were dismissed and I was ordered to stand to attention. He repeatedly slapped me on both cheeks until he was satisfied. My aunt stood by watching but did not lift a finger to stop him.

Aunty had two little boys at the time and it was my duty to carry them around on my hips whenever I was at home. It was very painful but there was no complaining. I was there to do her bidding; especially with the boys. She actually slapped me one day because I made the mistake of putting on one of the boy's trousers on back to front; the wicked cow!

## Teacher versus Vendor

Since there were no toys I improvised to amuse and occupy myself. Our landlady bought empty oil drums to collect rain water for her tenants who lived in the range. A surplus of drums was stored under our home and it gave me an idea to imitate a school teacher. I turned each drum on its side then pretended each round of the drum was a seat; that gave me three pupils to each drum. I sneaked a *pointa* (pointer) from the broom to substitute as a *Wil'-cane* (a bamboo cane used for corporal punishment in schools) and I was ready to teach. I asked the questions; shouted and beat the hell out of those drums . . . no one ever answered back. After all, wasn't that being done to us upstairs in real life?

Another favourite pastime was pretending to be a market vendor. My aspirations weren't too high back them. I picked the different weeds that grew prolifically along the gutter in our street to represent the variety of *greens* (vegetables) I was going to sell. I imitated the vendors by making neat bundles then arranged the *greens* on any piece of old cloth I could lay my hands on (this was a substitute for the sugah bags used in the market). I invited imaginary prospective customers to buy by yelling phrases such as, "Get yuh fresh callaloo, bora, shallot an' *bigan* (eggplant) or fish, look how it fresh; get yuh *bangamary an' strimps* (fish and shrimps) 'ere." I knew the market lingo to a tee because it was my duty to go to the market each morning before school to get the ingredients needed for that day's meal.

Making mud pies was another favourite pastime. I used the wild daisies to decorate the pies, and then left them in the sun to dry. I got a good *cut-tail* (whipping) one day for *nastyin'* (soiling) my clothes. When I wasn't teaching, I was selling; I was torn between the two professions. It was a wonder I wasn't certified and taken to the Mad-house.

## Greed and Diarrhoea Goes Hand In Hand

To supplement our boarding Mummy baked chickens, bread and her scrumptious pastries and sent the box once a month by air; with Art Williams of course. The Ruimveldt water ramp was quite close to our home but *greedy guts* (uncle) would have ridden his bike to the North Pole to collect the box if he had to. I actually saw that *scraven* (extremely greedy) bastard counting off the days on the calendar with his coloured pencils. He could not wait until the parcel arrived each month. Since there was no refrigeration on board the aircraft, Mummy used a liberal amount of salt on the baked chickens to preserve them.

Unbeknownst to Mummy Uncle always secured and ate most of the food she so lovingly sent for us. I still chuckle over this nostalgic incident. Mummy was a bit heavy handed with the salt on one occasion but that still did not deter the *hungish* (greedy) brute from eating it! We watched as that son-of-a-bitch once again enjoyed the lion share. But karma is a bitch; he got no sleep that night because he had *operation* (diarrhoea) all night long, and could not go to work the following day. That ungrateful sod had the cheek to curse my mother for her stupidity. Justice had prevailed at last! My brothers and I were overjoyed to see him in this condition. You bet it was secret laughter, but it was sweet revenge. "*We laff till we belly buss* (uncontrollable laughter)," and Mummy laughed even louder when we eventually had the opportunity to tell her.

## Mafia Censoring

We had no way of divulging any of the ill treatment. That bitch of an aunt had a custom of reading and censoring the monthly letter I was made to diligently write before she mailed it. Loud laughter broke out one evening while she was censoring my letter. I was about to go over to investigate when she called me to point out the mistake. In addressing my mother, I had written, 'Dead Mummy' instead of 'Dear Mummy'. That woman ridiculed and shamed me to tears for that simple mistake. Her life must have been very uneventful because she took the time to tell everyone she met about my mistake—in my presence.

*Ow meh goi*, I used to feel so sorry for Charlie when he got licks because he was so *likkle* at the time. Some of the incidents are too embarrassing and painful to talk about, especially where my eldest brother is concerned. Joel is no longer with us so I will omit that part out of respect.

## Memories of Uncle Deck and a Fudgicle

The quiet handsome man who sat on the tiny front porch was my Uncle Desmond, but we called him Uncle Deck. He is the first son that came along for my grandparents but he did not spend too much time slaving on the farm. I think he fled to Georgetown at a young age just like the rest of his siblings. I am not sure if he had a job; all I remember is him sitting there looking lost and lonely. He lived with us for short spells but was not one for conversation and kept to himself. My memories of Uncle Deck are fond and connected to my stomach. You see the Brown Betty ice-cream vendor came around every afternoon on a three wheel contraption that had a big silver ice-box. His arrival was signalled by the row of bells he jiggled on the handle of the ice-box.

There were only five items to choose from, an ice-cream cone, a small tub of ice-cream, Fudgicle, Creamsicle and a Popsicle. The price range denoted our financial status. Mummy had treated us once or twice when she was in town. She only ever bought the Popsicle because it could be easily broken neatly in two. How I longed for a tub of ice-cream or a Fudgicle with the crunchy delicious chocolate covering. My dreams came true once in a while when Uncle Deck was staying. I didn't go too far if he was sitting on the porch. I cocked my ear as soon as I heard the bells and waited for Uncle Deck to say, "Helen, guh an' get meh a'ice-cream cone, an' getta Fudgicle fuh yuhself." My hands were very dirty when I handed him the cone one day and he refused to eat it. What a bonus! I was happy to oblige. A Fudgicle was a whole twelve cents as opposed to the Popsicle which was six cents so we did not get one very often, but I was grateful for anything. I was able to lash out to buy a Fudgicle now and again after I started working.

Another vendor plied the streets selling *Shave-ice* (snow cone). He pushed a cart that contained a huge block of ice covered in saw dust which he wiped off before shaving the ice with the metal contraption. The man manipulated the crushed ice into a ball then poured cinnamon flavoured red syrup over the top. If we were at home we took a cup out for this treat, and IF Mummy was feeling generous she would pour a small amount of condensed milk over the top of the syrup; that was heavenly. The fast melting ball was otherwise handed over and frantic sucking was necessary. A Snow Cone in Australia is the equivalent to Shave-ice, but watching the ice being crushed by a machine is not as bewitching (or has the same germs) as a man shaving it.

## The Secret Is Finally Out!

We were not allowed to go home for the Easter break because an agreement had been made for us to return to the Rupununi for the long school holiday that began in July. That seemed a lifetime away; especially since our parents were oblivious to our plight. The letters were cheerful as I remembered; however, one of my father's sisters exposed the secret. This aunt who lived in the nearby Alexander Village paid us a visit a month prior to our departure. She was shocked at our black and blue condition. Aunty said nothing at the time, but secretly intervened on our behalf. My parents could do nothing but wait anxiously for our return on the scheduled flight. This plane ride was the scariest of all because we were on our own and my brothers had no sympathy.

Mummy wept buckets when she saw our condition. She was sorrier for Charlie because he was still so *likkle*.

My brothers and I acutely felt the physical and psychological pain suffered at the hands of these relatives. The ordeal lasted less than a year but it felt like an eternity. Needless to say, we never went back to live in that *big-big 'ouse* after the secret was out but we visited another aunt who lived there less than a year later. All will be revealed shortly.

# Chapter Five

*Every dog has its day.*—*Proverb*

## 1956—CALLENDAR STREET

### Living on Coconut Walk

There was only one alternative if we were to continue our schooling and that was for Mummy to live with us in Georgetown. Mummy was torn knowing she had to leave Cheryl in Rupununi. The crucial decision was eventually made and we set out for town shortly before the new school term commenced in September. In hindsight that must have been a daunting mission for my mother. She was going to be solely responsible for four young children plus she had to find us a home. Although I did not know it at the time, this would be my last flight in the Grumman Goose. Hallelujah!! I made four trips altogether in the *de duck* and never lost my fear of those air pockets.

We had lodgings with relatives while Mummy hunted for a home. The financial elastic was stretched to the maximum so we could not afford to rent anything that would further endanger the budget. Someone recommended a Negro couple who wanted to sublet one room of their home. The room was not that big, but the price was right and we had stairs for private access. It was basically four walls with no place to *put-*

*up* (store) anything. Our clothing was kept in the battered *grip* (suitcase) under the bed. We were allotted cooking quarters downstairs. I would not call it a room because it was dark and dingy, and the wall with the door was slotted so we had no privacy. This room housed a small table, a few chairs, a two ring kerosene burner, a few pots and pans, and our prized enamel utensils. The backyard was populated with fruit trees. A big breadfruit tree grew practically within arm's reach outside the sole window; a golden-apple tree graced one corner of the back *palin'* (fence), plus there were a few coconut palms. I inspected the bushy cherry tree next to the outdoor bathroom every morning for ripe fruit and prayed *Popeye* (our landlord) didn't catch me.

Our new address was 22 Callendar Street, although we did not actually live on that street. We lived in the lane that ran off the T-junction. The lane was called Coconut Walk and for good reason, the entire path was densely paved with discarded coconut husks. Living here was a nightmare in the rainy season, because it was prone to flooding. The area was a canal at one time, but it was not sufficiently filled in; therefore not suitable for a residential area. We always wore shoes and socks to school, but had to remove them as soon as we got to the junction in the wet season. Our nice warm feet were in for a rude shock as we gingerly picked our way across the almost submerged husks. Balancing to protect our *book-bag* and shoes was a futile effort at times. We sometimes had *putta-putta* up to mid calf, not to mention falling flat on our faces once in a while. I think my brothers actually enjoyed rolling in the mud, but I was never happy walking in the sludge. The residents threw pieces of timber and coconut palm branches over the husks when they succumbed to the mud; anything they could lay their hands on actually—just so we could get to our homes without sinking. East Indians predominantly lived along this lane and most of them kept livestock in their backyard. The animals were practically dragged through the mud when it was time to take them to market or out to the outlying pastures to graze. One fastidious neighbour kept a drum of water at his front gate so he could wash his animals' feet. He was a *mook* (silly person) in our opinion and did weird things; like putting a light in the fowl coop to fool the chickens into thinking it was day; they ate continuously and got fat faster so he could sell them to make a quick turn over.

## A Corrupt Address

This place was corrupt in more ways than one; a major problem was the address itself. Who ever heard of every house in a neighbourhood being given the same number? Our postman was a genius; he knew the names of all the residents at number twenty-two. This blunder led to serious *cufuffle* (kerfuffle) the Christmas we lived there. A store owner delivered a gift basket laden with ice-apple, grapes, pears, figs, dates, and other goodies to our home by mistake, while Mummy was out shopping at the market. We almost wet ourselves with excitement just peering through the cellophane at the beautiful fruit and other delicacies; some we had never seen, much less eaten. We knew we could not touch a grape before Mummy came home. Gripped by impatience, I decided to wait at the gate, and ran to meet her as soon as she was in sight. She was baffled, and wondered who could have sent us such a grand gift. We were hovering around the basket like vultures so Mummy admonished us by shouting, "A'watchin' yuh know; suh doan touch nutt'in'." As if we were that *schupid*. We did not have the luxury of a telephone so Mummy went in search of the rightful owner, and in true Sherlock Holmes fashion solved the mystery in no time. Unbeknownst to us, the recipient, a Portuguese family living on Callendar Street also had the same surname; although we were not related. We had seen this Putagee family, but were not friendly with them. I remember being envious of the small bicycles the children rode. I believed they were rich and that *out-ah-dis-worl'* (grand) gift certainly confirmed my suspicion. What a disappointment when we realised the gift did not belong to us. Mummy personally delivered the basket, but those ungrateful people did not even offer her a grape. We talked about that basket for a very long time—still talking about it now. Our entire family had to make do with the measly *ice-apple* Mummy got us for Christmas; we could almost see through the paper thin slices. The fruit was imported and kept in cold storage hence the name 'ice-apple'. We also called them 'C'ristmus Apple' for the obvious reason. I inhale deeply whenever I catch a whiff of a Red Delicious apple just to recapture the nostalgic memories of childhood and Christmas.

Many years later when I was fifteen, I met and began dating the boy from that *rich* family; *'old on* (wait), I promise to tell you about that saga later.

## The Family Servant

It was my duty to make *tea* (breakfast) for the entire family when I was nine years old. Many Guyanese called the three main meals, *tea, brekfus* (lunch) and *dinnah* and we were summoned for 'din-din' when the meal was served.

I was woken up each morning to go downstairs whether I liked it or not. This *tea* (breakfast) was not your basic coffee and toast. For starter we could not afford to buy bread very often. This was a substantial meal which varied depending on the taste of the family. The menu was decided the night before, because no one was getting *deh lazy behine* up before me. The rest of the family had the luxury of staying in bed while I slaved. Our substitute for bread was *bakes* (flour based). I learnt to make the three types which we called 'hard, fried and soft' bakes. The *hard bake* was rolled out with the *belna* (rolling pin) and made into a thick round shape to be roasted on a *Tawa* (flat baking grid), while the other two were cooked in *fry-ile* (Fryol was the name brand). *Salfish* was almost always on the menu; we enjoyed it very much, and cooked it in a variety of ways. I also prepared green or ripe *plantin* (plantains), and eggs; fried or boiled. Most important was the *tea*; my mother could not function until she had her first cup of coffee. Once in a blue moon we lashed out with a tin of Exeter sausages (eight in the tin) or Corned-beef.

Not all of the above was served on the same day; although I think *Big-'ead* would have devoured the lot. He demanded his *heggs* were to be fried and not boiled. Oh yes, there was a reason for that. It was because he was *big-eye* (wanted the lion share). Joel was convinced he got more egg, because it looked bigger when it was fried. He was so *hungish* he would even eat our *lef-lef* (leftovers).

After the family had eaten, it was also my duty to *scrub de wares*. This was done in a big basin of water and using a piece of old rag or dry coconut fibre and *salsoap* (salt-soap) to clean them. The basin was emptied into the yard and the wares were given a final rinse in clean water. No hot water was ever used to remove grease. We washed wares, clothes and bathe with cold water and no one ever complained, because that was our way of life. Today, I would not dream of washing or showering without hot water, but please don't tell my family in Guyana because they are going to say, "*Sh' playin' white* (pretending to be a foreigner)." Our soap dishes were made from discarded sardine or pilchard tins. We punched a few holes in the bottom for drainage and it was ready for use. We replaced them when they became rusty. Sardine or Pilchard tins also made excellent *puzzlin'-tins* (money boxes). A slit was cut on one side of the tin and it was nailed onto the wall.

I was only allowed to go to school when Mummy was satisfied I had completed my chores; this left precious little time to get ready. I walked to school and lived in fear of getting *de wil'-cane* for being late.

There was no use thinking I could leave the house without bathing because my mother was big on hygiene. We had to brush our teeth before breakfast; *bade we skin* (bathe/wash) before going to school and again at night without fail, because Mummy always said, "Cleanliness is next to Godliness." We were lucky enough to have toothbrushes, the more unfortunate used a twig from a Sage bush (I tried it in d'Riva and it's excellent). We also used *sweet-soap*; not everyone had that luxury, but we used ours sparingly. There was a tap in the yard so thankfully we did not have to *draw watah* (fetch) from the standpipe down the lane like some people.

I bet you think I talk strange so let me tell you the difference between *salsoap* and *sweet-soap*. One was for laundry purposes and the other was used as a toiletry. My mother's favourite sweet-soap was Lifebuoy. We only got Lux, which I preferred, when the shop ran short. Mummy always patronised the shopkeeper who was closest; this showed loyalty thus establishing a friendship. All calculated, because it enabled her to get *truss* (trust/credit) when she ran short of money. I used to be so *shame* when she sent me to ask for *truss*. Why was it always me who had to do the dirty deed? My eldest brother had no responsibility and this made me very resentful. We were never allowed to question our parents, their decision was always final. Grumbling after I was given a chore got me nowhere, because Mummy was always quick to remind me with this gem, "Yuh doan bark w'en yuh 'ave a'dog." I wanted to be a dog there and then so I could bite her. The sting from those hurtful and demeaning words planted the seed of malevolence. The incubating hurt contributed to the rift which led to the rocky relationship between me and my mother in later years.

## Going To Old/Small School

It was important to include the words, old/small and new/big to differentiate St Stephen's schools. They were two separate buildings located a street apart. Everyone knew the old/small school was the yellow two-storey building at the corner of St Stephen and Princess Streets. *Lil'* and *Big ABC* (kindergarten) occupied the lower level while first and second standard were above. This building was the original St Stephen's but it outgrew the students so a new school was built to accommodate the higher standards. The new/big school was at the corner of St Stephen and Evans Streets just down the road. You were classed as a *small fry* (nobody) if you went to the old/small school. My only ambition was to go to the new/big school where I would automatically become *big*. The new school also boasted a home economic class and since that meant food, it was going to be just up my alley.

## Reunited At Last

Life was a bed-of-roses for a very special reason. Remember I told you another aunt later lived in that big-big house? Jekyll and Hyde had vacated the house in La Penitence Street leaving Aunty Olga to sublet with Aunty Linda who had come up from the Pomeroon. It was pretty crowded because Aunty Linda had four children at the time.

I can still remember the day I saw Daphne again. We hugged as soon as we clapped eyes on one another, and then we held hands and danced around the room with joy. And if I thought that was wonderful, there was better news still to come.

You might also remember I said I was happy Mummy did not break her promise when the nuns eventually offered us a place. Call it a stroke of luck but Aunty Linda also had the same problem enrolling her children into the catholic schools. St Pius offered to take them but that school was too far away so she declined. Mummy suggested a visit to see Mr Giddings. He was so happy with Mummy's loyalty he agreed and Daphne and Eddie (Edward) joined us at St Stephen's.

It was not easy being the only Putagee children at St Stephen's School. We stood out like *horned albino monkeys* among a group of gorillas; but I didn't care because I had my cousin by my side.

## Donkeys Go To Heaven

The students lined up when the bell rang at 8 a.m.; the boys in one line and girls in the other. We were not allowed in the classroom until there was absolute silence. We marched left, right, left, right all the way to our desks then said, "Good marnin' tea-cha" in unison, and then we said the Lord's Prayer. We all *buss laff* (burst out laughing) one day when we came to the part that said, "Who art in heaven" because some wicked boy said, "Donkey dead in 'eaven." Mrs Thompson pretended to keep a straight face, but I am sure I saw her smile. We said the same prayer again at three o'clock when school ended.

The incinerator located across the road from St Stephen's belched black fumes all day long. All the rubbish collected from around Georgetown was burnt there. The smell was terrible when they were burning dead donkeys or dogs. We had to hold our noses some days and on top of that, the ash came into our classroom. I had a good view of the billowing black smoke from the window when I was in second standard. Huge mounds of the ash were piled all around the site. [Heavy fines would be imposed if that happened in today's society].

## Slates and Other Treasures

We used a slate and pencil until we went to the new school. I could not wait to be rid of those horrid slates. A new slate had to be ruled with a nail; the sound grated right through my body. Those slates earned me many a beating. They broke easily and we could not always afford a new one so I had to use mine if it had a big-big crack. Mummy reminded me often that slates didn't grow on trees. I was warned to avoid the children who were *'rang an' strang* (picked fights for no reason). The school was full of *ruckshun* (quick tempered) children waiting to break your slate if you looked at them too hard, and over your head at that! The slates had a wooden frame around them and Mummy made us keep ours clean by scrubbing the dirt off with a metal scraper . . . water and soap were applied first. The slate pencils were a nightmare, you practically had to hide it in your *bee-tee* (anus) if you didn't want it to be stolen. A new pencil became an inch long before the day was out; we shared it with our friends who did not have one. I spent many a lunch hour under the school searching for a small piece of slate pencil because I was too afraid to go to school without one.

There were long wooden benches and matching desks at the old school. We sat five or six to each bench and had to constantly ask someone to *dress dung* (move down) . . . we were always so *choked-up* (cramped/crowded) in those classes. Sitting close to *funkie* (smelly) children was not always pleasant; at times I could hardly *draw bret'* (breathe). First and second standards were divided by a long blackboard. Mrs Morrison and Miss Walks used the side facing them. Our blackboard was against the back wall so we would not be distracted.

A quick glance at the colour of our book cover told everyone what class we were in; it was a pale green in first standard. Our lessons were taught from the West Indian Nelson Reader. I remember reading about Twisty and Twirly being two screws, Mr Mike goes to school on a bike and Dan was the man in the van; it was riveting stuff! I especially loved the Brer Anancy stories. My favourite is the one where he conned his family into giving him their plantains. We changed to The Royal Reader when we got to fourth standard but don't ask me what was in those books . . . remember, I went to school to play. I hated it when I was too ill and could not go because I enjoyed school so much. I remember Joel getting into serious trouble for *skulkin'* (truancy). Mummy *washed 'e tail* (gave him a beating) with a stick whenever she found out. Those teachers did not make fun to tell your parents if you didn't show up for school. We weren't smart enough to forge notes and I have to tell you the joke about the boy who tried to forge one. He wrote, "Deer teecha, meh mudder said ah was sick yestaday so meh cudin come to skool." It was signed Mummy.

I used to tremble in my shoes when it was time for school reports. Everyone waited with bated breath to compare their *place* (graded number) with one another. My report never once read 1/22; it was more 9/22, depending on how many children were in that class. At least I never failed, some children had to *stay back* (repeat the class) . . . that shame would have killed me. I can tell you my report always said, "Very talkative." Me? How cyan dem tea-chas lie suh much? The Coolie children always got the best grades and that always made me wish I had paid more attention, although those thoughts only entered my head at report time.

The old school was built just off the ground but children crouched to go underneath to look for treasures. A cent or a *jil* (penny) sometimes escaped from the open floor boards from the classes above. I had the good fortune of finding one—I can still see that shiny cent.

A *scrawly* (puny) Coolie boy got stung by a scorpion under the school one day when we had recreation; talk about scream . . . thankfully he lived to tell the tale. Long centipedes were another danger, they were found lurking under a rock or a piece of wood. Mummy threatened us with *a cut-ass* (a severe beating) if she ever heard we went under the school, but that did not stop us. Who was going to tell her anyway? I think someone told her a boy looked at one of the girl's *pat-a-cake* (vagina) under there and she did not want the same thing happening to me. The boys would have had a job seeing mine with those big-big bloomers she made me wear; dem things went down to my knees. Don't think I was the only one wearing big bloomers, Mrs Payne who taught fourth standard had a habit of sitting with her legs apart and it gave us a good view of her *druzees* (bloomers). The entire class *skinned deh teet'* (snickered) when she sat down and spread her legs.

## Rules and Embarrassment

My school days at St Stephen's had some unpleasant memories. I started out on the wrong foot. Okay, it wasn't my foot, it was my bladder. At least I did not have to start off downstairs with the *small-frys*. I was passed the age for the ABC classes when I started school so I was put in first standard which was upstairs; directly over Lil' ABC. I have fond memories of my first teacher. Mrs Thompson was *dugla* (mixed race); she was soft spoken and very kind.

There were lots of rules to follow at school. You had to put your hand up if you knew the answer to a question; most of the children used to wave their hand while they jumped up and down yelling, "Me tea-cha, me tea-cha!" I never put my hand up because I was always *fryken* the answer might be wrong. Putting your hand up if you knew the answer was scary enough, but we also had to put our hand up and specify what bodily function we wanted to perform before we could be excused to use the toilet. If we wanted to urinate we indicated by holding up one finger and saying, "Tea-cha ah wan' fuh do numbah wan." It was *numbah two* if you wanted to do the other. I barely made it home some days!!

I was a very timid child; scared of my own shadow and much too afraid to raise my hand when nature called. Should I say more? Lil' ABC would have been surprised at the unexpected shower. The children started pointing to me while they chanted, "Tea-cha, dis gyurl jus' pee an' it runnin' dung." My sobbing increased when I was asked to stand in front of the class; I could have died from shame! The baggy change of clothing I was given caused more embarrassment.

There were two toilets in the school yard that were supposed to flush, but the children seldom used them because they were constantly blocked and filthy. I tried to hold on until I got home, but on occasion I had no choice. The door to the girls' toilet was broken so there was no privacy. A group of boys came to gawk one day as I was standing at the door trying to shield Daphne. We could not get rid of them so true to my nature, *a'buss cry*. Daphne repeatedly said, "Boys, please *wait* (move)," but the boys just kept pointing and laughing like a pack of hyenas. From that day onwards Daphne was jeered with those words whenever one of the boys saw her. She never lived down the embarrassment.

There was more embarrassment for me when a magician visited our school. I was in second standard at the time and Mrs Morrison was my teacher. A magician was performing tricks on the big stage along the back wall. I was laughing and enjoying myself until I saw him pointing and signalling for me to join him on the stage. I guess he couldn't help noticing me since I was the only *white* child in the crowd. He showed everyone an egg then made it disappear. I was dumbfounded when he pulled the egg out from my ear. Instead of laughing, I started to cry. Yes I made my debut crying on a stage and of course never lived that one down! Crying was my speciality; the teacher only had to raise her voice and I struck up a chorus. I am sure some of the licks I got were for crying and not because I did not know my sums.

Mummy came to the school every day at lunchtime to feed us, and I mean *feed us*. She brought a basket with the food and a spoon (yes, one spoon); we took turns getting a mouthful. Not to mention eating my brothers' *jutah* (germs), it was disgusting! I was so *shame* but if we didn't eat we would go hungry. The mothers who brought food all sat along the wall facing Princess Street. The Coolie mothers stood out because of their colourful traditional *head-tie* (a colourful scarf). One day Mummy wore one, *truh-truh* (the truth), she looked *coomerish* (comical) and I was so *shame* I wanted to crawl into a hole. Mummy was also famous for her umbrella, she did not go anywhere without one because she wanted to *stay white* (remain fair).

## Bata versus Yaatin' Boots

It was of utmost importance to attend school wearing the full uniform; failure to do so required a note from *yuh muddah*, otherwise you got the cane. We must have had the ugliest uniform in the whole country; bright yellow blouse that looked as if a baby with *operation* (diarrhoea) *kounced* (defecated) on it. The blouse was worn underneath a navy blue box pleated pinafore with a yolk neck; a narrow belt and a navy beret completed the uniform. The boys wore a white shirt and short khaki trousers. Shoes were optional. Some families simply could not afford shoes so their children went to school barefoot. That was against the law in our home, Mummy washed the one pair of socks we had every night so it was clean for the next day.

I have to tell you about my Bata shoes. [Come to think of it I think Bata should pay me for this advertisement]. The first pair of shoes Mummy got me fell apart in record time and she was having none of that. It was better to pay for one good pair that lasted a lifetime and she found the perfect pair at the Bata store. It was as ugly as a crappo. She bought the sandal version the first time, but my toes soon went over the edge. No worries, Mummy knew how to fix that problem too. She decided to buy the closed in version, and to crown matters she intentionally bought it in a bigger size. We stuffed the toes with newspaper until I *grew into them*. Not finished yet; after I outgrew them she cut the toes out so I could get some more wear; then when its school days were over the back was cut out to make it into a pair of house slippers. Don't let me tell you how long that pair of shoes lasted. I did everything I could to destroy those blasted ugly shoes but it was like the Ever-ready batteries . . . they just kept going and going. If my memory serves me right, I believe she only had to buy two pairs for all of my school days. I had to polish my shoes every weekend to bring them back to life.

We had *yaatin' boots* (yachting/canvas shoes) as a spare when our shoes got wet. Mummy might as well have stamped the word POOR on my forehead when I had to wear mine. I was so *shame* because everyone knew it was only *really poor* children who wore yaattin' boots. Dirty yaatins were forbidden; mine was washed every week. A product called 'Blanco'was used to keep them white. After the shoes were washed and dried a small piece of blanco was dissolved in water and applied to the shoes with a rag or sponge then left to dry, preferably in the sun. These shoes were seen drying on windowsills all over town at the weekend. Many years later a better whitener called 'Properts White Renovator' became available. This product came in a bottle with an inbuilt sponge applicator on the lid . . . we had arrived in the modern world!

## Picking Lice

At school I had to sit in close proximity with the other students and most of them were infested with lice, it was a major problem. I sat next to an East Indian girl in fourth standard and I used to stare at the lice doing gymnastics on her long plaits that shone with coconut oil. I took home a fresh batch of lice every day. All the mothers in the neighbourhood ganged together to *pick lice* (delouse) after school. There is nothing sinister about the act if it was done in private, but my mother performed this task by positioning herself on the front steps. This was so she could *gyaff* (converse) with our neighbour who was also doing the same thing. Apart from injuring my dignity, it prevented me from playing skippin' or hopscotch with my friends. I always tried to hide when it was my turn. Mummy placed me between her knees and locked me in tightly, it was humiliating. She was very rough and demanded I keep still so she could perform the task. She jogged my memory often by *konxin'* (rap with a knuckle) me on the head or cuffing me on the ears. A special *fine teet'* (fine tooth) comb was used when the lice was plentiful. I had to bend my head forward while she combed from back to front. That comb used to scrape my scalp and hurt like hell. A piece of white fabric was placed under my head on the floor for the lice to fall onto. Don't think for one moment Mummy flushed the lice down the toilet. Oh no, she took great delight in crushing them between her thumb nails to kill them. Thank goodness that custom ended when my school days were over.

This reminds of a funny story about my grandfather who had very little hair, about two strands. Granfaddah always called me to pick lice whenever I went to Pomeroon to spend the school holidays with them. He obviously enjoyed having his scalp massaged, and this was just a ruse because he knew fully well that I wouldn't find any. He was clever and drew me in by offering me a cent for each louse I found. Not a hope, this exercise was as useless as sheltering under a coconut palm without any fronds. Needless to say I never made a cent, but it proved valuable because it helped to form a bond between us.

## My African Coiffure

Our landlady was a Negro woman of ample proportions; we made fun of the *preggy* (a rounded frame) bicycle she rode. Everyone hated that old fashioned style and referred to it by that name because it was compared to a pregnant woman . . . I vowed never to ride one. This hefty woman was called a 'Madam'; although it was not of an illicit nature, she ran a hairdressing salon for Negro clients. I often went next door after school to watch her *press hair* (style hair). The equipment and technique she used for this process intrigued me. The coal-pot she used to heat the irons and pressing combs was lit long before the client arrived. Those ladies must have come with clean hair because she never *washed deh 'ead* (shampoo). Madam went straight into combing the wiry unmanageable hair with the *big-comb* (wide tooth comb). What a tedious job . . . those women looked like *Sen-seh Fowls* (a breed of chicken); all wild and fluffy. She parted and selected a section of hair then pushed the big-comb in tightly to hold the rest at bay while she styled. Some amber-coloured Vaseline (locally known as Brown Vaseline) was applied to the strands of hair before the straightening and the styling process began. The hair sizzled when the hot curling iron made contact and an unusual odour fouled the air. She occasionally wound the hair too close to the scalp when she was doing the sausage roll style and burnt clients. Apart from the women yelling, "Oh gawd yuh bun meh," no one objected too much and was generally very happy with the end result. Some of those ladies walked out with cultivated rows of hair so neat you wanted to plant a crop. A few of her clients preferred the crimped to the scalp effect or my favourite *de flip*. Watching these creations taking shape was a favourite pastime. I must have wondered aloud one day as to what I would look like with one of her creations, because she offered to style my hair. I was a bit sceptical at first fearing the hot iron, but I overcame that by visualising *de flip*. I don't think she even asked Mummy's permission; neither did I. I was over the moon when she finished and felt so *big* (grown up). I could not wait to visit my aunties and cousins later that afternoon to show off my new hairdo, Daphne was *bung fuh* (bound to/ guarantee) be jealous! We always walked down James Street; it was a straight route to my aunts' home. The homes along here were built close to the road and most people liked to *mole-up* (congregate) on their front steps or *landin'* (porch) to *poun' name* (gossip) or *ketch breeze* (keep cool) at that time of afternoon. It was the perfect time; everyone will admire my hair which was plastered down on my scalp with Vaseline and flicked up at the ends as stiff as a dead cat.

Have you ever seen a *white* person with *pressed hair*?

I was smiling from ear to ear as I walked down James Street with my head held high and could not understand why everyone was staring and *skinnin' deh teet'* (snickering/laughing). I thought I looked fabulous! Why did Mummy take me out if my hair looked so ugly? Maybe she was secretly laughing too . . . come to think of it, she probably took me out on purpose to teach me a lesson for going behind her back. What do you think?

Do you think I learnt my lesson? I hated my *arrow hair* so someone took pity on me and gave me a Toni perm. The results left me looking as if I had a load of sheep droppings dumped on my head.

## Homemade Coffins

Poor Madam desperately wanted a baby, but she had one miscarriage after another. Not that I knew what a miscarriage meant, but I was so *fas'* and forever eavesdropping on Mummy and her sisters. My mother would say, "De mistress loss baby again." It was no big secret, because

94

we saw *Popeye* (her husband) go out the gate with the tiny white coffin strapped to the back of his bicycle whenever it happened. It was twins one time, because he had two of the tiny white boxes. They were still births, but that lady never went to the hospital.

Madam's husband on the other hand was a long streak of misery. He had a *laang sour face* and his bulbous eyes looked as if they would pop out from the sockets at any moment. The bottom-'ouse was his domain and he checked often to see if we had done any mischief. I liked to pretend I was riding his bicycle; I sat on the saddle and rang the bell when he was not around. We did not step out of line for fear of a lickin' from him. Anyone could flog a child in those days and when your *muddah* found out you were *'ard ears* (disobedient), she gave you another lickin' just for the heck of it.

Popeye was always making something under the bottom-'ouse, but we never got too close to see what it was (probably making coffins in advance), because he did not tolerate children. We did not live there very long, so I am not sure if they eventually had children, but Madam was someone I really liked.

## Our Personal Dressmaker

Dressmaking was a home industry that supplemented many a household. Anyone who could not sew had a personal dressmaker. Aunty Sheila was our first dressmaker when we came to live in town. She was a beautiful East Indian woman with four gorgeous daughters and a husband that looked like a *star-bhai* (film star). They actually lived on Callendar Street. It was a good thing I only got a new dress twice a year because I hated having to stand still while the dressmaker measured me. I used to get vex-vex when it was time to measure the length because Mummy always insisted it had to be longer than I wanted it. She said I would "grow into it." The best part about getting a new dress was choosing the buttons; zips were only reserved for *big people* (adults). When I was sixteen I attempted to make a dress but I had to enlist the help of my friend Jean when it was time to insert the zip. What a tricky business, it came out all twisted but I was so proud of my first *strap dress* (shoe string straps).

Just like the grocer; our dressmaker too was changed when we moved. It was never anything personal just done for convenience. We remained friends with Aunty Sheila and our other dressmakers and visited them from time to time.

## A Mystery Cousin

My mother found a tailor for the boys but he lived some distance from our home. We called this couple Cousin Winston and Cousin Vee. He was African and his wife was what we called *duglah* (mixed race). Jackie (Jacqueline) and Andy (Andrew) are the only two children I can remember from that period. Carl was born later; I met him on my last visit to Guyana.

Their home had the longest set of stairs I ever saw. I did not enjoy going there (because of the distance) or walking up the stairs unless *genip* (fruit) was in season. The genip tree grew very close to the landin' so I was able to reach out to steal a bunch.

How Cousin Winston kept track of all that sewing, I would never know. He had several half made garments from one corner of the house to the next and the home was very dark. Mummy and Cousin Vee spent a lot of time *gyaffin'* (conversing) after my brothers were measured and I always got impatient.

My family rarely came in contact with Cousin Vee so I honestly never knew she was a blood relative until my in-laws migrated to Australia in 1980. I enquired as to who had bought their home and was surprised when Mr Martin said the lady was a cousin of mine. I was puzzled when he mentioned her name because I could not recall ever knowing a Victoria Anderson. He was adamant so I racked my brains but I became even more baffled when he said she was African. This mystery bugged me, and when in doubt I called Daddy for answers. To my surprise he said, "Yes, yuh Cousin Vee baut deh 'ouse." I was floored, because I only ever knew her as Cousin Vee and always thought she was just another adopted cousin.

When I visited Guyana in 1984 I decided to pay the family a visit for old time's sake. This home is built behind another so it was unsafe for me to venture into the yard after seeing the 'beware of dog' notice. I yelled and Andy came to the gate to greet me. Cousin Vee was visiting her daughter Jackie so he offered to accompany me to her home. Since this was a surprise visit, they were all very happy to see me. It was a wonderful reunion but what happened after we left Jackie is something I will never forget.

## Picked Up By the Police

This day stands out in my memory for more than one reason. It was the 26th May, the anniversary of Guyana's independence. Celebrations meant extra police, but I wasn't concerned. Dusk was approaching fast as I drove Andy home. I needed to turn on the car lights, but I could not work out where the light switch was in Charlie's Buick. I had just finished telling Andy that I will have to pull over to look for the switch, when I rounded the bend and saw a police walk out into the middle of the street to signal me over. I found myself at the gate of the prime minister's residence. The policeman came to the window and gruffly said, "Get outta de cyar an' come wid meh." I got out and meekly followed him to the gate where three other officers were standing around a motorcycle. This is the front entrance to the prime minister's home so imagine my surprise when I discovered they were admiring a box full of kittens. Andy was desperately trying to whisper instructions. He wanted to advise me how to respond. Satisfied he now had an audience, the officer proceeded to admonish me in his gruff police voice by saying, "Yuh didn't 'ave yuh lite on, show meh yuh lysin." I lied, saying it was at home . . . to tell the truth I did not have an international driver's license. One of the other cops fired a question that floored me. As if it was the most normal question in the world, he calmly said, "Yuh 'ave any w'iskey?" Anger flared up, and without thinking, I angrily shot back, "You must be joking, are you asking me for a bribe?" (Note my *white* reply). Andy knew the rules so he started prodding me in the back and began whispering more advice. I thankfully caught on and told them I would deliver a carton of cigarettes to the station at the earliest opportunity. This seemed to please them, but one of them adopted an authoritative manner saying, "Mek sure yuh tek yuh lysin to Brickdam stayshun fus t'ing Monday marnin'." I meekly promised to do exactly that. I guess they are still waiting, because the incompetent jackasses did not think to make a record of any of the particulars needed to track me down.

There was more drama waiting when Andy and I finally returned to the car. It was pitch black by now and I smelt the person before I saw her. A very old African woman was literally hanging onto the car; she was fumbling with the door. She was asking for a lift to Bourda Market where she slept on the pave in a cardboard box. I hesitated, because of the terrible smell, but Andy said she was blind and that persuaded me to take pity on her.

Charlie had given me permission to use his car while he was away in the interior, but my youngest brother who was living with him at the time took it upon himself to chastise me when he discovered the foul odour. I was called every name in the book for my stupidity and no amount of disinfectant could disguise the stink, it lingered for days.

## Hidden Memories at X Durban Street

It was the year 2000 when I saw Cousin Vee again. My husband wanted to see his old home for nostalgic reasons so we paid them a visit. We were both very surprised at the transformation of the property. Most of the trees in the yard had been chopped down. The sitting room had also been transformd by her artistic son Carl. The supporting pillars in the sitting room were now totem poles with Indian heads. The home was a hive of activity. Cousin Vee was boarding students and the Amerindians from the interior also came to stay. Daddy had told me the complicated family history, but I asked Cousin Vee to refresh my memory. She does belong to the family tree, but to tell the truth I think that branch is a bit crooked. She hails from the great-grandmother who was a half Amerindian on my maternal grandfathers' side. It is too complicated for me to untangle. There was another surprise in store when we were given a tour of the home. The doll belonging to my youngest sister-in-law Rowena was staring at us from the high shelf in the main bedroom. We naturally wanted to know why it was still there. Cousin Vee said it was there when they moved in and it is guarding the house for Good Luck; so Dolly Martin still keeps us connected to X Durban Street after all these years.

## Corner Store Establishments

Most people in Georgetown pinpointed the location of a corner store or some such establishment when giving directions. Personally, I cannot think of a corner without visualising a shop of some sort. One intersection could have four different types of shop.

The rum-shop was the most popular when it came to the men. Some went in after work with their entire pay packet and completely forgot they had a hungry family at home. The stench of vomit and stale piss always surrounded a rum-shop. Patrons stood in full view of the public and relieved themselves in the gutter outside the door. Some patrons could only afford to purchase a *snap-glass* (single serve of liquor) while others spent recklessly to show off. Most staggered out or ended up in the gutter after a fight with another drunk . . . It was a good spectator sport!

The housewives frequented the salt-goods (salted foods) shop almost daily to get small items or to ask for *truss* when they ran out of cash (husband drank the funds). The congestion of goods sometimes hampered one's progress to the counter. The heady aroma of these shops greeted patrons from the street. Casks with pig-tails and salt-beef in brine stood outside the door, while boxes filled with smoked herrings, marcel and salfish lurked inside to mingle with the foul aroma of rotting potatoes, onions and garlic. A blend of curry powder, roasted ground coffee and *kero* (kerosene) permeated the air adding to the confusion of ones nostrils. Hessian sacks with their collars turned down displayed flour, rice and sugar. Split-peas, black-eyed peas, chick-peas and other legumes were all on offer. *Fry-ile* (cooking oil), tinned and bottled goods along with cleaning products and toiletries competed for shelf space. A minority sold fruit and vegetables; most people bought those items fresh from the market.

It was the era of the scale; goods were weighed and packed in brown paper bags or wrapped in newspaper. Shopkeepers took pride in their shops, keeping them in pristine condition. The scrupulously clean wooden counter top held a cluster of sweetie jars in a variety of sizes. Most shopkeepers wore a white apron with a bib. My Kodak moment captured Mr Beharry wearing one while he swept the bridge in front of his shop.

A dry-goods shop sold harberdashery, household items, electrical goods and a host of other things. The proprietors did good business but they had a lot of competition from the stalls in the markets. People from the lower income bracket patronised the market vendors for several reasons. For a start things cost less than the bigger stores and the vendors were willing to give you *truss* if you were short of cash. Those stalls were tiny but they had anything your heart desired. Items were stacked so high they almost touched the roof.

Every neighbourhood had a drugstore or six. People had faith in these proprietors because most of them were qualified dispensers. Why go to a doctor when we had Mr Green who knew exactly what to prescribe for any ailment. The really big drugstores in town were, Jaikarans, Bookers, Latchmansingh, Narine, Kawall, Tangs and Twins. We lived around the corner from Cendrecourt and Jeeboo once; these were smaller drugstores but just as important. How did they all make a living when the population was so small? In hindsight, I can see our drugstores replaced the doctor's surgery we all flock to nowadays. In all the years I lived in Guyana I only visited a doctor once and that was to have my medical done for my immigration papers. It was not the best experience either. The *dotish* (doltish/senile) old coot gave me a utensil and told me to pee. All well and good; I understood that; BUT why did Methuselah have to stand and watch?

Green's Drugstore was a landmark in Albouystown; I remembered being sent there with notes for Mr Green from the time I was a little girl. The big-big sweetie jars were a drawing card. Sometimes Daddy told me to take a cent from the change to get one. This shop held a mixture of intrigue and fear. Mr Green was an old gentleman, jet black and had the whitest hair. His drugstore was so dark you could only see him when he smiled. He was a gentle soul who moved with the speed of a sloth. The beautiful jars that lined the shelves had unusual stoppers and each jar contained a different colour medicine. I often wondered how he knew which was which, but he always gave me the correct one.

Oh, there is something important you need to know. If you were given a prescription for a liquid medication you were expected to furnish your own bottle. I guess you want to know where you can buy a bottle. Well you are talking to the right person because I can tell you dat. Take a hike up to Public Hospital and you will be able to buy any size bottle from the vendors outside on the grass verge. These bottles were soaking in full view of the public; softening the dirt and rubbish accumulated from years of neglect. They were washed and clean as a whistle! The washing water may have come from Punt Trench, but that was no big deal because the immune system of the Guyanese people is the strongest in the world . . . No germ is powerful enough to kill us.

I can also give you advice on how to become a business entrepreneur in the bottle selling industry. All you need is a small cart or a big basket for that matter. Walk around Georgetown going from house to house yelling this slogan, "Bottles I buy, I buy bottles," then re-sell them to the vendors who clean them and sell them right back to desperate people.

My favourite was the cake-shop; I knew the location of everyone. Some even had a few chairs where patrons could sit and indulge in their favourite beverage and pastries. This was where you were guaranteed a cold sweet drink; my favourite was *Vimto;* it had a sort of a tart cherry flavour, red and *white creamin' soda* was my second choice. When it came to cakes, the tennis roll, collar, butterflap and bajans were the most popular items on the menu. My preference was *Salara,* a succulent coconut filled treat which was flavoured and dyed red. Aah!! What I would give for one of those!

The more modern shops were hygienic. The cakes were displayed in long glass cases along the counter top; whereas the shabby ones allowed the flies free rein. Guyanese talk with their hands so the shop owners shooed the flies while they carried on a conversation with the unsuspecting customers.

Back in my era our cake-shops sold butter/margarine according to what you could afford. The proprietor used a knife to put the butter on paper to weigh it. I used to get a penny's worth. I feel a story coming on, so I might as well tell you. This is a truh-truh story about a guy who went into a cake-shop to buy a *tennis roll* (small sweet bun). He didn't have *two cents to rub together* (not well off financially) so he said, "Gi'me a'tennis roll an' please cut it wid de butta 'nife." Only in Guyana!

Bakeries were also very popular because very few people had an oven. Children were kept busy transporting pans of dough to the bakery on a Saturday afternoon, where the bread was baked for a small fee.

My mother bought a small round electric oven when I was seventeen. She baked bread and pastries, but it was the pot roast chicken cooked with special stuffing and *surwa* (gravy) I remember most, it was delicious! The oven gave up the ghost when the element burnt out.

There was a popular bakery in James Street called 'Dictator'. That damn bakery dictated at every opportunity that I buy a *penny-loaf* which I enjoyed with *red salt butta* (salted butter). Nothing could equal that treat. I always went there first thing in the morning, and waited for the tiny loaves to come out of the oven.

Talking about fresh bread takes me back to when I first discovered sliced bread. I thought my friend was lying when she told me that Harlequin Bakery had a machine that was slicing bread. I was a 'Doubting Thomas' so the invention certainly caught my attention. Quick as lightening I was standing at the counter to witness this phenomenon. Right before my disbelieving eyes there was a machine performing this miracle; I was transfixed. I stopped for a loaf whenever I could afford it, but the novelty eventually wore off.

## Cumfa Dancin' and Other Spirits

*Cumfa Dancin'* was a strange phenomenon that took place around this district. That was the name the locals referred to it, but I believe the proper name for this custom is 'Saint Vitus Dance'. It is a custom introduced by the Africans when they came to British Guiana as indentured labourers. It is somewhat like a Voodoo cult in my opinion. The group dressed in white costumes with elaborate turbans. They danced and chanted until they went into a trance. Some even danced on broken glass and performed feats with fire. The ones possessed by the *spirit* fell to the ground writhing and started talking in strange tongues while others jumped into the canal. I witnessed these rituals on occasion when they were performed on the dam along Punt Trench;

it was street theatre at its best! The spectacle was frowned upon by some members of our society but it nevertheless always attracted a huge crowd. I enjoyed the entertainment but kept a watchful eye for any *news carrier* (gossip monger) who might report my presence to Mummy. I would have been doing my own cumfa performance when the licks for that deed were delivered. Whenever we were over excited or behaving in a rowdy manner Mummy used to say, "Wha' 'rong wit' yu'al, yuh got cumfa?" It always got a laugh, because we knew what she was referring to straight away.

*Jumbie* is supposed to be the spirit of someone who has died. A jumbie can make an appearance in a room full of people but the only person who will see the spirit is the one it is meant for. Some people believe this spirit is harmless while others fear it and will take every precaution to avoid a situation where they feel a jumbie may be present. They avoid the cemetery; especially at night.

We were even wary of the *magick* mushrooms (toadstools) that popped up everywhere. We called them 'jumbie umbrella' and believed that these spirits lived under them. No one ate them and I did not know mushroom was edible until I came to Australia.

*Backoo* is another spirit we feared. He was said to be a very short person who live in a bottle. Milk and bananas was a backoo's staple diet. This spirit performed wicked deeds when instructed by its master. I remember a very distressed African neighbour coming to see my mother; she was pretty shook up and said a backoo had turned her home upside down. Mummy told me the mischief was done by her jealous *sweet-maan* (lover). A rumour said his woman was *gi'in' 'e blow* (cheating on him) so he was looking for evidence.

*Fairmaid* is similar to a mermaid and is supposed to live at the edge of trenches or a *koka* (a sluice). Many superstitious people took food as offerings to placate this spirit when any disaster befell their loved ones. My father said he saw a Fairmaid brushing her long hair on a sand-bank then dove into the water and disappeared when she saw him. She left her comb behind but he did not touch it for fear of a curse being put on him.

I knew someone who made offerings of food at the *koka* close to their home. This same person told me her uncle was pulled to the bottom of the river and never seen again. Mummy said he ran away to Berbice with another woman, who do you believe?

**Queh-Queh** (Kwe-kwe) is another African custom my family had no involvement in. This celebration was held the night before a wedding. The bride was hidden from what I understand, but the bridegroom had a great time dancing with the unattached women who undulated in a vulgar manner that simulated the sexual act. I was forbidden to attend a queh-queh and since I wanted to live I obeyed my mother.

## Anti-men on Punt Trench Dam

Men impersonating women was another form of amusement we encountered on Coconut Walk, La Penitence and on Punt Trench dam. We jeered and called them *Anti-Man* (homosexual). They staged mock weddings, and dressed to suit the occasion; the entertainment was immense. Most children had no concept of what a homosexual was back then. We got to know the more flamboyant personalities and always tried to ridicule them by yelling out "Anti-man, Anti-man" if we saw them in the street. This taunting really annoyed the individual. They usually ran to hit us after we yelled the taunt. We were afraid of a beating and ran like hell in case they ever caught us. These characters missed their vocation as actors. I laughed when I saw the Australian movie Pricilla Queen of the Desert thinking what wonderful extras our flamboyant anti-men would have made and much more entertaining! Their names were the most exotic and their frocks were *out-ah-dis-worl'*. *Bundaree* was the most exciting personality. Most of us were very naïve and never realised this was a way of life; we thought they were dressing up just for the sheer entertainment. I had to come to Australia to be enlightened.

There were two other characters we taunted at every opportunity. The girl we called *Scaramouch* actually lived two doors down from us at a later address. She was a beautiful East Indian girl but she had a birthmark that covered one side of her face. I heard she was given the name after a movie featured a scarred character called Scaramouch.

Nose-Gay was not a pretty sight with half his nose missing. He was said to be a *t'ief maan* (burglar) who had his nose chopped off during a burglary. School children were very cruel; some even pelted him with stones.

Another notorious *t'ief maan* called Greasy Pole lived in a range not far from us at one time, and rumour had it he oiled his entire body before he went out burgling and he was too slippery for anyone to catch.

## The Walking Telegram

The Hindus had a novel way to announce a death. A man from their community was sent around the village with a gong to perform this task. After the gong was hit with a great force the person said the message in an almost singing tone of voice. The name of the deceased was announced, followed by the details of the funeral arrangements. Everyone ran out of their home to listen in case it was someone they knew. I guess we were way ahead of the western world with walking telegrams.

## My First Sexual Encounter

A strange incident occurred one day while we were living on Coconut Walk. We walked to school via Sussex Street, but had to *cross across* (cross over) the trench to get to that street. Our crossing was the only one without a regular bridge; we had to balance on a big roundish plank. There was a *lantin-post* (lantern post) on Sussex Street as soon as you got over the plank. I was way ahead of my brothers when I approached the post one afternoon and saw a man leaning up against it. He was wearing what appeared to be a very long grey coat; one I had never seen anywhere. I naturally assumed he was waiting for someone, and since we were taught to be polite I was going to say "Good afta-noon mistah" when I passed the gentleman. I was about to deliver the greeting when to my utter surprise the man smiled and opened his coat wide. I was so shocked to see the colour of his *lolee* . . . it was green and appeared to we wrapped in some kind of substance. He did not say a word, but instinct told me it was dangerous. I froze for a split second (long enough to look), but was so fryken, I took off and ran all the way home. Mummy had never warned me of such dangers but I knew it was sexual and did not feel comfortable telling her so she never found out. I never saw that man again, but I made sure I waited for my brothers until the day we moved. As I got older I thought of that incident and wondered if that man had a terrible disease. Why was his penis green?

## Cousins in St Ann's Orphanage

The mystery of St Ann's Orphanage would have never been solved if my mother had not taken me there. I was very young and the visit left a lasting impression. I thought of that visit every time I passed that place when I was older. One of Mummy's cousins had died leaving his wife with five young children. She could not take care of them so the three eldest had to be institutionalised. It was sad that the children had to be separated but the orphanages were segregated. The two girls were sent to St Ann's while the boy went to the St John Bosco which is located at Plaisance on the East Coast. Their mother lived in Pomeroon so I think other members of the family took turns at visiting the children from time to time. The girls' orphanage, the Ursuline Convent and St Rose's high school were all housed in the same compound (an entire block). Public viewing was restricted owing to the high wall surrounding the buildings. Access to the orphanage was gained by pressing a bell at the entrance on Thomas Street. We were let in by a nun the day we visited. We were told to wait at the gate after Mummy stated her business. The nun fetched the two girls then specified the allotted time for the visit. It was only a short time and the girls were both very shy so nothing much was said. Mummy did not give the girls any *luv-up* (hug and kisses), but she gave them a parcel with clothes and *sweeties*. I felt so sorry for them having no family in that desolate looking place. These cousins were reunited with their mother when they became teenagers. The eldest girl and I became close friends and we still correspond to this day. Their brother passed away some years ago after a motorcycle accident.

Orphanges and many other charitable organisations in Guyana benefit and maybe to some extent still exist today because of the generosity of the diaspora living abroad. Alma Maters have formed organisations in Canada, America and England to raise funds to help the needy. Please support them if you have the opportunity because they do an amazing job raising money and collecting items to send for the underprivileged in Guyana. We may have left our beautiful shores, but we will not forsake our fellow countrymen and women. God bless all those who do this wonderful work.

## Watching the Punts

We were cooped up in that small room like a flock of pigeons and really looked forward to visiting our aunts and cousins a few afternoons a week. It was customary for the five older children (Joel, myself, Charlie, Daphne and Eddie) to play in the yard while the adults gossiped, but if we heard chains clanking, we knew the *punts* (flat bottomed steel barges) were coming and ran down to the *Punt Trench* (canal) which was at the end of the street. We enjoyed watching the punts and counted to see how many there were. It was a favourite pastime for all the neighbourhood children; the dam was filled with spectators in record time.

We also knew the punts were approaching when we saw the overseer dressed in white from head to toe. He dutifully walked ahead in advance blowing a whistle to notify the residents of the impending danger, especially for the boys who did not mind swimming in the smelly canal. The boats were an obstruction so the owners had to move them onto the dam to allow enough room for the punts to pass.

These pontoon type vessels were used to transport sugar-cane; they also delivered tanks of molasses to the distillery. We always knew what cargo the punts were carrying from the direction in which they were travelling. And just for a point of interest, the Demerara sugar you enjoy is exported from Guyana. Although I must warn you, throw out the little lumps! I was told the workers don't leave the factory to relieve themselves—just kidding!

I enjoyed sugar-cane so I was happy when the punts came from the direction of the cane fields. All of the children lived in hope of snatching a piece of the juicy treat. I was never successful at snatching any and had to be content with a scrap when someone took pity on me.

Because of the scarcity of bridges some of the residents used a small canoe to get across. East Indians predominatly resided on the opposite side and many made a living by transporting goods and running errands for a fee. They crossed in record time using a long bamboo pole to propel them to the other side. The boats were tied up to sticks or to a platform if the owner had one. The women also used these platforms to do their washing at the edge of the dirty canal.

Punt Trench was not very deep so the sediments were stirred up when the punts passed; the swimmers had to wait a while for it to settle before they could resume swimming and performing their *Cuffum* (somersaulting like a fish by that name) tricks. Now you know why Mummy forbade us to swim in it.

My mother was also totally against eating *cackabelly* (small fish), *strimps* (shrimp) or anything else that was caught in the canal because many households emptied their *Poe* (chamber pot) in it. Trenches and canals were virtual dumping grounds. Some interesting objects were caught when the menfolk dragged in their *cyas'-net* (fishing net) to inspect their catch.

The closest bridge to our aunts' home on the canal was a street away. The more adventurous boys ventured to lie on it hoping to dip their hand into the molasses tank when the punt passed under. In those days a mule pulled the punts, then some years later tractors were used. The boys had ample time to dip their hands in because the harness had to be taken off the mule/tractor and put back on before they could clear the bridge. Jubilant shouts went up when they scored some molasses; the black treacle dripped from their hands and everyone gathered to have a lick. No one thought of *jutah* (germs) when molasses was sharing.

Punt Trench was filled in sometime in the sixties; I am not certain what year that happened but it was done long before I left in 1968. It is no longer called Punt Trench; the residents now have the prestigious address of Independence Boulevard if you please. I used to take my sister CeCe when she was a toddler for a walk along the boulevard (full of rubbish), every morning before I went to work. It was that time of morning when the men in the community met with their birds in cages. They congregated in groups and stuck poles in the ground to hang the cages on. For some it was just a hobby. Tiny birds called 'towa-towa' and canaries took part in whistling competitions. Men also met and stood at street corners holding their cages and waited on their birds to whistle. Many people spent hours trying to trap these little birds in the *backdam* or in their backyards.

## Charlie Has an Accident

We were visiting my aunts one afternoon when Charlie met his fate. We took off to the canal as soon as we heard the telltale noise of the punts approaching. I was very excited and took no notice as to where the boys went. It was molasses, because the punts were heading in the direction of the distillery. There was a clanking noise when the punts got to the bridge, nothing unusual about that. I could see the entire bridge was filled with boys; other than that I took no notice. I did not realise anything had gone wrong until I saw an East Indian gentlemen walking towards me. He was holding onto Charlie's left hand which was wrapped in cloth oozing with blood. I immediately realised something was seriously wrong. Charlie must have pointed me out to the gentleman because I did not know him. In a serious voice he said, "Is dis yuh bruddah?" I had stammered "ye-s," and the man said, "Run quick an' tell yuh muddah to guh to Public 'ospital rite away, yuh bruddah 'an' cut real bad." Charlie was standing there as calm as you please, not even crying. I watched the man lead Charlie to his car before running as fast as I could to give my mother the message.

The molasses tank on this occasion was slightly higher than the bridge. It appears Charlie was trying to get some molasses, but his hand got trapped and was almost severed. Although I was standing on the side of the trench I did not see when it happened.

## Mercy Dash on Mota-bike

It was a known fact my mother was deathly afraid of *mota-bikes* and had never been on one. That changed in an instant when she received the message. The only means of transportation around was Boysie's motorcycle. Mummy was frantic with worry and had no time to think, she practically begged Boysie to take her to the hospital. By now the word had gotten out and nosy spectators had gathered on the street. We all watched in amazement as Mummy pulled up her skirt and jumped on the back of the mota-bike. She held on for dear life when Boysie took off on the mercy dash. Watching Mummy go was the most excitement I had in a long time! I had forgotten all about Charlie. We slept at Aunty Linda that night because Mummy did not come home. I cannot remember when she actually got home, but it must have been the following day. That was when the full impact of the drama unfolded. I remember Mummy telling us Charlie's hand was sewn back on successfully. I asked when he was coming home but she could not say how long he would be confined to hospital. I was nine at the time and did not really understand the seriousness of the situation so I was not too concerned about Charlie. All of that changed four days later. Mummy came home visibly distressed after visiting. She said things weren't going that well and Charlie's hand had turned black. The doctor had told her infection had set in and it was travelling fast. I overheard Mummy telling someone it was "imperative" but I had no idea what the word meant until I heard her say, "Especially since it's 'is left 'an' an' close to 'is 'eart." That's when I knew it was a bad situation. The doctors had done their best to save Charlie's hand but gangrene was winning and swift action was required. A decision had to be made because it was now a matter of life and death if his hand was not amputated. A telegram was dispatched to Daddy in the Rupununi summonsing him to the city. The operation could not take place unless both parents signed. What an awful predicament for any parent.

We did not see Charlie for a long time after he had surgery. I will never forget the first time Mummy took me to visit him at Public Hospital. He and all the other children who were longing to see their family stood at the caged window of the children's ward. *Oh meh goi*, he looked so pitiful with his *likkle* face pressed up against the bars at the window. I could smell the ward long before we *reach* (got there). I must tell you, dat place stink! The children's ward had victims from every known disaster and I believe the smell was coming from the ones who had burns. Charlie met us at the door and he was allowed to walk about as long as his amputated hand was strapped to the sand-bag. I could see there was no hand where the brown bandage ended, but he was taking it all in his stride. Mummy gave Charlie some *luv-up* and a few sweeties then went over to talk to a nurse.

I had never been to visit anyone in the children's ward and I was so fas' I wanted to know what was wrong with all of them. Charlie said there was a funny looking boy he was fryken of and he pointed to the cot with enclosed bars at the far end of the ward. This, I had to see so I pretended I was looking for someone and causally strolled past the cot to take a peek. I was not prepared for the sight that greeted me. Apart from his Amerindian features, the rest of his appearance was nondescript. He was making a grunting sound and looked rather peculiar. He was naked and some parts of his body appeared to be covered in what looked like scales; the bleeding sores looked like raw meat. Someone said he did not have legs, but I did not hang around long enough to find out, *besize* people could have just been *bad-talkin'* (speaking ill) about the poor boy. We were told a hunting expedition had found him in the jungle left to die, so they rescued him. That could be true because in all the time Charlie was there no one ever came to visit him. He was treated like an exhibit; everyone went over to his cot to gape. I have no doubt some visitors came just out of curiosity after the news got out. I still wonder what became of him and wished I knew what caused his unusual condition.

Charlie waited in that exact spot every afternoon at 4 p.m. for his visitors. My brother was only seven years old, how sad and lonely he must have felt in that hospital. It was a long time before he was discharged but Mummy never missed a day visiting him. I went with her *wan-wan time* (seldom); especially if I got wind she was going to stop at *Rico's/Fat Maan* (Mr Baker) shop opposite the hospital to get sweeties for Charlie. We lived quite a distance from the hospital and Mummy could not afford a *Bookers* (name of company) taxi or a *drop-cyar* (taxi service operated privately) and I was too lazy to walk.

## Haffa 'an' Charlie

Charlie was back in school after his stump healed and the teasing began right away. Teasing and giving false-names was a form of entertainment for school children and in no time he became known as Haffa 'an' Charlie. But I am happy to say it ended as quickly as it began. Let me just say, you would not want to be at the receiving end, that stump packed a mean punch. I believe some of the winded recipients spread the word and that brought an end to the teasing. They still teased from afar and even then they ran for their lives.

Charlie did not indulge in self pity; he never saw his handicap as a disability. He could do anything he set his mind to. I am proud to say my *bruddah* was a champion cyclist among his many other achievements.

Charlie married a beautiful woman and is the proud father of three wonderful children. He still resides in Guyana.

Charlie wins another race!

## Brown Betty and Window Shopping

Some evenings we were taken *dung town* (the city) when the stores were closed to do some window shopping. This pastime was especially enjoyable around Christmas time. Bookers, Fogarty and Bettencourt were the biggest department stores in Georgetown. It was customary for us to walk slowly along the display windows admiring and making comments on all the beautiful merchandise. It was only eye candy; we knew full well we could never afford to buy or even ask for anything we saw displayed.

A stroll to Big Market eventuated if money was available to buy an ice-apple or a few grapes. The atmosphere of the market was vastly different at night. The kerosene lamps emitted a pungent aroma and the smoke from these lamps cloaked the perimeter of the market in a haze.

I was further seduced by the delectable whiff of ice-apple assaulting my nostrils while the cries of the flamboyant vendors further emanated the spirit of Christmas.

In the same vicinity as the stores and market was a well known establishment called Brown Betty. They sold ice-cream cones which were one of my favourite treats. Getting one was more realistic, as long as you did not ask. Begging was prohibited; it resulted in getting *nutt'in*. I was always on my best behaviour and prayed a lot because being rewarded with a Brown Betty cone was sheer bliss!

The Fernandes family owned this eatery and was probably responsible for introducing fast foods a few years before I left Guyana. You can imagine the commotion it caused because in my era there was no such thing as 'fast food'. We were very happy with 'slow food' and never complained at the length of time it took to prepare. A fast flying pigeon or parrot was classed as 'fast food' when I was a child. [Go to Guyana now and you will find a shop at every corner selling fast food, it's a disgrace]. That is not to say I did not indulge . . . I was especially fond of *chicken-in-de-ruff*. With a name like that, one would think the chicken still had feathers. It was merely presented in a basket as a gimmick.

### Bezette the Belching King

Here comes a story about one of our street characters . . . This one was called *Bezette* (Bezet). That is what it sounded like to my ears, but I've had others tell me it was 'Peas'ead'. I admit it does sound similar if you say it fast. Anyway my family know him as Bezette. He belched on request for money or a meal. The sound was so loud it could be heard a street away. He was famous for going into Brown Betty at lunchtime. I mean in the cafeteria where patrons were eating. This cunning character rubbed his belly to work up a melodious belch, then let one go in the hope someone will leave their meal in disgust. He scored a meal regularly because management was never quick enough to catch him. Bezette came to our home *wan-wan time* (now and again) for a meal. Our *Bezet* was a composer of a different calibre but it was ironic that he called my mother *Miss Carmen*. He was not the cleanest person so Mummy kept an old enamel plate just for him under the sink.

When Mummy was pregnant with CeCe she ran into Bezette at the market and he kindly offered to fetch her basket home. A few girls begun to taunt him and this angered him so he decided to fight them. He dropped the basket and the contents went in every direction; some items rolled into the nasty gutter and could not be retrieved. Mummy was vex-vex that day. Bezette came around to our home the following day to see Miss Carmen; he apologised profusely and Mummy forgave him.

Shoes did not interest him; he refused to wear any and sold the ones that were offered to him. Walking barefoot did not bother him. I was surprised to see him chatting away to spectators at the annual car races one year. This venue was held twenty-five miles from the city but he told me he left home at *fo'day marnin'* to walk there. He was an innocuous simpleton who survived on the sympathy of the community.

## Motor Racing at Atkinson Base

This once a year spectacle was mostly patronised by the younger generation; my mother was certainly not interested except to preach the perils of *likka* and lecherous men. I attended a few times when a lift was available. I will be honest with you, those cars whizzing around the track held little interest for me. I went there to *lime* (socialise) and to look at the boys. Not the ones racing; they were big shots and out of my league. It was a day to be seen in your most alluring threads; society page reading. That ladder was too high to climb so I never made it into the papers.

The food was another incentive; people cooked for days to go on this twenty-five mile journey. Anyone would think they would never see food again. The racing stars were held in high esteem; guys like Johnny Terril, Errol Ming and Elson and Errol Manson-Hing were the cream of the crop in my era. All I came home with most times was excruciating sunburn and chapped lips.

## Churned Homemade Ice-cream

I never had a birthday party until I was sixteen and then I had to organise and pay for it myself. Parties were not something my parents could afford. We did not know too many people who gave their children birthday parties, and if we were ever invited to one it was talked about for months. I honestly can't remember going to more than one when I was little. Cousin Sybil was living with a wealthy man and was able to give Donald a birthday party. We talked about it for a long time.

What we had once in a while as a birthday treat was *churned ice-cream*. That was *very special*.

Brown Betty ice-cream was beautiful, but the ice-cream I enjoyed as a child can never be recreated. We called this homemade delicacy 'churned ice-cream', simply because we had to churn for what seemed like hours before we could indulge in this utterly scrumptious treat. This once or twice a year treat did not come easy. A refrigerator was considered a luxury for most households in Guyana unless you were born into a relatively wealthy family. Apart from not owning a fridge, we were financially challenged so ice-cream was reserved for very special occasions. An ice-cream making day was as equally exciting as Christmas Day. The procedure began with my mother making the delicate custard. She used a large quantity of eggs among other *magick* ingredients. Great care was taken to ensure the custard did not curdle. Our one burner stove was really *botheration* (troublesome); Mummy had a job trying to regulate the heat to prevent burning. However the custard was slightly burnt on occasion which resulted in a not so perfect tasting ice-cream. Discarding it was never an option, but no one ever complained. It was Daddy's duty to hire and fetch the ice-cream churner. That chore was done early in the day, because the ice had to be fetched just before the churning began. The day dragged as we waited for the appointed time when Daddy would leave to buy the ice. It was a good distance to the ice company. The excitement built up while we waited anxiously for his return. Daddy always purchased half a slab which he securely wrapped in an old sugah bag. He brought it home strapped to the back carrier of his bicycle. The ice was usually covered in saw dust to prevent melting, but it was easily wiped off. The churner was a wooden bucket like contraption with a handle on the outside, and a steel chamber fitted in the middle of the bucket. The entire family and half the neighbourhood gathered to watch the operation. The ice pick was brought out of hibernation to be put to the test. We children could not wait for Daddy to start stabbing the ice; just hoping a piece would fly in our direction so we could start sucking! Mummy poured the cooled custard into the cylinder of the bucket then closed it securely. The chipped ice was packed in the space surrounding the cylinder and a layer of salt was added before the churning began in earnest. We were all eager to take turns turning the handle knowing the faster we turned the quicker the ice-cream will be ready!

# Chapter Six

*Action speaks louder than words.—Proverb*

## 1957-58 MIDDLE ROAD, LA PENITENCE

### Daddy Says Goodbye to Rupununi

My father threw in the towel and said goodbye to the Rupununi after five years of heartache and set backs. It was an unpleasant and fruitless experience especially since he still had to pay many more years of compensation to Uncle Leonard's family. As mentioned earlier Rupununi also claimed the life of my sister so it was bittersweet. Now that chapter was closed because Mummy had no intentions of ever returning and who knows, she may have given Daddy an ultimatum. Nevertheless, it was time he joined us in town so we could live as a complete family.

We moved from the one room apartment on Coconut Walk to a small cottage in Middle Road La Penitence shortly after Daddy joined us. It was no bigger than a doll's house, but we had it to ourselves—the top part anyway. This move came with an unforeseen problem. The new home was on the other side of Punt Trench; a place we were not familiar with. It could have taken us ten minutes from the old address but the bridge in that vicinity was for pedestrians only. The truck with our belongings had to travel over the big bridge at Hunter Street (where vehicles do cross) then back track to get to our new home which was in the opposite direction. My parents knew bridges were scarce here but gave no thought as to how we would *cross across* the canal to get to school. Needless to say we were not impressed with the long distance we had to walk to gain access to the closest bridge. Most of the permanent residents who lived on that side owned a boat, but we could not afford that luxury, *besize* our home was one street away from the canal. But we soon learnt to endure the long walk since we had no choice.

## The Goblin Landlord

It was no wonder we did not have religion in our lives. God couldn't find us because we were always moving. He could have seen us if he had eyes in the back of his head like Mummy, but my *muddah* was unique. This place was without doubt behind god's back, and if that was not bad enough we had to share a house with the Devil himself.

I will call this landlord Mr Goblin; it's close enough to his true name and nature. This pint size man had a Machiavellian personality. Not only was he cunning; he was a hermit and a mean miser who owned half the neighbourhood. He used a piece of rope to hold up his trousers and he went everywhere barefoot. Mummy was convinced he still had the first penny he ever made and said they would use it to *shut 'e eye* when he died. He made a living with his *donkey-cyart*. The donkey was kept in a stall in the backyard so we caught the full aroma of fresh manure wafting over our breakfast every morning. The dried up miserable sod passed us on the road many times, but he never once offered us a ride to school.

If we thought *Popeye* from our previous address was a demon, we had another thought coming. This miserable man lived in a tiny room below our house and slept with one eye open so he could spy on us from morning to night. We were not allowed to run in the yard or make any noise. He kept his hawk eye on the fruit trees and made a mental note of the fruit in case we picked any . . . he would give us hell and used the foulest language. AND that's where I learnt to *cuss* (curse). Mr Goblin was East Indian and used idioms such as this. "*Al'yuh backrah-pickney gon get a'good cut-ass if a'ketch yuh rass; an' doan t'ink a'mekin' fun, yuh bee-tee gon bun.*" It was sheer poetry. Now for the translation, 'You children will get a good flogging if I catch your backsides; and don't think I am joking, you will feel pain'. What a horrible little shit he was. By the way, the term 'backrah' was used when referring to a person who is Caucasian or *de white* people (European) I talk about. My grandfather on the other hand called us 'backrah-pickney' when he was angry and wanted to get our attention. The latter insinuated we were of half-caste parentage [dating back to slavery when slaves had children with their master/mistress].

Mr Goblin's threat of pain was not idle. I stepped on a broken bottle while playing hide an' seek one night. The pain was severe, but my mother had no sympathy. Oh no, she boxed me around the ears a few times as she angrily shouted, "It serves yuh rite fuh bein' suh 'ard ears, a'tole yuh not to play in de dark." The dreadful man actually placed broken bottles around the yard as traps; what a mean cunning man. I was cut by broken bottles when I was growing up more times than I care to remember and never went to the doctor or had one stitch; *scotch tape* (adhesive tape) sufficed. Any tape was called 'scotch tape' after we used the one with the Scottish tartan logo. That tape was used to patch everything.

A good game of hide an' seek livened up an otherwise dull evening. I always tried to get to the the big guava tree first. It was a bit dark in that spot and I hoped Kenny would catch me. Why? I wanted him to kiss me of course! Sure was a brazen *lil' t'ing*. The guava tree was just behind the goblin's hovel so we expected play to be curtailed when he came out waving a big stick, and boy we scattered in no time! We usually settled for playing cards indoors under the watchful eye of our parents after we were sent packing.

## No Plumbing Here

There was no plumbing in the homes on Middle Road so everyone had latrines in their backyard. A few cans of air freshener wouldn't have gone astray there. What about toilet paper; I hear you ask? Of course we had toilet paper. As a matter of fact we were so advanced we had special brands. I remember using, *Argosy, Graphic* and *Chronicle*; paper that allowed us the privilege of reading the news while sitting on the throne. The daily bulletin awaited us on a big nail. Mr Goblin kept a bottle of water in the latrine because of his religious belief. I always sneaked a little to soften my paper; it was cool too!

*Drawin' watah* was not a chore I enjoyed while living here. The standpipe used by the majority of this neighbourhood was located at *Crossroad* (an intersection), and that was a long distance from our home. We owned one good galvanised bucket and had to improvise with paint cans or discarded five pound *Golden Cream* (margarine) and *Klim* (powdered milk) tins. The coarse wire we inserted to make handles cut into our hands when the pails were full. My brothers and I had a quota to fill after school each day. The forty-four-gallon drum outside the back door was not allowed to go beyond a certain level. Remember, my mother did not bark, so that drum was kept filled by her busy little *pups* at all times. My father tarred those drums to prevent rusting but the water tasted foul and was not fit for consumption. Our drinking water was stored in a large terracotta goblet. The duty of filling it fell on my shoulders. My head actually, because that is where I balanced it while walking gingerly to prevent spillage. Mummy did not trust the boys with the goblet. She said they were too wild but she had no problem giving me the added burden of living in fear of breaking it. That goblet kept our water very cool because we did not own a fridge; not yet!

Our closest bridge was just beyond Crossroad. This was all well and good until the dreaded rainy season began. We were back to square one battling with the mud, and there were no coconut husks paving the way here. The residents threw pieces of wood here and there, but it was never adequate. We became experts at jumping puddles from Crossroad to Punt Trench and managed not to get too dirty.

Guyana has two seasons; wet and dry, the rainy season is terrible. The wet seasons are from May to August and November to January. The months in between make up the dry seasons, and note, Guyana is a country that has two rainy seasons.

## Our Adopted Uncle and Auntie

We lived next door to an African family at this address . . . The Trotmans. They owned a shop with living quarters above and we became very good friends with their five children; Jeanette, Victor, Oscar, Dennis and Pamela. In no time we were calling their parents Uncle and Aunty. I lived in hope of getting an *Everlastin' sweetie*; you could stretch it to thy kingdom come, and it lasted a long time. I was also hooked on *sigrit* sweetie. That was a novelty that caught every child's attention but I seldom had money to buy so it was wonderful having friends who had a shop.

We seldom saw Uncle Oscar because he was away running a sawmill somewhere in the Demerara River. Aunty Georgie had no trouble taking care of the children because they were well behaved. Uncle Oscar probably threatened them with a good *cut-ass* if they did otherwise. I had *typee* (passionate love) for Oscar Junior; that was in secret of course. Auntie Georgie/Gee and Mummy became firm friends; a friendship that lasted until my mother's death in 1981. I took up the correspondence after Mummy died and visited them whenever I went to Toronto. Sadly, they both passed away a few years ago. Those people may have been a different skin colour, but we were family.

Auntie Georgie's sister Ina was the image of her; she lived a few doors down and had twin sons who were a few years older than me. The children in the neighbourhood called them *Palm Bread* so I naturally assumed that was their name. It was some time before I found out their true names. Lennox and Leonard were given that false-name because their heads were shaped like a palm loaf. Why are children so cruel? Those young men were very decent and always polite.

A beautiful East Indian girl named Bibi and I walked to school every day when we lived at this address. Disaster struck one afternoon on my way home from school. Bibi and I were playing *chasie* on the road and I ran across without looking. A bicycle *licked meh dung* (knocked me down). The boy riding it was so distressed he offered to tow me home. However, my mother would have given me more pain so I told him I was fine. My mother never found out about that accident even though my shoulder bothered me for many years. Bibi, her mother and three brothers lived in the smallest cottage at the Crossroad intersection. *Ow meh goi* (echo of pity), my heart went out to that family. Their father had died and her mother was raising the four children. That poor woman worked from morning till night doing different jobs to support them. She was hardly ever home and Bibi had to take care of her brothers. She had no time to play; she did all of the cooking and household chores, but I never heard her complain once. I've often wondered whatever happened to them; we lost touch after I finished primary school.

## Frangipani Memories

We finally met a Putagee family we could relate to. This family owned a shop at the next corner. Like the Trotmans, they too had five children and also lived above their shop. I had a crush on their eldest son; unfortunately he never knew I even existed. Boy was that Putagee man strict, he did not allow his children to mix with the other children in the neighbourhood; we only really talked to them when we shopped. The two eldest boys had to serve behind the counter whenever they were at home. Their mother was a very tiny sickly looking woman. I don't think she knew how to smile, but that could have been because she was very ill. She passed away and a wake was held in their sitting room; that is the custom in Guyana. As I recall all mirrors and pictures in the home were either covered or turned face down. That was another custom to ward off evil spirits. Her coffin was open for viewing for what seemed like days. I dutifully paid my respect each day, hoping refreshments would be served. Food was always an incentive for any unpleasant situation.

The coffin was filled with frangipani; the perfume was over powering. To this day I associate the sight or fragrance of frangipani flowers with death.

Mummy attended her *finaral* (funeral) and said she had a good turn out. Funeral processions were very long at times but it was considered respectful to stand still and wait until it passed if you encountered one. It was also customary for the procession to drive past the home of the deceased so the person could pay their last respects before being laid to rest.

A scattering of Africans lived in this neighbourhood and I distinctly remember two families who kept Sunday school under their bottom-'ouse. I attended whenever I had the opportunity, just for the singing and the fun of colouring in the bible story pictures.

## Bowjie and Jumbie Spirit

A large family of East Indians lived two doors down. Some of the children were much older than me; I can only remember Kenny, Edith and Lily.

I had a crush on Kenny; he was a *star-bhai* in my eyes. I might as well warn you, my fleeting romances could be compared to the evanescence of Eno bubbles.

We called their mother Bowjie as a mark of respect. It meant 'sister-in-law' in their language.

Lily's mother died when she was a little girl and Bowjie *took sh' in* (adopted her). She and her cousin Edith were around the same age as me so we were playmates. Lily used to scare the hell out of me when she fell to the ground in the middle of playing *ketcha* (a game of chasing and catching). She started to *shake-up* (convulse) as soon as she fell; her eyes bulged, and she sometimes *dirty* herself. Bowjie immediately rushed to her side to put a spoon between her teeth to prevent her from biting her tongue. She said Lily was born with *caul* (membrane covering face); therefore she had the ability to see jumbie. She told us Lily was seeing the spirit of her dead mother whenever this occurred. This provided a bit of excitement mixed with fear, because I believed it was true. I did not know anything about epilepsy. Come to think of it I don't believe they knew either. It was sheer ignorance.

## Market Vendors

This district was predominately East Indians and most of them were market vendors; Bowjie was among them. She did her trading at La Penitence Market which took about twenty minutes walking from where we lived. The vendors inside the market had regular stalls and some used a trestle. Bowjie only had a regular *pavement lot* (a measured allotment). Vendors paid for these lots and no one else could use it without permission. Discarded rice and sugah bags or a length of plastic was laid on the ground before arranging their goods. The bundles of greens on offer were always neatly parcelled. Fresh fruit, vegetables, seafood, spices and livestock were all displayed in an enticing manner to attract customers. Vendors *waalked wid watah* to freshen up their produce periodically, because things wilted quickly in that hot-hot tropical sun.

The vendors left home very early in the morning carrying massive baskets on their heads; they sometimes had customers before they reach the market.

Bowjie got up at fo-day marnin', cooked for her family and was at the market before we woke up. The children took their lunch to school in a three-tiered food carrier. A lot of East Indian children took mouth watering curries to school in these contraptions; some were enamel, but the tin version was more popular.

Some vendors grew vegetables in their backyard or had a small market garden in another location. Failing that, they went to *Big Market* (Stabroek market) where they could buy everything wholesale. When *genip* was in season, vendors approached residents with trees in their yard and purchased the entire crop when the fruit was ripe. By the way, we said 'Big Market' because it was the biggest of the three markets in Georgetown. It is another of our famous landmarks boasting a tower with a clock on every side. Shopping at any of these markets was a unique experience. It was a case of the early bird catches the worm. Most housewives went to the market as soon as the children left for school. Not only were they able to select the freshest produce; it was also the coolest part of the day for anyone who had to walk. Everyone shopped around looking for a bargain before buying; a cent or two in those days made all the difference. A lot of bartering went on in the markets. Vendors enticed shoppers by offering to *t'row in* something extra with a purchase. Most times it was a sprig of thyme or two *shallots* (spring onion).

The perimeter of the markets were always more interesting. The hustle and bustle of the atmosphere was exciting, not to mention the *shovin' an' pushin'* that went on. It was a haven for the pick pockets.

I especially enjoyed the heady aroma of fresh thyme and shallots mingled with the exotic spices. This combined with the aroma of ripe fruit such as mango, pineapple or tangerine added to the intoxicating atmosphere. But be prepared for a change in aroma. These stalls were right alongside the road and the smell of fresh horse shit could, and did assault your nostrils from time to time. The animals were tethered to a *lantin-post* while their owners made deliveries. I knew people who hung around the market for the sole purpose of collecting the dung to use in their garden. That was good, because it helped to keep the city clean.

Indulge me this detour to tell you a wicked story. Nothing was sacred and anything left unattended was stolen; hence this prank. My late father-in-law once put a dead cat in a shoe box, strapped it to his bicycle carrier and leaned the bike up against a lantin-post in front of the busy market. He pretended to go about his business, but he was slyly watching. His back was barely turned when someone took off with the box; his job was done! Roast cat for dinner anyone?

Back to the vendors . . . Most of them were sold out by mid-day and some of them went home to bake for the afternoon trade. These ladies plied the streets with their pastry filled baskets after school. We looked forward and listened out for the cries of, "Get yuh fresh pine-tart an' salara, it still 'ot," and lived in hope that Mummy would buy some. These delicious treats were rare, but we appreciated and savoured those pastries. These delicacies were washed down with *swank* which Mummy made daily.

Vendors were not restricted to selling in the markets. They hawked their wares door to door all over town. Some sold *groun' provision* (vegetables) and *greens*, while others came around with seafood or fruit. You could get anything on your doorstep. Mango season was the best; great big mounds were sold for twenty-five cents. The varieties included, Buxton Spice, Julie, Turpentine, Foo-Foo, Pound Mango (very tiny) and Long Mango. My family adopted a *Buck* mentality during the mango season; *we ate till we belly buss!*

Another person who did brisk business was the man who came around to sharpen our scissors and knives. He had a little pulley system with a grinding wheel fitted inside his cart. Mummy only ever paid to have our scissors sharpened because Daddy had a file and he sharpened our knives. You see, he did bend his elbow for other things.

## Making Pointa (pointer) Brooms

Talking about our experiences at this address reminds me of brooms; *pointa* (pointer) brooms actually. There was an abundance of this resource in this region so we made the brooms ourselves, *besize* why buy one when you could make it for *nutt'in'*? Coconut palm branches were all we needed to make a broom. Oh, I almost forgot the piece of string to tie it together at the top. No, no, we certainly did not cut down branches from Mr Goblin trees. Bowjie next door had an ample supply of coconut trees so we got them from her or from equally generous neighbours. Making brooms is a community affair. Getting together under someone's bottom-'ouse to participate in this enjoyable pastime was a lot of fun. I have fond memories of us eating and talking in between stripping the fronds. Bowjie brought out her delicious *Mithai* (sweet treat) and *Phulourie* (spicy balls made from split pea batter) with hot peppersauce and mango chutney. It took a considerable amount of time and naked spines to make a decent size pointa broom. I am positive that every home in Guyana still has one of these brooms; although I can vouch that it is only used by the maids in the homes of the upper crust of society. I smile now at the memory of us finally getting a broom that was bought from a shop. Mummy differentiated by shouting, "Helen, bring de laang handle broom;" whenever she wished to use that one. What's more, she always said it loud enough so the neighbours could hear we had a broom that came from a store. We call people who do things like that *neva-see, come-fuh-see* (not accustomed to anything).

## Pointa (pointer) Broom Commercial

You may be forgiven for thinking that we only used a *pointa broom* for sweeping purposes. Did you know that Guyanese are the gurus of invention and improvisation? We replaced our brooms regularly because children stole the pointas to play all sorts of ingenious games. Walla! I just thought of that guy who advertises a set of knives on television and my warped sense of humour has kicked in! I could make a commercial demonstrating the versatility of a pointa broom that would make him look positively *schupid*. He captivates the viewers by telling them the knives can, peel, slice, chop, pare and core. Big deal, any knife can do that; just sharpen it like Daddy did! I bet that guy will want to sell these brooms if he knew what I am about to tell you.

Picture me plucking pointas from this insignificant broom as I deliver this sales pitch. "This viewers may look like a piece of rubbish, but do not underestimate its true potential until I show you how much money it will save you. It will be the best two dollars fifty you ever spend. Have you thought of your child's education? Then it's time you did. This is not only a broom but also a teaching aid. How, I hear you ask? You can encourage your child's interest in becoming a pilot, an architect or a veterinarian with these simply instructions. Make an instant airplane they can fly by simply inserting one of the pointas in the *bee-tee* (anus) of a *Palm-fly* (dragon fly). Watching the impaled insect struggling to fly might strike a chord of sympathy and lead them to a veterinary profession. Does your son have aspirations of becoming a professional cowboy in a rodeo? He can practice on those unsuspecting lizards lazing in the sun along the *palins* by making a snare with the more flexible end of the pointa. Slip it over the lizard's belly; tighten and watch them struggle to get away; not a chance! Does your financial situation hamper your child's chances of becoming a fencing champion? Here is the solution to that problem. These pointas make excellent swords. Please don't panic when they *jook* (poke/stab) one another in the eye. Use my muddah's simple cure. Spit in the eye. It worked fine for us so there is no need to waste money on a doctor. Does your baby suffer from constant hiccups? Worry no more! Break a tiny piece off the end of a pointa and insert it between one of its curls. If your baby is a Bald Eagle just use a piece of *scotch tape* to secure it. One pointa will last until the child is old enough to go to school. Have you ever fantasised about becoming a teacher in a third world country? No expense necessary and it is fun! A pointa acts as a *wil'-cane* to point to the pretend blackboard or to beat the children to your heart's content. (Remember, I am speaking from experience folks!) WAIT, THERE'S MORE! Spend quality time with your children and teach them the craft of making kite frames with the coarser part of the pointa; it is also perfect for making the mast for their sail boats. There is no need to buy toothpicks. A sharp piece of pointa is excellent and don't forget to always keep a piece handy to remove wax from your ear; (my father was lost without this device). But WAIT THERE IS MORE! I bet you did not think of pest control. Are you plagued by rats, *cakaroaches* and other pests? A pointa will do the job; push it into the hole where they are secreted and give them a sharp *jook* on their *batty*; you will get instant results. A word of warning children; just don't let yuh muddah ketch yuh taking any of the pointas, because you will get a good *cut-ass*; WITH THE BROOM! Make sure you go out and get a pointa broom today."

Now tell me where you can find another product on the market that can offer you so many opportunities.

After that bit of *schupidness* (folly), I would like to say we also used a broom obtained from the Manicole Palm. The blossoms on a stem made a very good broom. We swept the *bottom-'ouse* and killed *Ol' higues* with this broom. Folklore advises every household should have a Manicole broom in case one of these mythical creatures entered your home and attacked you. This was the only object that could beat them to death . . . it was our *silver bullet*. I know you want to know what an Ol' higue is so I better tell you.

## The Ol' Higue Myth

Our folklore is rich with myths and superstitions we actually believe. This one is in the same league as *Jumbie*, *Backoo* and *Obeah*, only a lot scarier since it involves fire. Mummy used to call my grandmother Francesca an Ol' higue, (behind her back of course). I guess it stemmed back to the beginning of her marriage. She said Gramuddah did not like her, although I never heard her say a bad word against Mummy and she was not an evil person in my opinion. Ol' higues are supposed to have supernatural powers that allow them to shed their skin [Maybe that is where the saying, *jump out of your skin* originated] and become a ball of fire after dark. They roam the city; letting themselves in through keyholes to suck blood from the necks of babies or anyone who has wronged them. A *love bite* was a dead give away that you were visited by an Ol' higue. Mummy always became alarmed when she saw one on my neck. She came up to me for a closer inspection, then enquired, "Wha' 'appen to yuh neck?" I always feigned ignorance of not knowing the bruise was there and always managed to convince her it was an Ol' higue. She was too naive to know what a love bite was and I couldn't tell her I was dating Ol' higues. People will tell you with a straight face that they saw a ball of fire in the sky and it was an Ol' higue. I never saw one, and I stayed out pretty late at times. We have several ways to capture and get rid of this mythical creature. It is said they hide their skin under a mortar after shedding it, and if you have the good fortune of finding it you should pound it into the mortar with the hottest pepper. The Ol' higue will have difficulty getting back into it and will recite this incantation, "Skin, skin is me; skin, skin yuh nah no me?" The chant cannot revoke the deed so the skin will not fit and the Ol' higue will perish. You can also trap them by leaving a big mound of raw rice in your home. They cannot resist counting every grain and will die if daylight catches them in the act. You could also fall victim to an Ol' higue if you wear your garments inside out.

I guess you are wondering how we determine who is an Ol' higue. They actually walk among us during the day and act normal so it's difficult to pick them. We are always suspicious of people with *mash-mout'* (no teeth); like the old African woman who used to visit Mummy. Rumour had it the woman was an Ol' higue so my sisters decided to set a trap to prove the theory.

This anecdote will explain another method of getting rid of them. An Ol' higue will not step over a line drawn with chalk so my sisters waited until the woman was safely in the house before they drew a chalk line on one of the steps halfway down the stairs. Those girls swore that the lady stopped dead in her tracks on the step above the chalk and went into a tail spin. She chanted and cursed until Mummy came out and intervened; she made them wipe the chalk off with a wet rag. They said the woman left very agitated and that was the last they ever saw of her. I wish I could have been witness to that.

It is not a compliment to be called an Ol' higue, so that is why you will never see me without my *false teet'*.

## Superstition and Ol' Wives Tales

Most people would experience what we call Ol' Wives Tales at some point in their life. *Maan,* I am here to tell you that Guyana will win the prize for those stories hands down. Here are a few. It was said that if you are beaten with a pointa broom you will pee the bed. That is a truh-truh story because I witnessed that with *meh own two eyes*. I saw my aunt beat my brother with the pointa broom every morning after she discovered his wet bed. That boy had to take some small blue pills (DeWitts or Carter Kidney Pills) to try and cure the problem, but I somehow feel it didn't work, because she kept beating him.

You will no doubt want to thank me personally for this bit of advice so in advance, you are welcome! We all have days when we spot a visitor coming, but we are just not in the mood for company or conversation. Well here is a very simple way to get rid of them. Turn your broom upside down before you let them in. They will want to leave before you open the door. That is another truh-truh story I tell you . . . I have friends who don't even bother to call anymore. And while I am on the subject of brooms I might as well warn all of the unmarried women reading this. If your ambition is to get married, please make sure that no one ever sweeps over your feet. I have a few Ol' maid friends because that happened to them.

My ever faithful friend *shame* walked with me hand in hand up to the day I left Guyana. I had heard if you wanted to return to Guyana you should *eat Labba an' drink creek watah* but my grandmother had a superstition that floored me. I had a very close relationship with Ol' Francesca but I was not expecting her to attend my wedding because she seldom left d'Riva. Except for that one time she went to England to stay with Aunty Rita (another story there). As I was saying, I was overjoyed Gramuddah attended our wedding, but shucks, did she have to embarrass me in front of the entire neighbourhood the day my husband and I said our goodbyes? The street was teeming with neighbours all wanting to hug, kiss and wish us good luck. I had sprung a leak long before I even opened my eyes that morning anticipating this scenario. The time had come for Gramuddah to say goodbye. That dear old lady hugged and kissed me, and then she whispered in my ear, "Ellen, yuh 'ave to look up at de 'ouse an' wave an' say, bye bye 'ouse, a'comin' back." She had to be joking right? No sir, she was dead serious! I shyly whispered back, "But Gramuddah, a'too shame to do dat." That old witch was not giving up. In her loudest voice she said, "Ellen, yuh 'ave to do it because if yuh doan tell de 'ouse yuh goin' it won't let yuh come back to Guyana." WHAT? The house had powers now? Never coming back to Guyana? I love Guyana; I can't allow that to happen. I was going to look like a big jackass in front of all those people, but it had to be done, if only to please Gramuddah. So there I was, a *big woman* waving to a house saying, "Bye, bye 'ouse, a'comin' back." I swear this is a truh-truh story. Maan, dat t'ing worked, because I've been back to Guyana three times so far and thinking of going again folks! Thanks Gramuddah.

Superstition was rife in Guyana. Let me give you some other examples. The *buryin' groun'* (La Repentir cemetery) ran parallel with our school on St Stephen Street. The wide trench that separated the road from the cemetery gave us some comfort, but it didn't stop superstition. Pointing at graves was strictly forbidden; you could be struck down by a *jumbie* (evil spirit). However, there was a way to reverse the curse should you make the mistake. This was done by putting all ten fingers in your mouth then biting them with all your might. I was particularly prone to pointing so my fingers were bitten raw some days. That cure really worked, because I am happy to report the jumbie never cursed me. I wonder where that one originated. Oh, another thing we used to do was go through the door backwards if we got home late from a *fete* (party). The jumbie could not follow you if it could still see your face. My mother was waiting for me behind the door one night and I almost *shite* myself when she tapped me on the shoulder!

Jumbie spirits were taken seriously; especially in the Pomeroon where I was born. Carpenters appeased the spirits by generously sprinkling White Rum before they put down the foundation of any building. My uncles and cousins also did this when they were building a new boat.

Certain dreams were interpreted and taken seriously. Whenever Mummy dreamt of fish, she or someone in the family will be pregnant, and someone will die if she dreamt of mud. And wherever her right eye was twitching she knew she would see someone she had not seen in a long time.

This next one is also supposed to be superstition, but I somehow believe it must be true because I personally suffer from this affliction. It is said you will not stop talking if your mouth is wiped with a *plate-cloth* (tea-towel). I would like to know which wicked person is responsible for doing this to me, and there is no cure for it!

## Hitching a Ride on a Jackass Cyart

*Dray* and *donkey-cyarts* were very popular. These were used to transport goods all over the city and competed with the cars on the road, but no one minded. There is a significant difference between a 'dray' and a 'donkey-cyart'. The *dray-cyart* has four wheels and was pulled by a horse whereas *donkey-cyarts* only had two wheels and were pulled by a donkey. Some people had two donkeys harnessed together on their 'jackass-cyart' as it was called by the unrefined. Those animals were overworked. Their masters flogged them to make them go faster so they could accomplish more in a day. From time to time a stiff dead donkey was seen on the street. They were picked up by the *M & T C* (Mayor and Town Council) rubbish truck and taken to the incinerator to be disposed of. Inhaling the aroma of roast donkey is not something I recommend.

Not many children were lucky enough to own a bicycle and there were no school buses. That privilege was reserved for the children who lived on the sugar estates. Hordes of school children walked to school each day and it was a favourite trick of some children, mostly the boys; to hitch a ride on the back of a donkey or dray-cyart if it was heading in the direction of school. A few of the owners were tolerant, but a lot of them used their whip on the children to get them off, because the extra weight slowed them down. Whenever I saw my brothers trying to jump on a cart, I yelled, "A'gon tell Mummy on yuh." Yes, I was a little wretch and wanted to get them into trouble. I was just jealous, and too afraid to jump on the cart myself. I was told I would be seen as another jackass if I stooped so low. Mummy said that only one jackass should be seen on the cart and that was the one pulling it, so I steered clear.

Mummy stopped bringing our lunch to school when we moved here because of the distance. We had to go home for lunch every day and get back to school in time; how we did it, I'll never know.

A donkey-cyart and a view of homes in Georgetown with 'jalousie' shutters

Me sitting on a dray-cyart in 1984

## The Backdam Was Forbidden Territory

The *backdam* (hinterland) held many forbidden treasures and adventures from what I heard, but Mummy forbade us to go there. The sugar-cane fields were not the only attraction in the backdam. Fruit trees grew wild on acres of unclaimed land. It was quite a hike from where we lived; you had to follow the route along the canal to reach there. Since the fruit trees did not belong to anyone in particular, the boys in the neighbourhood raided them constantly. We knew some of the boys who frequented the backdam and they sometimes brought back fruit when they could not eat it all themselves. The boys found a big *jamoon* tree and brought some of the fat juicy fruit for me. I was so *hungish* I wanted to go with them the next day to get some more, but that cut-ass wasn't worth it. My brothers got away one day and followed the *kangalangs* (ruffians) to the backdam, but they made the mistake of coming home soaking wet after swimming in the canal. That gave the secret away and they got a good *cut-tail*. I know they went again, but Mummy never found out.

*Maan,* I got brave and decided to go one time; Daphne was visiting so she went too. We found a jamoon tree halfway there; filled our bellies

133

and turned back from that point. My brothers continued, but I was too fryken Mummy would ketch me.

## Roasted Spurwing

Most of the older boys hunted birds with their *sling-shot* (a catapult). They shot Spurwing and Plover (small birds) which were plentiful. We were always looking for something to eat so I didn't mind helping with the plucking and cleaning. The tiny birds were roasted over a fire in someone's backyard. There was not much meat on those puny birds, but they were very tasty; pigeons and parrots made good eating too. There was a long neck bird we called a 'Gawlin'; another mispronunciation; I believe the correct name is a Gaudlin. The stork like birds foraged at the edge of any wetland so the boys had ample opportunity to shoot them.

We were all afraid of hearing the *Jumbie bird* (also called Ol' witch) when we were playing hide and seek in the night. That bird made the most ominous sound and was said to possess evil spirits. We all ran into the house and hid when we heard one, and wondered who was going to die.

Most yards had fruit trees in this district and raiding the fruit was a favourite pastime for children. Not everyone was tolerant and if you were caught you paid the price. Joel was caught stealing guavas one day in a yard across from the school. The owner threw a huge iron bar that hit him square in his back. He was in a lot of pain, but Mummy never found out. We steered clear of yards that had watchdogs because their masters were quick to *sic* them on anyone who tried to steal their fruit.

My cousin Richard found a unique way to raid the mangoes. A huge tree grew in his backyard and some of the branches were almost touching their landin'. His father had his eye on a very big mango but he knew Richard's weakness so he threatened him with a good cut-ass if he picked it. Uncle Joe inspected the mango each morning waiting for it to reach perfection. He went out to check one morning and was amazed to find a seed sucked clean hanging from its stem. Richard had cunningly found a way to eat the mango without picking it!

The *yowaries* (opossum) also had their feast when mangoes were in season. Killing them was another sport the boys enjoyed. Their foul odour gave away their secret hiding places. You knew you needed a bath if anyone told you that you smelt like a yowarie.

The *Salipenta* (Salipenter) and Mongoose were two pests who helped themselves to the eggs in the chicken coop. The boys tried to kill them at every opportunity, but they were quick and sly, especially the mongoose. That is why there is a calypso called 'Sly Mongoose'.

## Keeping Cows in the Backyard

Many people made a living from their cows by selling the milk. A rolled rag supported the huge urn milk vendors carried on their heads. A measuring cup made of tin was hung on one of the handles. Mummy made us listen out for the shouts of, "Milk, get yuh fresh milk" then sent me out to get a pint or two depending on her finances. Most people who bought on a regular basis knew the time and had their container ready. Some of these milk vendors were *cock-bran'* (con artists); watering down the milk and believing we wouldn't know the difference but we knew what pure milk tasted like, because we drank it often in the Rupununi. Apart from the flavour, the amount of cream it produced was a dead give away. There was never enough for me to steal without Mummy noticing. Anyway Mummy changed vendors when she thought the quality of the milk had deteriorated.

The people who had cows built a cow-pen in their backyard to house the animals. This was not pleasant if you happen to live next door. Apart from the putrid smell, the cow dung attracted flies that liked to decorate our meal.

The owners led their cows to the backdam to graze each day after milking them, and then brought them home in the late evening. Don't for a minute think the cow manure was dumped. It was sold to potential gardeners or used in their own market garden . . . nothing was wasted in Guyana.

## Kissing the Wicked Witch

We were not living here long when I saw a *drop-cyar* pull up in front of our home. I was playing under the bottom-'ouse at the time but I immediately ran to hide in the latrine when I realised who the visitor was. My blood boiled when I saw my aunt (the one we boarded with) and I wondered why she came because she was the last person I wanted to see. It appeared she had come to say goodbye; they were leaving for America. My mother knew I was home so she called repeatedly. I was fuming, and refused to budge until Mummy yelled, "If yuh doan come now yuh gon get a'good lickin'." Shit! That was all I needed to hear because you did not mess with Mummy. She had a temper, and could beat *real bad* if you provoked her. I was always *shame* when I got a beating; I cried silently because I did not want the neighbours to know. Apart from being ashamed, I knew Mummy would beat me more if I screamed. My brothers were screamers and she always said, "Yuh want sumt'in' to cry fuh?" It was fuel to the fire and the licks went on forever. Anyway, back to the saga of my aunt visiting to say goodbye. Mummy ordered me to kiss the wicked witch and I almost puked with hatred. That was the last time I ever saw that aunt.

When CeCe, Daphne and I visited my sister Anetta in New York in 1984, we decided to go to Baltimore to visit my dear Aunty Glerie (my mango peeler). Since the wicked witch also lived there, I thought it would be a good idea to bury the hatchet (in her head would have been good). I called to schedule a visit, but she made an excuse denying my request. Sad to say she died some years later without closure. I no longer hold a grudge; what good does that do? I had to forgive her to set myself free. I still have *uncle* issues; although venting here is excellent therapy.

## The Calabash Cut

A calabash is a gourd that we did not eat, but it had many uses. Daddy used one to give my brothers a haircut. The calabash was fitted to their heads and any hair visible was shorn off; a razor was used to finish the job. It was customary for the recipient of such a haircut to be tapped behind the head and teased unmercifully about his *calabash* or *roun'-de-worl'* cut, just another Guyanese custom. I brought a calabash back to Australia on my last visit just for nostalgic reasons. [I wished I had it the time I got adventurous and decided to give our eldest daughter a haircut; that poor child was too embarrassed to go to school]. I told you we had to *bade we skin* morning and night. Our outdoor bathroom had no shower; we bathe from a bucket and used a calabash or discarded can to *t'row de watah* on our body. The first dousing always made me jump, but it was very refreshing after that.

Calabashes came in different sizes and were used as utensils in many households; especially the Amerindians. We washed our rice in a calabash. Yes, I said "washed." I know we don't wash rice in western countries, but I am telling the truth; we washed rice in Guyana. Not only washed it, we had to *pick rice* every day. One would think we would be privy to perfect rice since we grew and exported this commodity. We had to make do with the crap that was rejected; it was full of all sorts of rubbish. I hated *pickin' rice*, but never escaped the task when I was home. The rice was spread out on the dining room table and I sorted it out grain by grain; like an Ol' higue. The clean rice was guided into the calabash (which I held under the rim of the table) after I had removed the imperfect grains, broken glass and the tiny stones. I often had the misfortune of getting a missed stone in my meal. I could never eat another bite after I chewed up a stone; it was revolting.

## Bottom-'ouse Activities

Our bottom-'ouse had to be kept clean at all times. We did not have the luxury of concrete; it was packed dirt. Water was sprinkled over the area before sweeping to prevent us being blinded by the dust. Most homes were built on stilts so we were able to hang a hammock under the bottom-'ouse. We had one here and Mummy enjoyed taking her siesta in it even though I heard her say many times that it was only *buck people* who used a hammock. How could she say that when I learnt some years ago that my great-grandmother was half Amerindian? Maybe that is the reason I love hammocks.

The bottom-'ouse had many functions. Most homes were small so we invented and played games under the house. Playing *dolly-'ouse* is what I enjoyed most. Our imagination was put to good use. Anything that was discarded was used as building materials. That meant scouting in the yard where there were hidden dangers. I hopped in pain many times after falling victim to broken glass or a *nail jook*. The nails were always rusty and that could lead to contracting lock-jaw. I had to endure the hot soft grease cure, because I wasn't ready to die. Mummy usually gave the area a good beating with a piece of wood. That was said to get rid of any *bad blood* before she washed my foot with dettol (another cure all). Then it was time to administer the dripping hot grease into the wound—ouch! I can honestly recommend *Soft grease* if you get a *nail jook* because I never knew anyone who died from lock-jaw. I hope you are all using it on your children so they know what true suffering means.

Look how easily I got off the subject of telling you how we made our dolly-'ouses. After we had collected all the building materials, we searched for *beddin'* (rags) which we expertly draped to make particians for our rooms. With experience like that, it is a wonder I never became a world renowned architect; then again, we could never afford the fees for college. If you haven't guessed by now, I always wanted to be the bossy muddah when we played dolly-'ouse.

The boys also had some very interesting and inventive games. I bet you didn't know you could have hours of fun with two rusty tin cans and a length of string. A hole was drilled in the top of the cans; the string was threaded through both cans and secured with knots on the inside and you had a pair of stilts. Insert your toes between the strings; hold the loop taut then start hobbling. Everyone wanted one of those toys.

The five pound margarine cans make an excellent *pull-along* toy. This toy was made with more or less the same principle as the stilts, except you filled the can with sand/dirt after you had threaded the rope through both ends. A length of the sting was added for pulling. [I was amazed to see a little boy pulling one of these contraptions when I went to Guyana in 2000].

The most exciting and dangerous game the older boys created was the *tin bomb* (carbon bomb). A discarded Ovaltine tin was used to manufacture the carbide bomb. Carbon from god knows where and other combustible items were added to the tin. Everyone took turns to spit in the tin before it was closed and given a thorough shaking. Someone brave was chosen to go close enough to light the match. We all ran anticipating the Big Bang and mothers ran out to investigate, but there was never anyone around because we had all taken cover. The cover of the tin sometimes blew off with the explosion. This led to a boy being hit in the face and seriously hurt one time. Funny; but I never saw a thing!

## Money Making Scam

We are famous for mispronouncing words and here is another example. The nuns showed films at the school from time to time. I did not realise the word was *film,* so I used to say, "A'goin' to see a'flim-show at Stella Maris."

*Flim-shows* were money spinners for the more cunning children. I guess when times are hard we become more creative. Some forward thinking children had the bright idea to make a few dollars. They foraged in the rubbish bins outside the cinemas and collected the discarded film strips. A section of their bottom-'ouse was darkened with flattened cardboard boxes and a bed sheet stolen from their muddah (if she has one to spare) was used as a screen. A large magnifying glass and a mirror were used to reflect and project the image. The unsuspecting children were duped into believing they were attending a *flim-show* but all they saw was disjointed bits of film.

My friend Norma said their dressmaker found a clever way to get free buttons with a flim-show scam. The lady got her son to set up a cinema under the bottom-'ouse and the patrons used buttons as currency to gain entry. Norma said none of her siblings clothes had buttons for a long time; they came off as fast as her mother could sew them on.

## De T'eatah-'ouse was Popular

In Australia we go to the cinema to see a movie; in Guyana we go to the *t'eatah-'ouse* to see a *pickcha* (movie). The next anecdote was told to me by a Guyanese friend. Joe came from a large family and like most of us, money was scarce. He said whenever he and his brothers asked their father for money to see *a'pickcha,* he would say, "Yuh want fuh see a'pickcha, come a'gon show yuh pickcha." He led them to the almanacs on the walls then turned the page of each month to show them the pictures. That was one item we used to get for *free,* what's more we looked forward to receiving the numerous almanacs offered by business places at Christmas. They served as wall decoration and art. Every free nail in our home begged for one of these treasures.

Going to the cinema was a bit dodgy at times. I was intimidated by the class of people who occupied *Pit* (the cheapest/lowest section). The name was suitable because it was the pits. No respectable person would be caught dead in that section. The patrons who frequented Pit were called *ranga-tangs* (unruly hooligans). Some of them were so *shame* they scaled the dividing wall after the movie finished to make it appear they were in the more prestigious section. It was advisable to sit mid-way in *House* (dress circle), because fights always broke out in *pit* and objects were hurled. Those ranga-tangs also used the patrons as targets after the lights went down. Staples fired with a rubber band really stung. I always sat in the *house* section. When I started dating a few of my dates sprung for *balcony* tickets because they had ulterior motives and had the privacy to do *t'ings* to you. My lips are sealed on that subject, someone might tell Mummy and she may *turn in sh' grave*.

A lot of people found an escape from their humdrum life by going to the cinema. Many young boys hustled to find or steal empty sweet-drink or liquor bottles for the refund which enabled them to *skulk* and spend the day in the cinema.

Our metropolitan cinemas were: Globe, Astor, Plaza, Metropole, Strand DeLuxe, Empire and Rio. I was happy when a comedy or romance was showing at Astor because I was able to get a small discount from my cousin Bernice who was the ticket seller.

Someone once told me a story about my mother and I tend to believe it is true. She said Mummy told them she wanted to see *a'pickcha* and took my baby brother. He cried and someone in *pit* got angry and yelled, "Put de bubbie in de baby mout'." I think Mummy had more class than that; then again she fed him in front of my boyfriend, and the cinema was darker.

When I was living opposite the Rio cinema in La Penitence I dreamed of going to see *a'pickcha* as I watched the movie goers lining up when there was a special attraction showing. Some kind relative gave me money to see a movie at Rio once. It was the 4 p.m. session and I was the first to arrive. I was walking along the seats trying to decide where to sit when I spotted a fifty cent piece. I could not tell you the name, or what the movie was about because I was so excited about that money since it was the most money I had ever had. Actually I tell a lie . . . Granfaddah gave me more than that when I was thirteen. I had said my goodbyes and was sitting in the bus waiting to leave Charity when someone knocked on the window. To my amazement it was Ol' Joe holding out a dollar bill. He gruffly said, "Heh Helena, by yuhself a'lil' sweet-mout'," as he passed it through the window. I thought I had died and gone to heaven. A whole dollar!

## The Big Fight at Crossroad

My parents must have missed their old farming life because they decided to lease a small plot of land to do a spot of hobby farming. It was enough to keep them happy, plus they figured we could eat the produce they grew to supplement the family income. For whatever reason, they chose a place called Friendship which was twelve miles from town. We had no means of transportation so they caught a bus every Sunday to tend their garden. Daddy took me one time when Mummy could not go. BORING! The only good thing about it was the *cook-up-rice* (pilaf) Daddy made on the camp fire.

My parents figured we were old enough to stay at home without supervision especially since we were left under the watchful eye of Aunty Gee. We knew better to disobey a neighbour so Mummy was confident we would be well behaved. My brothers and I usually kept out of mischief but one Sunday things got nasty. This would never have happened if *Big-'ead* did not go off *strayin'* (gad about) without Auntie Gee's consent. Of course I wasn't *tekkin' leff* (left behind) so I tagged along. One of the boys in the neighbourhood was a known bully; he and Joel did not get along. Every man jack congregated at Crossroad, including *Snake* who *fished-up* (insulted) Joel straight away. Blows started flying and Joel ran home for a knife. I was so fryken, I ran to alert Aunty Gee, who averted what could have been a potentially dangerous outcome. I witnessed the fight, but was not going to say a word to my parents. There was no need because Aunty Gee reported the matter to them the minute they got home. It earned Joel got a good lickin'. Auntie Gee was only looking out for us; we never held it against her.

Sure enough my detective mother discovered I knew about the fight. She was angry and said I should have reported to them straight away. She was exhausted after she gave Joel his lickin' so she left the job to Daddy by saying, "J.B., yuh 'ave to teach dat gyurl a'lesson; a'wan' yuh to gi' sh' a'good beatin'." I praised god for the lucky break, because the first time she asked Daddy to beat me she got mad and took over; she told him he was only *brushin' flies*. Daddy put on his pretend father face and sat down (you know he meant business when he did that). I had to stifle a laugh when he said, "Come 'ere an' ben' ova meh lap." (I guess he didn't want to bend his rubber spine). I dutifully did as I was told. Lucky for me, Mummy had left the room, because he gave me three lights pats on my *batty* and said, "Dat will teach yuh fuh nex' time." I actually got up and pretended I was crying. I walked passed Mummy rubbing my eyes and bawling so she could see what a severe beating Daddy had given me. The tricks children play on their parents eh?

My mother must have been exhausted at times I tell you. With her verbal shovel at the ready she called the culprit who had been reported doing something she didn't approve off. If we denied the accusation (we always did) she would say, "Ah goin' to dig until a'get to de bottom a'dis story." She dug and dug, but seldom got to the bottom, because we became experts at hiding things from her.

I know Mummy also spent a lot of time looking for a light, because she used to often say, "Doan t'ink a'gon be in de dark fuh laang; a'gon t'row lite on de matta soon, an' a'gon get to de bottom a'dis story suh yuh betta tell meh de troot now." She should have been a lawyer. Another thing she said was, "If yuh tell de troot, lies won't follow yuh." I didn't even know lies had legs.

## Beuzin' Was Great Entertainment

Most of our entertainment was provided by the local community. Houses were in close proximity to one another and since most Guyanese conduct a conversation using hand gestures we were privileged to free Marcel Marco performances when neighbours were *gyaffin'*. We could almost guess what the topic was depending on the intensity of their hand movement; not to mention the wicked laughing. If you were *fas'* like me you tried to eavesdrop . . . some of those conversations were really juicy. We got all the latest gossip on our doorstep. A video tape of this nature was intentionally made by my father-in-law to send to us in Australia. He secretly filmed my mother-in-law while she was *gyaffin'* with a neighbour over the *palin'*. I guess he wanted to remind us of the treasures we had left behind. We could not hear a word, but it was a priceless performance; we never laughed so much.

Let me tell you about Florence. She was an African girl a few years older than me; the family lived obliquely opposite us. Florence had a mother that made mine look like Mother Teresa. The poor girl met a nice boy and tried to go *strayin'* behind her mother's back but *cyat eat sh' dinnah* (ran out of luck) and all hell broke loose when some *news carrier* (gossip monger) reported seeing them together. No decorum about keeping things private. Her mother started *beuzin'*, (verbal abuse) with the intention of embarrassing her into submission. I was all ears, and nearly died laughing when I heard her mother say, "Yuh t'ink yuh is a'big woman now because yuh got big bubbie?" That poor girl did not show her face for days. All that gossiping sometimes backfired when people tell out. The once privileged information became public knowledge when a beuzin' broke out and the entire neighbourhood no longer had to eavesdrop. My mother never got involved in any of these frays. She said it was only done by *low-class* people and called women who indulged in that activity, *blagyard* (blackguard) or *bradar* (vulgar people). Mind you, even though Mummy did not partake in buezin' it never stopped her from secretly listening.

We simply hid behind our closed windows (no curtains) to listen and *skin we teet'*. Some of the things I heard about our neighbours made my ears blush. I was visiting a cousin one day when the peace was shattered. Two women living in the range behind her home *ketch case* and started *wrowin'* (quarrelling). I was all ears. The argument escalated when one said to the other, "Yuh 'usband *gi'in' yuh blow* (cheating)." By now the entire neighbourhood was listening. I was not prepared for her comeback when she said, "Well at leese a'ave a'usband, suh a'doan 'ave to use a'green plantin like yuh." It was all out war then but the rest has to be censored!

Please don't laugh at my ignorance when I tell you I never knew the term *buezin'* actually meant 'abusing'. I always thought it was just two people having a *free-for-all*. I got involved in a buezin' one day and almost died from *shame*; all because I owed someone four lousy dollars. This happened when we lived in Albouys Street so you will have to wait for that episode.

## The Window Was Our Cinema

There were no televisions back in my era but we did not miss what we did not have. Our windows were our television screen and it gave us a much better view of the world (narrow as it was). Mummy even positioned her rocking chair by our *gallery window* (sitting room vicinity) so she could *look out* (snoop); it was everyone's favourite pastime . . . CNN news had nothing on us. We could tell you what time a neighbour went to market and what time she came home and which boy peed in the gutter every day. On a visit to Guyana we knew within hours which gangster sold drugs opposite Daddy.

This next incident occurred when I was a teenager. We were living at another address at the time. A buezin' with sexual connotations broke out a few doors down on the opposite side of the road. I naturally positioned myself at the front window to enjoy the scenario. I could not hear properly so half my body was hanging out the window when Mummy caught me and bellowed, "Close dat window rite now, yuh 'ear meh?" I took no notice; I was a *big woman* now, and could do as I pleased. I forgot Mummy did not warn us twice. It wasn't so funny when the blows started reigning down on my backside.

## Times Had Changed

Customs evolve and it is always more noticeable after one has lived abroad for many years. I experienced this on a visit to Guyana in 1995.

The *gallery window* was replaced by television. A cousin offered us a ride to visit a relative, but there was one stipulation. She had to be home for 4 p.m. sharp. No, she did not have another appointment; it was so she did not miss The Bold and the Beautiful. We discovered that everyone rushed home or went to someone's home at that time every afternoon to watch the programme; it was bizarre.

Daphne and I had a surreal experience while we were home alone one day (that very holiday). A young woman we had never seen before opened the back door and casually sauntered in. She said, "Good aftanoon," and without further ado went directly into the sitting room and turned on the television. Daphne and I gave each other a quizzical look, but since the woman looked harmless we continued cooking and left her to watch the soap opera. She calmly got up and let herself out after the show was over.

I related the incident to Daddy when he got home and he said she was Shandrina's (his future wife) daughter and she came often to watch the show. That girl had the audacity to tell her mother we were rude, because we did not invite her to stay for a meal.

Things had certainly changed from my era. At four-thirty in the afternoon we got dressed and went for a walk or a ride to the Seawall, because there was no television. Failing that, we hung out of the gallery window to see if there was any drama happening on the street.

# Chapter Seven

*Blood is thicker than water.—Proverb*

# 1958 JAMES STREET, ALBOUYSTOWN

### Eavesdropping Heaven

Oh lawd! I almost forgot this next address; could it be because we were only there for five minutes? We lived next door to our landlord Mr Arjune, an amicable East Indian gentleman who owned the *salt-goods* shop at the corner of James and Non Pareil Streets in Albouystown. This small cottage was bursting at the seams, but we were thrilled to have plumbing in the kitchen. A small cottage and a double range stood behind our home. The amenities in the yard were used by all the tenants. Squabbles broke out daily at the standpipe; festering grudges were settled and new ones germinated. We shared this home with my Aunty Olga, her two daughters and one of Mummy's cousins.

It was here I honed my eavesdropping skills. You see my aunt was a single parent but her cousin was unattached and trying to find a husband. It looked as if *goat bite sh'* (imperfect/out of luck) because she wasn't having much luck. She enjoyed sharing her dalliances with the others who were more than willing to listen; you should hear them cackle. Nights were best, although I sometimes had to put my fist into my mouth when I got the giggles. My father was managing a rum-shop at a place called Diamond on the East Bank; he was only entitled to leave at the weekend. The three women took up their favourite pastime of gyaffin' as soon as the children were tucked in for the night.

With no men around the women indulged in gossip and told enthralling stories; some too risqué for my young ears. I was fascinated by the language they used during the day when the children were around. Try as I may I could never decipher the perplexing code. I was eventually enlightened by someone who told me they were speaking "gibberish." By the time the technique was explained and mastered we had long moved from this address. The language was banned in my presence after Mummy got wind of my knowledge. I knew a lot of their secrets, but I bet there were some very interesting stories I never learnt about, thanks to that *schupid* language. A lot of shenanigans went on in this home, but those memories will have to be censored because my mother always warned, "Doan wash yuh dutty linen in public."

How could I have forgotten this address? It was where I fell in love yet again. We lived in close proximity to a Negro family who had the best looking son, his name alone was romantic. I was obsessed with Oswald and took every opportunity to get a glimpse of him. I played *chasie* (tag) with him and the other children in the yard, but I am certain Oswald never knew I had *typee* for him. The love affair was short lived, because we only lived here for a short time. Memories of Oswald surfaced a few years ago when my husband and I took a cruise in the South Pacific. We spent a day on the Isle of Pines and were driven around by a man named Oswald; he was also of the same complexion. There are certain people you can never forget.

## Our Butcher Arthur

Mummy decided I was now old enough to do the shopping at La Penitence market so this became my duty almost every morning before school. Armed with a list and instructions, I was to buy fresh fruit, vegetables, fish or *strimps* (shrimp). And sometimes it was *a'poun' a'beef* (a pound of meat) when the budget wasn't stretched. Our favourite butcher was Arthur. Let me tell you about this handsome, charming, larger than life African man. Other butchers paled in comparison to our Arthur who had a flamboyant personality. Arthur knew me on sight and always greeted me in his big booming voice with, "An' 'ow yuh doin' dis marnin' darlin'?" I was always too shy to respond so I blushed; hung my head and gave him a sly smile. Arthur sprang into action with his dazzling performance the minute I gave him my order. He chopped and weighed with great flourish then handed over the carefully wrapped parcel as if it contained a Faberge egg. Since Arthur stood on a platform I could never see what went into the scale but I always accepted the parcel in good faith. On occasion he would give me more bone/fat than beef and Mummy always made me take it back. I was always *shame* when that happened but it was never a problem for Arthur. He just flashed *'e gol' teet'* while he took out one small piece of something, and replaced it with a different piece of fat or bone. Mummy was happy with the exchange, but I was not amused.

In Guyana there was no asking for any special cut of meat. We (my family) had no notion about different cuts of meat; it was simply called 'beef'; which meant you got a bit of this and a bit of that. [The first time I saw a butcher shop in Perth I stopped and gazed in total amazement. What the hell was a T-bone steak]?

I felt sick in the stomach whenever *fine strimps* was on the list, because that meant it would take ages to shell the tiny shrimps and I would take the lingering aroma to school.

I had to run all those errands and was still expected to get to school on time. I paid the price once or twice for being late. Mr Hope, the deputy headmaster always stood at the top of the stairs when the school bell rang at eight-thirty. His presence prevented any late comers from entering the classroom while prayers were being said. Hopie, as we called him took great pleasure in delivering the customary six lashes to the students who were late. He used a *wil'-cane* to administer the punishment and this really hurt, my tears usually started flowing long before the first lash.

Oh, I forgot to tell you that one of Arthur's fingers was missing, although we never found out how he lost it. Speculating is my forte; therefore I believe he must have been distracted while charming the ladies. I wonder who got the surprise of finding that extra bit of *beef* ???

## Live Chickens Equals Feather Pillow

Mummy personally went to the market on Saturdays. She stocked up on non perishable items and also bought chicken or crabs, which had to be transported home alive and kicking! The poor unsuspecting chicken hung upside down from the basket handle admiring the gutter all the way home. It was a wonder it wasn't dead from lack of circulation by the time she got it home. I will spare you the slaughter details. Looking back it was barbaric, but we did not know any better, it was a way of life. I did enjoy the chicken curry or soup, but how I hated plucking the feathers, and it didn't end there. We had to wash the feathers meticulously before we spread them out to dry in the sun, and then pray a strong breeze didn't blow them away. Removing the quill from each feather was a tedious job, but it is the only way to make a feather pillow; ours were the best! Chicken was not on the menu very often so it took a long time to make one pillow. But as Mummy always said, "*Wan-wan dutty does bill dam.*" It means, 'A dam can be built by adding one piece of dirt at a time'. Just like feathers from *wan-wan chicken* will eventually make a pillow.

I had a traumatic experience one day while returning home from the market. I was paranoid about losing the money Mummy always wrapped in the shopping list, but I must have been daydreaming and accidentally dropped some of the change into the gutter. What a predicament I found myself in. Anyone who knows Albouystown will tell you those were not ordinary gutters; they had their own life form under the surface of the murky water. I was prompted to fossick around in the black slimy waters after anticipating the *licks* I was *bung fuh* (bound to) get. I was only able to retrieve one coin. In defeat, I walked home crying from sheer terror. Apart from the fear, I also had to suffer the humiliation of the fas' people on the street pointing and *skinnin' deh teet'*. Needless to say that was the first and last time I ever lost any of Mummy's money.

## Mummy Sets Up Shop

By now you know our financial situation was not the best, my mother was finding it difficult to make ends meet. Of course, I am only now realising this because financial affairs were never discussed openly in front of the children. Everything always happened *out of the blue* in my family, and in an instant my mother was running a *groun' provision* (vegetables in general) shop. Location was very important, and she was fortunate to secure an ideal position. You could not get a better location than next to *Channa Maan* (he sold chick-peas) on the corner of Camp and Durban Streets. Mr Singh was his correct name. His astute business sense profited from knowing what the public wanted. He added popcorn, *candy fross* (fairy floss) and peanuts after the channa had caught on. Everyone who was going to the cinema made a stop to get some of his treats. The channa was either soft boiled or fried hard and crunchy; the latter was my favourite. This delicious treat was sold in paper cones for a few cents that I could seldom afford.

Mr Singh was given a rude false-name because he was of East Indian descent. An unfavourable rumour circulated as to why his channa was so tasty. He was of the same religion that kept a bottle of water in their latrines and for that reason alone he got the name Wash *   *   * Singh. If you can't figure it out you better find a Guyanese to ask.

The tiny cubicle that became our groun' provision shop was attached to his prosperous business; thus making him our landlord. An elderly East Indian woman we called Baby was employed to cook the endless supply of *channa*. The huge kerosene tins she used for this purpose were constantly bubbling over a roaring fire in the yard behind the shop. It was a stroke of luck that both back entrances to the shops connected because Baby secretly passed us bowls of steaming hot channa each afternoon after school. Poor Baby peeled and chopped mountains of onions and hot peppers to *fry-up* this delicacy. Her eyes streamed continuously but she never complained. She had no home so she slept behind the shop on some old beddin'.

Certain customers had fussy ways that made my mother very angry. There was an old African woman who could barely walk, but her fingers worked just fine. She squeezed every fruit to a pulp and drove Mummy crazy. You should have seen Mummy's face; it *swelled up like a crappo* (angry). She had to restrain herself because we were desperate for customers.

Mummy left very early for Big Market on the day she made her wholesale purchases. The fresh provisions were delivered by a *push/ drop-cyart* (operated manually). There were other modes of transport that was quicker, but the cart was the cheapest. They were good sized carts and sometimes those men strained to pull the heavy load. Mr Mack in Smyth Street had the monopoly on the push cart franchise. He made a living by renting them at a cost of five dollars a day; some clients rented on a weekly basis. I knew Mr Mack well because one of Mummy's cousins was his *sweet woman* (mistress/lover). Georgetown is a small place so it was no secret. This lovely lady held down a full-time job, but made time to take him a cooked lunch everyday. I think she had *typee* for him, because I don't know anyone who will go to that trouble in these modern times. My husband has to fend for himself most days!

## Ogling the Dead

We were obligated to go the shop every afternoon after school to wait until Mummy finished for the day. This route was in the opposite direction to the one home, but a damn sight more interesting. We had to pass Lyken funeral parlour which hosted one most afternoons. This was a big curiosity for school children and just up my alley. My friend Sattie lived quite close to Lyken's so we walked together. We went to take a look whenever we saw a big-big crowd, just to see if we knew the person. Lyken was known for its open concept which meant anyone could walk in off the street to see the person who was laid out in the middle of the parlour for the viewing. I always made sure I did not recognise anyone in the crowd, because I would get a good *lickin'* if someone told Mummy they saw me snooping. There was a small platform in one corner reserved for the members of the family who were mourning so it was a good idea to look up there first.

This embarrassing incident took place many years after my school days; I was already working. I was riding past Lyken and saw mourners spilling out unto the street. That had to be someone very important I thought. [Old habits die hard]. I leaned my bicycle against a lantin-post and went to investigate. The platform was obscured from my view by the crowd, but I managed to edge my way towards it. *Rant* (mild version of expletive *rass*), I got a hell of a shock when I *butt-up* with my good friend Pansy (another teacher) who was weeping with the rest of her family. I asked her who had died and she said it was her father. He had been killed in a hit and run accident two days earlier. I offered my condolences and went to pay my respects . . . this is what happened when you were fas' like me.

While I am on the subject of Lyken I will tell you about a character who worked there. We called him 'Spung-dung', so named because it was his duty to bathe the dead, he also informed the relatives of the deceased. It was said he once fetched a corpse from over the West Bank (crossing on the ferry) to the funeral parlour on his bicycle. He did not want to make this public knowledge so he slapped the dead man repeatedly while admonishing him to make him appear drunk. It is supposed to be a *truh-truh* story, but I have no proof; although that is not out of the ordinary in Guyana.

There was another character who worked at another funeral home called Bastiani, but his name escapes me. He was said to have nowhere to live so he slept in the unused coffins. He gave customers a terrible fright when they came in to book a funeral and saw him emerging from a coffin. I bet some of them thought they were seeing *jumbie* while others might have thought their loved one had come back to life. I will tell you about some of our more outrageous characters later.

## Wedding Proposal from Lot 12

Lot 12 is a very famous address in Georgetown. It is the address of our prison; located directly across the road from *Channa Man*. Imagine having a prison in the middle of a busy intersection. A high wall topped with barbed wire around the circumference enclosed this rather oppressive drab rust brown complex. There were many who spent their entire life in jail; for some it was better than starving. On occasion the gate to the main entrance in Camp Street opened to let the *Black Mariah* (police van) in while I was passing. I always craned my neck to get a glimpse of the inside, but the gate was always rudely shut so I never managed to see anything worth reporting.

The inmates on the highest level of the jail had the privilege of a cell with a window; a hole with bars is a more apt description. It was only a bird's eye view to the street from this vantage point, but this did not deter the jailbirds from hurling obscenities at passersby. Most of it was directed at women. A loud *pssssssst* is the first sign of the mating call; one that some Guyanese men think exudes romance when wooing women.

I shouldn't say that, because this *love call* actually worked for my friend Jamie who lured his now Australian wife Glennys with that very call on a London subway. They have been happily married for over thirty years and are the proud parents of a handsome son named Nathan.

I had many a proposition while passing Lot 12; some were so romantic I almost succumbed. Wouldn't you just swoon if you heard, "Marry meh darlin' an' yuh cyan wash meh *buckta* (underwear) fuh de res' a'yuh life." How can any woman resist that one? Just walk past the prison anytime you were feeling down and you will be laughing in no time. Some of the propositions are too crude for print, but you can use your imagination. The public enjoyed taunting the inmates; it was free entertainment and extremely amusing.

## The Nook

In the midst of all this madness there was a patisserie of renown called 'The Nook'. This famous establishment was run by the lovely Mrs Daniels. Her *patties* (small meat pies) were well known all over Georgetown. Scrumptious pine and coconut tarts and other *sweet-mout'* (tasty indulgence) such as black puddin' with *sour* (chutney made with green mango or kamaranga) were all on offer. The shop was never short of a patron. Many Guyanese have gone overseas and tried to emulate and capitalise on her talent, but they can never hold a candle to her pastries. I shouldn't have said that; I may never be offered another *patty* when I visit my relatives and friends in Canada. I am not talking about you Ernesta so you can come and fill up my freezer like you did on your recent visit . . . is that classed as crawling?

## A Melting Pot

While we are on the subject of food, I might as well tell you about some of our famous dishes. Guyana is a melting pot when it comes to culture and cuisine. Not only is it the 'Land of Many Waters'; we can also boast of being the 'Land of Many Dishes'. The people from several ethnic backgrounds who came to British Guiana as indentured labourers have all contributed to the cuisine that we proudly call 'Guyanese recipes'. The Amerindians taught us how to use the Cassava in various ways. Their cassava bread, atchee and pepperpot are very popular dishes.

The Africans introduced Metagee/Mettem, Konkee and cook-up-rice (peas & rice); fresh coconut milk feature in these Creole dishes. The East Indians win hands down with their dhal, curry, dhal-puri and roti. It's safe to say you don't have to be East Indian to enjoy their cuisine. Chow-mien, Low-mien and Fried Rice are done to perfection by the Chinese and the Portuguese are famous for black cake and the garlic pork which is traditionally served on Christmas morning. Salt-fish was also introduced by the Portuguese. In saying that, there are no boundaries when it comes to preparing any of this gastronomic delight. We happily embrace and enjoy the culinary expertise of each race.

No party or important affair would be the same without famous delicacies such as patties, black puddin', *stuffed eggs* (devilled eggs) chicken salad, channa and cheese straws. Prunes stuffed with peanut butter were thrown in to signify a *furrin* (foreign) influence. We washed down this delicious banquet with many homemade beverages. The most popular is *swank*, made with fresh lime juice, water and sugar. Sorrell drink is another brew we made from the Rosella plant. *Mauby* is made from a bitter bark and is an acquired taste. Fresh sugar-cane juice is also delicious and the *jamoon* (fruit) also makes a tasty fruit punch; not to mention jamoon wine. I got pissed, oops! I meant inebriated; after drinking jamoon wine made by my cousin Ann when I visited them in d'Riva in 1984.

The flesh of a pineapple is not the only part we consume. The discarded skin is soaked for a few days, then drained and sweetened with a little Demerara sugar to make a refreshing beverage. My husband still makes *pine drink* here in Australia whenever we pluck up the courage to buy a pineapple [they are always sour]. Ginger Beer was reserved for Christmas and for that reason we were all familiar with this ditty, "C'ristmus comes once a'year an' everyone shall 'ave deh share, but poor Willy in de jail drinkin' sour ginja beer." The majority of the populace made this brew a week or so before C'ristmus and left it to *set* (stand).

The more hard core drinkers preferred indulging in the famous XM or Russian Bear rum and our locally brewed Banks Beer. Mummy often indulged in a bottle of Guinness stout; especially when she was breast-feeding. She said it increased the milk supply, but I think that was just an excuse to drink Guinness. *Pac-pac* (homemade/generic fruit wine) was the last resort for hard core drinkers. Social snubs frowned on anyone drinking Pac-pac; it was considered an unfavourable brew because it was retailed cheaply.

My personal favourite was cider; the beautiful woodpecker gracing the label advertises the brand name.

## The Guyanese Vernacular

I think it would be appropriate to give you a run-down on our vernacular since you've just had the spiel on our cuisine.

Language differs vastly throughout the universe but that is not to say the official language of a country always remain intact. Travel around the globe and you will discover the native tongue in most countries has evolved to form an adapted version which suits the needs of the people for one reason or another. This is what happened in British Guiana. Under Colonial rule the British firmly established that English was to be our first language. The indentured labourers from different ethnic backgrounds found this very difficult to master (English education for the slaves was not encouraged) and found their own ingenious ways of forming a new language among themselves. In the beginning the language was basic communication known as Pidgin. Further down the track it evolved to a more understandable form. Strange words from the different races crept into the new language we now call Creolese. I can only assume that was how mispronunciation of words occurred, and since no one bothered to correct the mistakes, it has been passed down through the generations.

The vernacular in Guyana varies depending on the race. Although all Guyanese can understand one another when speaking Creolese, it is sometimes difficult to follow the East Indians (I must stress this is more noticeable in the country areas) who use words in a totally different manner. Most people spoke incorrectly so it was comical when my mother pulled us up if we used the East Indian idiom. Let me give you an example of the difference. The folks in town may say, "Come le'we guh 'ome gyurl." Although it is incorrect English, I am sure you understood what it meant. An East Indian will say, "Come gyal, le' a'we guh 'ome." Do you agree that is more difficult to understand? That's the explanation on our vernacular in a nutshell; the experts can give you the bigger picture.

Here's another example of a mutated word. My mother always said she was going to "chunkay" the dhal when she fried the garlic with the *jheera* (cumin) in oil to add at the end of the cooking period. It never entered my head that the word *chunkay* might not exist in the English language. That was until I saw a chef cooking dhal on television many years ago. He carried out the same routine at the end and called it a similar name, but I was not quick enough to catch it. I've been looking for that word ever since, so if you know what the correct word is for *chunkay* please let me know.

## Incorrect Pronunciation

We were famous for our malapropism. I gave you a brief history as to why our vernacular mutated and now I will give you a few more examples of mispronunciation.

On my last visit to Guyana I was having a conversation with an East Indian woman who was telling me she came from a large family and her parents could not afford to send them all to school. She was very proud of one of her sisters who was educated and was actually living in Australia. With a straight face she said, "Dat sistah is de only wan in we family dat *granulated* (graduated)." It was difficult not to laugh but this next one takes the cake. This Guyanese lady floored me because she was living in Canada and should have known better. Daphne took me to visit a friend of hers who was just out of hospital. I naturally offered her my good wishes for a speedy recovery on her latest surgery. We were enjoying some refreshments when she blurted out, "Did yuh know ah 'ad a'dictorectomy?" I nearly dropped my *patty* on her white carpet. Thank goodness I had been told she had a hysterectomy, because I was able to keep a straight face and said, "So I heard."

My stepmother cracked me up when she said, "*De revazar* (reservoir) mus'be empty J.B, de watah not comin' upstairs." Priceless gems.

## Understanding Our Patois

Guyanese are known for their peculiar and contradictory way in which they use words, for example . . . after enjoying a beautiful chicken curry, a Guyanese would say one of the following, "Gyurl dat was a'bad curry" OR "Gyurl dat was a'sweet curry" OR "Gyurl dat curry was sweet bad." You can be excused for believing that *bad* in the first example meant the curry had gone off, or that *sweet* signified the curry was cooked with lots of sugar in the second example. Nothing can be further from the truth; for a start we do not put anything sweet in our curry. Only *de white people* put apple and sultanas in their curries; that is a stew in my opinion. In all of the above instances, it simply means the curry was fantastic. Anything we enjoyed was classed as *nice* or *nice bad* regardless of it being clothes, food or a movie. I guess you are still scratching your head but you will get the hang of it; better still, make friends with a true Guyanese. [Ah 'ope somebaddy gon tell meh dis book is nice or sweet bad after deh read it].

I have the Australians eating every one of our dishes and pleading for more. I can't make enough *Black Cake* at Christmas. Marg Robbo buys for her entire family; although between me and you, I think the woman lies and secretly eats them herself.

Mummy used to quote this proverb to me almost every day because of my rudeness, she said, "De laangest rope gotta end," and this story about my husband's brother-in-law proves her right. In Down Under terms, Alan is a *fair dinkum Aussie*. When Mitzi married him in 1974 he did not know what curry was. Whenever she brought him to our home he sat in the sitting room holding his nose asking, "What is that stink?" What do you expect, he is *white,* you can tell by his perfect English. He refused to eat curry so Mitzi had to *waalk wid* (carry) something different for him, but I didn't take him on because I knew he would come around eventually. I continued making my Roti and Curry and he finally succumbed. You ask that man what is his favourite meal. GO ON, I dare you! Alan will tell you there is no other food like it on earth. The man is even saying a few of our words now but I still have to work on his accent. He and Mitzi were here the *odda day*, and I cooked them a chicken curry, he had to leave the table a few times to blow his hooter but he went back for seconds and that was when I heard the magic words and knew I had an Australian literally eating from *de palm a'meh 'an'*. I had to wait over thirty years to hear that man say, "Girl that is a bad curry." . . . truh-truh story.

I know how to get rid of him if Mitzi wants the job done . . . on second thoughts, the man was a detective so I better *shut meh trap*. But you didn't hear me say that okay?

If you invite a Guyanese to dinner and they tell you that your food was *sweet bad* before you serve dessert, take it as the highest compliment, *skin yuh teet'* and say "*t'anks*."

Another t'ing de white people don't understand, is our need to squeeze every bit of marrow from a chicken bone. I made a complete jackass of myself in front of my *white* (Canadian) brother-in-law. We sat down to a *bad chicken curry* and yours truly *mush up* (chewed) the bones in true Guyanese fashion, not realising I was being impolite. CeCe told me later that Doug wanted to know if I didn't have enough to eat.

My grandson Kyle calls me a dog whenever he sees me indulging in this practice.

## Emphasis and Double Meaning

A Guyanese may sound very impolite when speaking to someone who speaks the Queen's English. We are lazy in nature when it comes to speech so we shorten words and sentences. Here is an example of a word used to signify three different responses. Instead of saying, "I beg your pardon," a Guyanese would say, "eh?" And if we want to say "no," we say, "eh-eh." It could also be used to feign surprise, in that context it is, "eh-eeeeh." The tone of voice makes all the difference to the meaning. We emphasise to get a point across. Take this scenario for instance . . . after witnessing or hearing something out of the ordinary we would make our report by saying, "A'tellin' yuh wid meh own mout' dat a'see it wid meh own two eye," or "Ah 'ear it wid meh own two ears." Yes, we want you to know we are using parts of our own anatomy.

A friend in Florida was telling me of the death of a mutual acquaintance and I enquired whether this person was ill prior to his death. In proper English, the reply would have been, "He was not ill, he suffered a heart attack and died suddenly," but my Guyanese friend simply said, "No, de maan tek an' dead." I understood the nature of his death without question. We also say things such as, "Sh'/'e dead-dead or "Is gone 'e/sh' gone?" The latter is simply expressing disbelief. And I don't get jealous when my husband tells me he met a 'fine-fine' woman because I know that bitch is just bony. No, a *fine-fine* person is not a threat, they are just extremely thin. Just don't confuse the latter with 't'in-t'in'; this person is just very slim. A small person/object is, 'small-small' and 'big-big' means huge. We will also say something or someone is 'a little small' or 'a little big'. And you know someone is mega ugly when we say, "Sh'/'e ugly bad." We are only making sure you get an accurate picture. No explanation is necessary when we say, "We cross across de road" and "We bade we skin" because it makes perfect sense to a Guyanese. I know it's all very confusing so just keep your wits about you.

Then there is the unspoken language of *cut-eye* (a look of disgust) and *scheupsin'* (sucking your teeth), but I will enlighten you on those subjects later.

I am losing my grip on the lingo because I got fooled by this one recently. A cousin in Melbourne was telling me his sister came to visit them *de odda* day. I know she lives in Venezuela and was not aware of a recent visit so ventured to ask whether she had visited again and Maurice said, "No, she came 'bout t'ree years ago." So make sure you get specific dates when talking to a Guyanese. We will tell you a destination is "Jus' rung de korna" then proceed to gesticulate giving you directions to Timbuktu.

## Normal Guyanese Customs

I bet none of you have bananas or bread hanging on a line over your dining room table. My father was big on conserving energy (his own) and since we were short on storage this was the perfect solution. My father invited my sister-in-law Mitzi and her husband to lunch when they holidayed in Guyana some years ago. Alan was astonished to see my father reach above his head for dessert after the meal. I might as well tell you about the *cook-up-rice* (pilaf) Daddy made for them. Alan observed Charlie picking out and stacking the meat around the edge of his plate. He was a bit worried . . . you have to remember this man is *white* (Australian) and he became increasingly nervous and wondered if Charlie was doing this because the meat was contaminated. Alan said nothing but refrained from eating his meat. He said he was so relieved to see Charlie devouring the meat when the rest of the meal was gone so he followed suit. I could have told him Charlie was saving it for *bambye* (later). Saving the favourite part of a meal to eat last is a habit some Guyanese have; we want to savor it. If you ever had a food particle hanging off your mouth and someone saw it they would say, "A'see yuh savin' sum food fuh bambye." I did the same thing Charlie did when we had chicken curry; that little bit of chicken I got always tasted better at the end of the meal. I must tell you about that bit of chicken too. Mummy liked to think she was being *fair* so she asked us what part of the chicken we liked. To this day I cannot believe I asked for, *de neck an' de gizzard*, those blasted parts had no meat but it was *sweet* so I didn't mind. That never happened to Joel; he was *hungish* so he asked for the breast. I knew that Mummy loved us because she shared out all the best parts of the chicken to us and she ate the head; complete with the eyes staring at her on the plate and she didn't mind eating our *lef-lef* (leftovers). I keep reminding you *nut'tin* was ever wasted in our home.

We have many customs you might find peculiar. One is categorising our clothes as *house clothes* and *good clothes*; not forgetting *school clothes*; we all knew what to wear and when. I was surprised to find that was not the custom in Australia and it took some time to adapt. [Now dat a'white, a'wear good clothes every day.] We were in big trouble if we were caught wearing our *good clothes* in the house after we had been home more than five minutes. The backs of our bedroom doors had big nails driven into them; that was our wardrobe. Daddy actually strung a line up in the sitting room and hung up his *good clothes* to air as soon as he got home; our house looked like a *Chiney* laundry.

## Characteristics and Obversation of the Races

Guyana's population is ethnically diverse; our indigenous tribes might even be outnumbered if compared to the ancestry or the other races.

My observation pertaining to the qualities and characteristics of the different races may not be seen as accurate to some but it was how I perceived them in my era.

The Europeans: Anyone of European descent was referred to as 'de white people'. This group of people were held in high esteem simply because they were *furrinas* (foreigners). British Guiana employed the

Europeans because they obviously had no skilled engineers or qualified personnel to run their sugar estates. I believe all the overseers on the sugar estates were foreigners. They were regarded as Sahibs and exercised their power of authority in no uncertain terms. The sugar estates of Guyana would be an ideal setting for a Mills and Boon novel. It was common knowledge that many of the overseers who ran the estates conducted illicit affairs with the hired help and sired a few *backrah picknies*. My family knows someone who had a child by a supposedly very respectable overseer. She was naive and believed his empty promises. The man responsible for the deed supported the child financially; although it was only to a certain extent. Many were left *'igh an' dry* (stranded).

The foreigners I had the most contact with were the nuns and priests; most were from Ireland. They were placed in this category and were held in high esteem. The nuns ran the Catholic Schools; some were gentle while others dished out corporal punishment to the point of cruelty. In saying that, they also taught us many good values. The clergy was not held in high regard after my experience.

The British left their mark by implementing a sound education system. This regime gave us a good grounding and enabled many Guyanese to pursue a higher level of education that enabled them to become brilliant scholars.

The Africans: The Africans were easier to read. They wore their heart on their sleeves. What you saw was what you got. A bank balance did not interest them in the slightest; their motto was *live fuh today*. Dressing to impress was their main aim, not to mention loud music; a ghetto blaster and partying were far more important. They were what we called the *don-kay-dam* (not a care in the world) society, preferring to sleep until midday then step out to see what they could find. For some it was at the expense of the more industrious. That was not to say they were all tarred with the same brush. Many held positions in high office including former President Linden Forbes Sampson Burnham who gained a law degree at the University of London. My mother was right when she said, "There is good an' bad in every race." The Africans were expected to perform menial duties and were treated with contempt by the upper crust of society. They were prone to a lack of ambition, which unfortunately steered them in the direction of crime, but in their defence, this was mostly due to the lack of opportunity where jobs were concerned. The finger was admittedly pointed at them wrongfully at times because of their reputation for crime. In the later years of my life in Guyana, the racial disputes between the Africans and East Indians escalated and were publicly played out in a bitter arena of vengeance and hostility.

*The East Indians:* This race epitomized a somewhat subdued and amicable persona in public. The core of their true character was not displayed honestly in my opinion. East Indians could not collectively be classed as 'East Indians' as a whole because Mother India had failed to sever the umbilical cord of the caste system when they immigrated to British Guiana. An underlining nuance existed within the Indian culture, although I felt the hierarchy was well established and accepted.

On the surface we were led to believe they were peace abiding citizens, but it was a very different scenario in private where they conducted their beliefs and customs in an inner sanctum which excluded all others. The custom of arranged marriages still existed to a certain extent in my era; I personally knew couples who were married under that system. An underlying element existed when it came to religion. Many families indoctrinated their children in their faith by sending them to the mosques for private tutoring after school. To my knowledge none of this schooling was ever used for any purpose except for their inner circle.

Unbeknown to the unsuspecting public, seemingly harmonious families simmered like a pressure cooker of *Dhal* until it exploded in warfare and bloodshed. Entire families were often massacred by the hands of next-to-kin, leaving many to exclaim, "But deh were such a'peaceful family." One such episode took place right next door to where we were living; although we never did find out the origin of the blood bath. Gossip and hearsay was rife so we drew our own conclusion.

Their educational pendulum swung between scholars and illiteracy. The wealthier families were determined to educate their children at all costs, but then there were the illiterate whose only proof of indentifiction was a thumb print or an X marked on a document. I saw them as quiet achievers, hard workers, but frugal in anything other than acquiring property. Many chose to hold their trousers up with a piece of string and save the cost of the belt. Georgetown was a common place to see East Indian beggars, and it was a well-known fact that most of them owned properties and banked huge amounts at the end of each week. They also door knocked to collect food and money. Nine out of ten landlords in Guyana were of East Indian descent and were either shrewd or cunning. But when all is said and done they are the backbone of the sugar and rice industry in Guyana. Love them or hate them for whatever reason; no one can dispute their cuisine is superb.

The Portuguese: What I am going to say about the Portuguese is not very flattering, considering I belong to that category. Again, I am talking from my point of view. The more ambitious got down to opening businesses to become self-sufficient. Most stuck to the same line of work their ancestors were comfortable with. They opened bakeries, rum-shops and salt-goods shops. Many others were sales assistants or white collar workers. To be seen working for the municipality was classed as degrading; I cannot remember ever seeing a Putagee hanging off the side of the M & T C (Mayor and Town Council) garbage truck. Our fair complexion was a mark of social standing even if you didn't have a 'pot to piss in' as they say. I know Portuguese people who lived in abject poverty, but still had airs an' graces in public. They were capable of masquerading social status; as long as you didn't follow them home.

This anecdote will give you an idea of the prejudices held by the Portuguese. My husband was shot down in flames by one of his father's supervisors when he returned to Guyana after living abroad for three years. This person asked what work he did in Australia. The man was appalled to hear he was a labourer. He immediately exercised his superior complex by bidding my husband "good day" in a scornful and abrupt manner. He simply turned his back and left. We accepted these prejudices while we lived in Guyana, it was part and parcel of life, but in hindsight it was appalling and uncalled for.

Take this scenario for instance. The Catholic Cathedral held pews in reserve for wealthy families; their names appeared at the end of the pew they had paid for. No unauthorised person would even contemplate sitting in one of those pews, not even when the families were absent. How ridiculous is that in the house of God?

My Great Aunt Mats (Matilda) was another shining example of snobbery. She married Mr Korner (Uncle Howell), a *furrina* who should have been the snub but he was the nicest person. He always gave me a decent *freck* (a small amount of money) whenever our paths crossed.

The couple lived on Robb Street (considered posh) and owned a car, and that is why I was so surprised to see my biggety aunt on Sussex Street close to La Penitence Market. I thought I had encountered Mary Poppins! She sat ramrod on her preggy bike, serenely holding a parasol to shield her from the sun. I plucked up courage when we were abreast to say, "Good marnin' Aant Mats" but the angle of her nostrils indicated I might have been a bit of excrement on the pave for she pompously ignored my presence.

The older generation was also known for their guarded trait. Age especially was never revealed for whatever reason; some went as far as telling their children they were the same age for years on end. Many went to their graves withholding important family history. Who knows what they had to hide?

I am trying to think of a good virtue ... Oh, we made the best garlic pork and black cake and the women are gorgeous!

The Chinese: Where were they? I believe they were obscured by the woks in their cook-shops because I certainly did not come into contact with too many of them. However, I could tell you the location of every restaurant owned by these Chinese masters who had us mesmerised by their Low Mien, Chow Mien, Fried Rice and other enticing cuisine.

Like the Masonic Lodge, they too seem to have had a secret society. The Chinese Association headquarters in Brickdam was, and remained a mystery to me. I have a vague recollection of attending a wedding reception there once. The older generation that did not work congregated at this building during the day. They met to pass the time of day playing card games; hard core gambling from what I understood. There were no Chinese beggars on our streets; they were well taken care of by their families.

Apart from some neighbours, I never had a personal friend who was of Chinese descent, not unless I count the ephemeral friendship with Marilyn Nyguen who taught at Stella Maris for a short period.

Again, the cuisine was what I remembered most about the Chinese.

The Amerindians: The many indigenous tribes kept a low profile; preferring to live in the rain forest. There was an Amerindian Hostel in Georgetown where they were accommodated whenever they had reason to come to the city to conduct business. A *Buck* (Amerindian) was a rare sight in my era; a curiosity to most of the locals who had little contact with them otherwise. Some tribes never ventured into the city; they were isolated, but their wisdom for hunting the wild beasts in the jungle stood them in good steed. The cultivating of crops such as maize, cassava, plantains, bananas, pineapple, papaws and other local fare made them self—sufficient. These tribes lived in primitive conditions. Minimal clothing was preferred; the women skilfully wove these using resources from the jungle. Beads and feathers were used in abundance to fashion elaborate tribal costumes. There were the odd bones used for rituals or worn to signify status among the group. Each tribe had a *Touchou* (a chief) and a *Piaiman* (pronounced *pee-eye-man*) who performed their medical cures. Both of these men were highly respected and held in high esteem by the tribe. Amerindians lived in harmony with the environment and made use of every resource available. They painstakingly harvested vines from the jungle then put these through a process to produce fibres such as the *Tibisiri* which was used for weaving the beautiful hammocks they slept in, and other household items. Other resources such as Palm fronds, *Nibee* and *Mokru* were used in abundance. Cassava growing was given top priority because without it, there would be no Cassava Bread, Farina and Cassareep; these foods were their staple diet. They were adept in making shooting implements. Poison (curare) specifically made from certain plants were deadly when fired from their blow pipes or arrows.

The smoking method was used in the preservation of the wild meat and fish when there was abundance. The Amerindians are known to be bashful and peace-abiding citizens unless provoked. The habit of tribes walking in single file is attributed to the narrow paths through the jungle. (I grew up wondering why my mother called us Bucks when we walked in a single file).

As a point of interest there are nine tribes of Amerindians in Guyana. They are Carib, Arawak, Wai Wai, Akawai, Makushi, Warrau, Wapishana, Arecuna and Patamona.

Metagee: Guyana is also called the 'Land of Six Peoples' but since the races are not confined to the six groups selected above and there is no real definition to describe the ones not mentioned, I shall call the combined additional races 'Metagee'. Metagee is a Creole dish made up with a selection of local vegetables so what better way to describe a group of people who hail from all walks of life. If I were to identify each individual from the neighbouring islands who took up roots in Guyana, it will fill a book; therefore it's best to call that group *Metagee*, which in essence, is a collection of people with numerous ancestries. We referred to an islander as a 'blow in' because it was sometimes difficult to pinpoint where they hailed from and trust me; there were many who were not there legally.

## The Circus and Coney Island Comes To British Guiana

I seem to remember living here when the circus came to town; it might not be the correct year, but I know without doubt we were still called British Guiana. I can still smell the sawdust and see myself sitting under the Big Top. It's a wonder I did not want to run away with the circus because I was enthralled with those amazing acts. The agile trapeze artists had me spellbound; the performing animals were awesome, and I was struck speechless when a man rode a motorcycle in an enclosed ball called the 'Wall of Death'.

Coney Island also came, but I don't think it was the same year, or was the circus all part of that spectacle? . . . I can't remember. What I cannot forget is the image of Daddy after he got out of the *sputnik* ride. Only two people were allowed at a time, so he and my cousin Bernice took the ride and I waited. Daddy came out swaying; he had *eye-turn* (dizziness). He was laughing while rifling through his pockets when he realised his money had fallen out. He looked so funny he could have passed for an intoxicated hobo. Daddy decided the ride was too scary for me, so I was not allowed to go on it. I had to settle for rides on the tame Ferris wheel and the merry-go-round which was fine by me, I was just happy to be there and even had *fairy fross* too!

## Visiting my Great Aunt Victorine

The scent of naphthalene, a Peak Frean custard cream biscuit, beautiful crockery and the aroma of freshly brewed coffee always trigger the memory of my Great Aunt Victorine. This prim and proper aunt with her braided halo lived in a congested one bedroom duplex on Bent Street with her spinster daughter Lucille. Our visits to Aunt Victorine were random, because we did not have the luxury of a telephone to schedule times. As I remember, Aunt Victorine was always at home. These visits were not the most joyous outings; although it was worth the few guaranteed rewards. Mummy always reminded me not to forget my manners before rapping on her door. There was never any form of physical affection exchanged by either party; just the customary greeting to acknowledge the time of day. I was referred to as *chile* (child) and I wondered whether Aunt Victorine actually knew my name. I always chose the rocking chair in the corner closest to the front door. It was the best vantage point; especially since I would be invisible for the duration of the visit. The only bedroom was strictly off limits. There were no walls to distinguish the kitchen-cum-sitting-room and dining area. A bed with a beautiful patchwork quilt occupied a big portion of the tiny sitting area, and this was the focus of my attention. My aunt always wore her customary ankle length, long sleeved dresses made from patterned fabric. The belt, buckle and tiny buttons that fastened her dress at the front were all covered with matching fabric. Our unexpected visit propelled her into action to provide refreshments, although experience had taught me this was going to take a considerable amount of time. Aunt Victorine walked lethargically over to the kitchen area to the two ringed gas burner. She lifted the lid from a blackened cast-iron kettle with her long bony fingers then dug around the bottom of the kettle with a spoon to remove the *groun's* (grounds/stale coffee sediment) which she slung through the open kitchen window. The kettle was then filled with water and replaced on the gas ring with a flame.

She ambled over to the bed while waiting for the coffee to brew. It was time for show and tell and I was *all eyes*. Aunt Victorine slowly knelt to the floor before lifting the hem of the quilt with her speckled sun spot hand to reveal a treasure trove of unusual crockery. The ritual began, and the latest purchases were pulled out. Some items were still wrapped in newspaper or brown paper. Both women examined and admired the crockery from every angle with delight before a special tea set was selected for our afternoon tea.

It was obvious my mother shared her aunt's passion for beautiful crockery and there is no doubt these visits instilled the love I also have for crockery. When all the crockery was safely back under the bed, Aunty attended to the brewing of the coffee. She pried open the lid of a rusty tin, measured two heaped spoons into the kettle; gave it a quick stir, then poured a little cold water over the top to *settle* the coffee. I was taught this procedure at the tender age of nine when it became my duty to brew coffee for breakfast each morning. With dainty movements Aunt Victorine carefully placed an embroidered cloth on a wooden tray; followed by matching cups, saucers, and tiny cake plates with a beautiful floral design. She placed the tray with the *tea* (coffee) on the table, then ceremoniously handed me a plate with the long awaited cream biscuit and a sliver of cake. The anticipation of licking the cream from the centre of the biscuit made up for the otherwise boring visit. I was offered a glass of *swank* while the adults drank their *tea*.

## Ignorance in the Highest Degree

Cousin Lucille passed away some years later and I did not visit Aunt Victorine for quite some time. Mummy said she had given up the apartment and gone to live with one of her other daughters. The rumour mill was doing the rounds and it was said she was getting *schupidee* (stupid/senile). I heard she was saying and doing silly things which were not of her true character. Curiosity got the better of me and I asked Daphne to accompany me so it wouldn't be too obvious that I was being *fas'*. Cousin Dolores welcomed us, and then showed us to Aunt Victorine's room. I felt somewhat uncomfortable after she left the room because Aunty seemed to be dozing in the four poster bed and I wasn't sure whether I should disturb her; however I wasn't leaving until

I saw how *schupidee* she was. In a loud voice, I said, "Good afta-noon Aunt Victorine, we come to see yuh." Her eyes opened a crack, and after peering at us for a while she asked, "Who is it?" I replied in an even louder voice; as if she was deaf, "It's Helen an' Daphne, yuh know who we are?" The moment had arrived . . . she started telling us a story about how she had to go somewhere to do something; total rubbish. That whet my appetite for more; boy was she schupidee. I must have asked that poor woman ten times if she knew who I was. [Looking back I realise how stupid I would have sounded if anyone was listening. They would have thought it was me who had dementia, because it sounded as if I did not know who the hell I was]. I visited her once more before she passed away just for a laugh. I am now reflecting on those visits I made during her illness and realise how utterly disgraceful and despicable my behaviour was, but I didn't think so at the time.

## Titi Means Aunty and Mac-may Is More Complicated

I honestly thought my mother was being *full-mout'* when she addressed one of her aunts as Titi Shan. I assumed Titi was her name so to be respectful I called her Aunt Titi Shan. Another aunt finally enlightened me when I became an adult. I was saying aunt twice because Titi meant aunt in the Portuguese language. Our ancestors are from Madeira and spoke the language in the earlier generation, but it was phased out when my generation came along. I cannot understand why Aunty Shan or other members of the family did not point out my mistake from the very beginning. I should have picked up the discrepancy because Mummy addressed all her other aunts as Aunty. That was the same aunt my mother went to live with when she ran away from home at eighteen, so I guess she stuck to the Titi from that time. I believe she was also her favourite aunt.

Having a Mac-may and a Cumpay was another Portuguese tradition I never understood. My sister-in-law Mitzi patiently explained it to me recently. [A warning . . . you will need debriefing after reading this book].

Good *carta-lick* girls (like I was) acquired two *Nennens* (godmothers); one at baptism and another at confirmation. Your godmother's mother became your mother's Mac-may. That will keep you busy for a few minutes. And I spent all those years thinking the word meant 'friend'. Whenever Mummy was going to visit her friend Mrs Trotman (my godmother's mother); she would say she was going to visit her Mac-may. Doesn't that make perfect sense to you? [I threw that one in to send you to therapy]. GOOD LUCK!

## Time to Shut Up Shop

I will wrap up this chapter by finishing the shop story. This venture did not last very long; selling *groun' provisions* was not as fruitful as Mummy anticipated. She said too much perished and it was not worth her time. We met some very nice people in that short time and some shady ones too. A lovely young woman came in with her sister or mother most weeks. She told us she had some ailment called Bright's, but I had no idea what that meant. On occasion her face was so puffy we hardly recognised her, and her ankles were always swollen. I used to thank my lucky stars I did not have to follow her very rigid diet. She spent a lot of time choosing plantains because she was not allowed to eat the really ripe ones. She also said that the rice had to be washed and squeezed out several times after it was cooked to remove all the starch before she could eat it. We never knew another person who suffered from that disease, but I remember feeling really sorry for her.

I was not happy with the man who came too often to our shop. That fat crappo hung around for no good reason and Mummy seem to have plenty of time for him. I always gave him a *cut-eye* whenever I saw him. He told Mummy a sob story about his wife being very ill but I had to deliver some provisions to their home one time (they lived along the same street) and she didn't look too sick to me. I had a crush on their adopted son who was really cute, but he was out of my league. I am sure this man was hitting on Mummy; ugly big-belly son-of-a-bitch. He looked as if he could also be a *Freshie* (an older man who pursued young girls). There were quite a few of those around when I was a teenager. We lived next door to one when I was fifteen. That man sat at his window waiting to follow me as soon as I left my home. I was onto to him after he chatted me up the first time (he asked me to go to the movies with him) but he never got another opportunity. He was old and slow so I peddled fast and was able to hide in Jeeboo's congested drugstore before he came around the corner. I pretended I was looking for something in the shop while keeping an eye out. I waited until the lecherous sod went past then I took off in the opposite direction and gave him the slip. I was walking to the drugstore one evening just after dusk when a freshie I knew rode past on his bicycle and grabbed my right bubbie real hard. The shock made me so angry that I threw a few choice cuss words at him.

The demise of the shop was another closed chapter in our life; we moved from this address soon after that.

# Chapter Eight

*Spare the rod and spoil the child.—Proverb*

## 1958-59 SUSSEX & BEL AIR STREETS

### Flapping My Sexual Wings

This two-storey abode was owned by the Khan family who lived on the upper level together with Mrs Khan's widowed brother and his sons Laurie and Andy. We were the tenants in the bottom flat. This place was a palace, it had three decent sized bedrooms AND indoor plumbing . . . things were looking up.

We took possession of the biggest bedroom because there were more people in our family (five, plus Daddy when he came home). Aunty Olga and her daughters occupied the middle bedroom, and our cousin and her *sweet-maan* used the one facing the road.

Although our new address was on the boundary of Charlestown, it was still classed as Albouystown. That was because the street branched off from James Street. Bel Air and Albert Streets were the only streets built side by side in Albouystown. The two streets were separated by a wide green. [My brothers were in their glory at this address because they could play cricket on the green instead of the street].

We lived at the corner of Bel Air and Sussex Streets alongside the Sussex Street trench . . . not good when you can see the *buryin' groun'*. Money burned a hole in my pocket with shops gracing all four corners. The most tempting was the cake-shop at the end of our street, it was owned by Maurice and Dolly. In no time Daddy and Maurice were drinking buddies. Directly across the road was a rum-shop; I always tried to get a glimpse inside but could never see a thing because the saloon doors were too high. The liquor fumes wafted out onto the sidewalk but luckily patrons didn't have far to go to redeem themselves. The Church of God church was opposite our home and Brother Abdul was a very nice pastor.

My father was still managing the rum-shop and only came home at the weekend. Joel was now a teenager and was taking advantage of his absence. He was *own-way* (stubborn) and *fo'ce ripe* (acting like an adult) so his reins needed tightening. Not a problem in Guyana because one of the fathers upstairs volunteered to flog Joel on Daddy's behalf whenever necessary. What's more, he flogged him in the yard in full view of all the neighbours. [Can you imagine doing that to another person's child today]? Wayward boys were threatened with the prospect of being sent to Ondeneeming Boys' School on the West Coast and for a time I thought Joel would be sent there but he managed to escape.

The love bug hit me again, it was Andy this time. His father, brother and he occupied the bedroom directly above ours. Andy and I devised a system to fold notes small enough to slip through the cracks in the floor boards. This was quite a tricky operation since there was almost always someone in our rooms. What kind of things did you think we wrote in those notes? We were eleven and not very imaginative so we asked each other schupid things like, "What you doing?" As if it wasn't obvious enough we were passing notes. Just silly childish jargon, but we enjoyed the excitement of doing so without our parent's knowledge.

The *sweet-maan* saga was intriguing; I had listened to enough *beuzin'* on that subject to know what it was all about. At eleven I was more than a little curious about sex. Peeping through the keyhole of the lovers bedroom got me nowhere because I never saw a thing. Okay, there is no need to say it, I admit I was a very fas' child and one who didn't miss a trick. I slyly listened to the adults conversing at every opportunity. How do you think I know so much today?

Although this was a good sized home, it was not easy living here. It was no picnic having eleven people using one bathroom and toilet and as the eldest girl child I was expected to do the majority of the cleaning. This to me was very unfair and it added to my incubating resentment.

It was a good thing we only ever had to share a home twice!

## Going To the New/Big School

The day had finally arrived for me to attend the new/big school that I told you was built to accommodate the higher standards. My excitement was immense; I could not wait to get my hands on the items on my book list. It was the opposite for my mother because the start of a new school year always gave her a dreadful headache. Purchasing school supplies for three children added to her financial burden and I can still see her scurrying all over town scouting for bargains and ticking off each item as she found them. A brand new book was rare in our household. Requests were lodged with secondhand book dealers in the market as soon as she got our book list. Swapping with neighbours, relatives and friends was another option. School policy dictated all books should be covered to keep them in mint condition. We took great pride in revealing a new cover when the paper was changed. Books were either passed down to younger siblings or sold.

Going to the big school went to my head, and I think that was when I started *smellin' mehself* (feeling my power). You see being in third standard was IT!

Things were more orderly and civilised in this school. For a starter, we had a better seating arrangement; there were only three students to a bench. I started off sitting with my best friend Sattie and Daphne, but Mrs Fletcher soon got wind of our talkative nature and we were separated quick smart. Then I became close friends with an African girl named Joan Austin.

We had graduated from the scratching sound of pencil on slates to exercise books although I disliked the double lined version. I had to be very careful practicing my cursive writing. At the back of each exercise book were many useful tables, weights, measurements and other important facts. The desks tops lifted up for storage and had a groove along the edge to stow our pens and pencils and also a little ink well at one end. Using a pen was a novelty and we sure had some crosses to bear because these pens leaked and made a terrible mess on my school shirt. Mummy could never get the stain of the Quink ink out so it was a good thing the yolk of the pinafore covered most of the pocket on my blouse.

## Learning Etiquette

Home Economics rostered on Wednesdays and taught by the likeable Mrs Davis was my favourite class. Wednesdays couldn't come fast enough! I was impressed by the novelty of the food preparation and presentation more than anything, not to mention being able to eat what was prepared. Students were allowed to buy the prepared meal for twenty-five cents. Etiquette was also taught in this class. We learnt to set a table and were made to eat our meal with a knife and fork. It was tricky business and I was *shame* to admit I did not know how to use those utensils but I eventually got the hang of it.

We moved to a different room after lunch, where Mrs Cooke taught us the finer art of sewing and embroidery. I use the word 'sewing' with tongue in cheek because those lessons were sadly wasted on me. I never made a garment that needed a herringbone or blanket stitch. God knows I tried sewing, but my children wore creations that were only fit for the privacy of our backyard.

## My Practical Joke Backfires

The silly practical joke I played on a friend when I was in fourth standard will never be forgotten. We had to cross across a trench to get to our playing field which ran parallel to the *buryin' groun'*. This was where we played sports, but most of us went there to play *de fool* and I was no exception. We were sent over to play *rounders* one day, but I was not chosen by any of the team captains. I guess they did not want to play with a Putagee girl who could not run or catch. Grasshoppers were in abundance so I wandered around the perimeter of the playground and collected a handful which I carefully cupped in my hand and took back to school. My friend Kamala Khan was standing in front of me in the line as we waited to return to the classroom. I called her name to get her attention and as she turned around I released the grasshoppers in her face. Unfortunately the *schupidee* girl did not see the funny side of it and fainted on the spot. I almost followed suit when Mrs Payne called me and administered six lashes to my hand.

## School Bullies

School bullies existed even back then . . . someone was always willing to *buss yuh ass* (beat you up) after school. It was a regular occurrence, especially the boys in sixth standard; their fights attracted huge crowds. Joel's *passion* (temper) got him into a few fights but even his best efforts to keep them from Mummy failed at times and he paid the price with another lickin'. Joel's false-name changed from 'Big-'ead' to 'Cannon' when he went to the big school, but it was still in reference to his cranial measurement.

When it comes to fighting I was the biggest coward and was always fearful of being beaten up. I distinctly remember a *red skin* (mixed race with light complexion) girl named Ingrid Gaskin; she was feared for her reputation as a fighter so this chicken decided it was best to be on her good side so I befriended her. I must have stepped out of line one day because she threatened to beat me up after school. You never saw anyone run so fast when the school bell went at three o'clock . . . I could have broken Roger Bannister's record!

The majority of school children went home for *breakfus* (lunch) at midday; some unfortunately did not get a hot meal. My brothers and I were fortunate to always have one waiting although I disliked some foods, especially *Karilla* (gourd/bitter melon); no amount of seasoning could disguise the bitter taste. *Bolanja/bigan* (eggplant) and Okra was also unpalatable, and I know this is going to sound ungrateful but I hated it more when my mother cooked soup. *Cutty-cutty soup* (soup cooked with vegetables cut into small pieces) was fine, but if she said she was cooking split-pea or black-eye soup, I knew she would leave the *foo-foo* (boiled green plantain pounded in a mortar) for me to pound. Mind you, it was my favourite. [I heard people in Guyana are now using a blender to do that job].

## A Taunt for Each Race

Children today are taking drugs and weapons to school, we never dreamed of such things, but that does not mean we were all innocence. Our weapons were verbal, and inflicted just as much pain if you had a sensitive nature like me. Children made up taunts that really hurt and I cried when anyone taunted me with the Putagee chant below.

## The Putagee (Portuguese)

Putagee bumba fart cucumba
Putagee potax ten poun' a wax

## The Coolie (East Indian)

Coolie watah rice, poke-n-spice
Wash yuh batty wid dhal-n-rice

## The Black-man (Africans)

Black Man sala, poun' massala
T'ief 'e muddah choka an' run a koka

We were very scared of the African children so we started running before we got to the second line. You bet I gave as well as I got!

The more naive children were asked silly questions such as, "Yuh want sum jamoon." When they answered "Yeah," we said, "Jam de moon" or "Yuh want a'mango?" "Dance de tango." We thought it was hilarious back then. They say simple things amuse simple minds and I fitted into that category without a doubt.

## The Games We Played

A lot of our games were invented simply because we could not afford the luxury of shop bought toys or equipment. My brothers made their cricket balls from scratch using a *kurio* (Akuyoro) seed, twine and strips cut from discarded bicycle tubes. It was painstaking but they had a ball to play *bat an' ball* in the street. The more affluent boys had balls made from *balata* (rubber from the bulletwood tree). A bat was fashioned from the thicker end of a coconut branch or shaped from a piece of wood if you were lucky to find a sturdy piece. Discarded timber or the cover from a drum made a wicket. A *sling-shot* was constructed from the fork of a branch, some string, and pieces of rubber obtained from the discarded tube of our punctured bicycles. There was no shortage of ammunition, the boys used pellets we called 'buck bead'; these were obtained from a weed that grew prolifically in any field, mainly the cemetery. [I had the crazy notion to make a sling-shot recently to show my grandson Kyle but it wasn't my best inspiration. He used the cats as target practice and his muddah was not amused so it was banished]!

We played Rounders which is similar to Softball, and the usual games like London bridge, Brown girl in the ring, Ring-a-round-a-rosy and Blind mans' bluff. No one wanted to be chosen as the dog when we played 'The farmer takes a wife' because children were cruel, and patted the dog in a rough way on purpose. I always wanted to be the wife. We also enjoyed games such as, skipping, hopscotch, and littie which we also called jacks. It was called 'littie' when you used pebbles instead of the proper little spikes that were the *real jacks*. I only ever had pebbles and that was not much fun. You had to be quick to catch the stone (representing the ball) before it hit the ground. Those tiny balls were hard to come by and I envied anyone who owned one. That game was also played with bones and was called 'Knucklebones'. The one inch bones were collected after a meal, but we must have eaten ours because I never once found a knucklebone.

Another favourite game played mostly by the girls was Rick Chick-chick. Where it originated I cannot say with certainty, but after recently viewing the YouTube Video featuring an annual Guyanese picnic I came to the conclusion it must have been introduced by the African slaves. My mouth watered when I saw all the familiar Guyanese dishes in that video, but I wasn't prepared for the nostalgic tears when the rendition of this soul sounding ditty started.

This is how I remember the game being played: Someone was chosen to be the Fowl Mamma and she picked ten chickens. The person chosen to be *de ketcha* (the catcher) will ask for one of the chickens (naming the person) and Fowl Mamma's job was to protect and prevent that person from being caught. [I apologise in advance if this is incorrect].

Fowl Mamma and her chickens had to yell "congatay" after each line was recited by the de ketcha.

A rick chick chick-chick Congatay!
Meh bin a backdam Congatay!
Meh see fowl mamma Congatay!
Wit' ten fat chickens Congatay!
Ah beg sh' fuh wan Congatay!
An' she wun gimme wan Congatay!
Yuh see dat gal deh Congatay!
Name (name the person) Congatay!
She fat lak-a butta Congatay!
An' she magga lak-a chow Congatay!

The chosen child is then chased after the last line until caught. She then becomes the catcher and the game starts again.

Here are two variations of another game we played call *Chirren, chirren* (Children, children)

| | |
|---|---|
| *Chirren, Chirren* | *Yes, Mama* |
| *Whey yuh been* | *Grand Mama* |
| *Wha' she give you* | *Cheese an'bread* |
| *Where is mine?* | *On the shelf* |
| *How can I get it?* | *Climb on the chair* |
| *If I fall?* | |
| *Bruk yuh foot, I doan care!* | |

---

| | |
|---|---|
| *Chirren, Chirren* | *Yes, Mama* |
| *Whey yuh been* | *Grand Papa* |
| *Wha' he give you?* | *Crappo guts an' salfish tail* |
| *Where is the Crappo?* | *In the bush* |
| *Where is the bush* | *Fire burn it* |
| *Where is the fire?* | *The water out it* |
| *Where is the water?* | *The cow drink it* |
| *Where is the cow?* | *In the stable* |
| *Where is the stable?* | *In Bent Street* |
| *Where is Bent Street?* | |
| *A big fool like you doan know were Bent Street is?* | |

## No Trophy for Me on School Sports Day

Certain primary schools in Georgetown participated in a big School Sports Day held once a year at the Teachers Association Sports Ground. The excitement building up to this venue was immense. Apart from being allowed some special treats we would not have any school work for the entire day. Children not participating in the competition sat in the stands to cheer their school to victory. Trials were held before the big event and the weakest runners were weeded out. The not so weak ones were allowed *adge* (advantage) which gave them an equal chance of winning the race. I never qualified for anything and was always a spectator. The winning school got the trophy which was gloated over until the next school carnival. I can't remember ever winning a race at school, although I enjoyed the egg an' spoon (using a potato) and the *sack race* in the big *sugah bag*. The t'ree legged race was a good one too.

The most common sport played by the boys was marbles. Terms such as *gam* and *jummin'* were used in play. The version called 'holes' was serious and I was only allowed to watch. The aim of the game was to sink marbles into a course of holes (similar to golf). Measurements were taken with thumb and forefinger to determine who was closest to the target when opponents missed the hole. Bets were paid with buttons or marbles. The most coveted prize was called a *Taw* (steel marble or big ball bearing scavenged from abandoned vehicles). When the boys ran out of buttons to pay they tore the ones off their clothing! My brothers got some good licks when the deed was discovered. Fights broke out when someone did not agree with the correct form of play but that was added excitement for spectators. Playing marbles was the rage for a long time but not everyone was fortunate to have marbles bought from a shop. The boys improvised with the *kurio* and *awara* (fruit) seeds. Those seeds needed no more cleaning or polishing after we had scraped the fruit off with our teeth! Seeds deposited into an ant nest were also polished to perfection. The cunning boys challenged the ones who had real marbles (glass or steel) and became experts at playing to win.

Children used whatever resource was available and invented all kinds of toys. We could not wait for our muddah to finish a reel of thread. Those empty wooden cotton reels came in very handy to make a *spinnin' top* among other things. A discarded bicycle wheel and a piece of stick gave children hours of enjoyment. In the rainy season the gutters on the street filled to overflowing proportions. It was perfect for sailing boats fashioned from discarded newspaper. The soft, but firm stalk of the *Moca-Moca* (a wild plant) which grew abundantly along the moist gutters also made superb boats. A *pointa* from your muddah's broom and some newspaper made the mast and sails and away you went sailing. Some of the designs were quite creative. Children were seldom bored in those days.

## Pocket Money

Some children were given pocket money but not on the weekly basis we do today. We got what was called a *freck* (a pittance) and it was given to us to buy treats at school. Every child enjoyed buying a treat from the vendors who sat with their tray of goodies in front of the school. My brothers and I seldom got money, and we knew Mummy well enough to know begging was not an option. We lived in hope that she would offer us a *jil*; even a cent was appreciated.

[The amount of pocket money given to children today astonishes me. I would have been able to purchase a bike with it when I was growing up. Besides it is appalling to see parents paying their children to make the very bed they sleep in. I never had the privilege of having a bed to myself. My children usually bring out the violin at this point].

## The Phantom Flutee Vendor

The word had gotten around that *palin' flutee* (ice-confectionery sold over the school fence) was the juiciest. That's another thing we knew; the quality of a flutee. You may laugh but some of those vendors used to water down the mixture and it tasted like crap so when we found someone selling a good quality flutee we patronised them. This icy treat was basically made from Kool-Aid, water and red food colouring; how I loved sucking on one of those dripping red blocks. The red stripe down our arm, along with a red tongue and lips was a sure sign we had indulged. The girls pretended they were wearing lipstick which was a no-no until you were *big*. Who discovered palin' flutee remains a mystery since this was a phantom vendor. Then again school children in Guyana had a nose for sniffing out food. We would find someone even if they were selling something in a dark hole. If I was lucky enough to have a cent I spent it buying a flutee from the phantom. This is how the transaction went . . . you stood behind the palin' at the back of the school and yelled loudly, "Pleeease fuh a'flutee." A tong materialised over the fence offering the tiny red block. As it came into view a voice said, "*Heh, gi'me de money.*" That simply meant, 'Here, give me the money'. [I will digress to explain our speech in case you are wondering why our English is so broken].

We were taught to read and write perfect English. It is our first language, but most Guyanese were more comfortable with the local parlance. I never spoke correct English even though I was a teacher (without going to Teachers' College). I adhered to the correct form when I was teaching or talking to my superiors at work, and definitely when I came to Australia. On second thought I might have stuck to the Creole because my accent was too strong and the Aussies did not understand one word I said. And that just reminded me of the bad grammar incident that took place one day at Stella Maris. The junior teachers liked to get to school early to congregate in the lunch room to gossip. The entrance to this room was just outside the steps that led up to the second storey of the school. We were chattering away like parrots one morning; most likely *talkin' sumone's name* (gossiping about someone) when Sister Roseanne materialised out of the blue. She was about to mount the stairs but stopped dead in her tracks when she overheard me say something in broken English. This apparition decended on us and in a stern manner shouted, "Teachers! Who said that? That is disgraceful English; you should be ashamed of yourselves speaking like that!" I jumped and then froze with fright. She was so angry she gathered up her habit in the most ungodly manner and stormed up the stairs. I could have died from embarrassment. That incident made us more aware of our conversation and we kept a close watch for anyone coming around the corner unexpectedly after that.

I am still on the topic of school vendors so forgive me for strayin' again.

The most sought after treat was green mango served with a mixture of hot peppersauce and salt (peeled and sliced in sections on the seed). The hygiene of these road side vendors left a lot to be desired. I watched the ones with *big-foot* (Elephantiasis) scratch their afflicted leg with the same knife they used to peel the mangoes. Not a thought was ever given to cleaning the knife afterwards. We turned a blind eye at such things because we didn't know any better . . . who knows it may have even added to the flavour!

Those cheerful ladies provided a feast for a child's palate. On offer was, black chipped and grated sugah-cake, tamarind and gooseberries fresh or stewed, phulourie with sour, channa, methai, jamoon, guava, dunks, awara, akurio, loquat, genip, golden apple, cherry, mango (several varieties) sapodilla, cashew, banana, papaw, pineapple, carambola (star-fruit/five finger), karamanga, star apple, psidium, soursop, fat poke, whitee . . . It was difficult to decide what to buy when or if you only had a cent or two. Not all vendors had the same fare on offer, some were patronised solely for specialities such as *Tambrin* and *gooseberry syrup* (stewed in sugar), black puddin', *bal-am-acha* (a pink and white combination of delicate sugar ribbons), *rock-ress* (coconut-ice), cassava pone and black chipped sugah-cake.

Custard blocks were another favourite; although I seldom could afford those. They cost a whole penny and more if they had raisins.

Then there was a big red sweetie called 'Neva-dun'; the rubber band attached to the top allowed you to hang it from your arm so it could be sucked at your convenience. Let me tell you, the name of that sweetie did not disappoint, you could suck it forever. My friends and I shared a Neva-dun many times. We saw nothing wrong with taking turns to suck, and we did not mind each others jutah one bit . . . those were very special times.

A few of the vendors offered us truss when they thought we were honest enough to repay the debt. I never allowed my truss to go higher than five cents and lived in hope of a generous relative visiting to get a *raise* (offer of money) so I could pay it off. Miss Marjorie remembered who owed her by writing our names and the amount on a piece of brown paper. She crossed off whatever amount of the debt you repaid; it wasn't always possible to clear the whole debt in one hit. I am surprised she didn't charge interest! It was high finance. You know something? I have a feeling I left St Stephen's still owing Miss Duncan a *jil*.

A selfish child must have started this trend and it caught on. After making your purchase a friend or an acquaintance (one with courage of course) could come up to you and say, *stings* (asking for some). You broke a tiny piece off and gave it to the person to save face, but if you were not feeling generous or did not like the person, you simply said, *no stings* and that was the end of the matter.

I seldom had money, but I always envied the girls who had a pocket in the skirt of her uniform. Having a pocket to put my hand in would have looked so cool, but the dressmaker charged more to do that so I

NEVER got one. I always look for clothes with pockets now . . . It's part of my therapy.

## School Curriculum and Frivolous Pastimes

Looking back, our primary school curriculum was basic; although it was adequate and in my opinion gave us a far better foundation than the present education system. A calculator was unheard of in my days; we had *mental arithmetic* to keep us on our toes. Our school subjects comprised of: English, Arithmetic, Mental Arithmetic, Spelling, Nature Study, Geography, Woodwork (boys only) and Home Economics (girls only).

Milk was supplied to the underprivileged children. At first it was just a big bucket of water with a few scoops of milk powder, and all the children had to drink from the same cup. I had *kinna* (an aversion/ scorn) and refused to drink anyone's *jutah* so I never took any. But it was a different story when it changed to flavoured milk in bottles. Children could purchase any surplus for six cents. I am ashamed to say I sneaked into the line for the free milk on occasion because I could not afford to pay. Isn't that underprivileged? The milk came in three flavours; vanilla, chocolate and strawberry and I was barefaced enough to take strawberry which was my favourite.

At school Daphne and I were always talking about which boy we *liked*. She had a crush on a cute red skin boy name Colin Stuart in fourth standard. He never returned after the holidays and we never found out what happened to him. Maan, there was a Coolie boy named Victor Rampersaud who had *typee* (passionate love) for me. That boy drove me crazy and gave me *tizzick* all day long. The entire school knew he liked me, but I was not keen on him. I used to *fish-up* (insult) that poor boy but he was persistent. I ran into him many years later and accepted a date out of pity. We went to the movies, but nothing came of it. Victor was really a very nice boy; I was just a bitch. Imagine my surprise when I saw his wedding picture in the Chronicle right next to mine. It was almost as if he was saying, "Look Putagee gyurl, a'got mehself a'beautiful wife, tek dat." Victor might be pleased to hear he came with me to Australia because I brought and still have the yellowed newspaper.

## Barbaric Teaching Tactics

The teachers were becoming more feared as I climbed to the higher standards. Mrs Moriah, Mr Hope and Mr Durante taught the higher standards. Mr David was the *pupil teacher* (a trainee teacher) but he was still allowed to flex his cane. I still associate each teacher at St Stephen's according to the degree of corporal punishment they dished out. Almost all of them were ruthless and feared. I praised god I was not smart enough to be in Mr Giddings class, he taught the scholarship class and his lashes were legendary. Some of the older boys stuffed their trousers with their exercise books in an effort to outwit the male teachers who made them bend over for the lashes. That ruse was soon discovered and the extra licks left them unable to *siddung* on *deh behine*.

Mrs Dennison was quite docile. I can still remember standing at the blackboard in fourth standard trying to work out a long division with Mrs Payne standing over me with the wil'-cane. My legs were shaking and the tears were streaming; sheer fear made me put my mind to it and thankfully I got it right. It was so traumatic, I can still remember the answer to that sum; it was *t'ree*.

Mrs Moriah was my last teacher; a demon in the classroom but a really lovely lady. I visited her after my school days just for a chat. What a pity the teachers I encountered never took the time to encourage or inspire me in any shape or form. Unfortunately, I was one of those children who could never be inspired by such barbaric treatment.

## My Best Friend

There were a few nice friends, but my best friend right through primary school was Sattie Naraine. That was after Daphne of course. Sattie was a beautiful East Indian *gyal* (girl) who came from a very large family. Two of her older sisters and two younger brothers also attended St Stephen's. My eyes popped out the first time I visited her home, not as a guest. I waited at the gate for her so we could walk to school together. Their two-storey home was a mansion in my opinion. St Stephen's School was located between both our homes when we lived at this address so I ran home for lunch, gobbled it down then ran to Sattie's home. After a period of time, Mrs Naraine took pity on me and told Sattie to invite me to wait in their kitchen instead. I was a nervous wreck sitting next to that severe looking lady; we exchanged smiles but never had a conversation. Not only was I shy, I was scared of her because she was so strict with her family.

The three older girls were not allowed back to school until the wares had been washed and the kitchen was tidy to her satisfaction. Mrs Narine dutifully prepared the mid-day meal, but the children did all the household chores. Sattie had many brothers, some much older than her; a few of them were already working when I met the family. I had a crush on the one with a killer smile and a big *muff*; he was in the class below me. Mr Naraine owned a salt-goods shop in Albouystown and on occasion it was Sattie's duty to deliver his mid-day meal. She was of course allowed to leave home earlier on those days and I accompanied her. I looked forward to those days because a reward of one of my favourite treats such as a fowl-cock sweetie, nuttin, sour-stick or butterscotch was guaranteed. When Mr Narine was feeling generous he offered us a freck and although it was only a cent or a penny, it was a windfall to me.

Can you imagine a child of eleven performing that duty for a parent these days?

## Hula Hoop Craze

We were living here when the hula hoop craze hit. I never knew what envy was until this insipid plastic ring appeared on our street. Although unspoken, we knew it was no use asking for a luxury like that. The next best thing was to befriend the girl who owned the hula hoop. I already knew her in passing; she may have even attended my school. Lucky for me she was very accommodating. I guess it was no fun having a hula hoop if you had no competition. She needed to test her skills against someone else and I was just the person. Let me tell you, I could work that hoop from my ankle to my neck in no time; we played for hours. I think the craze was just about over when we moved from that street. How I wished I could have entered the competitions that were so talked about.

## Muddah Rat Goes Home

It was here my brother Charlie gave me the false-name *Muddah Rat*. Don't go jumping to conclusions that I was a *waabin* (prostitute/rat) because I was only eleven at the time. It's a known fact that rats can be found in dark secluded places, especially sewers and I was compared to one of these creatures when Charlie caught me foraging in my secret hiding place. There was no private place in our home to hide my few precious possessions. Now you may be wondering what I could possibly have had that was so precious. It was no more than a much loved hair clip, a kerchief, a few glass marbles (I still had a few marbles you know) and I also had a beautiful *likkle* toffee tin I kept odd buttons and my money in; IF I was lucky to have any. Nothing was sacred where my brothers were concerned; *find and destroy* was the name of their game. It was by a stroke of luck that I discovered that the water hydrant outlet on the grass verge outside our home was accessible. The cavity under the lid had a narrow ledge around it, just big enough to put-up small items. The lid was made of steel which protected my belongings from the elements. The fire men only tested the hydrant periodically so it was safe to hide things there.

My guard must have been down the day Sly Fox caught me in the act. Loud laughing broke out and quick as a flash he yelled out, "Suh dat is weh yuh hide yuh stuff, a'gon call yuh muddah rat because only rats guh in deh."

To this day I have cousins who still holler "Hi Muddah Rat!" when I telephone them in Canada. [No damn respect I tell you].

That reminds me of my visit to Guyana in 1984. A group of relatives and friends took me to the popular Belvedere nightclub which I frequented in my younger partying days. Maan, I was having a great time when my dear Uncle Joe got up and asked for some *hush* and in a loud voice he announced, "Ah buyin' drinks fuh everybaddy to welcome 'ome meh niece muddah rat, sh' come all de way from Asstralia." How can anyone forget a welcome home like that? I wished I did have a hole to hide in that night.

And now it's pay back time Uncle Joe or should I say *Pokey Joe*. Uncle Joe is only five years younger than Daphne and I, so we used to socialise with him. We thought he was loaded because he worked in the *bush* (interior/gold fields). Whenever he was in town we badgered him to buy us Carnation milk and *white creamin' soda* to make our favourite drink. I guess that combination is the equivalent to what we call a 'Spider' in Australia. This little anecdote involves his false-name. His *saga-bhai* personality earned him the nickname 'Pokey Joe' which is not very flattering (he is going to kill me). That may sound innocent to you but *pokey* is the rude word for a woman's private parts. No self respecting person would want to answer to that name, but Uncle Joe thought he was a stud so he good naturedly accepted and answered to it. That was until Charlie who was living in New York at the time made a collect call to him in Guyana and embarrassed him. In those days the operator had to connect the call. Uncle Joe picked up the telephone and a lady with a strong American accent said, "I have a collect call for a Mr Pokey Joe." He was enraged and told the woman there was no one there by that name and slammed the phone down. He failed to realise she was American and would not have the faintest idea what the name signified. Charlie had to call back using his correct name before he accepted the call.

We had some interesting false-names. Aunt Phil was married to a man named Cecil but his peers called him 'Bruk-up', and for good reason, he was the nicest person but the deep crevices in his face gave him the appearance of a jig-saw puzzle that had been put together haphazardly.

The most unusual nickname was given to Aunt May's de-facto husband. His real name was Ulric but someone nicknamed him 'Fluckum-pump'. I am sure there is a priceless story attached to that one but who do I ask? Almost all of that generation have gone.

Joseph D'Agrella (Pokey Joe), my mother's youngest brother

## Puberty Blues

Aunty Olga had a habit of coming to our bedroom to gyaff after we got home from school. I was always on *tenderhooks* (tenterhooks) in case Andy decided to pass a note through the floor boards from above. She and Mummy got onto the subject of puberty one time . . . you know, talking about starting to grow hairs and other embarrassing things; that is puberty right? Rant maan, I don't know what got into them, but Aunty Olga asked me if I had *started*. Shucks a'shame, yuh know wha' a'mean?

I shyly said "no" and thought that was the end of the conversation but the next thing I knew they were wrestling me to the ground to see for themselves. They just did not have any respect for anyone's privacy. And that was not the only time. When I was thirteen; Aunty Olga was living in Agricola, a village three miles out of town. I walked there to spend a few days with her and her two daughters Donna and Sharon. Out of the blue one afternoon Aunty lifted up my arm and laughingly said, "W'en yuh gon grow sum 'airs gyurl?" I could have died from the embarrassment but I had to learn to live with it. That whole family is very wicked so I guess that's where I inherited my warped sense of humour.

## Sugah Bowl Catastrophe

The relationship between my mother and I was already rocky when this incident took place. It was no secret she favoured her sons and she openly extolled their virtue. Maybe that fact made me more sensitive. I picked up on the smallest discrepancy if it was connected to my brothers, my eldest brother to be exact.

There was one injustice I never forgave her for. We were having breakfast one morning when *de mastah* (Joel) said, "Weh is de sugah?" I was already seated but sure enough Mummy ordered me to fetch the sugar bowl. I saw red but an order from Mummy was never disobeyed. I stamped my feet as I stood up, pushed my chair back angrily and shouted, "Wha' 'appen 'e legs bruk, why 'e cyan't get it 'e self?" Then I got the bowl and slammed it down onto the table. The glass bowl had already met with a sad fate and lost its lid. You guessed right, it smashed to bits. There were beatings I rated one to ten, but this was a twelve without a doubt. [Don't ask for *de sugah bowl* if you visit me because I don't have one].

## Castor Oil and Cascara Agony

There are childhood memories I cherish dearly, although I can say the memory of Mummy waking me up at *fo'day marnin'* to administer a dose of Castor oil, a brew of Senna pods or that nasty Cascara is not one of them. Most Guyanese children were subjected to these nasty tasting purges their parents inflicted with regularity. The Senna pods were soaked overnight and drained next morning. I could not stomach the taste and had a dreadful time swallowing. I retched and retched, and it took a few good slaps before I swallowed. Drinking any one of the above was bad enough, but the gripe was even worse . . . I will choose childbirth any day. This was a monthly occurrence and was supposed to purge us of worms and to prevent colds. What a lot of rubbish. All it did was make you *kounce* (open bowels) all day long. No use thinking I was going anywhere that day because I had to stay close to the latrine. You would not believe what I am going to tell you, but it is a truh-truh story. I want to tell you why we were woken up so early when it was worming day. Mummy still thought she was a fisherwoman in d'Riva so she had to *bait de worms*. I saw your eyebrows go up so let me tell you how she accomplished that amazing feat. She gave us a piece of uncooked salfish about half an hour before the castor oil. Can you believe she was actually baiting worms that were in our intestines? Mummy said that the worms would come out to eat the salfish, and while they were in a mad feeding frenzy we would drink the castor oil and *ketch* the culprits red handed! I thought long and hard about that one and finally found the answer. Those blasted worms did not die; they drowned in the oil slick. That wasn't all folks. We had to *kounce* in the *Poe* that day. I know you will not believe the reason, but it was so Mummy could count how many worms we passed. It was a competition to see who had more worms, although we never got a prize.

Have you picked yourself up off the floor yet?

I am sure all the Guyanese from my era will remember *Broklax*. That was a chocolate laxative (in case you didn't know), but it was one thing I never had to use because my bowels are regular and reliable as *fowl-cock crowin' at fo'day marnin'*. One of the boys in our teenage gang was *scraven* so the other boys decided they were going teach him a lesson. He was a bit naïve and did not know about Broklax so he ate the whole block of *Cadburys* that was kindly offered to him. I heard he never left the toilet for a week . . . and that's also a truh-truh story.

## A Spoonful A'Sugah Works Magick

Canadian Healing Oil was always looking out for us when we had a chest cold. Mummy insisted on putting a few drops on my singlet before I went to bed. I had to inhale the nasty scent all night long. She also made me take a few drops in a *spoonful a'sugah*. I only recently found out this product was to be administered externally. My sister-in-law said she almost killed her young son thirty years ago after administering a dose. He vomited non stop and had to be taken to a doctor who gave her a stern warning. I think that only happened because the child was *white* (Australian); his constitution couldn't handle it. No Guyanese child ever suffered side effects from taking it.

Sacrool was another remedy for colds. Red in colour; the unpleasant taste was disguised in what else, but a *spoonful a'sugah*. We used that *spoonful a'sugah* for every cure known to man. Tell me what you think of this one. We were given *sugah watah* (water sweetened with a spoonful of sugar) whenever we had a bad fall. I am still in the dark with that one. Talking about *sugah watah* reminds me of another story, Charlie (who else?) told me. He said a young man fainted on the street and a passerby came to his aid . . . when he heard a woman was bringing him a glass of water he raised his head and said, "Tell sh' to put a'spoonful a'sugah in it." I think he faked the fainting just to get sugah watah. I know I faked a few times???

*And how do you think Mary Poppins started singing "A'spoonful a'sugah?" She did not know a damn thing 'bout it until she butt-up with a Guyanese in Queens. She was complaining 'bout de children always falling down those hills that were alive with sound of music and he let de cat out of de bag 'bout our sugah watah remedies. Not only does she have healthy children now; she is rich and famous because of our ingenuity. Just thought I would throw in that bit of schupidness.*

Vicks was very popular; it came in a small tin or a jar. Not only did Mummy rub it on our chest and under our nose, she made us put a little lump of it in our mouth before we went to sleep. That was also only supposed to be used externally. I don't think they bothered to read the instructions.

## Guardian Angels in Abundance

My friend Norma and I were talking de *odda day* about these dangerous cures our parents used in Guyana and she said, "Gyurl, we only survived because we 'ad a'lotta guardian angels." I somehow think she is right.

We were also subjected to some unpleasant tasting tonics. There was Ferrol Compound; it was said to increase your iron if you were a bit anaemic and also good for coughs. I don't think that was ever proven. What about other remedies such as Milk of Magnesia for constipation. I refused to drink dat . . . a bucket of ripe mangoes for twenty-five cents worked just as well and was enjoyable to boot! Then there was Sanatogen for building you up if you were *run-dung*. I have a joke on that one. A man met his friend who had come to town from Berbice and thought he was looking a bit on the sickly side so he said, "Bhai yuh look like yuh run-dung." Quick as a flash his friend replied, "Nah bhai, a'come dung wid de train."

I was grateful our financial situation saved us from Seven Seas Cod Liver Oil and Malt. My cousins were given a spoonful of malt each day; the smell alone made me want to puke, but they actually enjoyed it. What an era, I wonder who the hell concocted all that bullshit.

The evanescence bubbles in Andrew's Liver Salts captured my attention. I used any excuse to coax a spoonful from the tin my mother *gyarded wid 'er life*.

Daddy's favourite purge was Epson Salts. I always knew he was feeling a bit sluggish when he said, "Helen, go to Mr Green an' get meh sum salts, a'feelin' bilious, a'need a'good clean out." We teased him about this remedy when we were older if we saw he was looking a bit *run-dung* (weak). We said, "Daddy, yuh look like yuh need a'good dose a'salts." We always got the same response, which was, *"Yuh mekin' yuh eyes pass meh chap."* [You are being disrespectful]. But we could never make Daddy angry.

Hear this joke Daddy told us about a man who took the entire bottle of Epson Salts; the man said it would save him having to take any for six months. Daddy was laughing so hard when he told this story. He said, "Chap, dat man dare not caaff; everytime 'e move 'e shite 'e self!" Maybe it actually happened to him and he turned it into a joke because he was too *shame* to tell us the truth.

There is a similar story connected to Uncle Naysh, except it involves cough medicine. He had a terrible cough he could not shake off so he decided to go to Charity to see Dispenser Joseph who gave him a big bottle of cough medicine. Uncle Naysh stood in the kitchen and after reading the instructions put the bottle to his mouth and drained it. His pharmaceutically enhanced state sent Gramuddah into a panic. In a timid voice I heard her say, "Why yuh do dat fuh Natius?" His reply verbatim, "Muddah, a'is a'busy man, t'ree tablespoons a'day gon tek a'laang time to wuk suh is betta if a'jus' tek it all in wan shot; a'gon get betta fasta." I heard that with *meh own two ears* and must agree there is some logic to his way of thinking.

It's time to tell you about Red Lavender and another miracle product called Woodward's Gripe Water. These were two items no mother in Guyana could live without. The *Red Lavender* was rubbed on the soles of the baby's feet to relieve colic or wind. Mr Green who owned Greens Drugstore in James Street around the corner from us did brisk business selling those things by the tablespoon. Mummy sent me to Mr Green armed with a small bottle to purchase these items when she had babies in old age. [Wait for that saga]. There were *nuff* (enough) babies in this neighbourhood to keep him in business. No television in those days. Everyone went to bed by 9 p.m. in the evening; just after the death announcements on the radio. Maybe it was a gentle reminder that the population needed increasing.

## Cures for Every Ailment

We had cures for every ailment under the sun; most were simple and cost nothing.

Almost everyone I know in Australia owns a dog, but I bet no one knows that their dog is a barking anti-biotic. Indulge me while I brag about Guyanese dogs. They should be in the Guinness Book of Records because they are the only dogs I know with magical medicinal tongues. Our dogs cured all of our cuts, bruises, open wounds and sores by simply licking them a few times. No pain inflicted in this treatment either; it tickled and felt as rough as sandpaper. We could not afford the luxury of owning a dog when we moved to town so Mummy sent us to use the neighbour's whenever our sores needed a lick; she only wasted an *M-am-B* (M and B) tablet if the dog was out strayin' down the street. She ground up the tablet to the consistency of talcum powder then she used one of our table knives to pack the substance tightly into the cut or sore. That treatment really hurt I tell you, but it was a very good cure. My sores always took longer to heal because the M-am-B powder formed nice scabs which I enjoyed picking. It was for that very reason my brothers called me, 'Sorey-Sorey' when I was little. That was long before I became *Muddah Rat*. I hope you weren't disgusted to see Mummy used one of our table knives to pack the sore; we only used that one to butter bread. The M-am-B tablet actually had a groove in the middle and the initials M and B were engraved on either side; just don't ask me what it stood for. [More Bullshit]? We said the name quickly and it sounded like M-am-B; it was used for other things, but I can't remember what. We had Phensic and Whizz for headaches, fever, pain, toothache; take your pick. Cloves and rum also cured our toothache. How do you think we learnt to drink?

Ringworm was constantly on the prowl. A blue liquid called 'Gentian Violet' was applied but it was very difficult to cure. I had the odd one, but my brothers were always infected, mainly because they were forever fossicking in some nasty gutter or rubbish dump.

There was a *Yaws* (sores) epidemic from time to time and it was *ketchin'* (contagious) so great care was taken to prevent the sores from spreading. That *mus'be* what we call 'school sores' in Australia.

We were also afflicted with hard boils. A hot poultice made with flour and water was applied to bring it to *a'ead* (maturity); what abscess wouldn't erupt after all that heat was applied; it was savage.

And when all else fails bring out the trusted Mercurochrome. No self respecting household was without a bottle of that *red stuff* you painted on with a feather. I must not forget Iodine and Dettol.

Now it's time to give you the low down on my father. He used special tonics only talked about in hushed tones or in a joking fashion. Whoever invented Viagra was too late because Capadulla and Cungapump were blazing a trail long before that; what's more you could get it *free* in the jungle. The capadulla jokes were still flowing when Daddy got married for the second time at the age of eighty. My brothers openly asked him if he had a good supply for his honeymoon. Daddy laughed at the wicked humour and as usual said, "Yu'al eye pass meh or wha' chap?" 'old on, yuh gon 'ear all 'bout de weddin' before dis waalk is ova.

*Chiney Brush* was another sex aid talked about with a cupped mouth. I was never really interested enough to ask what it was or how it worked until now . . . research for the book, and not what you t'ink. This potion is said to sustain an erection when applied to the organ . . . only passing on what I have been told. See how you learn something new everyday? A wicked Calypsonian sings about Chiney Brush; the lyrics will make your ears blush.

And who can forget the panacea we call Limacol. My sister-in-law Mitzi cannot live without it; she asks anyone coming from Canada to bring a bottle. The slogan on the radio used to say, "It's de freshness of a'breeze in a'bottle." Yes, we sold *breeze in a bottle*. I bet the Yanks haven't thought of that one yet! I despise the stuff for the simple reason it reminds me of illness. Whenever I had a fever, a kerchief doused with Limacol was put on my forehead and that was done to *bring dung* (lower the temperature) *de feva*. [My mother *sapped* the kerchief when it dried out]. The minute my mother saw one of us cloaked-up she ran for the Limacol. She also had a sniff of it if she had *bad feelings* (nausea) that t'ing had a multitude of uses. And it cooled you off if you were feeling hot; don't forget the breeze is captured in the bottle so you just had to let it out. Ladies, I left this cure for last because I am on your side. I am going to give you some valuable advice without any cost because we Guyanese like anything we can get *fuh free*. I want to implore you not to ever keep Limacol in your home. The damn t'ing cures a headache and none of us want our husbands to bring the Limacol when we say, "Not tonite darlin', a'ave a'eadache." You can practice safe birth control because you can have a permanent headache. You see how I am trying to help you out? There is no need to thank me; you bought the book so that is t'anks enough; well I hope you bought it and didn't borrow it from a friend. I know you Guyanese well!

## The Mystery of Nara

Have you ever heard of Nara? I must confess that this is one subject that has me stumped. I have been able to look back and make the connection to quite a few of the ailments we suffered; ailments I actually laughed at and thought was funny. For instance, I now know it was not a jumbie spirit that caused the symptoms little Lily displayed; she was suffering from Epilepsy. I also researched the Bright's disease to see what that lovely young girl with the swollen ankles and a puffy face had. And I hang my head in shame, because I also know without doubt that my dear Aunt Victorine who I thought was *schupidee,* suffered from dementia.

I on the other hand was suffering from something totally different and after a case of self diagnosis (thankfully no anti-biotic was needed since I was only suffering from something only *eddicashun* can cure). Yes folks, I was solely afflicted with a case of Monumental Ignorance which I am happy to say has now been cured.

Now it's time to *eddicate* you on the subject of *Nara* (stomach ache). I can also tell you how it was cured because I had it on two occasions. Indulge me for a moment because you might need to have your Nara *rubbed* (massaged) some day and this information will come in very handy. I distinctly remember the very first time someone rubbed my Nara. At least the cure is relatively cheap; although you must have two hands . . . *de clock* (Charlie) cannot rub Nara. Not everyone can perform this task. Extensive training in con artistery is needed to become such a *quack*. We had not yet left the d'Riva so I was no older than five when my parents took me to the home of a certified quack. I remember being taken behind a curtain made from a *sugah bag* . . . who takes their children to a place like that? The decrepit Coolie man did not even own a bed. He laid me out on the floor and without any warning pulled down my underwear just below my navel. I watched in terror as he pulled out a length of string. That man was ahead of his time because I bet practitioners in the western world have not thought of using string to make a diagnosis. Again, this is important . . . it might save your life someday?? The quack proceeded to measure the gap between my nipples and navel. Holy crap, the man confirmed my parent's suspicions. An uneven measurement was a dead give away. I had Nara. You have to remember no one had told me what *Nara* was or how it was treated so I was a nervous wreck by this stage. He applied warm Coconut Oil (Red Lavender can also be used) to my abdomen then began to massage. Make no mistake; it is not just any run of the mill rubbing. The action is performed in an upward fashion to coax the *spirit* up to your navel. A lit candle was placed on the navel region and a glass was placed over the candle. The man recited an incantation before the glass was removed. Now this is the baffling part; the glass had to be pulled off with great force because suction had built up during this process. If the candle was extinguished before he removed the glass it meant the *spirit* had been expelled. Hello! Does it take a fool to figure that one out? I'm sure there was a scientific explanation for the suction. [I can see everyone wanting to experiment with this one]. I cried throughout the procedure because of the excruciating pain, but my parents were happy because the quack had cured my Nara. Lawd! I got Nara when I was around thirteen for the second time. I had started sprouting seeds for my bubbie so I was a bit self conscious but since I was still tongue tied at that age I had to suffer the embarrassment. Wait for it! Daddy had mastered the art and was now a guru in this field. After all, we got Nara often and money *didn't grow on trees* to keep paying quacks. *Maan* let me tell you, no one was measuring my bubbie or rubbing my belly after that. Funny but I never ever had Nara again.

That sexy Dr Oz who appears on Oprah was wrapping up a discussion as I entered the room one day and my ears pricked up . . . he was telling the audience that having an uneven measurement from nipple to navel is medically correct. Well there was certainly nothing uneven about his gorgeous physique, but what the hell was he talking about? I wished I had paid more attention but I bet he wasn't talking about Nara . . . or was he? Anyway he had said enough so I rest my case about those quacks and their piece of string.

## An Angel in the Nativity Play

The mention of guardian angels reminds me of my acting debut.

A halo might catch afire if it was put upon my head, but all children have aspirations and mine were no less. At assembly one morning, our headmaster Mr Giddings announced that the school was going to stage a play. He said the characters will be chosen from the children in the higher standards. I was so excited because I was in fourth standard and most certainly qualified. This was not any play; it was going to be a depiction of the Nativity. God only knows why because it wasn't a catholic school. Mind you, that didn't stop me from wanting to portray *Mary* (Our Lady). The catholic schools paid homage to Mary each May by having a procession around the church and my secret desire was to be one of the angelic looking Putagee girls. I especially envied the girl who was chosen to crown the statue of Our Lady because she looked like a bride in her special dress and veil.

Speculation was rife as to who will play the lead roles. This was a perfect opportunity for me. I thought I had the part of Mary in the bag ... hello! I was *white* and as far as I knew so was the *real* Mary. I am not certain how they chose the characters; all I know is, Daphne was picked to be an angel and I got squat. I was so angry I was spitting chips, big ones too! I stamped my feet angrily as I sobbed, "Mummy how cyan de tea-chas pick Daphne fuh a'angel, but leave meh out?" She seemed genuinely sympathetic, but children are cruel and I heard a whisper on the grapevine that I wasn't chosen because we could not afford the *schupid* angel costume.

I have a feeling Mummy must have greased sumone's palm after she saw how devastated I was, because Mrs Payne called me up two days later to say I can be an angel too. The dressmaker made me a long white satin gown and I helped Mummy to fashion a pair of wings from an old cardboard box. We asked everyone who smoked to save the little bits of silver paper (alfoil was not invented then) that came in Lighthouse *sigrit* boxes. Enough was collected to cover the cardboard wing. We had a job getting the silver paper to stick because we ran out of Gloy and the *Glamacherry* (berries used as glue) and flour paste was not sticky enough. However we persevered and did the best we could.

The big night finally arrived. I was so nervous I wanted to vomit but cried instead ... well as you know it was what I did best. Daphne and I were the only two 'white' children in the play. Have you ever seen an angel dripping silver? Thank goodness I did not have to speak because my teeth were clattering, my knees were wobbling and my wings were slipping because the blasted elastic was too slack. It was a surreal experience but I was proud as punch to be in the nativity play. Sorry there was no camera to *tek out de pickcha*.

Plaiting the Maypole was another thing I would have given anything to be a part of. I may have stood a chance if I attended Dolphin Government School in Broad Street. That was another *Black School* that had a lot of *ruckshun* children but they held a fair every May and showcased Maypole plaiting to perfection. It was not as simple as it looked. The little girls in their multi-coloured dresses weaved in and out with precision and it was simply beautiful to watch.

## Sex Education on the Streets

Sex education was not part of our school curriculum, we got ample tuition within the family circle, or from watching the animals fornicate on the streets. This will tell you how naive we were. My younger cousin called her mother one day to show her a dog *towin' 'is fr'en'*. I used to watch those dogs towing their friends at every opportunity; we even had to throw a bucket of water on them at times to allow the friend to go home. If Mummy was at home I hid behind the *jalousie* (a slatted window) and peered through one of the slats hoping she would not *ketch* me in the act.

Georgetown was full of horses and donkeys, and as children we always laughed and pointed when we saw one of these animals displaying an erect penis. We had nothing better to do so found our amusement on the streets; it was sideshow alley without having to pay.

It wasn't just the animals who displayed their organs in public; a few flamboyant characters on the streets of Georgetown mimicked the animals. This embarrassing experience happened when I visited Guyana in 1984. I was invited to have lunch with two former colleagues and Sister Kostka who was my supervisor at the school where I taught. The venue was the popular Palm Court; a well known eatery in the heart of the city. Charlie was going to pick us up in the avenue in front of the restaurant but since Guyanese are notorious for being late he was not there when we came out and I suggested a stroll along the avenue which was lined with beautiful *Flame* (Flamboyant) trees. Two minutes into our stroll I spotted a hefty Negro man casually approaching. He was shirtless and that was acceptable in the unbearable heat. As he came closer I realised he was wearing trousers with in-built air conditioning for his private parts. I could not help but notice the man had a *donkey lolee*; it was hanging to his knees. Charlie arrived at that precise moment and took swift action. He quickly put his arm around the nun and turned her in the opposite direction. Convulsed with hilarity he spluttered, "Come Sistah, we doan want yuh to guh bline yuh no." I hope she wasn't enjoying the scenery. The rest of us pretended it was a disgrace but we collapsed with laughter after *Sistah* was safely dispatched home. Charlie told me that man is given a new pair of trousers very often, but he cuts out the crutch the minute he gets it. He must have seen that movie Born

Free. Charlie did tell me his nickname, but it has slipped my mind so I will call him, Free Willy.

## No Law and Order Here

Let me tell you about some of the famous characters from my era. My favourite was definitely Law an' Order. If a crowd was gathered near the law court building you can expect to find yourself witnessing an execution. Law an' Order staged performances several times each day. This dear old black gentleman pushed a small cart around town laden with all the necessary paraphernalia to stage a hanging. His subjects were puppets; whips and a replica of the gallows were all part of the spectacle. The execution took place only after he had berated, ridiculed and informed the victims on the correct laws of the justice system. He accused the culprits of the most heinous crimes and showed no mercy. No two crimes were ever the same so you never knew what to expect. He treated those puppets as if they were human and referred to them by name. He thrashed them with all his might while ridiculing them. I noticed he was particularly hard on the ones accused of adultery, leaving me to wonder if that was what happened in his life. The crowd threw a few coins after the performance. Everyone thought it was hilarious, and did not miss an opportunity to witness one of Law an' Order's executions. How sad, the poor man must have been suffering from mental illness.

Another well known character was Bertie Vaughan. This man was said to be a scholar in his younger days—a headmaster, but I believe too much *eddicashun* sent him round the bend. His gimmick was shaving with a broken bottle; not only his head, but different parts of his anatomy. He walked around town wearing nothing but rags which he washed in the dirty canal. When Bertie asked you for five cents he meant five cents, if you gave him more he refused. No amount of reasoning convinced him to take a different amount to the one he asked for; very strange indeed, and no one knew why or what caused him to go *funny in de 'ead*.

How about Pussy in de Moonlight? What a sexual image that one conjures up but I can assure you he was not looking for sex after dark. He was a Putagee man who sold sweepstake tickets when he wasn't drinking the local brew. He was unkempt and wore a very colorful ensemble. School children teased him mercilessly with this taunt, "Pussy in de moonlight, pussy in de dew, pussy neva come 'ome before 'alf pass two." He had a multitude of children and a few followed him around town. Cato was the one I feared the most because he was definitely mentally unhinged. This character was always half naked and exposed himself to passersby while chanting, "A'want sum money fuh buy a'panty fuh meh sistah." Cato also had a fetish for rubber and the school children wanted proof so they jeered and threw their erasers at him.

We had many more of these strange personalities, but it would take another chapter to tell you about each individual.

## Going To Pomeroon for School Holidays

This was going to be an adventure of a lifetime for Joel and me. We had been begging Mummy for a long time to let us go to Pomeroon to spend the school holiday with our grandparents. She finally thought we were old enough to travel unaccompanied. The arrangements were put in place and it was agreed we would travel on a Monday. Monday is Market-day at Charity and Granfaddah will be there to meet us when the bus gets in around four in the afternoon. This trip is very long; Mummy took us once so we knew what to expect. I was so excited I could not sleep for nights.

What bliss, just me and Joel with no *muddah* to do all those hundred and one embarrassing things to you in public. Things like boxing you if you want to *play de fool* or having to feel *shame* when she *dressed yuh dung* in a loud voice in front of everyone. Mummy also had a habit of *spittin' in sh' 'an'* and wiping your face if it was dirty; *maan,* how I hated her doing *dat!*

Mummy packed the little grip the night before with a few changes of clothes then sat us down to go over the instructions on how to get there along with *de leckcha.* She began with, "A'want de two a'yuh to open yuh ears suh yuh cyan 'ear wha' a'ave to say." I had gone stone deaf after the first word. Her preaching always got on meh nerves. I was just waiting for her crystal ball to come out. Yes, that woman was a clairvoyant. Hear what she said next, "A'no as soon as meh back turn de two a'yuh gonna be'ave like jackasses, but a'ave eyes in de back a'meh 'ead suh doan t'ink a'won't no." I was certainly special having the only mother with eyes in the back of her head, I hope you are jealous. I was seething inside and silently thought, "A'no exactly wha' a'will do as soon as yuh turn yuh back; a'will tek off dat schupid kerchief yuh pin on meh dress fuh a'start." I had a habit of wiping my nose with the back of my hand so this is how she solved that problem. "'ere, blow yuh snot on dis kerchief insted a'yuh 'an'"; she usually said as she pinned it on roughly and *jook* (stab) me in my chest with the safety pin. Are people supposed to admire the snot? Why else would you want it on show to the public? [Would you believe I pinned a kerchief on my first daughter? I even have a picture to prove it! I have to admit that is butter calling the margarine greasy]. We had gone quiet so she said, "Yu'al lissnin'?" With my bottom lip quivering I stammered "Ye-s Mummy." Daddy who was *lallin' off* (relaxing) in a corner wearing his silly *sliders* (underwear) saw my face and took the opportunity to say, "Look, sh' gon spring a'leak any minute." He thought it was funny and always said that when he thought I was going to cry. But Mummy wasn't finished yet. She still had to tell us about the consequences so she went on to say, "As a'was sayin', yuh betta not let anyone come an' tell meh deh see yuh doin' nutt'in' schupidee or a'gon cut yuh tail w'en yuh get back 'ome." These weren't the most endearing words for two small children going off on their first big adventure. I for one couldn't wait to get to Gramuddah.

## The Big Day!

We were awoken at fo'day marnin' to wash our face an' 'an's, and have something to eat before we left to get the first ferry. Mummy slit some left over fried bakes and filled them with salfish then wrapped them in a big brown paper bag and gave it to me. That was our food for the journey and I was in charge of it. I put the parcel in the nylon string bag along with my *purse* (a toffee tin). We had to *kerry* the grip all the way to Big Market because we could not afford a *drop-cyar*. We were accustomed to walking everywhere so we did not mind; *besize* we were humming like a spinning top with excitement. Maan, if yuh see how much people deh round Big Market at dat time a'marnin', deh shovin' an' pushin' from every direction. Meh nose open up w'en a'smell a'nice ripe mango, but a'know a'gon get plenty weh a'goin'. In a stern voice Mummy said, "Yu'al 'urry up or yuh gon miss de boat," so we followed her at a faster pace to the back of the market where she joined a queue to get our ticket. I was somewhat nervous, so I started looking around to see what everyone was doing. The old Coolie woman standing in front of Mummy took out a nasty kerchief from her dress pocket . . . even she had a pocket I tell you. She tried to undo a knot in the corner of the kerchief to get her money. That is where most East Indians keep their money. Mummy said that some of them have that knot tied so tight you can't get any money out of it. East Indians are known for their frugality, but in all fairness they work from sun-up to sun-down and deserve what they have.

Mummy handed her money to the man behind the cage and said, "Please fuh two 'alf fare ticket to Adventure." He shoved his hand through the hole in the cubicle to give her the tickets. She said "t'anks" and then led us through the crowd to the turnstile where we had to go through to board the ferry. The Demerara River is located behind Big Market and the ferry is moored alongside the wharf there. The ride over to the other side of the river takes about twenty minutes . . . but felt like forever when I was a child. Mummy gave Big-'ead some money so we can buy a treat along the way. She said twenty-five cents was for me. *Rant!* She must have won the sweepstake! It was time to say goodbye to Mummy so *a'buss cry.* She must have kissed us, but I honestly cannot remember. My mother was not an affectionate person; not towards me anyway. I voiced this observation to my sister CeCe recently and she begged to differ, but as I said earlier every one of us seemed to have had different parents, and I will never doubt what any of my siblings say. We all have our own story and this is my experience.

## Flying Solo

One ticket will take us all the way to Adventure so we don't have the problem of having to join queues at the next two legs of the journey. Mummy said Granfaddah will pay Patsy when we get off the bus at Charity. Mummy went as far as the turnstile with us to make sure we went through. We handed the man our ticket which he clipped on the end before giving it back. Mummy told us we had to *gyard it wid our life* until we got to Adventure. My dress did not have a pocket to put it in and that was Mummy's fault. I wrapped my ticket up in a clean kerchief to keep it safe . . . I always carried kerchiefs. I was not even on the ferry when I got hurt. The *kiss-meh-ass* (no good) parrot the man behind me was carrying on his arm *pick meh* (pecked me) on the top of my head as I was crossing the gangplank to go on board and of course . . . What do you think? I started crying, but I made sure Mummy didn't see because she would have taken me back home. A nice black woman ran her fingers over my head; looked at them and tried to *cochore* (encourage/flatter) me by saying, "Is a'right, it ain't bleedin', siddung an' suck dis sweetie darlin'." She reached into a big pocket and handed me a *sour drop*. I could see Big-'ead was jealous, but I wasn't giving him a suck of my sweetie. I was a *hungish* wretch when it came to food.

The vendors came close to the windowless ferry to ply their wares. That money was burning a hole in my pocket I tell you, but Big-'ead said I had to wait until we got over to Vreed-in-Hoop because the vendors had more to choose from. Those were not his exact words, but it will take too long to tell you how he said it, he was always bullying me. The ferry was packed that day so we were all *choked-up* like *pigin peas* in a pod. Two cute looking boys were standing next to a nice bicycle *brace-up* (leaning) on one of the big posts. It looked as if it was brand new and I wished it was mine. Although I was eleven, I still didn't have a bike, nor could I ride. I could do *chip-chip* (one foot on the pedal and the other on the road) on Daddy's bicycle under the bottom-'ouse so I was sure it wasn't hard to ride a bike like that. I never attempted to ride a *constant* bicycle. You could be thrown over the handle bar if you did not know how to change the gears. Joel knew how to *stickle* (hover) while sitting on a bicycle, it looked very difficult. Don't ask me how we came to use the word *stickle* but we also said the same thing when we saw a hummingbird that appeared to be motionless while sipping nectar.

Vendors waiting on the stellin' for the ferry

We reached Vreed-in-Hoop and it was a mad scramble to find a seat on the rickety train that will take us on the next leg of the journey to Parika. I couldn't wait to get there to buy some of those tiny *speckled bananas* (overripe bananas with black specks) we called *sweet-fig*. The vendors started swarming outside the train windows with their baskets full of mouth watering delicacies. I pushed the bottom half of the window up to get a better view. The tantalising smell of fresh salara and pine-tart climbed up my nostrils, and the other sweet-mout' winked at me from big *Mokru* (local fiber) baskets. I had to *cut-meh-eye* on the fried fish and bread. The chanting was intoxicating; someone shouts, "Get yuh fresh channa 'ere, a'ave nice 'ot peppersasse fuh yuh green mango; wan cent gon get yuh t'ree phulourie; look at dis nice fresh pine, a'jus' peel it fuh yuh, by sum nah." Another Coolie lady is yelling at the top of her voice, "Who lookin' fuh sum sugah-cake, a'got de chip an' de black kine, only wan cent each; 'urry befoe de train pull out." I asked Joel for my money, but he said he had to change it first. My *passion* (temper) rose and I shouted, "Well 'urry, a'want fuh by a'sugah-cake." He bought two awaras and gave me my money when he got the change. The train was starting to shake so I quickly handed over the money for the sugah-cake. A'barely 'ad time to get it; de train was movin' an' de lady 'ad to stretch sh' 'an' out laang to gi'me de t'ing. I quickly put-up the change in my tin then settled down in my seat to enjoy the sticky treat. Joel started eating his awara and in no time his mouth was orange from the fruit. He is lucky Mummy wasn't on the train to use the spit treatment. The train clonked along at a steady pace and we passed village after village.

Children and people came out to wave as the train goes by. Everyone was smiling and so friendly that I shyly waved back at them. I desperately wanted to pee, but there was no toilet on the train so I had to hold it in until we got to Parika. I squeezed my legs tight and prayed I didn't pee on the train. The man with the ticket clipper came around to put another hole in our tickets, so I fished mine out from my kerchief. This leg of the journey took forever, but the next part was going to be even longer.

We are finally at our destination. Parika stellin' is a *mad-house*. I am a bit nervous as I am not sure who to follow. That nice black woman who gave me the sweetie on the ferry was walking a little way ahead so I told Joel we should follow her. I was right because she was going to the same place. All the stalls that lined the path to the stellin' had bananas, mesh bags full of rosy oranges and tangerines, and fat juicy pineapples hanging from the roof. Plenty of bananas, but I couldn't see the tiny *sweet-fig* variety I was looking for. They were always hard to come by. I finally spotted some closer to where we had to get on the big-big steamer. I bought a whole hand of them so I can take some for Gramuddah and Granfaddah. Joel had the grip so I put them in the holey string bag I was carrying. I couldn't wait to get on the steamer to eat a few. They are so small, one fits into my mouth. Joel bought a penny *hard channa* (fried chick peas) in a paper cone and I was hoping he would give me some, but he was too *hungish* to share. Alright, I know that is *de lime callin' de lemon sour*. I stuffed a banana in my mouth and left him in peace. I still had a few cents to buy something from the snack bar on the steamer.

## The Slow Boat to China

Joel and I joined the long queue to board the big black vessel which is called the M.V. Malali. A man clipped our ticket and gave it back as we went through a small gate. We walked a short distance before we crossed the gangplank to get on the steamer. I was so happy we were safely on board.

I had to wait until we got on the steamer to look for a toilet because I was too afraid to use the one on the stellin' in case the steamer took off. Can you imagine if that had happened to me? The steamer has a top deck so I was going to go up there as soon as I finished peeing. *Maan,* it was so easy to find that toilet; all I had to do was follow the smell. How anyone can pee up a wall is beyond me; I had to hold my nose. I climbed up on the seat and squatted to pee because there was no way I was sitting on that seat. I made a vow never to have to pee if I go to Pomeroon again! You bet I meant it. I went to Pomeroon many times after that and never once used that stinking toilet.

The cafeteria was a small cubicle just by the foot of the stairs. The smell was so enticing when I went past; I wondered what I would be able to buy with the few remaining cents. I joined Joel who was already upstairs leaning over the rails to see what was going on below on the stellin'. A big lorry was crawling into the bowels of the steamer; the boards on the gangplank made a rattling sound as it entered, then a line of cars crawled in . . . okay it was three cars but it was a line to me. After a lot of shouting and some big ropes being removed the Malali moved off like a sloth. We were now in the mighty Essequibo River where the water was the colour of rich chocolate. The captain cruised close to shore guided by the giant mangroves along the route. At times it was so shallow the mud churned up behind the steamer. By this time my worms were getting restless. We had eaten the food Mummy gave us on the train and I was looking forward to buying a nice treat. My mouth watered just from looking but I could only afford a Salara and a Vimto; my favourite sweet drink. I still had five cents left over; not bad at all. I was so *shame* because Joel was so *big eye*, he pointed to the biggest *white-eye* (a sweet bun) as he stammered, "Da, da, da wan be-be be-ine de te-te, tenis roll." Thank goodness he didn't have to ask for a glass of sarsaparilla. He mercifully ended my shame by pointing to the bucket of mauby. We went back upstairs to mole-up on the back deck behind a big drum to eat because I was too *shame* to eat in front of everyone. How I enjoyed that treat.

After what seems like an eternity we stopped at a place called Hogg Island, but I didn't see any pigs on the stellin'. What I did see was a man standing on top of a big pylon throwing a *cyas'-net* into the river. I was hoping he would fall in so I could laugh at him; I always enjoy a good laugh you know.

The next stop was at Wakeanam; a well known East Indian settlement so a heap of Coolie people got off there. Adventure was not too far from there; we could see it in the distance shortly after leaving Wakeanam.

## Patsy Is a Man

Everyone picked up their bags and started heading for the gangway of the ferry like a herd of elephants getting ready for a stampede. They were all anxious to get a seat on the bus. I remembered Mummy telling us we had to hurry here. She said to find the yellow buses that belonged to Kass and to tell Patsy we are Jose D'Agrella's grandchildren. I was squashed between the other passengers as I followed them out through the gate. I heard a voice saying, "Dis way, tickets please," but I couldn't see the person. I followed the crowd and finally saw a short black man clipping tickets; I gave him mine as I squeezed through. He kept the ticket because the fare ended here. We didn't have to walk far to get on the road. I spotted the yellow buses right away. There were two, but it didn't matter because they both belonged to the Kass family who live at Charity. Mummy said we should ask for Patsy, but I forgot Patsy was a man so I was still looking for a lady when Joel beckoned to indicate he had found Patsy. Joel was standing next to him so I went over to his bus and said, "Good afta-noon mistah." Patsy gave me the biggest smile, ruffled my hair and said, "Gyurl, yuh resemble yuh muddah bad, a'went to school wid yuh muddah yuh no, guh 'pon de bus." I smiled shyly and climbed aboard hoping for a front seat, but the bus was already half full. I found a seat down the back but Big-'ead beat me to the window seat so I had to sit on the end. I had to crane meh neck to see out 'pon de road. More people came on and they were all puttin'-up things above my head on a slatted rack. Joel was trying to put up our grip when a big-big tin of Golden Cream margarine slipped off the rack and just missed my head by inches. The Coolie man who the tin belonged smiled broadly as he apologised, "Sarry lil' gyal, yuh lucky de t'ing didn't 'it yuh 'pon yuh 'ead eh?" Rant, de man 'ad some fire-rass gol' teet' an' nearly bline meh wid 'e smile. Patsy yelled out, "All aboard, 'old on," and the bus took off. Maan, I don't know how that bus moved. Every seat was full, and people were crammed together in the aisle. A stout black lady stood next to me holding on to the rack above for support; her armpit was level with my face. She was using the same deodorant Mummy used; the smell of MUM was strong. I took a sly look and saw a strip of the pink cream under her armpit. I *sucked meh teet'* in disgust but not loud enough for her to hear.

Everyone was quiet for about five minutes before they started making friends with their neighbour. My ears pricked up for any juicy gossip. I heard a lady say, "A'went to tung to see meh dauttah who 'ad a'bouncin' baby bhai in Public 'ospital, 'e name Leroy." I remembered that because I had a cousin name Leroy in d'Riva. We called our Leroy by his false-name which was Zex. He got that name because he was partial to *salsoap* with that name. Aunt Maud could never find her salsoap where she left it at the waterside when she went to wash clothes. He probably couldn't get sweeties; poor boy.

I wanted to eat a banana, but I know everyone would stare at me so I didn't bother. I thought a man was looking at me until I realised he had bad cock-eye. He looked so funny I wanted to laugh, and then I gave Joel a nudge to show him the man so he could laugh too.

We were travelling on the Essequibo Road en route to Charity. Lush rice fields and coconut trees paved the way on either side of the extremely bumpy road they called 'Abortion Highway'. An array of colourful flags fluttering on *Jandhi* (religious) poles gave the densely populated villages an air of carnival. People wave all the time, and we even had to stop a few times to allow cows or donkeys to get off the road.

Fishermen sitting in groups on the beach, mending their seines and cyas'-nets can be seen whenever the road nears the river.

I saw a small boy take out his lolo to pee in the trench that ran in front of his home. A bit further down a lady was *beatin' clothes* (washing) on the bridge over the trench. Someone at the very back at the bus yelled, "'old up, 'old up bhai, yuh pass meh place, stap quick." Patsy pulled up and a fat-fat black lady waddled off the bus; arms straining with several shopping bags and a *lil' bhai* clinging to the hem of her colourful skirt.

We took off and a few minutes later reached Suddie where you find the closest hospital from Charity. This is a bustling intersection with a cacophony of traffic sounds; horns are blaring and vendors are shouting. A good thing some passengers had gotten off at Anna Regina because the bus filled up again. Family and friends travelled long distances to visit their loved ones in hospital.

Halfway to Charity the seat in front of me became vacant. I took it quickly so I can get near the window. A big wad of chewing gum was stuck under the ledge. Some child was probably saving it for *bambye* and forgot to take it; we always saved gum for later. This window seat gave me a perfect view and then Patsy stopped to buy a *watah coconut* (fresh coconut) from a man selling at a busy intersection that had a standpipe. Children were queuing to draw watah and that reminded me of my water fetching days; I felt sorry for them. Patsy leaned out the window to guzzle the drink. A Coolie woman had a stick in her hand and she was *runnin' dung* (chasing) a little girl to beat her while a bigger girl with a baby on her hips looked on from the top of the stairs, it was all very familiar to me. Joel tapped me on the shoulder to tell me something but by the time he stammered, "Heh-heh Helen, look at da-dat maan wi-wid de go-go-dee;" the man had sat down, so I missed out. Okay, I won't leave you guessing because only a Guyanese will know what the word 'goadee' means. You would often hear people in Guyana say, "Yuh gon get goadee if you lift dat 'eavy t'ing." Contrary to that belief, this affliction was not caused solely by lifting heavy objects. The correct medical term is Hydrocele or Elephantiasis. Sad as it was, school children knew how to spot a *goadee* and loved to make fun of the unfortunate person. I always thought it was men that suffered from such an ailment so I was surprised when a friend told me recently that *Fogaty-bun-dung* (a street character) had a goadee. Since this person was a woman I thought that was impossible. I was all ears as she explained it to me. The woman suffered from a hernia which descended through her private parts. I remember the woman well; she was homeless and was accused of causing the fire that burnt a store called 'Fogarty'; hence the name *Fogaty-bun-dung*. The rumor mill said she was cooking too close to the building but it was never proven. She did not wear underwear so her unfortunate situation became public knowledge when she stooped to do her washing in the canal.

We are still travelling on the Essequibo Road with Patsy; that was just a small detour to explain *goadee.*

Patsy was now refreshed after enjoying the watah coconut; I wish I had one because it was hot in that bus and I had no water. Bottled water wasn't invented yet and even if it was we could not afford to buy any. People got off at almost every village and the bus was almost empty by the time we reach Charity.

## We Meet Granfaddah

I spotted Granfaddah first; he was leaning on a post smoking one of his nasty smelling Capstan sigrits. He stomped on it before coming to greet us. This man does not know how to hug or kiss so he ruffles my hair and gruffly says, "Suh yuh come to see meh gyurl, yuh gettin' big." He turns to Joel and says; "A'ope yuh gon 'elp meh wuk bhai, a'got sum caffee fuh pick."

With greetings out of the way, we began making our way to d'Riva to find his famous boat. I was tired, but happy we were finally getting to the end of our journey. I couldn't wait to see Gramuddah. As we were heading in the direction of the river I saw a person with *white-white* hair walking towards us and I knew right away it was Aunt Phil. Her false-name is 'W'ite-'ead'; she is Daddy's sister who lived at Charity. She was coming to say hello before we *went in d'Riva* (started the journey) to go home. She gave me and Joel some *hug-up* and handed me a big Mammee. She has a big tree in her yard and she knows I love this fruit. I mustn't forget my manners or she might tell Mummy, so I said, "T'anks Aant Phil." Granfaddah was getting impatient so he said, *"Come pickney a'we betta guh now, it gettin' late an' meh nah want dark fuh ketch meh."* [Come children, it's best if we leave now because it's getting late and I don't want night to catch me].

I hope you are getting the hang of the lingo because it takes too long to explain everything.

## Granfaddah in Hospital

Grandfather was a *bush maan*; he never went to Gt. (Georgetown) unless it was absolutely necessary. Like the time he broke his thumb and had to spend four days in hospital. Yes, for a broken thumb; they probably

214

couldn't figure out what was wrong. Granfaddah made it clear that it was my job to take him three square meals a day. I had never heard of a square meal until then. I might have been a *big woman,* but that was of no concern to Granfaddah. He refused to eat the hospital food and expected me to comply. You better believe he got three squares meals each day. Lucky for me I was on school holidays. Granfaddah stayed with us the day he came out of hospital, but only for one night. He came out of the toilet the next morning and had this gem to declare, "Well ah cyan tell yuh dat Jargetung only good fuh wan t'ing; yuh cyan shit in yuh 'ouse an' it go out to d'Riva w'en yuh pull a'chain." Thank goodness we had something that impressed Granfaddah. That was the only time I remember seeing him in town in the twenty-one years I lived in Guyana. He refused to come to town to attend my wedding.

## Gramuddah Philly Teaches Me to Tell Time

I would like to tell you about my maternal grandmother Philomena, known as Philly to her peers. She was the most gentle and loving grandmother you can hope to have, I honestly cannot remember her ever raising her voice to me. There was only one thing she said that baffled me. She constantly advised my mother to put the fear of the Lord into us.

When I was a teenager Gramuddah shared something very special with me. She showed me the letter my father wrote to ask for my mother's hand in marriage. [I wonder what ever happened to that letter].

This was the first school holidays my brother and I spent with them and I remembered my age because of this incident. Gramuddah wanted to know the time one day so she called out to me "W'ata clock Helena?" [That is how Guyanese asked for the time]. I reeled out the numbers where the short and long hands of the clock were pointing. She was in the kitchen cooking but she dropped everything and came into the room where I was, and in a calm voice she said, "Yuh mean to tell meh yuh is eleven years ol' an' doan know to tell de time Helena?" And just like that, she took the time to teach me. I was an expert in telling the time when those holidays were over.

Gramuddah had very long hair and wore it in a plait wrapped around her head like a halo. I enjoyed watching her loose it out at night;

she always made a fresh plait after brushing and left it hanging. I spied on her one evening when she was washing her *face an' 'an's* by the big drum in the yard; she looked up, but I don't think she saw me. She had a big four poster bed and I sometimes slept with her when Granfaddah was up at Red Hill (his other property). My brothers and I liked it much better when he wasn't there because he was very strict and didn't think twice to *cut we tail* if we misbehaved.

In the beginning we only spent school holidays with these grandparents at Siriki, but alternated with our other grandmother who lived at Try Best when we were older. Some of my best memories were from those school holidays.

## Granfaddah's New House

When I was very little (before we left Pomeroon) my grandparents' house was very different to this new house. The old house was level with the ground and had fewer, but bigger bedrooms. The kitchen was completely separate from the main house and Gramuddah cooked on a big-big fireside.

The new house was very modern. It boasted a row of glass windows along the entire front of the house and had three decent size bedrooms. There was a huge sitting room with a narrow walkway that led into the kitchen and dining room (these two rooms were on opposite sides of the passage.) The kitchen had a kerosene stove and boasted modern cupboards, shelves and hooks to hang the cups. The dining room had a solid table with chairs to match and was of great interest to me. Granfaddah always bought an assortment of cakes home on Market-day and stored them in the basket that hung from a hook over the dining room table . . . to keep the ants out. You bet I helped myself to those, but only when Granfaddah was in the backdam. I enjoyed sitting at the bottom of the back steps because I was able to pick and enjoy the oranges from the huge tree that grew at the foot of the stairs. The big *Katahar* (Kathal/Durian) tree was also close to the house. I enjoyed that fruit as a child but it left me feeling queasy for days after eating it in Singapore some years ago.

The latrine was over the trench on the first *bed* (field) from the house. The bathroom was not far from the stairs behind the house. My brothers and I did not use it; we preferred bathing and swimming at the waterside.

There was an enclosed staircase which led into the sitting room. The stairs were divided halfway up by a *landin'*; it was the perfect place for me to play dolly-'ouse.

Granfaddah kept a big-big tin of Wieting and Richter's *salt biscuits* (savoury) at the foot of the stairs in a corner. I always helped myself without his knowledge. The sweet biscuits were even nicer, but that was a rare treat; he only bought those in a small quantity. Solid concrete blocks held the house up at a safe distance from flooding. It was a very impressive house in my humble opinion.

There was ample room for storage under the house, but it was quite dark for some reason; it was not my favourite place. Lurking under a barrel, old corial or stored timber were the biggest crappos you ever saw. I could have learnt to love them but Granfaddah took the wrong approach . . . His favourite game was to pick up the biggest ugliest *crappo* and put it close up to my face. Then in his scariest tone of voice he threatened, "'e comin' fuh get yuh!" That sent shivers down my spine and caused me to start screaming in fear. Do you think my screaming deterred that old bugger? No way, it only egged him on because he thought it was hilarious. Gramuddah would eventually hear my screams from upstairs and come to my rescue. Ol' Joe left me the legacy of a phobia for frogs. To this day I cannot look at a frog even if it's on a television screen.

## Market-day at Charity

I did not grasp the importance of 'Market-day' until I started going to Pomeroon for the school holidays. Monday was and still is, Market-day at Charity. It is the biggest event of the week for the Pomeroon community. I should tell you where Charity is situated . . . it is as far as you can go by road on the Essequibo coast. The road comes to an abrupt end at a T-junction and the Pomeroon River lies just over the edge so be careful. Almost all the inhabitants who live in the river district own a boat; it is the only means of transportation. I say almost, because there are people who cannot afford a boat. Some pay for *passage* (ride on a passenger boat) or dependant on the generosity of a neighbour.

Charity is the hub of this small farming community. This is where you will find the post office, dispenser, police station, school, market and rum-shops. Everyone residing along the river came to Charity to collect their mail because there was no mail delivery to the farmers back then. Anyone seeking minor medical attention paid a visit to Dispenser Joseph (everyone called him that). Patients with more serious problems were sent to the hospital at Suddie which was half an hour away.

The Charity market itself is a building that operates during the week. There are numerous stalls (cubby holes really) stocked with all sorts of groceries, haberdashery, tools, fishing and boating equipment and a host of other things. These jam packed stalls obscure the vendors behind the counter, but don't let that fool you, they know where every item can be located, and if by chance they did not have the item in question they will kindly direct you to another stall that stocked it.

Vendors with trestles positioned themselves at a convenient spot on the perimeter of the market. These vendors sold fresh fruit, vegetable, meat, fish, fresh livestock, clothing and all sorts of other interesting merchandise. How can anyone resist some of the gems these vendors shouted to the shoppers? Pretend you are a vendor and say the following out loud. "Get yuh fresh strimps, bangamary an' bhagee 'ere." Now you are a jolly East Indian woman peeling a pineapple offering, "Tas'e befor' yuh by." My favourite was always, "Sugah-bowl-covas, ladies get yuh sugah-bowl-cova;" as some hefty blackman waves an armful of panties in the air. The intonation in their voice was a sweet melody. The friendly smiling faces of those humorous people were the pillars of the community. My favourite vendor was Mr Harrop; his jet black wavy hair was slicked down with Brilliantine and shone like a beacon. He was married to Mummy's cousin Celine, but I still called him Mr Harrop out of respect. He once paid me a nice compliment which I never forgot. It was a welcome change to be told I had a beautiful smile because my biggest pet peeve was having everyone remind me I was the image of my mother. The ambivalent relationship between my mother and I was responsible for the doubt.

The market opened daily, but is dead as a doornail until Market-day rolled around. No one needs to be reminded it is every Monday because it is public knowledge in that region. And don't think for one minute that it is only the farmers who come out to sell their produce. The rest of the community descend like red-ants making their nests around the perimeter to sell their home made craft and anything that moved or was edible.

Colourful makeshift stalls were erected complete with roofs made from pieces of flapping plastic, bed sheets or whatever they can lay their hands on. It all added to the atmosphere and excitement of the day. I loved the spectacle of Market-day, but it was a rare privilege. Merchants from the city made the journey by sloop to the Pomeroon fortnightly to purchase fresh fruit, vegetables, coffee beans, copra and livestock from the farmers. The captains of these vessels formed close friendships with farmers they liked and conducted business with them on a permanent basis. The stellin' at Charity was a hive of activity on Market-day. It was an operation of pure precision with men forming human chains to load these vessels with provisions, and whatever else had to be loaded onboard that day. Most people are isolated on their farms, especially the housewives. Shopping for the weekly groceries was the number one priority on Market-day. It also provided a much needed outlet for socialising and the exchange of gossip; not forgetting the opportunity to show off their latest *dan-dan* (dress).

The rum-shops did a roaring trade. Many farmers sold their produce and spent most, and in some case all of the money getting intoxicated. I have first hand experience of that where my grandfather is concerned. Gramuddah was left at home most times and was always nervous when he was expected home. She never knew what mood he would be in and made sure she had his caffee-tea ready. My job was to keep out of his way.

A trip to Pomeroon is a must whenever I visit Guyana; allowing the time frame to coincide with Market-day. The atmosphere is even more electric than back then. The girls are certainly more fashion conscious now. I was amazed to see a young woman wearing knee length boots in the blistering heat strutting up and down the road as if she was on a catwalk in Paris.

There is bound to be a fight or someone falling in the trench after a drunken spree. No one takes any of these things seriously; it provides a good laugh.

## Granfaddah Takes Us to Red Hill

Granfaddah had bought another farm and told us it was way up at the very head of the river. The place was called Red Hill. He told us it took hours to get there. I was curious and wanted to see it but Granfaddah kept saying, "W'en yuh come nex' time." I was around fifteen when that day finally arrived. Daphne, Joel and I went to d'Riva on that holiday so he took the three of us to spend a few days at Red Hill. I thought we would never reach de place. The river got narrower and narrower the closer we got. We finally arrived and had to climb a steep incline after getting out of the boat. The dwelling was a *logee*; just a structure with a thatched roof and a fireside for cooking. This place was what I called *de jungle*; nothing but forest from where the cassava field ended. There were a few Amerindians around the place including a very young woman who lived in the house. I assumed they were workers on his farm and I did not think anything of it, but that visit came back to haunt me forty years later.

I stood on the bank of the river on Granfaddah's side one day and was amazed to see the rain pouring down on the opposite side of the river. Not a drop fell on my side. I have never forgotten that phenomenon. Looking back, I believe that happened for a reason, because I never forgot that place even though I never went there again until the year 2000. I will tell you about the saga that scandalised and rocked the D'Agrella Empire a bit later.

# Chapter Nine

*The early bird catches the worm.—Proverb*

# 1959-60 MIDDLE ROAD, LA PENITENCE

### A Sisyphean Move

On reflection, this next move was a calculated one, although it appeared to be Sisyphean in my opinion. Moving back to Middle Road did not appeal to me; we had lived here once and it was not the most desirable address. Why would my parents want to return to a place without plumbing I wondered? There must be a good reason for this move but I wasn't game to ask.

Daddy and this dark skinned gentleman who became our landlord met in the market, and a friendship was formed over a period of time. For that reason we were given first choice of this apartment when it became available. Mr Kansanally, a widower and successful market vendor lived on the upper level of this home with his extended family. He had sole occupancy of the large bedroom, while the remaining two were divided among his five daughters and their families. There was his eldest and recently widowed daughter Pearly and her children Claudette, Dennis and Roy; Mavis with her husband and their five children. Then there was his unmarried daughter Lucille with her daughter Colletta.

His twin daughters; Nora and Lottie completed the household. Lucille ran a hairdresser salon for African clients upstairs. When we lived there it was never of any interest to me as to where they all slept. Until now the thought never entered my head that they might have been a bit cramped with sixteen people.

Who else but Charlie could think of a suitable nickname for Mavis? He gave her the name 'In time', and for good reason. The woman had the knack of being omnipresent and always appeared just in time to catch us in the act of doing something wrong. There was only one time she didn't catch us in an act, a very dangerous one at that. The bigger boys had discovered a new game for the more unsuspecting, namely, me. They waited until my mother was out then invited me to see their new trick. The light bulb in the bedroom was removed and I was told to put my finger in the empty socket. I was gullible enough to try it since they told me it was fun. Praise the Lord our voltage was low or we could have all been electrocuted.

This address was a playground in itself; we had no need to leave the yard with so many playmates at our finger tips. Lice must have been invented here because there was never a shortage in my hair. Just the thought of them makes me want to scratch.

Downstairs was divided into two apartments. The one facing the road was rented by a *fine-fine* (extremely thin) elderly red skin woman named Mrs Johns, who cheerfully washed and ironed mountains of laundry for a living seven days a week. She washed clothes by hand with the help of a wooden washboard, a *beatah* (wooden bat) and elbow grease. Mummy used to say, "Dat poor woman got sh' wuk cut out;" whenever she saw her bringing home the basket loaded with dirty linen on her head. Only the affluent society sent out their clothes to be laundered by a washer-woman such as Mrs Johns. She always placed the huge tin tub on the steps to do the washing so it was convenient for me to *cock-meh-leg-up* (put my feet up) and chat while she washed away. I never thought to help the poor woman. I think she gave the older boys upstairs a *small piece* (small amount of money) to fetch the enormous quantity of water required for such a mammoth task. I liked to admire all the fancy clothes after she hung them out on the palin'. That was our clothes line.

We were living closer to Crossroad this time, and that meant a shorter distance to *draw watah*, although that was no consolation. I was a teenager now and I thought it was degrading to be seen doing such a menial chore. It was wonderful when the rain fell then the tanks were filled and I got a reprieve.

We lived in the one bedroom apartment at the back of the building. The latrine in the yard was communal and had a few stories of its own. Not to mention needing pegs for your nose. What I hated more than anything while living here was the humiliation of having to take the *Poe* out every morning; that was mega *shame*. Queuing for the slimy bathroom was an everyday occurrence and I hated it.

There was a disgusting smelling fowl pen at the side of the palins and a *magga* (meagre) looking *dunks* (fruit) tree. I burrowed in among the few hibiscus bushes to find a bit of solitude and to do *private t'ings*. I see you're getting fas' just like me, but *'old on*, I will tell you what it is later; you know I can't keep a secret.

## Daddy Starts His Coffee Business

We were not living here very long when Daddy decided to start his own business. Didn't I tell you it was a calculated move? My father had been contemplating going into the coffee business for some time, but I was accustomed to him procrastinating so never took him seriously. Guyanese are big coffee drinkers so Daddy decided he was going to cash in by producing and marketing ground coffee. Did this mean he was planning to give Ricks some competition? Mind you, Ricks had already moved from his humble beginnings to a more modern establishment and we were financially challenged so a factory was out of the question.

We were among the many households who parched and ground their coffee so Daddy was already acquainted with the simple process. How and where was not a major concern, he was only going to do it on a small scale; a 'backyard venture' really. The fact that we were renting did not deter him in the least; *besize* he was only using the yard. Parching coffee beans involves fire and one would assume that would pose a major problem, but not in this neighbourhood, or in this country for that matter. Councils had no concrete rules or regulations that prevented anyone from building a fire in their yard. I doubt whether Daddy even asked permission from our landlord before taking the plunge.

We used a *canaree* (Carahee—a cast-iron type wok I believe every household in Guyana owns) to parch our coffee. Ours was a decent size, but not big enough for commercial use. Maan, Daddy lashed out and bought a *fire-rass* (exaggeration of size) canaree and began parching coffee in the yard. He ground the coffee then made up small packages which he took to the two smaller markets to sell (I guess he was testing the market). It was a humble beginning, but before long Daddy had built up a clientele and needed to do things on a bigger scale. Parching in a canaree would not suffice. I wonder if it was Daddy who thought of the construction of the apparatus he had made for this purpose. He casually arrived home one day with this contraption strapped to the carrier on the back of his bicycle. It was to parch coffee he said but I did not ask how because it held no interest for me. I was thirteen years old when this happened out of the blue. Out of the blue for me because children were kept in the dark at all times. Would you believe I found out it was my birthday when Mummy said, "Today is yuh birt'day Helen;" up to about ten years of age anyway.

I was a typical teenager daydreaming with the fairies and living in a world of my own and didn't have a care in the world as long as we had food on the table. What more could I need? I had also started attending one of the more prestigious high schools for girls and thought I was *Miss Prim* . . . well Mummy called me that.

That contraption Daddy brought home was obviously important because I came home from school one day to find him sitting on a box manually rotating the drum. The drum was suspended on the rim of the guard he used to contain the blazing fire underneath. This coffee parching device was made from a forty-four-gallon gasoline drum; cleaned thoroughly of course. Holes were drilled in the centre of the top and bottom of the drum and a steel rod was inserted. One end of the rod was soldered onto the drum sealing the hole, and a handle was soldered on to the protruding end. A section of the drum was cut out in the middle to make a flap which was held in place with hinges. The raw coffee beans were inserted into the drum via the flap then secured with a bolt (a piece of coarse wire) before the parching operation began.

Parching the beans to perfection was crucial; burnt beans were no good. This process was especially tricky in the beginning when Daddy had no concept of how long it would take. He had visual access when he used the *canaree* but this was different. Testing had to be done periodically to make sure the coffee beans were sufficiently parched. Help was enlisted during this process because the drum had to be lifted off the fire. The hot flap was carefully opened with an old rag, yes an old rag; no one gave a thought of safety back then. The surroundings and method used by my father were definitely a hazard; one that would not be tolerated by the Health and Safety regulations of today.

We all took turns at grinding the beans in the large mill that was screwed onto the bench top in our kitchen. I am transported back to those times whenever I smell the aroma of coffee brewing. The ground coffee was then weighed and packaged into brown paper bags of various sizes to accommodate the needs of his customers. Daddy strapped a carton with the packages onto the back of his bicycle carrier and rode around town making deliveries. He could also be found selling the coffee on the perimeter of Bourda Market on Saturday morning. This was where he befriended an elderly African woman we called Mother Gladys. She had a permanent stall in the market and eventually sold the coffee for a commission.

Daddy parching coffee in the yard

## Mummy Throws 'Box-hand' for School Fees

It was at this address I became a teenager and sat the common entrance exam for St Joseph High School. I passed, but it was not a government scholarship, therefore fees still had to be paid and this posed more financial difficulties for my parents. The fees were paid quarterly so sacrifices had to be made. There was only one way my mother could guarantee having the money. She had to join a 'box-hand' group. I have no idea whether this is the proper name for this practice but I know trust played a big part. One person was selected from the group to be the *purse holder.* This person hands over all the money to the person *drawin' box-hand* that week. Mummy's group had twelve people and each person contributed three dollars each week. My mother always drew the last hand, thus ensuring she had the thirty-five dollars to pay my school fees. She had a whole dollar left over! Going to this school was rather prestigious and Mummy was especially proud of this accomplishment. You could hear her at every street corner telling someone, "Helen pass de cammon entrance exam yuh know." There wasn't a cap in town big enough to fit her head. Daphne had also sat the exam; unfortunately she barely missed out. This saddened me because I was hoping we would attend this high school together.

## Becoming a Carta-lick

It was obvious the nuns were not impressed with me passing the common entrance exam fair and square; they still had another criteria waiting before I could be fully accepted. The principal, Sister Mary Consolata Muldowney allowed me to commence the school term after she extracted a submissive promise from my mother. The mission was to have me converted to the Catholic faith as soon as possible. I was desperate to attend this school and would have shaved my head if the nuns wanted me to. Carmel primary school was in the same compound as the high school and since the nuns taught there, Sister Cecelia was commissioned to teach me Catechism after school. When I was able to answer all the questions parrot fashion I was ready to be baptised. Only another staunch Catholic was allowed to stand as a godparent and we didn't have too many good *Carta-licks* in our family. Mummy's uncle in Bent Street must have been the only family we knew who went to church so she asked their daughter. Elizabeth was only a few years older than me but that didn't matter so she stood as my *Nennen* (godmother). One of Daddy's nephews name was put on the paper as my godfather, but that was only a formality. Cousin Cleo was not obligated to attend my baptism. Only Beth, the priest and I were there on the appointed day. I was baptised at the prestigious St Marys Catholic Cathedral (also called Brickdam Cathedral) if you please; the same one I was married in eight years later.

## A Proud St Joseph High School Student

Attending St Joseph High School was one of the most nerve wracking periods of my teenage life. It was a known fact that only wealthy families sent their girls to this school. I learnt different many years later. Let me tell you, I was so happy Mummy did not know someone who had an old uniform to give me. That happened later though so I did not escape completely. The dressmaker made me the navy tunic but we bought the two white shirts. No damn pocket in my uniform skirt again! It was compulsory to wear the correct uniform which also consisted of a navy *berette* (beret), a belt and a school badge in the shape of a shield. I still have my badge; the only tangible item to prove I actually attended St Joseph's. My inferiority complex got the better of me in this environment. However, I became friends with a girl named Naline Kawall; her parents owned Kawalls Drug store opposite La Penitence market. I met her every morning at the drugstore so she and I could walk to school together. Naline sometimes offered me a sweetie or some *Max* (chewing gum). I think she found different friends when the school moved. By the way, *Max* was a popular brand of gum. We found it simple to call all gum by that name, just like we called all chocolate *Cadburys*.

I never had pocket money like the other girls so I kept to myself out of sheer embarrassment. There is one highlight I treasure from my time at the old school (a new one was built). The daughter from the wealthy Khan family in Lamaha Street who was in the fifth form actually drove a little red sports car to school. How rich were these people? I was hurrying to get to school one morning after running an errand for Mummy that took me out of my way. To my utter surprise the red car screeched to a halt next to me. I was dumbstruck when this beautiful girl smiled sweetly and opened the door to invite me in. I was *shame*, so like an idiot, I began playing *brigah* (feigning interest) and said, "No t'ank yuh;" but she insisted, so I climbed in. I was overjoyed and overwhelmed by her kind gesture. She was lucky her car was still dry when we got to school. I felt like a million dollars and secretly hoped all the other students saw me getting out of her car.

St Joseph High School was a big rambling two-storey building. The lower forms were downstairs. I never got to experience the upper level because by the time I was ready to progress to the third form upstairs the school was relocated to Thomas Lands. I was disappointed not being able to experience being on the upper level because it had prestige and an air of superiority. I was asked to deliver some papers to an office upstairs one day and that was the only time I got a glimpse of what it looked like. To tell the truth it was dark and gloomy.

## Teenage Blues

My early teenage years had begun, but life was not always as joyful as I would have liked. This period of my teenage life was laced with melancholy. Communication between my parents was the number one problem in our family. Each member seemed to be living a separate life. As our anchor drifted, I floated aimlessly on another planet feeling isolated but there was no one to confide in.

The relationship between my parents had begun deteriorating a few years earlier; although I believe I was the only child who absorbed and recognised the dynamics between them. My siblings seemed to have breezed through their childhood without any adverse effect. I enjoy playing the *rememba w'en* game when my siblings and I meet, but it is almost as if we all had different parents. None of them have any recollection of the deep issues that affected our family. Does this happen in every family? Why did I absorb and retain all those miserable times? I can only conclude my over sensitive nature is responsible. Not only do I spring a leak at the drop of a hat; I despise conflict or injustice of any nature. It rattles my cage!

My parent's marriage was fractured beyond repair at this point. It was another of their silent treatment periods and I was made to do Daddy's washing and ironing. Claudette Murray and I had become good friends and although she was only a year or so older then me, she could run their household single-handed. I was struggling to iron one of my father's shirts one day when she came downstairs to visit and told me I was ironing the shirt incorrectly then took over to show me how it should be done. To this day, I still think of Claudette whenever I iron a shirt, which is not very often; we can afford *wash and wear* now.

## Attacked By Hairy-worms

All sorts of adventures took place here and we were lucky to have had very nice neighbours. We did not know the ones behind us with the big jamoon tree (notable for *hairy-worms*) and wished we did because this fruit was too tempting to resist when in season. While my mother was resting one day I decided to steal some jamoon. Our back palin' was almost touching the tree so I could use that for leverage. I had barely begun climbing when I felt a severe stinging. I dropped to the ground barely missing the spiked palin'. *Rant!* Those blasted *hairy-worms* (dangerous caterpillars) had zapped me. My knees tripled in size in no time and the pain was excruciating. Vinegar was supposed to be a good cure and since we had none I squeezed a lime on the rash. OUCH! I had to hide my swollen knee caps and bear the pain in secret or face a good *cut-ass* from Mummy. Stealing is one thing she did not tolerate; although I stole a few times without her knowledge.

This memoir is a confession for all of my sins so I will tell you about the day I could have been arrested for petty theft. Mummy sent me all the way to Big Market to get an item she needed. We seldom patronised that market which to me was Disneyland. Those stalls were jam packed with many tempting items to feast my depraved eyes on. Don't ask me why I did it, but I had sense enough to wait until the lady was distracted by another customer before I t'ief the tiny mirror, which by the way was a replica of the one Helen had given me in the Rupununi. I slipped it into my basket then causally sauntered off . . . that theft has haunted me to this day.

## A Questionable Character

At thirteen I was perceptive enough to know when something was not quite what it seemed. Mummy was due home from the market one

Saturday morning so I stood by the gate to wait for her. I did a double take when I caught sight of her in the distance. A man was walking alongside her, he was pushing a bicycle and had Mummy's basket hanging on the handlebar. I could tell they were conversing by her hand gestures. I had never seen this man before, but I took an instant dislike to him when he came within close range. For a start he had *cock-eye* and he looked *sly;* you know the look I am talking about. Mummy said, "Dis is meh big dauttah;" as if I didn't have a name. I practically snatched the basket out of that man's hand as he handed it to me. I *sucked meh teet'* (under my breath of course) and flounced off into the house. Mummy stayed and chatted with him for a few minutes before she came indoors. I asked who he was and she said his name was Verdie. Is that so I thought to myself; he may be Verdie to you, but I am going to call him Mr Cocky.

Well, wouldn't you know it; I was in the front yard by Mrs Johns a few afternoons later when a man on a bicycle stopped. He remained sitting on the bike while balancing with one leg on the road then he beckoned me over. When I was close enough I realised it was none other than Mr Cocky. He gave me a slimy smile and said, "Is yuh muddah 'ome?" Not for you she isn't! I angrily thought. No way was he chatting up my mother; so I said, "No, sh' an' Daddy gon to de Seawall to ketch breeze." I would have liked to tell him to go and jump in the canal, but I didn't have the guts; *besize* he would tell Mummy and she had repeatedly said, "A'gon still beat yuh even if yuh big as a'coconut or cabbage tree." Now, that is something I want to tell you about because that message was somewhat confusing. I knew how *big* (tall) a coconut tree was, but I had never seen a cabbage tree in Guyana. I certainly never saw any growing on either of my grandparent's farms. The nuns always had cabbage on their menu and I wondered how they could afford it as it was always very expensive. We only ever bought a small piece when we wanted to cook Chow-mien. But since Mummy said it didn't matter how *big* I was, I assumed cabbages grew on tall trees. Imagine my surprise when I came to Australia and saw these cabbage plants growing close to the ground. I felt cheated and ripped off by Mummy, BUT, I was doing some research de odda day and found there is a Cabbage Palm so it looks like she was more *eddicated* than I thought, and I am not just saying that, I mean it. Mummy was taken out of school in fourth standard to work on the farm with Granfaddah so her education was limited. She read everything she could lay her hands on so she could learn about things in the world. She always told me that reading is the best thing anyone can do. I have only just become a voracious reader and she was right, I just wished I had taken her advice sooner.

Oh, Mr Cocky did stop by once or twice, but Mummy was NEVER at home; then we moved so he couldn't find her. That is what I would like to believe anyway.

## Schupid T'ings Mummy Told Me

My mother certainly had some strange ideas. I was running late for an appointment recently but could not leave the house because I hadn't done the dishes. It was while washing them I made the connection. There were two things Mummy had to do before she left the house and this was her warning to me, "Helen, yuh mus' neva leave de 'ouse until yuh mek-up de bed an' wash yuh wares." That was so-so advice, but there is no logic in the statement that followed. She would say, "A'would feel suh shame if a'went out an' got killed an' deh 'ave to bring meh back because deh will see meh dirty wares an' de bed not made." Looks like she thought she would still have powers when she was in her grave.

The tapes in my head are getting weaker. I have stopped listening to the one where she said, "Neva put off till tomorrow w'at yuh cyan do today." These days my housework is not only put off for tomorrow, it gets done when I am in the mood, and most times it's only *a lick an' a promise* (minimal cleaning) because I have more important things to do . . . like living! The last thing she wanted to know before I left the house was if I had on clean underwear. I used to think, "Mummy, it might be clean now, but yuh betta believe it will get dirty if a'cyar lick meh dung."

Like most teenagers, I was starting to sprout wings and was beginning to *smell mehself* (feel my power) and *playin' de fool*, but Mummy always warned me by saying, "Monkey know which lim' to jump on." I knew what she meant and quickly learnt to be careful when I was dealing with her. I don't know how many times my mother threatened to clip my wings. I was almost expecting to go under the scissors like poor Laura; thank goodness I never grew feathers. That didn't matter because she used metaphorical scissors to do the job. She threatened to lock me out of the house. Now that is a scary thought in Guyana because I would have had nowhere to go. That threat would not faze the youngsters of today. A visit to Social Security and they would have a nice place of their own before the day was over. They might even get the police to come and sort me out. We simply did not have that option.

My mother used to say things like, "Stap brayin' like a'jackass or doan *mek bassa-bassa* (stir up trouble)" if I was talking too much or trying to defend myself. I brayed a lot, it was my favourite occupation. I made the mistake of *brayin'* too close to her one day and her wedding ring split my lip. I had some vicious thoughts about Mummy and I lived in fear of her finding out because I know she was a mind reader. She was forever saying, "An' doan t'ink a'doan no wha' yuh t'inkin' because a'cyan read yuh mine." Shite, that one sent shivers down my weak spine.

While we are talking about weak spines I might as well tell you what she said about ribs. Mummy caught me giving away our last cake of sweet-soap one day. She called me after my friend left and said, "*If yuh gi'way yuh batty yuh will 'ave to shit troo yuh ribs.*" I could see you scratching your head so I will explain. It means, 'You will have to improvise if you no longer had what was important to your needs'.

I was sick of hearing her say, "Every dog has its day" when I was rude, and that was almost every day. It can't be that bad; those dogs seem to have a lot of fun on the street so I was looking forward to having my day too. I tried everything to floor and outsmart my mother, but I could never win because she said, "A'ave a'plasta fuh every sore." That woman had a whole drugstore full of plasters; she must have had shares in one of those big drugstores I told you about.

Did you know you could measure the length of your memory? Whenever I did something really bad; like suckin' meh teet'; Mummy would say, "Yuh t'ink a'gon fuget yuh rudeness, a'got a'laang-laang memory suh yuh gon pay fuh it wan day." Well, Mummy wasn't the only one who had long memory; Aunt May had one that was even longer. I went to Guyana in 1984 when things were grim. Stocks on shops shelves were depleted so I filled up an extra suitcase like all Guyanese do when they are going home . . . especially when you have relatives coming out of the woodwork, but I love them all and wanted to take something for each one. I went to see Aunt May in d'Riva and took her a cake of sweet-soap, a tube of toothpaste, some salfish (all the way from Canada) and some sweeties. The woman took the stuff, looked at me with a straight face and said, "Ellen yuh cudden bring a'dress lenk fuh meh?" I was crushed, but I humbly apologised and told her I will bring one next time. The next time I saw Aunt May was in 1995, and the first thing she said when she saw me was, "Ellen, a'ope yuh rememba to bring de dress lenk." A *truh-truh* story folks; not everyone has family with such a good memory; I am blessed. By the way a *dress lenk* (dress length) is three yards of fabric which was enough to make a dress, and if you were lucky like me you might get a matching panty. How I longed for the day I could buy a real silk panty from a store. I know yuh fas' and want to know if I remembered the dress lenk . . . well yes I did, you think I want that woman to haunt me from the grave. I already have enough baggage of my own to *kerry*.

When I was in my teens, my mother never asked me outright whether there was any truth to the rumour she may have heard. Her skilful means of questioning was always done in a diplomatic fashion. She fished and baited me like a true fisherwoman, knowing her tactics would wind me up and make me spill my guts. When I couldn't take anymore I usually said, "An' a'guess yuh believe dis person rite?" Let me give you an example. She bailed me up one day and said, "Sumone seh deh saw sumone lookin' jus' like yuh on de seawall wid a'bhai in de dark." I was so damn vex, I retorted with, "Dis sumone mus'be a'owl to be able to pick meh out in de dark." She allowed me to go on and on in anger before she smugly said, "A'didn't seh it was yuh, but if de cap fit pull de string." Cap, what cap was she talking about I wonder; I never wore one. She just assumed I was guilty because I got angry and challenged her. Another time she told me she could *smell a red 'errin'* a mile away when she didn't believe my story sounded genuine. Daddy on the other hand was forever saying he could *smell a rat*. Why not? Our home was infested with them.

I admit I went to the Seawall often, but it wasn't always to meet boys. My girlfriends and I went there to *pampazet* (show off) and *ketch swank* (to be seen). Sure we met boys we knew; that was because EVERYONE went there; we had nowhere else to go. I promise to give you the spiel on the Seawall as soon as I finish *poun'in'* (pounding) Mummy's name. I hope she doesn't find out I am telling the whole world about her or she may rise from her grave and really punish me.

## Dead Men Walking

Seeing I mentioned the word *grave*, I better tell you Guyanese believe it is a breach of etiquette to talk ill of the dead, but I only want to tell you that we have a lot of restless people in the Le Repentir cemetery. And how do I know that? Simple, I listened to people *talkin' name* (gossiping) and I can't begin to tell you how many times a day I would hear someone say, "Sh'/'e muddah/faddah mus'be turnin' in sh'/'e grave rite now." A person will say that if they see the offspring of a deceased person doing something they know would have disappointed them if they were alive.

You may not know this, but every time someone dies, two other people will get jealous and get into the act on purpose, because the superstition 'It always comes in t'rees' has to be confirmed. I must admit I still think in those terms today, but it always happens. In the last fortnight *t'ree* people I know died, one after the other. Laugh all you want, but I believe it is true. Looks like I need some more *eddicashun* eh?

All the *schupid t'ings* my mother said back then can provide a good laugh now, but there is truth in some of her sayings. Now that I am a mother myself I can see clearly what she meant when she punished me and said, "Yuh t'ink a'enjoy doin' dis, a'doin' it fuh yuh own good." She took her parenting role seriously and went to great lengths to raise us with the little education she had. True, she manipulated us with bullshit and ruled with an iron fist, but she did an amazing job of raising six children who all turned out decently. There are no visible framed diplomas hanging on any of our walls, because there are no scholars with a degree (except for Charlie's B.A . . . Bullshit Artist) among us. None of that matters one bit because Mummy accomplished much more than that. We all graduated with a degree in RHDAC (Respect Honesty Decency and Common Sense) which is something sadly lacking in most children today. I may not have agreed with Mummy's policies at the time, but I would like to humbly pay tribute to my wonderful mother for making me the decent and honest person I am today. I take my hat off to you Mummy; I am deeply sorry for making it so difficult for you. THANK YOU MUMMY.

## Guyana's Most Notorious Landmark

Yuh still wid meh? A'ope yuh enjoyin' de waalk suh far; we reach halfway a'ready. Ow, doan siddung now, come . . . walk wit' me." Meh mout' gettin' a'bit dry suh a'gon stop fuh a'cup a'caffee-tea before a'tell you 'bout de seawall because dat story is a'bit laang.

I bet you are dying to hear about the Seawall where Mummy and Daddy went to ketch breeze. That was a lie by the way. Yes, I knew how to tell a lie. Daddy was most likely out drinking with his friends that day and Mummy would have been inside the house angry, and looking like she was *suckin' 'pon a'tambrin*.

This wonder we called 'de Seawall' was the perfect place to *spot a'bannah* (meet a handsome boy) or *a'bini* (beautiful girl); especially on a busy Saturday afternoon. Boys also liked to take their *bake* (girlfriend) to de Seawall with the pretence of *ketchin' breeze*, but girls knew it was to practice their romantic skills.

*Maan*, if that seawall could talk I would have been in big trouble with Mummy after I became a *big woman*. That was one romantic venue I tell you. The name alone should tell you it is a wall, and I can also tell you it was built to keep out the Atlantic Ocean because Guyana is below sea level. The seawall was there to protect our coast line, but it turned a blind eye when it came to protecting our young women and their virginity. Mothers will tell you it was used for *commonness*. I bet you want to know what that means right? We have several words to describe what is natural between two consenting adults, but we NEVER used the correct word, it is too vulgar. When the rooster mounted the hen, we said, "De fowl-cock treadin' de 'en," and we all knew what 'de dogs jookin'" meant, but no one said the word "sex," it was taboo. My mother referred to it as "commonness." Any word that had the slightest sexual connotation was removed from our vocabulary. I can honestly say I never heard the words *penis* and *vagina* until I was an adult. It was, *punny, pum-pum, powder-puff* and *pat-a-cake* for a female and *lolee, willie, birdie, soti* and *lolo* for male, and those are the tame versions.

Like I said, if that concrete structure could talk there would be a lot of divorces and a lot of mothers would be in jail for killing their *gyurl chirren* (girl children). That is very true because I will tell you some juicy stories as we continue this journey together . . .

The gossip mongers who wanted to *run-dung* (degrade) other people's daughters would say, "Sumbady shud tell dat woman w'at sh' chirren ge'up to w'en sh' back turn." Those girls were lucky they didn't have a mother who was a clairvoyant like mine. However the more perceptive mothers did go in search of their daughters on de Seawall. They always took a stick or a belt concealed on their person to cut-ass when they found them *soorin'* (romantically embracing) with some *good fuh nutt'in'* (worthless/loser) boy. There are a few girls I know personally who were embarrassed by their mothers in that manner and I lived in fear of my mother following me, because I knew how far she could walk.

Thank goodness my mother never followed me, but a *choke-an'-rob* (bandit/thief) did. One night, my fiancé and I parked just below the wall on an empty stretch of land. Ours was the only car parked there. Most lovers had a bicycle which they parked against the actual wall, but I was now *shittin' in 'igh grass* (circulating in high places) and could neck in the privacy of a car. Shortly after we parked we saw a young African man approaching and I was advised to wind up the window. The man casually glanced into the car as he walked passed. I looked back until he had disappeared into the darkness. We had more important business to attend to so I thought no more about it. My right hand was cramping so I decided to remove it from my fiancé's neck. I turned my head and *meh eye mek four* (eye contact) with a man who was crouching and creeping up to the back window. I knew in an instant we were in BIG trouble; I kept my cool and whispered, "Drive now Johnny, drive quick!" Thank goodness he wasn't *schupidee; besize* we weren't doing anything that warranted such a command. He understood and took off right away. The bandit rushed to Johnny's window and started banging on it in anger when he realised we were leaving. We were gone in a flash. I was never so fryken in my life. We could have been killed and god knows what else. It was sheer common sense that saved us that night. A good thing

I had that diploma from Mummy. That happened not long before we got married, but we never told our parents.

At the far end of the seawall there was Fort Groyne; better known as Dixie to lovers. It was a very dangerous place for more than one reason. A No Swimming notice was up as you approached the long jetty. Most people went there for an evening stroll, but many went there to take their lives. A friend of mine did that after I left Guyana. Because of its seclusion it was an ideal place for a tryst, illicit affairs and for lovers who wanted to do *commonness*. Dixie was the bushy section before you reached the jetty; I recently learnt it is also aptly called Scandal Point. Some lovers paid to go to a *short-time-place* (house of ill repute), but that cost money; besize, everyone knew everyone in Georgetown so someone was *bung fuh* recognise you. A close relative of mine lives across the street from a house that conducts that sort of business. The last time I went to Guyana I had fun counting how many times the same *freshie* (old man) brought a different young woman in one week. He must have been a star-bhai because he rocked up twice one day. I wonder where he was buying his Capadulla from!!

I went to Dixie *wan-wan time* with friends out of sheer curiosity because as you know 'Fas" could have been my second name. Maan, those bushes were alive with the sound of romantic noises, but making love in a bed of *pimpla* (thorns) was not my *speed* (preference); besize, Mummy would have skinned me alive . . . *commonness* was out of the question.

## No Good Beaches in Guyana

You will be mistaken for thinking we had a beautiful beach on de Seawall but nothing could be further from the truth. It was just a mudflat and the water was murky. My friends and I attempted to swim there on one occasion but were put off when we sunk deep in the mud and had no where to wash off when we got out.

It was said Bee Hive beach was the place to swim so a group of us took the train to go there on a picnic. Although the tide was in, it was still too shallow to swim. We had to wade out in the mud to deeper waters. While swimming the gold ring I was wearing slipped off; I quickly lunged after it and must have dug up half the ocean trying to retrieve it without success. The jeweller had engraved Helene by mistake, but since it was a birthday gift from my mother it had sentimental value.

On my last visit to Guyana, Charlie and family took us to *B.V.* (Betaverwagting) beach for a picnic but nothing had changed; we still had to wade out a great distance before we could swim in the ocean. If you are looking for nice beaches please go to Barbados where the water is crystal clear.

## Going To Shell Beach with Uncle Mike

The sight of a massive dead whale on Shell Beach in Guyana was something I never expected to see. I received that picture via e-mail recently and it brought back memories of the three wonderful days I spent there with Uncle Mike when I was fifteen.

I had a few memorable trips before I married and going to Shell Beach was one of them. Uncle Mike had started a venture growing watermelons so when Joel and I went to d'Riva for a holiday he took us to help with the harvest. The trip itself was a bit scary because we had to venture into the Essequibo River and that meant leaving the relative calm of the Pomeroon River. It was a fair distance from the mouth of the Pomeroon and it was rough going until we reached Shell Beach. The name did not disappoint. It was not safe to swim here but the ecstasy of walking on a carpet of white shells while listening to the crashing waves has remained with me. The remoteness and tranquillity of Shell Beach was reminiscent of being a castaway on an island.

Daddy had grown the odd watermelon on his hobby farms, but this place was watermelon heaven. The vines were endless, bearing fruit of every size and shape you can imagine. No need to be conservative here, there was enough to feed an army. Joel and I began chopping watermelons at random. If one wasn't red enough, we discarded it and split another; there was enough to do this all day. The field looked as if a massacre had taken place when we were finished. We were both *buck-sick* by the end of our stay and never wanted to see another watermelon as long as we lived.

*I think of Shell Beach whenever I eat watermelon.*

It was August so crabs were marching while we were at Shell Beach. We waited for the tide to go out then went crab ketchin' in the mangroves.

I was up to my ears in mud but it was a heap of fun. The only negative aspect was trying to avoid those giant *tengaleh* (tentacle). I was supposed to fill my *Quake* (a *Mukru* basket with a small opening), but I did not bag too many because those crabs pinched me too often and would not *le'go*. The young buck woman who lived with Gramuddah around that time had gone with us to do the cooking. I cannot remember her name but I had never seen anyone so excited over crabs; not to mention her expertise in catching them and even quicker at cooking them. What a feast we had on the beach.

Mummy roared with laughter when I told her about the buck girl. She said, "Dem buck people cyan ketch crab wid deh eye shut."

## Malaria Attacks Cousin Jim Struck At Santa Rosa

I was around age twenty when I made my maiden trip to Santa Rosa; a well known Amerindian settlement. We must have hired the boat because no one I knew in town owned one. It was a motorboat and big enough to hold Daddy, Joel, Daphne, Cousin Jim, Fedna and myself. We had to *cross across* the Demerara River to enter a creek that led to our destination. The motor speed had to be cut to a crawl to navigate the narrow creek which looked like a giant meandering snake. We had a few close shaves going around the sharp curves, but we got there safely.

The Amerindians materialised from nowhere and greeted us shyly. Before long they were offering us water coconuts for refreshment. There wasn't much to see at the mission except for the little school house and a few logees scattered around. Cashew trees laden with succulent fruit grew in abundance. The bashful Amerindian children covered their mouths with their hands and giggled as they followed us around the compound, and the nun in charge also chatted with us. Our visit was cut short when Cousin Jim *tek-in-sick* (suddenly became ill). He shook uncontrollably with a severe case of ague. We laid him in the bottom of the boat and covered him with whatever we could find to make him comfortable for the trip home.

Cousin Jim worked in the gold fields where malaria is prevalent. The incubating type is unpredictable and can flare up suddenly. Malaria is the biggest pitfall when you work in the interior and many of my relatives, including my two youngest brothers who do that line of work, repeatedly fall victim to the virus.

## Religious Rigmarole at Easter

Writing this memoir has been a revelation, until now; I did not realise how much my life has changed direction. On reflection there isn't a specific occasion I truly celebrate in Australia, although the *footy* (football) grand final is spectacular, especially if my favourite team is playing. The fireworks display on Australia Day is also grand, but nothing bears the same significance compared to events celebrated in Guyana. Back then we celebrated everything under the sun. Two Palm-flies mating the longest was cause for celebration. Easter and Christmas were the biggest celebration so choosing one over the other would be difficult. It was the kites, not eggs that were the main attraction at Easter. As a matter of fact there was never an Easter egg in sight. I am not certain that another culture celebrates Easter like we did in Guyana, but you have to experience it to know what I am talking about. For me, Easter in Australia is just another long weekend; a competition to see who would collect the most chocolate. In Guyana it held great religious significance and rituals that were taken seriously—by the devout. When I became a Catholic worshipper I was expected to follow all the religious rules and ceremonies connected to Easter. Lent officially began on Ash Wednesday, but my ancestors kicked it off on Shrove Tuesday, better known as 'Pancake Day'. Naturally we made pancakes; these were different to the flat ones we eat now. A yeast based batter was used for the ones we made. The tiny blobs of batter were deep fried then steeped in heavy syrup. This recipe originated in Portugal so we called them 'Portuguese pancakes'. I have never made or eaten that type of pancake since I left Guyana, but I can still remember the taste. The next day was Ash Wednesday so I made my way to Mass with syrup oozing from every pore. The compulsory dash of ash had to be rubbed on my forehead and it was proudly worn as a badge of honour. Heck, I even visited family and friends after receiving the ash because it clearly said, "Look how holy I am." I will tell you how holy I was back then. I did not know the origin of the ash until recently, and would readily admit I did not realise it was administered in the shape of a cross. And I was further educated by Ruth (Life Writing tutour) when she said the palm crosses from the previous year were burnt to produce that ash. You learn something new every day. You would be correct if you called me a hypocrite, but in my defence, you have to remember I was cajoled into becoming a Catholic.

What I am about to say may sound like an abhorrence to Catholics but that is not my intention. Consider this a confession because I won't be doing it in a confessional. Again, I hasten to add that this is solely my personal perception of the faith. There were sacrifices to be made at Easter; the bigger the sacrifice, the better a Catholic you were in the eyes of your peers. Note, I said *peers*, because it was more a competition than for reverent reasons from what I gathered.

Lent meant abstinence; this sacrifice won points for Catholics. You had to forego something you really enjoyed; giving up kissing did enter my mind, but that was too big a sacrifice so I chose sweets instead; I could never afford them anyway. To tell the truth that was never taken seriously either because I always cheated before Lent was over. There was more praying and pretending on Holy Thursday when a service was held for *the washing of the feet*. I guess the priest who coached me for confirmation was too busy mauling me to explain the significance of that ritual. Some of the men having their feet washed were the biggest hypocrites; they were only concerned with doing good deeds for themselves. For some of them it was the first time they had their feet properly washed in weeks. Certain aspects of the religion do not resonate with my personal beliefs; secular religion is more to my liking.

Next came Good Friday. That was bigger than Ben Hur!! Every man, woman and child attended Mass. For me, it was an opportunity to show off my latest dress and that new mantilla (veil/head scraf). The dress code was strict; no woman in their right mind would dream of wearing anything other than black, white or shades of purple . . . unless you wanted to be called a whore. A woman could not enter the church without having her head covered back then. Attend a mass anywhere today and tell me if you can see a *mantilla*. I recently asked a niece who is considered 'a good Catholic' if she had a mantilla, she looked at me as if I was speaking another language or from a different planet! Then she asked, "What's that?"

We hated having Gramuddah (Ol' Francesca) around on Good Friday because she watched us like a hawk; we were not allowed to even cough. Anything we did reflected in the suffering of the Lord. I remember Gramuddah came to town one Easter and made Good Friday absolute hell for everyone. I was around fifteen, but she would not allow me to do anything. I wanted to cook something, but she said you should never cook on Good Friday because the fire would burn Jesus, so I turned off the stove. I got out a needle to sew up a hole in my dress, but she said I couldn't do that either because every stitch would pierce him. I honestly couldn't believe she was talking about the same man who didn't flinch when he had two big-big nails put in his hands on the cross. But I dared not argue with her, and did as I was told.

Holy Saturday was another day of restraint; I had to put off going to a *jump-up* (party/dance) for another week. Such sacrifice I endured all in the name of being *a'good carta-lick gyurl*.

To be truthful, the anticipation of flying a kite at Easter was over shadowed by the religious aspect.

## Flying Kites on de Seawall at Easter

The build up to Easter was very exciting for children. Making or buying a kite took priority over everything else for weeks. Various types of paper for making kites were displayed in stores and sold by all the street vendors. The Barbados (thick and glossy) paper was especially popular; although it depended on your budget. For my family it was the nastiest, cheapest paper; just looking at it too long could rip it apart. Our kites were shredded before they left the ground. Boys will be boys, so my brothers practiced their kite making skills weeks before Easter. Bamboo or the coarser pointas from our broom was used to make the frames and since we seldom could afford to buy Gloy, a substitute of thin flour paste or *Glamacherry* berries was used to glue the flimsy paper to the frame. The boys raided Mummy's beddin' for the bits needed to make the kite tail. The twine was a bit more difficult to come by; they scrounged and joined whatever they found. That ball of twine was always multi-coloured, but their only aim was to get that kite in the air.

The Easter celebrations began in earnest on Easter Sunday; this was the day we sinners were all waiting for. The more devout worshipers attended church, but for the pagan worshippers it was time to get *de likka* flowing. The population congregates on de Seawall because it is a space devoid of electrical wires and has ample room for kites to soar. A steady procession of kite flyers made their way to this rendezvous at *fo'day marnin'* to secure the best position. By the time we arrived at mid-morning there was a kaleidoscope of colour in the sky. All eyes turned upwards to watch the aerial ballet choreographed by the trade winds that blew in from the Atlantic. Kites of every style and description undulated as if in a hypnotic trance. As a child I was enthralled by the entire spectacle at Easter time. The *box-kite* was my favourite, but there was never too many of those because they were difficult to make. The *singin'-engine* was the Rolls Royce of kites because of the noise it emitted.

Does this all sound innocent to you? Think again. This is a crowded place with wall to wall people, kites and just as much venom in the atmosphere. Not all kite flying was for pleasure; there were competitions and dirty tactics. The more astute pooled their resources to build the biggest and most powerful kites, and businessmen paid to use them as billboards. There were competitions, but sabotage was the name of the game for most of those competing. Attaching a razorblade on the tail of your kite is one sure way of bringing down a competitor. Beautiful kites were seen plummeting to the ground after it became the target of an unseen assassin.

The competitions took place on Easter Monday; the final day of the official celebration. Children crying and clinging to battered kites were dragged home by exhausted parents. Fights broke out providing more entertainment. Guyanese are voyeurs and do enjoy the spectacle of a good fight. Yes, it was a perfect end to another fabulous Easter. Remnants of kites dangling from trees and power lines made colourful buntings and reminded us of Easter for many weeks.

The Bandstand (also called *de Round House*) was also located on the Seawall. This rotunda was the venue for Saturday afternoon concerts performed by the Guyana Militia Band. This group of men were always immaculately dressed in full uniform and looked impressive when they performed. There was no cost involved, the band played solely to entertain the public and were rewarded with good attendance. That tradition died a long time ago so I was lucky to be privy to such a spectacle.

## Christmas and Flower Power

Christmas in any other part of the globe can never compare to what I experienced in Guyana. It was almost sacred in my opinion. The poorest of the poor made some sort of effort to prepare for this magical time. Bottom-'ouses became a hive of activity when people started sandpapering their old chairs and if you were lucky an old coffee table. These items were varnished or painted. My skirt was ruined one Christmas when I visited a friend and sat on a varnished chair that was not quite dry.

The intricately woven cane centre of our *Morris-chair* needed replacing, but that was wishful thinking. Christmas came and went and we were still sitting with our backsides hanging through the hole.

Sales for *lino* (linoleum) went up at Christmas; it was a priority for most people. We proudly fetched ours home on our shoulders. The look and smell of the new floor covering on Christmas morning added to our good cheer.

Artificial flowers at Christmas were a must. In the early days they were made from crepe paper, and then the wax and plastic variety made its way onto the market a few years before I left Guyana. No household was without a vase or six displaying these unsightly creations. The wall vases were extremely popular. We had two in the sitting room but they were obscured by the multi coloured wall.

Our flowers were mild compared to the Coolie people. Their homes could easily blind you with the bright colours they chose; there was hardly a place to stick a pin because they had never heard the term *less is best*. It was a standing joke whenever I visited an East Indian friend, but they knew I was pulling their leg when I said, "Yuh sure yuh 'ave enuff flowers?"

My youngest brother is married to an East Indian woman. I saw pictures of their new home recently and thought it was the Taj Mahal. I can afford to laugh at them because I have silk flowers and think that is classier. Some traditions never die so you don't dare laugh at my flowers.

We never had drapes to pull at night; instead curtains were a simple frill at the top and two longer lengths draped down the sides at both ends of the window. To be able to replace your curtains each Christmas was considered prosperous, so naturally Mummy wanted to impress. Secrecy and surprise was the name of the game at Christmas. No one divulged their purchases to their neighbours. Every item purchased was secretly brought into the home. This buying began months in advance because some bigger items had to be taken on hire purchase.

The house was securely locked up on Christmas Eve while the *titivating* was done. Opening our window on Christmas morning was similar to an opening ceremony of a new building. We knew the neighbours were peeping behind some crevice, because we were doing the same. How pathetic was that? That was bad enough but we had the gall to see if we recognised where the neighbours got the fabric for their curtains because no one wanted to be called, 'cheap'. I loved the whole concept of the Christmas conspiracy.

The year before I left Guyana we actually bought a *small-small* Christmas tree, it was so small we could barely see it, but hey, it had a string of lights and we were damn proud of it. The only thing missing was the *Angel Hair* (like gossamer). I was envious of anyone who had that *white stuff* draped over their tree.

Bing Crosby filled the airwaves with his rendition of 'I'm dreaming of a White Christmas' but the lyrics were as foreign to me as *crappo wearin' shoes*. I was only dreaming of having *garlic-pork* on Christmas morning.

Mummy always expected Daddy to give her some extra cash at Christmas so she could shop at one of the big supermarkets. That was a once a year treat. The shops were called Yong Hings and Kwan Hings; both shops were at the same intersection and owned by Chinese, as if you couldn't tell. The shopping fell to me one Christmas when my parents were giving each other the silent treatment. I was in awe of all the *furrin* goods and took the liberty of buying a small can of baked beans. I had no idea what it was but I was very anxious to taste it. The contents of the can barely afforded us a teaspoonful each. I also bought a tin of thickened cream, although I did not have a clue what to do with it. Those were all luxuries in our household.

My mother always *set* the *ginja beer* and *garlic pork,* and made the *black cake* the week before Christmas. The tedious job of *washin' de butta* always fell to me when she was ready to bake. The butter and water were stirred together to remove the salt content. The salted water was discarded and the process was repeated until the butter reached the desired taste. We could have used the tasty Blue Band margarine but my mother was convinced *washed butta* made a nicer cake.

The biggest extravagance was the Dutchman Head (Edam) cheese. It must have been reasonably priced because we always had a whole one. We could never afford ham but it didn't matter because the garlic-pork was traditional in our household. The *meche-meche* (residue) was always the best part.

I also recall my father making a special Hot Toddy on Christmas day. He heated milk with other ingredients, and then used the *swizzle stick* to make it *fraffy* (frothy). It was garnished with nutmeg.

## Muddah Sally and de Santapee Band

We began listening for the distinct sound of drums and flutes a week or so before Christmas. This was a telltale signal that the *Santapee* (Centipede) *or Maxkaraid* (masquerade) band was making its annual rounds. These colourful street characters attracted huge crowds wherever they appeared. The bands were in competition, so there was big *backanal* (trouble) when two bands clashed in the streets. Members of these bands were said to carry concealed weapons and sly injuries called 'stings' were inflicted when fighting broke out, hence the significance of the name 'Centipede'.

These bands comprised of African men who masqueraded as women. I encountered this theatrical spectacle in different neighbourhoods and assumed the central character was changed each year for variety. It wasn't until I was older that I realised there were more than one band.

One band featured a character called 'Mad Cow/Bull' and another kept us enthralled with the 'Laang Lady' (men dressed as women balancing on very tall stilts).

My favourite was Muddah Sally or Buum-buum Sally as she was more commonly known. This character mostly danced in Albouystown where I lived. Buum-buum Sally wore a dress and her underwear was padded to surreal proportions. Her *bamsie* (bottom) took on a wobbling appearance as she performed an energetic and suggestive dance. We were all captivated by this spectacle. At times, Buum-buum Sally seemed to go into a hypnotic trance and since this is an African custom, I guessed it was another form of Cumfa dancin'.

The repetition of the following sequence was the essence of the performance.

One of the characters dramatically recited a poetic incantation (something pertaining to Christmas or folklore) while there was a lull in the music. After reciting the ditty, he shouted, "Meeew-zick!" This was the cue for the flautist to put on a performance and build to a crescendo. It was a revenue raising act so the performer showed off his flouncing skills at this point. Spectators were happy to throw a few coins and cheered louder if the character was capable of picking up the coins while still in motion.

The offer of liquor from residents or shop owners enhanced these performances and provided excellent entertainment.

## Visiting Over the Festive Season

It was tradition to stay at home on Christmas day; in our family anyway. I attended midnight mass so I had no reason to leave the house. Celebrating the festive season began in earnest on Boxing Day and lasted until New Year. Boxing Day was also a very popular day for weddings; my brother and father both chose that day.

I revelled in visiting family and friends during the festive season. It was one time of the year where perks were guaranteed. The anticipation of a slice of *black cake*, a walnut, a cream filled biscuit and a glass of sweet-drink or ginger beer was heavenly . . . just don't forget your manners. The drink could have been the most delicious but it was considered *good manners* to leave a little portion in the glass. That is one custom I left at Atkinson Airport.

I always took the walnut home because I was too afraid of breaking my teeth in someone's presence. Every time I break a walnut I remember those times.

Any hostess serving a drink and a biscuit was considered stingy. I wanted a *real treat* so steered clear of those misers the following year.

As you can see I was always thinking of my stomach. I wonder what nostalgic memories the children of today will have.

## Hindu Ceremonies

There were a lot of Hindus living in this area; some built temples in their gardens and practised their religious beliefs daily. We had such a family living directly opposite us. I learnt a little about their customs by spending time in their home. One of the girls and I played cards so she explained a few things. Following in the Hindu tradition this family hosted feasts for the poor from time to time. A steady procession of people dressed in traditional robes started trickling in to the appointed venue from mid-morning. It looked as if it was a pilgrimage to Mecca with the men in their white Dhotis and turbans and the women in their Saris. Fires were built in the yard and huge cast-iron pots were used to cook the Indian cuisine. The delicious aroma wafted over the neighbourhood and I sharpened my teeth.

A bamboo pole with a piece of coloured cloth tied to the end was erected alongside the temple after a *Jhandi* (a religious celebration/thanksgiving). Hindus also held a *Pooja* celebration. I never took the time to find out the significance of these ceremonies; I was only interested in the food. The poor were fed on such occasions and the neighbours were also invited to partake. I especially enjoyed the vermicelli with raisins.

There was, and still is a place called the 'Dharam Shala' in Albouystown. A wealthy businessman donated this building for the *down an' out*. The people who took refuge there went out begging each day because food was not provided; it was mostly a place to bed down. An invitation was always issued to the Dharam Shala inmates when someone performed one of those aforementioned ceremonies. There were two other Indian celebrations I enjoyed; one was called Phagwah and the other was Deepavali or Diwali, as it was most commonly called. The *Diwali* (festival of lights) was spectacular; especially if you lived in an area where there were many East Indians. Hundreds of *diyas* (tiny mud/clay cups filled with ghee) were lit around their entire home and garden. Traditional sweets were always shared with neighbours the day after the celebration.

The Phagwah festival was to celebrate an important victory of importance in their culture. Red Kool-Aid was made in large quantities to represent blood and unsuspecting passersby got doused; although this game was mostly played among the respective families. Talcum powder was substituted for guests who were not too thrilled about having stained clothing. I copped stains a few times when I played Phagwah with my East Indian friends; it was great fun!

Talking about the Dharam Shala reminds me of the elderly in homes. Nursing homes did not exist. The one establishment I distinctly remember was the Alms House (also called de Palms); although you wouldn't send your dog there. The building looked as if a bomb had ripped through it. Praise the Lord we never had to put any of our relatives in there. It is traditional for families to care for their elderly parents . . . the lack of facilities had no bearing on this custom, it was a given. The reverence for our ancestors was genuine; we enjoyed having them in our midst and would never dream of putting them in a home unless it was absolutely necessary.

The closest I ever got to de Palms was sighting it on my way to the Botanical Garden and that was also unpleasant. Magnificent Cannonball trees grew opposite the Palms but I was always revolted by the aroma in the vicinity. The heady fragrance of the Cannonball flowers was distorted by the overuse of disinfectant from this oppressive building.

When I began dating my husband I discovered his mother sent his younger sisters to *de Palms* to take a little sweet-mout' for some of the residents. Mrs Martin did not know any of the residents personally; it was simply a gesture of pure kindness. I want to spring a leak just thinking of her generosity and good hearted nature. She was one in a million and treated everyone with dignity and respect. My memoir would not be complete unless I pay tribute to this wonderful lady named Carmen Martin. Just recently in my Life Writing class we were asked to write about a legend and I would like to share what I wrote about a very inspirational lady who happened to be my late mother-in-law.

## A True Legend

There are many legends or people that have inspired me over the years. I can reel off the top of my head many as I was born in a part of the world where legends and myths are plentiful. As a child I was regaled with stories of Obeah, Jumbie and Ol' higue which I believed to be gospel. At a deeper level I believe there are certain supernatural powers; especially since I encountered such a mystery. However, I have no desire to delve into those mysteries; I relinquish the hocus-pocus to the witch doctors and those who truly believe.

Some legends are fictitious, and many become legends for the wrong reason. I would like to sing the praises of a *true legend*. We, our family that is, all affectionately called her 'Mops', but her real name is Carmen. I first met this amazing woman one evening when my boyfriend took me to his home. Carmen was his mother. She was certainly not a striking beauty in my eyes, but she captured my heart the first time we met. I did not know it then, but Carmen was to become my mother-in-law and greatest ally. This unassuming woman had the capacity to love anyone she came in contact with, and in turn everyone who crossed her path gravitated towards her. It didn't matter whether you met Mops in the street or in a crowded room, it was all the same. She gave you her undivided attention, making you believe you were the only person on earth that mattered to her . . . It was magical. I believe I was the luckiest daughter-in-law in the entire world, and that wasn't because I was her only daughter-in-law. She treated me as equally as any of her five daughters and in time I thought and felt like I was actually her daughter. Mops accepted everyone exactly as they were; I never heard an unkind word spoken by this wonderful woman in all the years she was alive. I learnt not to complain about broken crockery because Mops pointed out that businesses will have to close if nothing ever broke. She saw the good in every situation and taught me valuable lessons that I live by today.

Mops immigrated to Australia and in no time captivated everyone she came in contact with. She was smitten with her grandchildren whom she loved unconditionally. Her unique way of loving was such that each child believed he or she was her favourite. It didn't seem fair that our dear Mops lost her life after being reunited with her family after only two years. It may have been a short period but it was long enough to leave her imprint in their hearts.

They say beauty is in the eyes of the beholder. Some judge a person by their exterior beauty, but after knowing Mops I can tell you there is no beauty as pure as the inner beauty, our beloved Mops possessed. That dear lady told me six weeks before her death that I would never want for anything. It's been twenty-eight years now and her prediction is spot on so far. I firmly believe she guides and looks over us each day. Legends like Mops are rare in these modern times. We were truly blessed.

## Elvis Is Alive and Well

Talking about legends, I will ask for your discretion with this privileged information I'm about to share with you. Mummy always said, "gyard it wid yuh life" when something was special so I am begging you not to *waalk wid yuh mout'* (spread gossip) after you hear what I have to say. I couldn't keep this secret any longer. Would I be correct in saying, everyone wants to know the real truth about Elvis? Well I am only going to tell you okay, come a bit closer because I don't want anyone else to hear. There are a lot of *schupid* people looking for Elvis, and many have claimed sighting him in all corners of the globe. All wrong of course, and why? No one has taken the time to look for him in Guyana. I guess Elvis knew it was safe to go there, because it's behind god's back. When a Guyanese says, "A'swear to God" you know they are telling the truth and they wouldn't lie to you. I have proof that Elvis is in Guyana because when I visited my father in 2000 I heard his muddah yelling, "El—vis, yuh dinnah ready bhai." You know me, I was at that window in a flash, but it was getting dark and all I saw was his shadow. I think he changed his colour. And don't let me tell you how many imposters there are in Guyana. I asked Daddy what he knew about the Elvis living next door. He laughed and said, "Yuh mekin' sport chap, gyurl a'loss count how many Elvis livin' round dis naabahood." I guess the only way we could know the truth is to start digging like Mummy to get to the bottom of the story. I think we should put all of them in a room and play that game we see on television; the one where they ask the *real* person to stand up. But it still won't be easy because every Elvis in Guyana is black!

## Changing a Child's Name

While we are on the subject of names, I will tell you what happens to the perfectly good name our parents bestow on us at birth. In no time someone shortens it or it disappears completely. I noticed the East

Indians always had at least one child in their family called, *Gyurlie, Boyie, Boysie* or *Brudsey*. They are too lazy to remember the child's name, so if it's a girl, it is easier to say *Gyurlie*, you get my drift? Another thing they do is call their last child 'Baby'; that name stays with them to adulthood. Eh eh, ah jus' rememba anada funny story. This anecdote is connected to the name Buddy. I can't begin to tell you how many men I know that are called *Buddy*, but this is a truh-truh story that happened to me. A friend asked me to accompany her to an East Indian wedding at B.V. The name of that place is so long, but in true Guyanese style we abbreviated it to B.V. Okay, I'll tell you the correct name. It is Beterverwagting; now, can you see why we had to shorten it? Try pronouncing it. Don't bother because only a Guyanese or the Dutch can do that. I will break it down to the closest sound for you. It sounds like, *Betta-fuh-actin'*. Most of the names of our villages are derived from the Dutch influence, some I have forgotten how to spell, but this is not a spelling lesson so I won't bore you with that. Let's get back to the story about me going to the wedding. I was not invited by the bride or groom; never met either one, but in Guyana no one needed a formal invitation to attend a wedding in those days, especially when it came to Indian weddings. A family member of someone named Buddy came to ask me a favour when she heard I was going to the wedding. Buddy was an invited guest so she asked me to deliver a small parcel to him. Her instructions were, "Jus' akse anyone at de weddin' fuh Buddy, deh gon no 'e by 'e *push teet*' (protruding teeth). Like I said, I was going with a friend and didn't know anyone. East Indian weddings are huge affairs that last for days. This wedding was especially large; there were people spilling out into the street, but I finally found an opportunity to ask a lady if she knew Buddy. To my surprise she asked, which one? Since I was not given a surname I told her I did not know. She offered to call him via her vocal cords; no loud-speaker was necessary. "Buu-uudeeee, a'gyurl want fuh see yuh, come to de backstep now if yuh 'ear meh." Within a minute there were five men named Buddy standing in front of me. Sheila was right, it would have been easy to find him, but in the excitement I had forgotten her instruction . . . sorry Sheila.

Also if you are looking for a place to stay in Guyana, I can tell you that 'Buddy's International Hotel' looks like a good choice; this hotel was built specially for the World Series cricket a few years ago . . . I hope they send me the advertising fees!

Identifying people by their infirmity is another t'ing Guyanese are famous for. I have been sent to look for people with *cock-eye*, *big-foot*, *finnie 'an'/leg*, *faffey-eye* and *cocabey* to name a few. I will have to explain those to you if you are not Guyanese. *Big-foot* in medical terms is Elephantiasis; a *finnie 'an'/leg* is someone with a withered limb. *Cocabey* is a term we used for leprosy. And how did we know if someone had this affliction? We simply assumed that multiple patches of pink skin were enough of a telltale sign. Missing appendages also gave rise to speculation and there were quite a few who displayed that trait. I personally knew an old *ropey* (extremely wrinkled) Putagee woman who had all of her fingers missing and it was said she had cocabey. The Leprosy Asylum was in Berbice, which was quite a distance from Georgetown where I lived. I never went there in all the years I lived in Guyana so I can't say in all honesty that I've seen or been in contact with real leprosy cases.

I personally had a few relatives who had *faffey-eye* (rheumy eyes) and it was not a pretty sight. Lack of medical treatment was a contributing factor in many of these ailments.

## My Darling Gramuddah Francesca

Just typing that heading makes me spring a leak; I adored *Ol' Francesca*. That was what Mummy called her. Behind her back, it was *de Ol' Higue*. There wasn't too much love lost between those two, but at least there was a healthy respect. I heard through the grapevine that Gramuddah thought Daddy was too good for one of Jose D'Agrella daughters. Gramuddah was a staunch Catholic and I believe that was another reason she didn't like Mummy. She believed Daddy was led astray from the Catholic faith to become a Seventh Day Adventist. I met this grandmother when we lived in Pomeroon but we rarely visited her because she lived way down d'Riva and since we lived closer to Mummy's parents we visited them more often. When my brothers and I began spending school holidays in d'Riva we stayed with Mummy's parents but they always took us to spend a few days with Ol' Francesca. We even spent a day or two with Aunt Maud at Buxton. When I was thirteen I wanted to spend equal time with both grandmothers, and it was easily arranged because our school holiday was over two months long. I think Mummy was happy to see the three of us go because it gave her some peace and she didn't have to feed us. From that time onwards I really got to know Daddy's mother. That was when I realised where my trait of crying came from for that woman cried at a drop of a hat. Mummy had no patience for her, and once said, "Ol' Francesca cries for everyt'in'; she wood cry if sh' see a' dog punishin' to shit." Yep, that is exactly how Mummy said it; no one minced words in our family. *Ow meh goi*, that was cruel, I have to defend Gramuddah as she and I were so much alike. We have a soft heart and feel sympathy for any kind of suffering, regardless of it being a constipated dog.

I've told you about my grandfather and his reputation. Everyone knew everyone in d'Riva and stories got around. Daddy always cracked up whenever he told this story. Like me, Gramuddah was deathly afraid of crappos and Granfaddah got wind of this information. He chose the biggest crappo, put it in a box and took it to Charity. He knew Gramuddah always went to Charity on Market-day so he went in search of her and after the usual greeting was exchanged, it was time for business. Granfaddah took the crappo out and told Ol' Francesca he wanted her to kiss it. She was petrified and could not bring herself to do it, but she knew Ol' Joe was a persuasive man so she tried to compromise. Fear got the better of her and she tearfully said, "Sarry Mr Agrella, a'just cyan't kiss de crappo, but a'gon shake 'e 'an'." Can you imagine allowing someone to bully you like that? Especially when that person was her son's father-in-law; he was only a few years younger than her. She always called him Mr Agrella and was scared of him because of the things she heard he had done to other people. It was mostly wicked pranks like the crappo stunt. I will admit, I have a warped sense of humour, although I would never overstep the boundaries like Granfaddah.

Here is a bit of family history for you . . . one of Granfaddah's brothers married Daddy's oldest sister, Mary (the one we called Aunty May); remember the dress length saga? See how they had to remove one letter from Mary to shorten it to May? Anyway the family tree does have many close branches!!!

## Gramuddah's Fashion Sense

A few years after I left Guyana Aunty Rita invited my grandmother to go to England for an extended holiday; all was well until it turned cold. The Ol' woman from d'Riva could not take it; she refused to leave the house. One day Aunty Rita put her foot down and told Gramuddah to put on her coat and boots because they were going out. No problem, she was ready in no time. Aunty Rita found her waiting by the front door wearing her dressing gown and bedroom slippers . . . guess she figured they were warm enough.

This old lady was very modest; most of her ankle length dresses were floral patterns in subdued colours. All of them had high necks and long sleeves; a belt in the matching fabric prevented her bubbies from escaping below her waist and she always wore a hat to church.

Talking about *bubbie*, I almost forgot I was going to tell you what I got up to under that dunks tree. Fantasising and titivatin' was what I did under those bushes. I wanted to have bubbies too, so I pretended I had some and was wearing a brassiere. I took one of Daddy's belts and tied it across my chest just to feel the strap. Come on, I bet some of you have done that too, and I think I used that stolen mirror to check for pimples.

Gramuddah must have had her bath before I woke up or after I went to bed because I never saw her using the bathroom. Only one personal routine was performed in my presence. She undid her braided hair each evening when she got into bed; brushed it and slept with it undone; it was pure white and beautiful. It was always plaited and coiled onto her head by the time I got up in the morning.

It is amazing how a person can say very little yet convey so much. Ol' Francesca was one such person.

My Grandmother Francesca on holiday in London

My Grandmother Francesca & Uncle Mike going to Charity

## Holidays at Gramuddah's Farm

When my brothers and I began spending time at Try-bes', we broke the journey at Charity by spending the night at Aunt Phil. I can still picture her white hair as she stood on the side of the road when Patsy stopped at the end of the line. As soon as we got to her home, one of us had the job of *runnin' dung* (catching) the fowl she pointed out in the chicken pen. On occasion she asked me to *ketch* a peel-neck-fowl and that meant we were going to have chicken soup. She always said they were *sweeter* (tastier). Within an hour I was enjoying a beautiful chicken soup or chicken curry. A *peel or clean-neck-fowl* is a species that has a small section of its neck devoid of feathers.

Gramuddah picked us up early the following morning in her big *bulluhoo* to take us to Try-bes'. This seemed to take forever; the anticipation was as exciting as the trip itself. The first time we went to Gramuddah she advised us never to swim in the waterside if the tide was high when we arrived. She explained the hidden dangers my uncles might have added in our absence; stumps for instance. She said we might land on one when diving and get seriously hurt. The tide is not consistent in d'Riva; one week it would rise in the morning then the following week it did the reverse. We could not swim when the tide went out because the landin' becomes a mudflat.

Having the distraction of the farm was good because we could only swim once a day when the tide was high. My brothers and I could not swim when we first went to Pomeroon, but with the waterside close by we learned to swim in no time. Looking back, I realise that none of the adults bothered to supervise us when we went off to swim. I have even more reason to believe what Norma said about us having a few guardian angels; we could have easily drowned. Again, it was common sense that prevailed. We checked to see what part was the shallowest and started practicing tentatively until we became expert swimmers. I don't mean Olympic standard, just enough to keep our heads above water and save ourselves. We spent hours in that waterside; we did not get out until our lips were blue and we were shivering. On the rare occasion Gramuddah had to tell us to get out, but she was mostly tolerant and allowed us to have fun.

Saying goodbye to Gramuddah at the end of the holiday was a very traumatic experience because we both leaked so badly; it was not a pretty sight. Anyone watching would think I was going overseas and never coming back.

## Try-bes' was The Best

My grandmother lived at Try-bes' with three of her adult children when I was growing up. There was Aunty Agnes who we also called *Glerie*, *Gler* or *Banks* and uncles; Mike (Michael) and Naysh (Ignatius/Natius). My cousin Compton also lived there. The women occupied the main bedroom; Uncle Mike and Cousin Compton had the little bedroom and Uncle Naysh slept in a hammock in the sitting room. I can't remember him ever using a mosquito net; he was really tough. Extra hammocks were hung up for my brothers, but I slept with Gramuddah. When Aunty Glerie left home I took over her bed. Uncle Mike and Cousin Compton eventually built a small logee down the dam and moved out, but Gramuddah still cooked their meals. Cousin Compton is Aunty Mary's eldest son but he called his grandmother 'Muddah' because she raised him from a baby.

Gramuddah's home was especially welcoming and cosy; I loved everything about it. The bedrooms were completely enclosed, while the rest of the home had low walls. It was an open plan that allowed full view of the farm from every angle. My emotions were akin to reverence whenever I was ensconced in Gramuddah's bedroom. It was sacred to sneak a peek into her antique dresser; nosing around the naphthalene scented embroidered items. Best of all, I enjoyed reading the news on her walls. Recycled newspaper was not only used to block up the cracks to prevent a draft; it was also used as wallpaper. Insects eventually ate the paper because the paste she used was made from flour and water. I knew every news item by heart before it was renewed.

The sitting room was sparsely furnished with a few *Nibee* (local fiber) chairs and Uncle Naysh's permanently hung hammock. The floor boards were bare of rugs or polish; Gramuddah or Aunty Agnes had to get down on their hands and knees to scrub them; they were always spotless. I helped with the scrubbing when I got older.

There was no need for an alarm clock in d'Riva or in town for that matter. We were awoken by fowl-cock crowin' at fo'day marnin', and alerted by the ever reliant six o'clock bee at dusk. The pitch black canopy at night was illuminated by myriads of twinkling *candle-flies* (fireflies) reminding us it was time for bed. Although no reminder was necessary; we went to bed pretty early to escape the mosquitoes. I didn't mind because it was so cozy under the net, and the night serenade always picked up speed soon after I retired. It was sheer bliss listening to the harmonious symphony of the night creatures. The orchestra was led by the frog quartet croaking in tune; the crickets played bass and the mosquitoes buzzed in harmony; the odd owl hooted for the heck of it. No music was sweeter.

There was so much to do on the farm that we always planned our agenda the night before. It might be to check on the sapodillas to see if they were ready; those mangoes that were not quite ready two days ago, or that bird nest with the pale blue eggs to see if they had hatched. Fishing was always on the agenda, and we were always so proud when we caught a few to take home to Gramuddah. The day after we arrived at Try-bes' I always went out and picked a heap of *full sapodillas* (mature fruit), wrapped them in banana leaves then hid my stash under a thick bush. There is no other fruit to equal a sweet sapodilla.

It was no secret that Ol' Francesca idolised me. She had dozens of grandchildren; she loved them all, and I am sure the others will tell you she idolised them too. That beautiful lady was very generous with her affection; she gathered us all to her naphthalene scented bosom and loved us dearly. Spending school holidays with her was sheer bliss. I got to sleep in the cosy four poster bed with her. I always slept by the wall so Gramuddah could creep out at fo'day marnin' to get breakfast for my uncles without disturbing me. I stayed in bed until I heard, "Ellen, get up, yuh fry plantin an' salfish ready." I went to the kitchen; said, "Marnin' Gramuddah;" then I leaned over the windowless wall of the kitchen to wash away the *boo-boo* (gunk from eyes) and brush my teeth before sitting down to enjoy the amazing breakfast only Gramuddah knew how to prepare. She did this every single morning for me; sometimes it was bakes an' salfish. She always had the hottest peppersauce to doctor it, so I was in heaven.

No prodding was necessary to get me to visit the bushy *wiri-wiri* (variety of pepper) tree. Plucking a handful each day was sheer pleasure; no other pepper can equal its unique flavour. When in season the tree was magnificent; the tiny peppers resembled baubles on a Christmas tree. She also had a *bird-pepper* tree, those peppers were hot!

We dined at a huge table in her spacious kitchen. There was a big fireside in the corner where all of the mouth watering dishes were cooked in big blackened pots. My uncles often brought home a pigeon, plover or spurwing they had shot in the backdam. It was plucked and hung over the fireside to be smoked. Sweet-corn season was something to look forward to. We ate copious amounts so the cooking was an outside job; in the yard that is. Gramuddah cooked the corn in a large kerosene tin over a roaring fire. The corn was made even sweeter when she cooked them in fresh coconut milk. We enjoyed sucking off the rich curdled cream that clung to the kernels. The corn was sometimes boiled in salted water, and sometimes roasted on the glowing embers of a dying fire. Roast corn was my favourite. Then there was corn porridge; definitely not my favourite unless it was served with lashings of Carnation milk and that was a luxury. We certainly lived like the Amerindians when corn was in season; it was served at every meal. The kerosene tin was also used to cook crabs when they were marching. Crabs always marched in August when we were there and we enjoyed feasting on fresh crabs cooked in coconut milk.

There was an abundance of dried coconuts on the farm which Gramuddah used to make her own cooking oil. We helped to throw the coconuts into the trench so they could float down from the backdam with the tide. We pulled them out when they arrived in front of the house and piled them close to the kitchen steps. Making the coconut oil was a tedious and back breaking job. A spike implanted in the ground was used to remove the coconut husk. Breaking the nut in two even halves was tricky, but Gramuddah had the knack of knowing just where to hit it with the back of the cutlass. I waited with my cup to catch the sweet juice. She sat on a flat piece of iron with fangs and expertly grated the flesh from the shell. A large number of coconuts were needed to produce one decent bottle of oil. At the end of the cooking process there were some *meche-meche* (residue) we called *chanchie*. I enjoyed eating it with a sprinkle of sugar. It was very rich and I always got *buck-sick* from over indulgence. There was nothing nicer than green plantains fried in the fresh coconut oil, with a bit drizzled on for good measure.

Parching coffee was a weekly chore, because it had to be fresh. The coffee beans were grown on the farm, but Gramuddah did not have a coffee hulling factory like Ol' Joe, so she took hers to be hulled at a neighbour. The old cast-iron mill she screwed onto the kitchen rail had a little half tray that slotted in neatly at the bottom to catch the coffee granules when it was being ground. The aroma was ever present and clung invitingly to the kitchen.

Sitaram and Maria were Gramuddah's closest neighbours; they were an ancient East Indian couple, *Surra an' Durra* (devoted to one another). They lived *'an'-to-mout'*; but no one would know because they never complained and always had a smile on their faces. As a mark of respect we called them Mac-may and Cumpay. One of Maria's arms was *finnie*, and although Sitaram very old and had a *faffey-eye* he was he still able to earn a living by doing odd jobs on neighbouring farms. He sometimes worked for Gramuddah when it was harvesting season. I used to run down to the dam to see them in their tiny hut and one day I slipped and fell into the trench; Sitaram was quick to the rescue.

There was always billowing smoke coming from their home, probably to keep the sand flies at bay. Sitaram was so happy to see me one holiday; he gave me one of his prized chickens.

Returning to Try-bes' in 1984 is something I have always regretted. I don't mean d'Riva; I will always want to go to Pomeroon. My sisters cannot understand the attraction; they went once and were attacked by mosquitoes so they never went back. I am talking about *Try-bes'* where I spent all my school holidays when I was growing up.

Gramuddah was aging and had become dependent; she had to move to Charity to live with Aunt Phil. Dolly (Aunt Maud's daughter) now lived at Try-bes' and I assumed she had taken over Gramuddah's home. Melancholy set in when I saw the modern house on stilts instead of the old familiar homestead. My little bit of paradise was gone. Try-bes' was not the same, but the memories still remain as strong as ever. No one can take that away except for Mr Dementia, and I am praying he never visits. I have the broom turned upside down, so let him try.

We were asked to write a fictional story titled: 'A cheerful place to visit' in my Creative Writing class. I could not think of another place more cheerful to visit than Try-bes', so this is what I wrote.

## A Cheerful Place to Visit

The rising tide is slowly covering the exposed roots of the mangrove trees along the river bank. They all look alike until the boat comes to the next bend in the river. Standing guard at the end of a long stelling is a lone giant mangrove. This is the landmark for Grandmother's place. The noise of the motor alerts Teddy who comes running; tail wagging in greeting.

The water level in the boat house is perfect; Uncle Mike kills the motor then expertly guides the boat into the narrow mooring. Three of the six steps leading up to the stelling are covered today, but the tide will fall before it reaches the top. The thatched roof of the little home is barely visible above the built up dam that runs the length of the property. The high dam is necessary to keep out the river that sometimes overflows in the rainy season. The dam between the homestead and river is a mosaic of discarded coconut husks; it prevents slipping in wet weather. A slight incline from the dam leads to a bridge over a narrow trench before entering the yard. The fish and tadpoles darting between the beautiful water lilies are interrupted by humans on wash days; not forgetting Teddy who enjoys plunging in to cool off. The sight of brightly coloured pots made from discarded oil drums overflowing with every variety of croton and other tropical flowering shrubs takes my breath away. These huge flower pots are dotted around the freshly swept yard that is bare of grass. A beautiful humming bird appears to be frozen in mid air as it sips nectar from an obliging hibiscus. The ducks and chickens are happily scratching in the dirt looking for a morsel. Washing is flapping between the two giant golden-apple trees that are used to harness the clothes line. A small fat piglet waddles off to join its mother and siblings lying under the star-apple tree that shades their sty. A hammock slung on the open verandah beckons invitingly. The huge mango tree on the right of the cottage is straining with bunches of half ripened fruit which a hungry flock of colourful parrots are trying to devour. Sturdy young banana suckers can be seen in the first field of the farm which begins just beyond the back of the house. Smoke billows from the kitchen into the cloudless blue sky and the smell of Grandmother's cooking reaches my nostrils. Grandmother materialises on the kitchen steps wiping her hands on her apron as she prepares to greet me. The sound of laughter startles me, but to my surprise it's Laura the parrot. She is sitting on top of her cage under the house laughing as if she were human. Uncle Mike deposits my bag on the stairs, whistles for Teddy and leaves for the farm as Grandmother and I embrace. We climb the stairs to enjoy a cool drink and a long chat in her airy windowless kitchen that overlooks the tranquil river.

I do not have a single picture of Gramuddah's place, not that it matters, because it is etched into my memory forever. That was my little *cocoon of love* where I always felt secure and welcomed.

## Aunt Maud and Her Tribe

Spending time with Aunt Maud and her tribe was a foreign experience. I never went to boarding school, but I have a feeling the sleeping arrangements and atmosphere would be the same as that household. I cannot remember Uncle Jose; he died when I was very little and Aunt Maud was left to raise eight boys. God bless her sweet nature; she still had room in her heart and home to include us. Aunt Maud cooked in huge pots and had the longest dining room table I've ever seen. That table looked like a feeding trough at meal times. She managed to feed everyone, and if we weren't satisfied, we always had the fruit trees on the farm. The older boys had to weed the farm, so we spent most of the day in the fields. That was when we weren't swimming at the waterside. The older boys swam out to the middle of the river to show off, but I was scared to venture too far; especially after *Spida* (Harold) gave me a duckin'. The depth in Aunt Maud's waterside seemed to go from shallow to drowning and I swallowed a lot of water while swimming at Buxton. I preferred the familiarity of Gramuddah's waterside.

Sleeping head to tail was standard in large families; there were no spare beds for extra guests, so we just wedged in wherever we could find room. We got up to all sorts of mischief under those mosquito nets. I was the only girl and it was a bit intimidating. The boys told dirty jokes and egged me on to show them my naughty bits, but I threatened to tell Aunt Maud. I was more than curious but scared of them at the same time.

Aunt Maud reared pigs to sell; the pen was huge with sows and boars the size of small rhinoceros. Those pigs stank and tried to attack us if we went too close to the rails. I braved the stink just to gaze at the beautiful piglets and was allowed to hold one if an adult was around. The pigs were fattened up to be sold at Christmas. One was always slaughtered to make *garlic pork* (pork marinated in vinegar, garlic thyme and peppers) for the tribe. You should see the giant size *jimmy jar* (an earthenware container) my aunt marinated the pork in.

Aunt Maud tied the knot for the second time with a man who was half Amerindian. Uncle Teddy finally gave her the daughter she always wanted. They christened her Dolores but in no time she was being called Dolly. Toty (Theodore) was next but Aunt Maud closed the maternity shop after that.

This aunt made the best cassava bread and that was what she was doing when I paid her a surprise visit in 1984. The thatched roof of her home was a mosaic of cassava cakes when I arrived. Cassava bread is dried in the sun before storing. Aunt Maud was standing alongside the roaring fire tending to the cassava cake on the pan. This distraction gave me ample opportunity to creep close to the breadfruit tree next to the little cooking hut before I yelled, "SURPRISE!" Her face lit up when she saw me, and in between her joyous laughter she said, "Yuh sly bitch; yuh come to see meh at las'." Then we embraced and cried our hearts out. It was to be the last time I saw that darling woman.

Aunt Maud baking Cassava Bread at Buxton in 1984

## Visiting My Cousins at McKenzie

Guyana's Bauxite Mining Company is located at McKenzie; a place only accessible via the Demerara River when I was growing up. A highway was built in the late sixties, but I never had the opportunity to travel on it. I had heard all sorts of intriguing stories about this mining town and my curiosity was piqued . . . I wanted to see McKenzie, and I wished we had relatives or friends living there so I could visit. Anyway the opportunity finally presented itself when Aunt Maud's sons Kenneth and Brian got jobs and went to live there in a house owned by the Bauxite Company . . . overnight guests were not allowed. That was not a problem because Daphne and I only wanted to go on a day trip. McKenzie is only sixty-five miles from Georgetown, but the trip seemed to take forever. We boarded the motor vessel R.H. Carr pretty early in the morning and got there by midday. The return journey to Georgetown departed around 4 p.m. (I think), which didn't leave us much time to see the place properly. Brian came home to have lunch with us and returned to work so we were left to our own devices. We took a walk around the streets, but there wasn't much to see and we had no means of venturing further to explore. I left McKenzie very disillusioned and came to the conclusion it was a boring place. I thanked my lucky stars I was not stuck there. Recently, thanks to the World Wide Web I read some fascinating stories of people who grew up in McKenzie and felt I missed out on the opportunity to explore a very interesting place.

## My Unforgettable Uncle Naysh

My memoir would not be complete unless I delight you with a few tales of my vagabond uncle; the one christened Ignatius. Most of the family called him Natius, but I called him Uncle Naysh. Wickedness lurked in his eyes and in his smile. In all of Guyana he was the most *lawliss* (lawless) and *wutliss* (worthless) person I ever knew. He is Daddy's little brother, the last child in their family. He never grew up; another Peter Pan character. His many older sisters spoilt him rotten; unfortunately it back fired and he thought he could get away with murder. I almost thought I would be witness to one on more than one occasion. I praise the Lord it never came to that. Uncle Naysh was over six foot tall and *magga-magga* (very thin); he drank gallons of *caffee* from an old chipped enamel cup that was big enough to be a posy. He lived at home with Gramuddah when I was growing up and I can tell you, he ruled the roost. That poor old woman lived in fear of him. Gramuddah got up before cock crowed to have Uncle Naysh's *caffee* and breakfast ready because he always left at *fo'day marnin'* to go to the backdam. He occasionally overslept and I would hear him say, "Dayclean a'ready muddah?" *Dayclean* is another word that means *daybreak,* but it was mostly used by the country folks. He came home for lunch depending on the distance of the field he was working in on a given day. If he wasn't coming home, he *waalked wid* some cassava bread or left over bakes and salfish to eat in the fields. He drank coconut watah to quench his thirst. Uncle Naysh always had a cutlass and a *fawk-stick* (a stick with a forked end) in his hands. This device is used to rake the vines and branches together; all the farmers in Pomeroon had fork-sticks. Uncle Naysh always wore *laang-boots* (gum boots) to work in the backdam. It must have been uncomfortable in that heat but it was a safe guard from snakes. If Uncle Naysh came home for lunch he always sat on the steps to take off his boots; sometimes when they were full of mud he rinsed them off in the trench, then turned them upside down over the two sticks he had planted in the yard for that purpose. He never ever wore socks, so I guess moisture would have built up and he turned them upside down to dry them out. I am figuring this out now because I never stopped to analyse any of these things when I was a child. I just remember it was something he did with regularity. My uncle was known to be a scoundrel; he had no shame or inhibition. He stripped stark naked whenever he got the urge. Whenever he did this Gramuddah would say, "Natius, yuh gon bline de chirren, put yuh clothes on bhai." It was water off a duck's back; he just gave one of his wicked belly laughs and replied, "Deh shud shut deh eye if deh doan want to see meh cack." I always hid in Gramuddah's bedroom so I could peek through the hole where the paper had peeled and cracked. Gramuddah could not stand the humiliation so she usually found a chore out in the yard and left him to the airing. When he had enough he retired to his hammock in the sitting room; that was his bed. This was all very normal behaviour to me when I was growing up; boy did I laugh.

Uncle Naysh was always diggin' *pimpla* (thorns) out from his hands; the farm was infested with them. Mummy used to have a field day removing the ones embedded in my feet and hands when I got back to Georgetown.

The vagabond always had a story to tell and they were mostly wicked; not vulgar; mostly stories of practical jokes he or others had played on people. [I was cursed with a warped sense of humour from both sides of the family]. I don't think Uncle Naysh would mind me telling you this story. He went out on a drinking spree one night and did not get home until late the following morning. We smelt him before we saw him, and it wasn't the rum fumes this time. His face was dirty, so I innocently said, "Wha' is dat on yuh face Uncle Naysh?" He ran his hand over his face, smelt it, and exploded, "A'gon get dem fuckers fuh dis." It appears his drinking buddies had given him a fowl-shit facial while he was out cold. I am laughing so hard I can barely type. A'need a'caffee-tea, but a'comin' back to tell yuh more.

Uncle Naysh, Grandmother (Francesca) and Aunty Rita

Uncle Naysh hugging my sister-in-law Gale, his defacto wife Bibi
and three children on right

## A Tiger Called Natius

The temptation of strayin' to the backdam was ever present while we lived at this address; my brothers went many times without Mummy's knowledge or consent. *Tambrin* (tamarind) trees were plentiful so they always brought some back. I dipped the acid fruit into a mixture of hot peppersauce and salt . . . *maan*, don't let me tell you about the *edge teet'* (sensitive teeth) I had afterward, this condition lasted for a few days. Drinking *ice-watah* was very unpleasant, but it never stopped me from enjoying tambrin. [My husband and I found Tamarind trees growing on the beach in Cairns when we holidayed there some years ago. I was in heaven and as you know I always *waalk wit'* peppersauce. It was a trip down memory lane for me].

I constantly suffered from *edge teet'* when we spent school holidays at Try-bes' because Gramuddah had the biggest tambrin tree and if the mangoes were still green I made *chow-chow*, so that added to my misery.

To this day I am intrigued by that tamarind tree for it held secret fears. We were told a ghost was *gyardin' a'Dutch jug* (guarding treasure) that was buried under the tree. Gramuddah said she saw the ghost on occasion. She also warned us to be extra careful and not to venture far, for tigers roamed the backdam. That intrigued us even more; we could not resist the temptation and sneaked a trip from time to time. I always had my stash of peppersauce and salt wrapped in a piece of newspaper so I could start eating as soon as we got to the tree. Joel always had a sharp cutlass so he could kill the tiger that may attack us (wink-wink) because he was the *big bruddah*.

Uncle Naysh always left for the backdam at fo'day marnin' so we did not see much of him. That man was a wicked sod. We were on a mission one day to get tambrin; armed with salt an' pepper we bade Gramuddah farewell. Our first stop was the *psidium* (fruit) tree to fill our bellies before continuing the long walk along the dam. We were coming up to the tamarind tree when a low deep growl stopped us in our tracks. My heart started pounding with fright, but we didn't panic—not yet! We had a good look to the field of banana trees on our left, then to the neighbour's field on the right, but there was no sign of the tiger. Joel was starting to use bad words; only when he was out of earshot of Mummy or

Gramuddah. He was feeling really brave so he said, "Le'-le' 'e co-come, a'go-gon chop 'e fu-fu-fuckin' 'ead off'!" With that show of confidence we decided it was safe to start walking again. We hadn't gone more than five feet when a loud growl turned our jelly legs running towards the direction of home. I started shouting, "Run quick boys, run quick-quick!" *De Clock* had gone with us on this holiday and boy you should see us run. We stopped running as soon as the sound of hilarious wicked laughing reached our ears. Only one person laughed like that and in an instant we knew who the tiger was. I could have strangled Uncle Naysh with my bare hands. My heart was still thumping and my legs were trembling from the terrible fright we had when we spotted that rascal. He was standing behind a big banana sucker disguised in banana leaves and was laughing so hard he could barely stand up. Uncle Naysh said he wanted to teach us survival skills and to see how we would react if a real tiger had been close by, or tried to attack us. Who needs an uncle who makes you wish yuh muddah had pinned a spare pair of panties on your dress.

## Battles at Try-bes'

Uncle Natius provided me with many laughs when I was growing up; some of his antics bordered on the mentally insane at times. I was sitting in his hammock one afternoon when he appeared over the rim of the dam fully clothed but dripping wet. It was Monday, so he had gone to Charity for Market-day, to do what he did best. Someone gave him a ride in the morning, but he got *passage* (paid a fare) to come home in the afternoon. He was a bit worse for wear from heavy drinking, and had a misunderstanding with the boat driver who refused to pull into his waterside to drop him off. He was so angry; he threw his shoes in the river then jumped overboard and swam the short distance to the stellin'. Don't let me tell you the cussin' that driver got; a good thing he couldn't hear him.

He also terrorized Gramuddah on a regular basis. The reason being, he wanted *a raise* (money) to buy rum, but she seldom had any to give him. The *wrowin'* always started at dusk after he had built the fire in the front yard to smoke out the swarming sandflies that descended in droves every evening. Gramuddah only had to say "no" and he was off on a tangent. He didn't care that we were children and may have been scared of the abuse he dished out. He got out his big-big cutlass which he began sharpening to let Gramuddah see he meant business. He paced the yard as he hurled the verbal abuse at her. He ranted and raved and shouted these gems, "Muddah, yuh skunthole betta gi'me sum money or a'gon chop yuh fuckin' 'ead off now OR "De cutlass nice an' sharp now suh a'ready fuh yuh; yuh betta 'urry an' bring de money ol' woman." This one is my favourite. I think this threat really made Gramuddah hand over the money, "De cutlass suh sharp a'gon cut yuh skunt up in small pieces an' t'row yuh in d'Riva weh de perai gon eat yuh rass." How can anyone not take a threat like that seriously? I used to run and hide in Uncle Mike's bedroom when he started. Poor Gramuddah did not *pick sh' teet'* (did not say a word); I guess she was too *fryken* to add to his fury. I believe she gave him the money in fear, because he always went out not long after he started cussin', and peace reigned once more on the trembling house.

I am happy to report that my grandmother was buried as a whole person when she finally died around the age of ninety-six (she did not know her year of birth); only six weeks after I last saw her in 1984. She went straight to heaven.

## Lugga-Lugga

Like everyone else, Uncle Naysh also had a false-name. It was Lugga-Lugga. Apparently he was floundering under the influence of the local brew and had taken on the appearance of a fish by that name.

He was another one who hated the city, and only went to town *wan-wan time* out of sheer necessity. I must have seen him twice in town in all the years I lived in Guyana. CeCe said he came to town after I left for Australia and she still laughs at the memory of this incident. She said he was wearing his *laang-boots* and was fully tanked-up when he said his goodbyes. He no sooner got out the door when she heard a crash. She looked out to find Uncle Naysh folded up at the bottom of the stairs. He broke out laughing and sang, "Honey you're de reason a'doan sleep at nite;" when he saw her. Nothing fazed him.

Uncle Naysh had found himself a woman when I visited Pomeroon in 1984. The scoundrel never married, they just shacked up together. He and Aunty Bibi had their third child shortly before I arrived. I went to pay them a visit in the little hut he had built a little distance down the dam from Gramuddah's place (Dolly's now). He was entertaining three other relatives when I rocked up at his humble abode. After he hugged me he said, "We wettin' de baby 'ead." There was no room in the dwelling so I joined them on the stairs to *gyaff*. A very dark East Indian woman poked her head out of an opening, smiled shyly then disappeared just as quickly. I never saw the baby. The drinks must have been flowing for some time because I could see Uncle Naysh was tanked-up. Bless his heart; he still wanted to give me some gifts. He picked up his cutlass, grabbed his door-mat (sugah bag) and said, "Le'we guh to de backdam, a'wan' fuh get yuh sum nice *pears* (avocados) an' aringes." We left the others drinking and I followed Uncle Naysh to a field that looked like a jungle. The *special* pear tree he mentioned came into view so he began chopping to make a clearing to get to it; he miscalculated and chopped his leg. All I heard was, "Oh skunt, a't'ink a'chap meh foot." He wasn't wearing his *laang-boots* that day. He *t'ink* he chopped his leg? I guess the likka had anesthetised him because I took a look and that was no small cut. The blood was gushing out of the long wide gash and it scared the hell out of me. Uncle Naysh calmly jumped over the trench and chopped down a *Moca-Moca*. He cut it up, squeezed the juice into the wound then wrapped it up with some of the leaves and went on picking my pears as if nothing had happened. He never went to the doctor. The Moca-Moca plant is a well known bush cure.

Seeing Uncle Naysh's home reminded me of something my cousin Diane had said the day before when I visited her and her husband Shaun in their newly built home on the dam at Charity. Diane was proudly giving *Cousin Helen* the royal tour and I stepped out on to the verandah to admire the surroundings. I spotted the tiniest structure on the next block. There was a shirt hanging on a bush so I asked Diane if it was someone's home. Diane's answer sent me into fits of laughter. With a straight face she said, "Yes Cousin Helen, sumbaady does live deh; but we does call it de Chicken Hawk Palace." It was cruel but so damn funny!

Well I figure if that small place had such a prestigious name, then Uncle Naysh's home deserved to be given an appropriate name too. I just cannot make up my mind what to call it. *Carrion Crow Castle* has a certain ring, but *Barely Inn* is also suitable. Which name do you like best?

## Birds of Prey

There were certain birds we disliked and were wary of because of their habits. The 'Chicken Hawk' is one of them; the name gives away the bird's profession. He cleaned up the chickens whenever they were left to forage on the farm. Gramuddah used to keep a watchful eye from the kitchen when she was cooking and the minute she saw one circling she ran out to chase it and gather her precious fowls. I witnessed a chicken being snatched one day; the poor thing did not stand a chance. The spectacle took on the appearance of a hot air balloon as the hawk ascended clutching its meal.

Mummy compared us to a Chicken Hawk whenever we were squabbling or being vicious to one another because of the nature of that very bird. I have been called a Chicken Hawk once or twice when I was trying to snatch my belongings back from the clutches of my wicked brothers.

Another bird we are wary of is the 'Carrion Crow', it's a scavenger; you know without doubt that if you saw one or more circling above there must be something dead close by. In a way that was good because it helped to clean up our roads; especially with the amount of dead dogs lying around.

On my visit to Guyana in 1984 Charlie wanted to take me to a nightclub as a *welcome home* gesture. On the way to the venue I spotted an object in the distance in the middle of the road. As we got closer I realised it was a dog lying on its back; rigor mortis had its legs straight up in the air. I was appalled and asked *de Clock* why the dog hadn't been removed. Charlie gave one of his wicked laughs and said, "Gyurl, yuh cyan't see de dog sunbadin'; de carrion crow gon pick 'e up tomarrow." It was an everyday occurrence to him and he thought it was funny.

Superstition was rife in Guyana so no one liked to see a Carrion Crow circling above unless there was a dead carcass lying around; it was a bad omen and it meant someone was going to die. That bird preyed on vulnerable animals; picking their eyes out before they were dead.

That is why we called a person a *Carrion Crow* if they tried to obtain an inheritance from a relative before they were dead.

## My Tiger Died

I often wonder if Uncle Naysh ever tried using Moca-Moca for the cancer he had on his shoulder blade. The last time I saw my rascal uncle he was crouching under a tree on the dam in front of Aunt Claudia's home where Daphne, my husband and I were staying. Daphne and I had to walk past him so I stopped to ask if he was alright. With pain etched on his face he said, "Dis t'ing 'urtin' meh bad today gyurl." Up until then, I had only heard about the *bad sore* on his shoulder, but had not seen it. I was not interested in seeing it either, but Uncle Naysh pulled down his shirt without warning to show it to me. I felt sick to the stomach and Daphne had to walk away. That wound was so big I could have put my fist into it. I wondered how he was still able to walk. I went back into the house to fetch a packet of pain killers for him. Uncle Naysh passed away a few months later without ever going into hospital. I called to talk to Daddy after I heard the sad news and he said, "A'went dung to d'Riva to see 'e before 'e died an' chap dat maan looked olda dan me;" then he tearfully said, "Yuh Uncle proppa punish in 'e las' days Helen." It broke my heart. Uncle Naysh was twenty-two years younger than Daddy but he abused his body and paid the price. I loved that scoundrel uncle dearly.

I wrote the following poem about fifteen years ago in a nostalgic moment.

## Holidays in Pomeroon–by Helena Martin (DaSilva)

*The long August school holidays had arrived and off we went*
*To our grandparents in Pomeroon it would be spent*
*We will have the greatest adventure of our lives*
*My brothers will jump off the mangroves to do their dives*
*You see, we are going where we can swim*
*No lessons for us; we learnt when someone pushed us in.*
*Gramuddah Francesca lives in a thatched roof cottage*
*No windows or doors nor place to store our measly luggage*
*Boys stop wasting your time with that silly bet*

*You know I always sleep with Gramudda under the mosquito net*
*First we take the ferry across the Demerara River to Vreed-en-Hoop*
*That is one step closer to Charity and Aunt Phil's hot chicken soup*
*It's a mad scramble here to catch that rickety train*
*Vendors with huge baskets on their heads all shout the same refrain*
*Trees laden with fruit and villages with children are things we will see*
*Friendly people, I wave and they wave back at me*
*There are goats, donkeys and cows ambling along the road*
*Heading for the market where man and beast unburden their load*
*Tiny speckled bananas are waiting at Parika our next stop*
*Sweet sensations that always make my taste buds pop*
*The Parika to Adventure leg is travelled by sea*
*The M.V. Malali is a big steamer but this is the most boring part for me*
*Nothing to see except rotten mangroves that stink like hell*
*We are on our best behaviour in case someone knows Mummy and tell.*
*Delicious smells wafts from the snack bar on board*
*But a sweet-drink and a Salara bun is all I can afford.*
*This little treat is a luxury so I savour it even more.*
*No such treats at Gramuddah, she is wholesome to the core.*
*Gramuddah lives on a huge farm which we call Try-bes'*
*It's laden with fruit trees and baby birds in their nests.*
*Sorry I rushed ahead because we are not at Charity yet.*
*I haven't told you 'bout the long yellow bus we have to get.*
*Missing the bus is a disaster as walking is just too far.*
*And only the wealthy can afford a drop cyar*
*The buses owned by Kass are always full to the brim.*
*Patsy our driver packs us tightly like sardines in a tin.*
*Passengers without a seat stand and they hold on tight.*
*Sitting is great but gazing up at someone's armpit is not a pretty sight.*
*This last leg of the journey takes 'bout an hour an' a half*
*But everyone is full of good humour so we all have a good laugh.*
*We'll see Aunt Phil waiting as we go around the last bend.*
*And I just know this is going to be the best holiday I am ever going to spend.*

# Chapter Ten

*The longest rope has an end.*—*Proverb*

# 1961-63 CHARLES & HOWES STREETS

### Another Cantankerous Landlord

We lived at the intersection of Charles and Howes Street, above a shop owned by a man of Chinese descent. This obnoxious and cantankerous character had a habit of bathing stark naked every morning at the standpipe in the yard, cussin' in a loud voice the entire time. Since I was always up early to make the family breakfast, I took the opportunity of sneaking a peek. However it wasn't worth the trouble; instead of getting an eye-full I only got half. Don't forget I had seen those donkeys. The madman was incensed by Anetta running around the yard. He fixed the problem by meticulously placing pieces of broken bottle in strategic positions around the yard to cut her foot. She still bears the scar to this day.

My parent's passion continued to leach and brought with it another episode of the 'War of the Roses'. This posed a problem since there was only one bedroom. My father improvised by making a partition in the sitting room with a sheet of *tentis* (Masonite) to conceal his bed. Our dining suite was wedged into the narrow passage leading into the kitchen; our supposed dining room. The restricted shower cubicle in the kitchen had to be vacated before we could dry ourselves. The kitchen sink was fitted on the outside of the sole window and had a drainpipe (always blocked) that emptied into the street gutter. The communal toilet was in the yard.

An elderly black gentleman named Mr Griffin occupied a tiny cubicle directly underneath our kitchen. The cobbler was almost invisible in the cramped quarters. How he remembered who those shoes belonged to is still a mystery to me . . . the pile reached up to the ceiling so he must have had an ingenious system. A lot of people used to re-sole their shoes—more than once. We were regular customers. My Bata shoes spent time with the likeable Mr Griffin during the school holidays. Mummy took pity on him on very hot days, offering a snack and a glass of *swank*. That dear old gentleman always rescued Anetta and hid her behind the shoes when Mummy was *runnin' 'er dung* to give her a beating. How that girl could scream.

The Spooners lived on the corner opposite to us in a spacious home I called 'de Mansion'. I never went inside, but I could picture how grand it might have been. Mr Spooner was well known for his *drop-cyar* service. If he wasn't driving, he was cleaning or polishing the car; it was always immaculate. St Joseph High School was also at this intersection, directly opposite the Spooners. The school unfortunately became redundant just as we moved here.

Ricks had *gon-up-in-de-worl'* and now had a new factory in close proximity of this home. We inhaled the rich aroma of coffee and curry daily.

## Confirmed By a Hypocrite

Being baptised does not make you a fully fledged Catholic; Holy Communion followed by Confirmation completed the process and the tenacious nuns made sure that mission was accomplished. I dutifully presented myself twice a week at the presbytery to receive instructions for these sacraments. This was a most unpleasant period in my teenage life. I had to endure being locked up in a tiny cubicle with a short overweight priest who looked like a garden gnome. He lived up to his name, what a 'pain' he was. That blasted man pretended he was cuddling me at the end of every lesson, but contrary to belief, I was not *schupidee*; I knew he was fondling me when he tickled me under the ribs and surrounding area. [I wonder if I can sue and cash in; everyone else is exposing those dirty bastards so I can't see why I shouldn't]. Do you think I told my mother? Not on your life! Those priests were held in high esteem, and no one would ever believe me. I would have probably gotten a good *cut-ass* for having such a wicked thought. This same priest had married my parents in 1944, and much to my disgust he was still alive when I was ready for matrimony in 1968. My mother was overjoyed and felt it was an honour to have him officiate. I was not amused but my hands were tied.

At fourteen, time was running out so the nuns decided it was best to combine Holy Communion and Confirmation on the same day. I was the picture of innocence wearing virginal white and holding a prayer book. Mummy had asked Auntie Georgie's eldest daughter Jeanette to stand as godmother. I finally had a second name; it is Bernadette. I have never used it because second names are only recognised when you are baptised and I never got one. My confirmation day was not a happy one, especially when it was time to *tek out de pickcha*. I had a nasty sore on my lip (probably due to stress) and tried to hide it by pressing my lips together and ended up looking like an *Ol' higue*.

With my Godmother
Jeanette Trotman

## A Big Bicycle Dilemma

St Joseph High School was relocated at Thomas Lands. A great location and a modern building, but it posed a major problem. From my perspective the school might have been at the other end of the country. The distance from my home definitely required transportation. Cash was short, so I already knew a bicycle was not forthcoming. I had no choice, if I wanted an education I had to walk. A bicycle finally materialised a few months after I commenced. To say I was embarrassed, is putting it mildly. Every part of that bicycle was either donated or bought from a second-hand dealer before it was assembled. It was quite a disappointment, because it did not compare to the newer models most of the girls rode. That may sound ungrateful, but hey, I had my pride. I was so *shame* riding that blasted bicycle but I quickly swallowed my pride when I realised its true value.

That bicycle was what we called *cock-bran'* (unreliable) and caused a few embarrassing experiences. The first one occurred while going home at lunch time one day. Most of the girls sported a sweater when it rained, and I naturally wanted one. Aunty Olga was working at Elias Brothers and was able to get me one at cost price; a lovely buttercup yellow. It had stopped raining so it was draped over the handle bar. This was common practice with all the students; we just wanted to *pampazet* (show off) when we weren't wearing the sweater. I was among a big group of girls making our way out on the potholed road that led to the main road when my bicycle tube bubbled. The full blown bladder brought my bike to a sudden halt in the middle of a puddle. I was caught unaware, and with no time to think, the sweater fell off into the mud. That was the end of it. Sweaters *didn' grow on trees* and that one was beyond cleaning.

A watch was another luxury for which I hankered. *Tide* (soap powder) ran a competition for a watch but we never had enough coupons to enter. My mother relented on a rare occasion and allowed me to wear hers for the day.

Our sport factions were divided into three colours and were referred to as *house*. The *house* colours were red, blue and green. I belonged to the *green house* which was the weakest team; we always came last at the school sport carnival. Dusk was fast approaching when sports practice finished one day. I was in a panic because my bicycle was not fitted with a light and that could result in a fine if I was stopped by the police. There was only one sure way of speeding things up. Getting off the saddle enabled me to pedal much faster. There I was in top speed when my foot slipped and I went down with a thud. The pain was one thing, but did it have to happen in front of the Queenstown Fire Brigade station in full view of the young fire fighters? I could not rub *you know where* and did not know where to look as the tears stung my eyes.

## Mega Embarrassment

The new school was much bigger and more intimidating. I was even more self conscious in that alien environment and became *a' jackass dat couldn't bray*. The cafeteria was enormous. It had a selection of tempting treats on offer but I learnt to *cut-meh-eye* because there was no way I could afford to indulge. A good thing my mouth watered so much from drooling; at least I had something to swallow. Recess was hell. I could not bear the embarrassment of not having pocket money, so I wandered off most days to the furthest corner of the school grounds to avoid the other students and pretended I was reading. Some of the more affluent students remained at school and purchased their lunch each day. In the beginning I did likewise because it was not possible to walk home and be back in the time allotted for the lunch break. Daddy did offer to bring my lunch but I begged him not to as I was too *shame* because he had a *bruk dung* (old and rusty) bicycle and he reeked of coffee. I did not want anyone to know he was my father. I pray I don't go to hell for that indiscretion.

Twenty-five cents was all my mother could afford to give me for lunch, and that was a lot of money back then; it made a big dent in her weekly budget. I bought a *Dhal Puri* and a small carton of milk most days. I can hear you saying, "Why didn't you take some sandwiches for lunch?" They weren't invented yet . . . I'm just kidding. Sandwiches were a luxury we read about; something we thought only *de white people* ate, *besize* there was no extra bread lying around; we mostly ate bakes. As much as it was a painful experience I did enjoy eating lunch at school. It gave me the illusion of fitting in with my peers. That lark came to an end after I got my bike. I was expected home to eat the meal my mother prepared for lunch, or stay at school and starve.

## Please Forgive Me Bruddah

I have no doubt that there is something each and every one of us has done that wasn't our proudest moment. I am no exception, so it's time to confess. This incident has been plaguing me for almost fifty years, and all because of *twenty-five cents*. I was not a very clever t'ief; you could say I was *schupidee* because I did not stop to think my mother would miss the coin I took from her purse when she only had two. I was sick of being poor and wanted money to spend at the cafeteria like all the other girls. The missing money was discovered before I even left for school. Joel had already left for work and I was scared shitless. I vigorously denied taking the money and Mummy naturally assumed Joel had taken it to buy cigarettes. Poor Joel was no sooner through the door that afternoon when Mummy made the accusation. He hotly denied the allegation, and he was telling the truth. I was standing there feeling very guilty but did not have the courage to own up. I am so very sorry, because my brother died without me ever confessing. I had no justification for my actions that day.

## Kindness I Appreciated

A group of older girls from a higher form showed me kindness I will never forget. These beautiful girls must have observed me and realised I never bought anything from the tuck-shop. I would like to think they befriended me in a kind way; others may see it differently. One of the girls from the group approached me, casually at first; she smiled and made small talk. Then one day she asked me to purchase something for her from the cafeteria. She handed me the money after I shyly agreed. I cannot really remember how it came about, but before long I was joining the queue at recess to purchase food for a group of girls. They always bought more than necessary and insisted I had a share. I still *spring a leak* whenever I think of their kindness and generosity. All the girls came from wealthy families but there was never a derogative comment from any of them; I was accepted for who I was and it felt good. I truly wish I had the courage to tell them what this kind gesture meant to me because I was so desperate to fit in. I am going to say "thank-you" here, just in case one of them reads this and remember *de lil' Putagee gyurl* who was always *bruk* (broke).

Navigating the labyrinth of our social climbing society was painful. I became a social cripple in high school all because of my inferiority complex. Most of the girls in my form were friendly but I was afraid of the consequences so refrained from getting overly chummy. Inviting them to my home was one of my biggest fears because I assume their homes would be beautiful. I actually knew where some of them lived and I would rather die than allow any of them to see my location. Why did I feel such shame? Very simple; my self esteem was very low, not to mention stupidity and ignorance in great abundance. Our home was always very clean, so that was not the problem. However we lived in a lower class neighbourhood and I was keeping that a secret at all costs. Our furniture was another cause for embarrassment; I thought no one would want to be my friend after they visited my home. You see what I mean about ignorance?

The friendliest and most popular girl in the class was an East Indian girl named Janet Singh, she was full of the confidence I was sadly lacking. She wanted to be a hairdresser so she took me home to practice perming hair . . . I looked wired for action when she had finished with me.

## A Friend for Life

I found a wonderful friend when I finally found the courage to let my guard down. Her name is Barbara; I say "is" because we are still friends to this day. She became family when she married my cousin Desmond. We confided in each other and I was invited to her beautiful home and made to feel very welcome by her parents and her sister Lana. Barbara lived in the Lodge Housing Scheme which was considered too far from my place so she never visited my home. Barbara was very knowledgeable, especially on sexual matters. Don't get me wrong, she was not promiscuous; as a matter of fact her mother would have *skinned her alive* if she even thought of having a boyfriend. Her mother informed her on matters I knew nothing about. There I was at fourteen and still in the dark about menstruation. Yes, yes, I was a late bloomer. Barbara filled me in but I honestly thought she was making it all up. She also decided I needed some beauty treatment and brought a razor blade to school. Waxing had nothing on this razor blade; she left me looking like a Bald Eagle. I was greeted with raucous laughter and teasing when I got home from school that day. Choking on his laughter, Charlie said, "Look, Muddah Rat 'ad sum a'sh' w'iskas shaved off!" Who else had a *bruddah* like him?

Attending chapel was part of the curriculum, but I hated going and always sat in the very last pew, hoping to go unnoticed. I was overcome by *bad feelings* (nausea) one day and fainted. What a *cufuffle*; I almost *loss away* again from sheer embarrassment when I *ketch meh-self* (came around) and found the entire class staring at me like I was an exhibit at the zoo. That was the very first time I can remember ever fainting; and it was probably due to lack of food.

My parents made the devastating announcement of the axing of my high school education at the end of fourth form. They could no longer afford the school fees. I was broken hearted at having to leave school knowing I would not be able to sit my G.C.E (General Certificate of Education) to complete my education. This was to be one of my biggest regrets in life. I never had the opportunity to test my true potential but I was determined to have a certificate one day. I finally achieved this goal in 2004 after completing a six month course at TAFE (Technical and Further Education) for Certificate III in Aged Care.

## Joel and I Joined the GUYS

The former St Joseph High School became the headquarters for the GUYS (Guyana United Youth Society). The organisers of this group were Compton Young and Winston Rodrigues. Joel and I became involved with this group mostly for the camaraderie; we never had any real interest in political issues. Political meetings were held at street corners and members of the different parties drove around Georgetown in vans fitted with loud-speakers announcing the venue. It was a time of political unrest so it was a safe bet there would be a scuffle by the time the meeting ended. Mummy always warned us to steer clear of these gatherings but some of them were very entertaining, so I attended behind her back. There were political demonstrations from time to time and we felt obliged to join in. I actually remember one such demonstration vividly. The GUYS blocked off a road and we all sat and sang songs such as, 'Solidarity Forever' and 'We Shall Not Be Moved'. We thought so until a good dose of tear gas moved us on. I never attended another demonstration after that.

The GUYS headquarters was bombed one night during the riots in 1962. We felt the full blast of the bomb because we lived across the road. Joel was attending a meeting at the time, so Mummy was frantic. Pandemonium broke out, but we were able to get through the crowd just as the ambulance was pulling away. Joel was sitting in the back and he assured us he was not seriously injured. He was released the same night since he only had minor cuts and bruises.

We became friendly with most of the members of the GUYS. Some of our friends were: Raymond, Michael (Mousie) and Joseph Gonsalves; Joseph and Carlos (Collie) D'Oliviera; Aubrey and Angus D'Aguiar; the Mendonza brothers; Tony Faria, Terrence Romalho (Bread), David, Maureen and Aubrey Small; James Conyers (Konya), Norma, Hazel, Desiree and Carl DeAbreu; Michael DeNobrega, Pauline and Michael (Mickey) Texeira; Gloria Gonsalves, Evelyn DeSantos, Famena and Paula DeFreitas; David and Bernadette Jardine and Terence (Terry) Joaquim. I am still in contact with some of the above mentioned.

## Black Friday

In 1962 the political situation had reached boiling point with the unions calling a strike. The frequent blackout gave rise to the crime rate, and schools and most businesses were closed. The culmination of all the hardships eventually resulted in a full blown riot. Looting broke out and the main shopping centre was set alight. This happened on Friday, February 16th 1962. It became known as 'Black Friday'. It was a most terrifying experience, everyone feared for their lives and homes.

Never mind the house, my *puzzlin'-tin* was more important and had to be saved at all costs. The fire was definitely getting closer and my *magga* savings were all in a sardine tin nailed to the bedroom wall. I quickly fetched the crow bar and pried it off. The coins flew everywhere and I had to be quick before my brothers pounced on them. To this day my sister Anetta accuses *de Clock* and me of trying to steal hers. No memory of *dat! Besize,* where the hell she would get money to put in a puzzlin'-tin; she was eight years old.

What I do remember, is my cousin Eddie bringing home a box full of shoes taken from a store display window during the looting. Poor Eddie did not realise that shoe shops only displayed one side of a pair of shoes. There was only one person who was overjoyed after the disappointing discovery was made. Muddah Evans who lived in the *range* (housing unit) across the road was the only person who benefited from this venture; she only had one leg and was seen sporting a new shoe each week! That's another *truh-truh* story.

People possessed the strength of Samson that day. We watched in amazement as a parade of looters passed our home carrying refrigerators and other heavy items on their backs. When the law threatened to take action a few days later, the trench on Sussex Street became congested with the discarded stolen goods.

## Living in a Range

I was always grateful we never had to live in a *range*. We had relatives living in such an environment at one time, so I got first hand experience of what went on when I visited. It was akin to a commune; several buildings were arranged in a big yard and each one had a few units which comprised of two small rooms. Kitchens were a tiny detached structure at the foot of the steps. It was so small one barely had room to turn around. The entire community used the standpipe in the middle of the yard to wash clothes, dishes and bathe the younger children. The outdoor amenities were shared by everyone, and the cleaning was done sporadically, thus the hygiene left a lot to be desired. The close proximity of neighbours in this environment meant that everyone minded *deh matty* (fellowmen/friends) business. It was a breeding ground for *buezin'*; some were so vicious it led to blows.

We lived across the street from a huge yard that had several ranges. Some relatives of ours lived there so I know what they endured. How those people suffered when it rained; the yard flooded and became a muddy quagmire. A flashback of Mrs Drake and her brood has left a lasting impression and reminds me of the abject poverty I escaped. Mrs Drake, the matriarch of the clan shared the *magga* dwelling with her many unmarried daughters. The girls frequently produced an additional mouth to feed. There was limited room in the tiny unit so the *bung navel* (protruding) snotty nose, pot bellied children ate their sparse meals sitting on the door stoop. The family lived *'an'-to-mout'*, nibbling on a few Edger Boy biscuits and drinking *bush tea* (tea made from wild daisies or lemon grass) which grew alongside the gutters. My heart went out to them and the many families who lived under those conditions.

## Weird Religious Sects around Town

Different religions intermingled with the regular and more accepted denominations; although anything out of the ordinary was cause for curiosity. We found some Orthodox religions very intriguing. Three doors down from us was a little church that I was not allowed to set foot in, but I sure enjoyed listening to them sing. At a certain time of the year the church was filled with fresh produce. It signified something to do with harvesting. They sang "bringin' in the sheaves" so loud I learnt the words. I forget what denomination it was, however, I do remember the *Jordanites*. This mob dressed in white from head to toe and lit kerosene lamps at dark street corners where they preached their sermons. I stopped out of curiosity when I came across one of these gatherings. I liked hearing them say "Amen" or "hallelujah" after the preacher said something profound; I even joined in a few times. One night the preacher was really worked up and he warned, "If yuh doan repent deh is goin' to be gnashin' of teet'." One man in the crowd was not worried because he yelled, "Praise de Lord a'ain't got no teet'." The preacher heard him and said, "Den yuh gums will feel de squeeze." Where can you go nowadays to be entertained like that for free? There was another sect we called the *clap 'an' church*; they were a jovial lot. The congregation for these religions were predominately Africans. We also had a secret society called 'Lodge'; our first landlord (Popeye) belonged to this sect. I asked mountains of questions but nothing was ever divulged. Members of the congregation wore ceremonial robes to meetings and their deceased members were driven to the cemetery in a long carriage with glass windows. I have a vague memory of the driver holding a red rose between his teeth.

## Smoking In the Botanical Garden

I laughed when I heard that Queen Victoria spent time lying flat on her back at the bottom of the Botanical Garden; the same garden my mother forbid me to enter. Her statue was finally restored and she was once more seen regally standing in front of the Law Court.

A *Putagee* family lived in the tiny cottage between us and the church, and I became friendly with two of the girls. Paula was about my age, but Famena who was almost three years younger liked *limin'* (hanging out) with us and since she was a lot of fun we included her. She and I have been friends ever since. My mother would *turn in sh' grave* if she knew the things we got up to. We decided to go to the Botanical Garden one day just for the fun of it. The zoo is next door, but we did not have the entry fee so we stayed out in the gardens to *ketch swank* when boys passed. We happen to *butt-up* with a group of Chinese boys who were smoking, and wickedness took control of us. We began goading Famena, telling her she did not have the guts to ask them for a *sigrit*. The next thing you know she was sitting with these guys and smoking! Alright, I won't lie; I had a few puffs too. Famena left not long after this happened to reside in England where she met and married her husband some years later. She now goes by the name of Penny, and she said I'm allowed to tell you that. The new name she chose fits her perfectly because that girl was a *bad penny* from the day she was born.

Famena (Penny) smoking in the Botanical Gardens

## Monkey Business in the Botanical Garden

The Botanical Garden holds special memories for me. The garden itself did not hold as much interest; not until I was old enough to date anyway. I enjoyed the zoo as a child, but that was a rare treat. A tame (so I thought) black monkey held in check by a long chain sat on a dead branch at the entrance waiting to greet patrons. When I was sixteen I asked Lita to take a picture of me holding that monkey. He clung to me for dear life after the picture was taken. I had to peel him off to put him back on the branch. He was obviously peeved because he punished me with a whopping bite on my finger which bled for ages.

My parents took me and my siblings to the zoo for an outing when I was around ten or there abouts. Monkeys are my favourite animals so I was always impatient to get to their cages. I could watch their antics for hours. I was wearing my brand new red *berett* (beret) one day and must have ventured too close to the cage because a monkey whipped it off my head. I sobbed and watched helplessly as he took it to the water trough where he washed, rung, and washed it again and again. I was devastated, but he was having so much fun. What a shame I was so unhappy and did not see the beauty in his actions at the time. I just wanted to strangle the little bastard!

We acquired a black monkey in the last home I lived in before leaving Guyana. That monkey was out of control . . . Jacko was kept under the back stairs and he terrorized me each time I passed. There was a serious personality clash between us. I had a vendetta against him because he broke his chain several times and reeked havoc; pulling down the washing line into the muddy yard. He was very cunning; he dumped his water bowl full of *kounce* (feces) on me when I tried to get past him one day and he bit me on more than one occasion. I love monkeys, but they don't seem to like me. I had another bad experience on the Malali coming home from Pomeroon. I wanted to touch the Sakiwinki monkey a man was holding. It was restrained on a length of rope so I figured it was safe. I ventured closer to ask the man the name of his monkey . . . which (surprise, surprise) was Jacko, and of course he bit me. After that I did not mess with monkeys!

Me holding the monkey that bit me at the zoo

Me, Lita & Daphne in the Botanical Gardens

## My Mother's Clothes

I was cryin' like *bird-pepper was bunnin' meh eye*; snot was pouring out but the stiff organdie fabric I was blowin' my nose with was not as absorbent as a kerchief. *"Dis will teech yuh bitch,"* I thought as I sobbed and blew my nose repeatedly all over my mother's fancy-dress. Mummy always said things such as this, "A'will beat yuh as laang as yuh live unda meh roof." What's more, she meant it. I cannot remember why I got the *cut-ass*; however, I do remember being very angry at the time and this was the only form of revenge I could conjure up. My mother must have had this dress made for a special occasion because it was made from good quality fabric. I may have only been fourteen but knew what expensive fabric was supposed to look like. Funny, but this dress is the only one belonging to her that is etched into my memory—guilt? The colour was candy floss pink with gold thread woven through the pretty pattern. The style was short sleeves, a collar and a belt with a buckle covered in the matching fabric. It was indeed her finest dress but it didn't look so pretty after I doctored it with my snot.

Although my mother was forty-four years old when I left Guyana, she had never worn a dress bought from a store. In Guyana, the women who could not sew engaged a personal dressmaker. I feel very guilty whenever I look at my bulging closets because Mummy never owned more than two or three decent dresses at any given time when I was growing up. I know one thing; I didn't get my fashion sense from her. I still cringe when I think of a wedding we attended in 1967. The phrase, *pregnant pause* took on a new meaning that day. The bride was *up de duff* and my mother was wearing a maternity dress because her pregnancy was even more advanced. And if that wasn't embarrassing enough, I had to endure the sight of her legs. Why? She wore stockings without giving any thought of shaving her hairy legs. She could have killed the black tarantulas trapped under her stockings with the *stone crushers* (shoes with wide heels) she was wearing. I just remembered what she said on that subject . . . she said a person became "weak" when they shaved any part of their anatomy. I am sure she only said that because she read the story of Samson and Delilah; how else would she concoct a bullshit story like that?

My mother and I enjoyed window shopping at our largest department stores, Bookers and Forgaty's. We admired, drooled and fantasised when we got to the expensive fabric section. Kirpalani in Camp Street also had cheap *eye-ketchin'* fabric but you had to wear sunglasses when entering that store because you could be blinded by the bright-bright colours on display. We had to make do with buying our material from the stalls in the market where the vendors had a unique way of measuring. An accurate yard was measured from the tip of the nose to the full length of an out stretched arm. Fabric of a certain calibre was cheaper when I became a teenager and for good reason; it was rubbish. The vendors sold three yards for one dollar and in true Guyanese style it quickly became known as 't'ree fuh D'. Buying *t'ree fuh D* was an art. Friends teased you if they thought your dress looked *cheap,* so Mummy became an expert at choosing a pattern that appeared to look more expensive. She wasn't fooling anyone because everyone knew we were strapped for cash and could not afford anything better.

Women from Mummy's era did not wear trousers so you can imagine the surprise we had when my mother came out of the bedroom one day wearing a pair of Daddy's shorts. We thought it was hilarious and could not stop laughing at her. As you can see, it didn't take much to entertain us.

## I Became a 'Big Woman' Here

A Guyanese reading this will know what *suckin' yuh teet'* means. It was also called 'stewin' yuh teeth' or 'scheupsin'.' I can only tell you it is a sound we make when we draw air through our teeth. Guyanese use this sound to signify various moods. A *suck-teet'* can speak volumes, not one word is necessary. The duration and intensity of the delivery will leave the recipient in no doubt as to its meaning. A vindictive woman's *suck-teet'* can leave a man's manhood dangling as useless as an anchor made of cork.

We suck-teet' a lot and it's almost an automatic and acceptable gesture depending on the conversation. However, it was not done while you were being berated by your parents. It was classed as insolence and was certainly not tolerated in our household.

I was getting a *dressin' dung* from my mother over some silly matter, but since I was not allowed to back chat I voiced my annoyance by suckin' meh teet' and she heard me. Without missing a beat she indignantly said, "Suh yuh t'ink yuh is a'big woman now; well big women does wash deh own clothes." I knew she was dead serious when she brushed the palm of her hands together to signify washing, before she angrily added, "A'wash meh 'an's of dat from today." An' le'me tell yuh sumt'in' reada, w'en meh muddah said sumt'in' sh' meant it. I was fourteen but from that day onwards she never washed another piece of my clothing. If only I had stopped to consider the dire consequences. How I wished I had heeded her warning when she said, "If yuh mek yuh bed 'ard, yuh will lie in it." This was a hard bed indeed.

## Starching Cyan-Cyans (Can-Cans)

Washing my own clothes wouldn't have been a big deal if we owned a washing machine, but that was another luxury we could not afford. A zinc tub, *'ard-brush* (scrubbing brush), a *beatah* (heavy wooden bat) and a cake of *salsoap* were our only tools—I forgot *elbow grease* (Tide and Rinso were a luxury). If you were lucky you had a wooden washboard; we did not own one. I joined the other occupants who congregated at the standpipe to *buck-up clothes* (wet and soap dirty laundry), bathe children and fill their buckets to take to their respective living quarters and my life of drudgery began.

*Cyan-cyan* petticoats were in fashion; the stiffer the better to make my circular skirts stand out. The tulle version needed no starching but getting one of those was out of the question, and since there was no spray starch in a can I had to make it from scratch. Making starch is a tricky business; you had to know exactly how much boiling water to add to the powdered starch to obtain the right consistency. Then there was Ricketts Crown Blue which was used on white clothing to make them whiter. Don't even try to figure that one out. The cube of blue was placed in a small piece of cloth and secured with a string. This cloth was then dipped into the water used for the final rinse. Not as easy as it sounds because you had to know just how much *blue* to add and some times my *whites* ended up being *blue*. Didn't I tell you it wasn't simple?

Then there was the time I won a competition on the radio for a whole gallon of Javex. We bleached everything in sight and I even ended up with a skirt that looked as if it had *cocabey* (leprosy) after I added some to the washing for good measure.

## Flying Mother Nature's Flag

Here is more embarrassment to share with you. When girls got their first menstrual cycle they became a 'yung lady'. That was one *big-story* (very important) because your *muddah* delivered 'de talk'. I would have preferred the boiled egg I heard some girls got for breakfast. I was well past my fourteenth birthday and thought *goat bite meh* because all of my friends had become a *yung lady* long before me. When it finally happened I was so *shame* I asked Daphne to tell my mother. I waited for the call, and with my head down to my knees I heard Mummy solemnly say, "Now dat yuh is a'big gyurl yuh mus' not le' a'bhai touch yuh or yuh gon get a'baby." Shucks, that was going to be difficult because I knew a lot of boys. Oh, I forgot the other bit, she also said, "An' doan *wash yuh 'ead* (shampoo) w'en yuh 'ave it."

The *lap-cloth* (rags/cloth napkin) I had to use made me look as if I had *goadee*; I was convinced that everyone knew when I was *flyin' de flag* (menstruating).

I lived in fear of *gettin' a'baby* whenever any boys came too close. Thank goodness Barbara straightened me out on that score or I might still be a virgin. Another bit of advice Mummy classed as sex education was this gem, "Rememba, a'man only want wan t'ing from yuh." I am still trying to figure out what it is because my husband wouldn't tell me. How about this one, "If yuh mek yuhself grass, ass will eat yuh." Don't worry Mummy, I had no intentions of going out with an Ass . . . I preferred men. I had a hard time explaining that last one to my daughters. It simply means, 'You will be taken advantage of if you let your guard down'.

The older, wiser and uncouth boys made jokes when they knew girls were menstruating. Many girls were embarrassed when one of these louts shouted, "Sh' flyin' de flag" to their friends. It was even worse when word got out that some unfortunate girl was pregnant. The rumour mill said she was "up-de-duff." I thank my lucky stars that the only *duff* I ever had to deal with was the ones my mother made with cornmeal to put in the soup.

I heard about *Crab-dogs* (equivalent of a Dingo in Australia) from an early age and knew they existed in Guyana. However my mother's reference to this animal did not extend to the canine variety. Judging from what Mummy said, these dogs were held in low esteem. She attached the label 'Crab-dog' to any man who had nothing decent to offer a woman and warned me several times not to marry one. I know without doubt she approved of my naturalised Dingo.

## Buying Unmentionables at Cendrecourt Drugstore

Ask anyone from Georgetown where Cendrecourt Drugstore is and they will tell you. We lived just around the corner from it at this address. The proprietor was a tall handsome duglah gentleman. I've mentioned duglah people before but I will explain it to you just in case you haven't got a clear picture. They are people of African and East Indian parentage with a light brown complexion and soft hair. I was partial to duglah men and dated a few.

Becoming a *yung lady* meant you had to buy your *unmentionables*, and that was an embarrassment I had to overcome when I started working and could afford *real pads*. The attendants in Cendrecourt drugstore were often young men, and I definitely didn't want them serving me. No one was going to buy sanitary pads for me so I eventually found a solution. Lucky for me, Mr Cendrecourt was the only person on duty the day I plucked up courage to buy *my t'ing*. With a charming smile he asked, "W'at cyan I do fuh yuh yung lady?" Holy hell, I wonder who told him! I handed him the note and nervously said, "Mummy aksed meh to ge' dis." The proprietor politely wrapped the packet of Modess and handed it over without a fuss, but he had a knowing smile on his face.

I did exactly the same thing when it was time to buy my first bra. Not that I had anything to put in it . . . but hey I was fifteen and the boys needed to see a strap from the back. This was another big lie I had to go to confession for. I told the girl at Bookers Teenage Department I was buying it for my sister because she was too shy to come herself. I hope Anetta knows she was wearing a bra at eight years old!

## My First Love and First Date

I know you have been waiting to hear all about that boy from the *de rich* family in Callendar Street, well you can relax now. This boy's name was Delano; he was a Putagee like me and the most handsome boy I had ever seen, *star-bhai* material. My heart did flip flops every time I thought of him. He was without doubt, 'my first love'. He rode past our home on his way to work each morning. I had no idea who he was until I met him while swimming at Luckhoo pool. This was the only public pool in Georgetown and a great place to meet a nice *bannah*. Delano and his friend Victor were experts on the diving board and were *ketchin' swank* (showing off) no doubt. You could say I stalked him because I became an expert at timing Delano in the morning. I could see all the way to the corner where he turned into our street. This gave me ample time to run down the stairs to pretend I was just leaving for school. He probably saw right through that ploy but he never let on. We rode side by side and chatted until we had to go our separate ways. I was on cloud nine for the rest of the day. He finally asked me for a date. *Rant* that was going to be almost impossible; how will I tell Mummy? You already know I am devious, so it is no surprise I lied and said I was going out with other friends. There was only one problem; I had no *good clothes* to wear. Well, that is not exactly true, I had ONE good dress, but you would not believe what that *schupidee* dressmaker did. She measured my waist just under my *bubbie* so it looked like a maternity dress. And that was not all, it was the most hideous colour; it looked as if someone vomited green all over me. If that wasn't bad enough I had to wear flat-shoes because I did not get a pair of *'igh-'eels* until I started working. Charlie said I looked like *monkey waalkin' 'pon iron* (walking very clumsy) when I was learning to walk in my heels. I can only see the funny side of that now.

There was no way I could tell Mummy I was going on a date. I wore the dress in desperation and hoped Delano wouldn't notice. We went to the movies, but I don't remember what movie it was because I was more interested in holding his hand. And I was not going to get a baby by doing dat!

Delano eventually invited me to his home to meet his family, but his mother was not at home on the day I decided to visit. That was when I met his sister Lita (Estrelita). Would you believe they had a fridge? I was on a roll with this guy. That wasn't all, they had *jell-O* (jelly) and blamange; things I had only ever heard of. I played *brigah* when Lita offered me some. Although I was dying to try it I demurely said, "No t'ank yuh" ... you're laughing at my stupidity right? I was painfully shy in those days; too shy to eat in front of a stranger. It was getting dark so Delano said he would escort me home. To my utter surprise, he decided to kiss me just outside their front door. You *fas'* lot; I bet you want to hear about that too. Now you have to remember this was going to be my very first kiss so promise not to laugh. I did not know I was supposed to keep my mouth open so I closed it in the middle of the kiss. I am still cringing!

## Bikini Disaster

Luckhoo pool was only recently opened when I went to swim there for the first time. I borrowed a bathing suit from someone to begin with because I was still at school and had no money to buy one. Some of the girls were wearing nice bikinis, but that was only a pipe dream in my case. That was until I got the bright idea to make a two-piece bathing suit. That wasn't so difficult I thought; all I needed was someone to do the sewing, because we did not have a sewing machine. Lita's aunt who was only a few years older than us sewed so I begged Claudette to make it for me. I managed to find a nice floral pattern (more suitable for curtains) and made sure it was thick enough so nothing would show through when it got wet; you get my drift? The bust part was so simple, a fool could make it. A straight piece of fabric joined together with elastic threaded at the top and bottom. Wow! I looked HOT in that strapless two-piece; eyes were going to pop! I could not wait to show off my creation so Daphne and I went off to Luckhoo for the afternoon. Delano and Victor were already up on the diving board at one end so I went to the other end where I was going to dive in to make a splash. I came up all smiles and did not realise my top had disappeared until Daphne pointed it out. Didn't I tell you eyes were going to pop? How I didn't drown myself that day I will never know. After that I did not show my face at the pool for a very long time.

The *hobble* (pencil skirt) was high fashion at this time and naturally I wanted one. Girls were not allowed to wear them until they were *big*;

that happened when you stopped wearing socks. Well, I certainly wasn't wearing socks anymore. Only to school and Mummy did say I was a "big woman" so I qualified for a hobble. How to get one was the sixty-four dollar question. My aunt in Kingston who had married into relative wealth had a dozen step daughters so I got most of their *cast-offs*. That was where I got one of my high school uniforms from. Where was I? Oh! I was telling you about the *cast-offs*. It was a stroke of luck that a *full-skirt* (gathered skirt) came in the next lot they sent. Since it couldn't fit anyone, I decided to *loose-it-up* (unpick) to make my hobble. Once again Claudette came to my rescue. She did a great job because it fitted my curves perfectly and boy did I have curves! I was so proud of that skirt I wanted to show it off so I asked Lita to *tek out meh pickcha*. The fire hydrant in front of our home was the perfect place to pose. Daphne and I posed for a picture (she was wearing a *full-skirt*). My little cousin Donna was looking on so like *a neva-see cum-fuh-see*, she begged, "Tek out wan wid meh nah." I obliged because she was cute and I envied her beautiful curly hair. I bet she has that picture because I can't find it.

Another rite of passage for every Guyanese child was, *gettin' big* (becoming a grown up); none of us could wait for that day. You already know that was when girls stopped wearing socks. The boys became a man when they were allowed to wear *long pants*. If a boy tried to wear one without his parent's consent, he was said to be 'gettin' mannish' or 'fo'ce ripe'. My husband has a priceless story when he *became a man* but he might kill me if I tell you. He is a very private person; not a big mout' like me.

## Chubby Checker Concert

Our annual attraction was called the L.C.P (League of Coloured People) fair. My friends and I went to *lime* (socialise) and check out the boys; you never know where you may find a nice one.

The best and biggest attraction was when Chubby Checker came to Guyana. We were definitely living here when this event took place. The evening is etched into my memory. I was nursing a big-big hard boil under my left armpit and the abscess chose to erupt halfway through the concert. What a mess! I was wearing a sleeveless top and had nothing to mop it up with. As if that wasn't bad enough, I had to ride home after the concert praying the police didn't stop me, because my bicycle still had no light. But hey, I saw Chubby Checker in concert; he was fantastic!

## My Gambling Streak

My gambling streak emerged during this time. I made bingo cards from cardboard boxes and organised the gang from the GUYS to come over to my home on Saturday afternoon to play. This home was very small so we all *moled-up* on the front steps; no one complained. I only charged a penny a game. Where would you get good honest fun for that price today? No gaming license required. I was *chief-cook an' bottle-washer;* I ran the show and called the numbers. It was a business venture; so don't think I didn't make a profit. I took a small *cut* (a percentage) before deciding how much the prize money would be for each game. I must have made at least fifty cents every Saturday. [I am still pondering my failure to become a tycoon in the business world].

## The End of the World

My mother was a very religious person while she and my father belonged to the Seventh Day Adventist faith but too many bad things had happened in their lives and religion went by the wayside. I was now the only holy one in the family! I was a confirmed Catholic who went to confession every Saturday without fail, and church on Sunday because you had to fess up on Monday when the nuns asked if you went to church. Severe dressin' dung was expected if you gave a negative reply.

I had heard every bible story over the years and knew some of them by heart. From the time I could remember, Mummy had told me what to expect when the world came to an end; she obviously heard this in a sermon. She said we will hear a noise a million times louder than a bolt of thunder. Lo and behold the day finally arrived out of the blue. I was in the house day dreaming as usual when an almighty thundering noise turned my knees to water. It went on for what seemed like an eternity. I was rendered helpless and started praying; I honestly thought my mother's prophecy was coming true. Mummy was in the yard washing at the standpipe but she lived long enough to come running up the stairs to tell me what had happened. The roof of the huge wood shed two doors down had collapsed and gone down in a domino effect. Halleluiah! (I had some underwear to wash afterwards!)

## Daddy Matchmaking with Chivalry

I was almost sixteen before we moved from this address; Daphne and her family were living across the road so we spent every spare minute together. That was until I became best friends with Lita.

My father had gotten into a habit of drinking and was never home; this did not help matters between he and my mother. They never talked but conducted all of their conversations through me. It was a very sad period of my life, but looking back I now realise that the deterioration of their marriage began with Cheryl's death. Cher died ten years after their marriage (the ten blissful years Mummy always talked about). There were other contributing factors, but it's not my place to tell their story. They have taken those stories with them to the grave and that chapter is now closed.

Anyway I wanted to tell you about Daddy trying to marry me off to his friend. I was going home after visiting Daphne one day when I *butt-up* with Daddy and a duglah man (I had never met him) on the pave outside her home. After I had greeted them, Daddy turned to the man and said, "Dis is meh big dauttah." Imagine my surprise when the man took my hand, squeezed it and cockily said, "So you are the woman I am goin' to marry." [Yuh see how de man tried to sweet-talk meh wid 'e perfect English]? I quickly pulled my hand away, *sucked meh teet'* and dropped a good *cut-eye* on him before walking off in a huff.

We lived just across the road from Daphne so Daddy only had to *cross across* the road to get home but he and his friend must have gone to the rum-shop at the corner because there was no sign of him for hours. I challenged him as soon as he got home, wanting to know what his friend meant by that remark. My father had the nerve to tell me his friend was *a'good ketch* (a good prospect), because he was a school teacher. The subject was dropped and I did not see Brent for a long time after that.

Two years or so may have elapsed when I decided to pay some very good friends of my parents a visit. And who do you think was *moled-up* at Uncle Cecil and Aunty Dolly's home; it was Brent of all people. It turned out he was a relative and was boarding (just meals) with them.

Until then I did not know the connection. He was about ten years older than I am, but still a *batchie* (bachelor). Brent came over to our home a few times after that meeting. He was alright so I eventually accepted an invitation to the movies. Wait for it, another embarrassing experience. We were walking, yes, walking! You would think the man would at least own a bicycle seeing he was a teacher and supposed to be *a'good ketch* at that. Anyway, we were strolling on a carpet of scarlet petals along the avenue in Camp Street when we came to a big pool of water. Brent picked me up and carried me over the puddle. His unexpected action surprised and embarrassed me in front of the crowd queuing for the cinema. A man walking towards us laughed and said, "Chivalry is not dead." I am begging you, PLEASE do not laugh; I asked my date who Chivalry was, I certainly had never met him. Aah!! You learn something new every day, I remember Sir Walter Releigh; he was the guy who was looking for El Dorado (the fabled city of gold). The Raleigh I was more acquainted with was a brand of bicycle; I dreamed of owning one of those, a Hercules, Rudge or Humber would have been just as nice. Bicycles called Pink Witch, for obvious reasons came and went out of fashion in the twinkling of an eye; no one could afford them. But I bet I was the envy of all the girls in town when I got my Blue Witch!

# Chapter Eleven

*A drowning man will clutch at a straw.—Proverb*

## 1963-64 DRYSDALE STREET

### Communal Living

My father who had only ever managed rum-shops in the past few years had now taken a job at Sprostons Wharf. From what I remember, it was a flash in the pan. I broached the subject a few years ago and he confirmed the job only lasted nine months. I never thought to ask what his duties were; a Stevedore maybe?

The two duplex apartments and cottage in this yard, along with a good portion of the neighbourhood was owned by a dodgy East Indian man. The rotund money swindler did the rounds monthly with the rent book pretending to jot down notes for jobs needing urgent repair, but his insincere promises always evaporated.

Although this apartment was *frukudy* (dilapidated) it was a palace in my opinion. It boasted two bedrooms and a minute sitting-cum-dining area, but most important was the indoor plumbing. We had gone up a notch in society and on top of that, Aunty Lin moved into the adjoining apartment so Daphne was just next door. Life couldn't get any better.

The gutter was the only thing that separated our duplex and the road because the dilapidated palins in between were really an apology for a fence. A little hop from the landin' would have catapulted us into the street.

The second duplex was set back a little distance from the street. The Khans, an East Indian family, lived in the back apartment and an elderly lady we called Grannie occupied the front section. The Fernandes family lived behind us in the small cottage that looked like a doll's home; how I wished we had it instead.

This was a multi-racial environment but in no time we all became friends. The children in our yard amounted to twenty after Grannie took in a wayward young relative and her two small daughters. We had no need to leave our yard to find playmates, although I wasn't playing hopscotch anymore. At almost sixteen and a big woman according to Mummy, I was well and truly ready to start my hunt for a husband.

*Squash-Squash* (Uncle Sonny—he was short of stature) hated the teenagers who *moled-up* on his landin' to gossip and make his life hell. Daphne and I were pretty popular but our homes were too small to entertain our friends indoors. Admittedly, the man worked away during the week and only had the weekend to relax and enjoy his home. He thought we were a nuisance and was determined we should feel his wrath from time to time. Not only did he hurl abuse, sometimes there were objects. We were all *lallin' off* (relaxing) one evening when I experienced the phrase *time flies*. I was sitting on the rail that divided our landin' when a clock flew pass my face missing it by an inch. It sailed over the *palins* and landed in the gutter . . . it was time to call it a night. Aunty Lin said it was still ticking when Uncle Sonny retrieved it the following morning. The glass on the face of a *Westclox* clock was the only part that ever broke; those clocks lasted for donkey years. That was the same brand of clock I decorated that earned me a cut-tail from *de Jackass* (uncle) so how can I forget that?

Squash-Squash surprised us on occasion with a generous dousing when the noise became intolerable but nothing deterred us. Just as well, because it has provided me with an anecdote for my memoir. Didn't I tell you everything happens for a reason?

## Sweet Sixteen for Daphne and Me

A girl's sixteenth birthday was a big deal in Guyana; in my era anyway. I guess we were so deprived we needed a milestone to celebrate while waiting for the only significant birthday parents recognised and celebrated. That was our twenty-first birthday. It was called the 'comin'-of-age' and we were officially given the key to the door. I had double cause for celebration on my twenty-first birthday.

As you know Daphne and I were born less than a day apart. Our parents did not make a fuss of birthdays. To be honest they could not afford the expense. A lot of our friends had celebrated their 'sweet sixteen' birthdays; Daphne and I even organised a surprise *sub-party* (monetary contribution) at the Small's home for Lita whose birthday is also in March. Our parents were not even going to entertain the thought, so we decided to plan a party for ourselves. Aunty Lin gave Daphne permission to use their sitting room for the venue.

Daphne and I loved one another but there was no denying that there was healthy competition between us. I am speaking for myself, so you will have to ask Daphne how she felt. We used to *ketch case* (fall out) in primary school and not talk to one another for two days but we always found a way to patch things up. Anyone who had a close relationship or were inseparable like us were called *Batty an' Poe* (anus and chamber pot). The reference is an indication of the close association between the two. That is an endearing term in our rather warped vernacular.

We decided to keep our cakes a secret until the night. I said "we," but it was most likely my bright idea; wanting to show off that mine was going to be nicer. The cakes were going to be sponges; that was the intention anyway. I told you in the beginning that I have no patience for certain things and cake decorating is one of them. I cannot wait until one layer is dry to start on the next. As a result my cakes end up looking as if someone vomited on them after a hard night of partying. [CeCe, I am going to tell them you inherited the same virtue. I just wanted you to know I am not the only one in my family with that affliction].

We could not afford printed invitations so we relayed them verbally to our mutual friends then we went about planning the sparse menu. The party fare consisted of a big pot of cook-up rice, patties, channa, stuffed eggs, pine-tarts, and maybe a few peanuts. We bought a case of Juicee and I-Cee sweet-drinks and I seem to remember the boys sneaking in a few bottles of our famous Banks Beer.

It is customary in Guyana, to *stick-de-cake* (cut the cake) with someone of the opposite sex. We had already decided who our victims would be; I am sorry, I meant to say handsome boys. Would you believe I did not have a boyfriend at the time? I had broken up with *de rich* boy, but I was working on the *duglah* boy who lived across the street.

Strange, but the icing on my cake ended up being a similar colour to the maternity dress I wore for my first date; nevertheless I thought it looked beautiful. That was until Daphne brought hers out. She had kept it hidden until it was time to *stick-de-cake*. I was never so *shame* in my life. My cake was a dismal failure compared to hers. To begin with, Daphne's cake had height, whereas mine looked as if a cannon ball had dropped on it. She chose a lovely pink colour scheme, and the sly wretch had used a piping bag to decorate around the edges . . . it was simply beautiful. By this time, I had turned the colour of my cake with envy. We lit the candles on both cakes and the usual happy birthday was sung. After blowing out the candles, I grabbed and yanked the lot out, leaving a gaping hole in the middle of the cake. As it is customary, the boy shoved some cake in my mouth. Shucks, I did not remember using cement.

I blocked out the entire party from that point and can't even tell you who I stick-de-cake with. I must ask Daphne if she remembers because there are no pictures to mark the auspicious occasion. Just as well because the memories are bad enough.

## Teaching at Stella Maris

My departure from St Joseph's had left me in a bit of a predicament. I had no high school certificate and this posed a problem finding employment. Most young women with a similar problem resorted to commercial lessons (shorthand and typing) to improve their chances of finding a job. This seemed like the only option so I decided to give it a try. A school in Thomas Street came highly recommended so I enrolled. How anyone learnt anything at that place is beyond me; no teaching was ever done. The tutors gave us the books, sat us in front of a typewriter then never bothered to explain anything . . . it was hopeless. Before long, money became a problem; my parents could not afford the fees so I had to drop out. Jobs were hard to come by and I had no skills; it was a terrible time.

The saying, "It's not what you know; but who you know," came into play here. Aunty Hermina came to the rescue. She was married to a staunch Catholic who was a prominent member of Sacred Heart Church; this prestige enabled her to 'pull a few strings' as they say. She had already done this favour for Daphne the previous year so I guess she thought it was only fair to help me. She recommended me to the nuns at the Sisters of Mercy Convent in Kingston, asking them to consider me for a position as a kindergarten teacher at Stella Maris School. An interview was arranged and I met with the principal, Sister Mary Ursula. She was a rather stern character but she agreed to give me a chance. I was put on a probation period of three months. I started in September 1963 when the new school year commenced; it was a relief I tell you.

The school was a two-storey building with two additional classrooms located behind the convent. Mrs Hill and Miss Annette Adjodia taught those classes. In later years Mrs Ferreira joined the ranks to run a commercial class and canteen.

I taught a beginners class on the lower level of the school. My colleagues were Glenda Gonsalves, Pat Gaskin, Vera Gajrag, Noreen Bacchus and my cousin Daphne Gomes; Sister Kostka was our supervisor. The upper level teachers were Mrs Gill, Mrs Isaacs and Sister Ursula. The teachers who later joined the staff were, Pansy Pelay, Elizabeth D'Andrade, Norma DaSilva, Sue (Sursati) Singh, Elizabeth Rodrigues and Marilyn Nyguen who all became my friends.

The teachers went through the same ritual with Sister Ursula at the end of each month when wages were received. The sombre mood in which she conducted this task led us to believe we were being called to a death chamber. We were individually summoned by one of the pupils on the upper level to appear before her desk. I was always a nervous wreck when it was my turn. My knees shook as she delivered the compulsory pep talk, then it was time to sign for the paltry salary. I could almost hear the words, "consider yourself lucky" as she ceremoniously handed over the envelope. The probation period was hell; I lived in fear of her terminating my services. Thank goodness she never gave me the chop. I credited her wisdom for recognising a good worker.

Sister Kostka was strict but fair, she was a younger nun who had spirit. She was the first nun to play the guitar on the altar when the church relaxed its rules. Her sense of fun led her to do a most unpredictable thing one day. The junior teachers were in the lunch room trying on the new hats Lincoln had made us for the fair, when she came in. She whipped off her veil and donned one of the hats. Our mouths were still open when she cocked her head and said, "Well, does it suit me?" We were dumbfounded to see she had hair; we were told all nuns are bald.

Children from wealthy and prominent families attended Stella Maris. This afforded the teachers some perks. We received Christmas gifts and were invited to the occasional birthday party. Denise Gillette's generous parents invited all of the teachers and served the best food!

A wealthy family engaged me for a short period to give their daughter extra lessons leading up to the common entrance exam twice a week after school. That earned me four extra dollars. Their maid Thea offered me a beautiful snack on the first day, but when she asked me the next time if I would like something to eat, I was embarrassed and timidily said, "A'doan mine," meaning I would, but the *schupid* woman obviously took it as a negative and I am still waiting! A snack was subsequently omitted and I was not impressed.

To my knowledge none of the kindergarten teachers had a teaching diploma. The teaching was well structured and the nuns made sure we were trained with up to date methods. Sister Kostka even went on an overseas holiday one year to learn about improved teaching methods. Any knowledge gained was passed on to the teachers. We were in awe of the Cuisenaire Rods and Flash Cards. The children lacked nothing and had a good foundation at Stella Maris; it was no fly-by-night school. I taught at Stella Maris until my marriage in 1968. Those five years were one of the most enjoyable periods in my life. I loved those children and the camaraderie of the other teachers. My salary went from forty to eighty dollars a month after five years. I would not be able to buy a loaf of bread with that if I lived in Guyana today!

## Extra Duties without Pay

Those nuns were very cunning; they utilised our services to their advantage. The junior teachers were made to do all sorts of extra jobs for the value of a meal.

We all dreaded the last two weeks of the long school holidays because Sister Ursula made us report for duty. We spent everyday scrubbing and varnishing every bench and desk on the upper level and then had to clean everything on the lower level. The only thing we looked forward to was the meal she bribed us with. That dreadful job was all included in our *scrawly* pay packet. We called her a slave driver behind her back. There was no union to complain to, *besize* no one would dream of lodging a complaint against the nuns.

Sister Kostka did take the teachers on a trip to Mahaicony, but I am not entirely sure it was free of cost since we had to travel on the train to get there. Two enjoyable nights were spent at a guest house. Pictures were taken of those carefree days; in one I am wearing a Coolie hat (god knows where I got it) but that is no surprise because I was always the rebel teacher who led the others astray.

St Joseph High School (the one I attended) held an annual fair on the school grounds at Thomas Lands. This was a very big event so the nuns capitalised on the action to raise some revenue of their own. They conned us, in not only running their stall, but to also do all the preparations leading up to the event. In the beginning it was me, Daphne and Noreen. Norma joined us when she started teaching at Stella Maris. In hindsight I can see we were used, but we didn't complain back then. I actually enjoyed and looked forward to the friendliness the event provided each year. Noreen's clever brother-in-law Lincoln always designed and made a special hat for us for the occasion. We went to great lengths to make sure our wardrobe was coordinated to create a theme. One year tent dresses were the rage. I look pregnant in the picture we had taken; that style just didn't suit me, but I had to follow like sheep just for the sake of fashion . . . You're not seeing that picture folks!

Teachers in Michoney, me wearing a 'Coolie' hat

Me, Norma, Noreen & Daphne wearing the hats
Noreen's brother-in-law Lincoln made one year.

## Getting a Telephone Call at Work

We did not have a telephone at home but it was an instrument we had great respect for. It was seen as an object to be used only in an emergency. That is why I panicked the first time I was summoned to the convent. The maid the nun had sent to fetch me sheepishly said, "Sistah seh yuh must guh ova to de convent now, becaze sumone want fuh talk to yuh 'pon de fone." My legs instantly turned to jelly and I was panic-stricken; I honestly thought someone in my family had died. Why or who would call me at work otherwise? My best friend Lita was on the phone . . . her brother who I used to date (*de rich bhai*) had been knocked down by a cow. He was injured and he wanted to see me. Why I wondered? I was no longer officially his girlfriend and I was not too thrilled about the fright this call gave me. Lita was my best friend and Delano was a very nice person, so I relented and went to visit him after work.

I only had a handful of calls in the five years I worked there, and each one of them frightened the daylights out of me.

## A Nun in Our Family

Having a nun in the family was a sort of safeguard for my job. Sister Mary Rita was Daddy's eldest half-sister. She was stationed in the Northwest; a place called Hosororo but spent her annual holiday at the convent in Georgetown. I was always invited to have a meal in the convent kitchen so she could pump me for all the family secrets. My aunt never ate with me and I was always very self-conscious because the servants were condescending.

Those nuns ate things I had never seen or heard about. Cauliflower was one of them. I wondered where it came from, because I never saw it in our markets. As for cabbage; we certainly could not afford to serve big portions like they did.

I did not know it at the time, but this incident took place at what was to be our very last meeting. Sistah Rita had heard my parents were finally buying a home, and that Daddy was having some trouble with the man he was purchasing it from. She asked me what had happened and in my haste to *talk white* (to speak perfect English) I disgraced myself by saying, "De mon was tryin' to raab Daddy" instead of, "The man was trying to rob Daddy." She was getting on in age, so I prayed she was deaf and did not hear me. I still cringe when I think of it. She was a sweetheart who always had a little gift (something holy) for me and I always enjoyed seeing her.

## Pickcha Tekkin' with Phillippe

Another thing we had to endure once a year was *pickcha tekkin'* (a photo session). These were official pictures of the teachers and their class. The photographer Philippe was very well known around town and was very good at his job. He just didn't know when to stop. That man took a million pictures. I was sick to death of smiling by the end of the ordeal. But did I learn from that experience? No, I commissioned Philippe to come to my home to take pictures on my birthday. There weren't many places to pose in our tiny sitting room so most of my pictures were taken standing in front of the same plastic floral arrangement, or sitting on the hot pink Chesterfield suite. I looked like a statue with the handbag draped over my arm like the queen. I never had my picture taken as a child so I was making up for it in my teenage years.

Teachers L to R Vera, Noreen, Pat, Annette, Pansy, Elizabeth,
Norma, Me & Glenda (Daphne absent)

My class and I enduring our annual photo session at Stella Maris School

## Mummy Had Major Surgery

My mother was very proud of the long scar she had on her lower abdomen. She regaled us with stories of the magnitude of her gall bladder operation and said the stones they removed were huge. I listened in awe; although this period of my life is vague. For starters, we were not living at this address. Anetta was very little when my mother had this surgery and she went to live with Aunt Hermina in Kingston. Pat told me many years later they never knew a toddler who could bawl so much, they nicknamed her 'Ann de Balla'.

To tell the truth I can only remember going to my aunt in Cowan Street to visit Mummy while she was recuperating. I have no recollection of visiting her in hospital and cannot remember who looked after us during that period. However, I remember sleeping once or twice at the Rodrigues family in their huge two-storey home in Cowan Street. Children came out of the woodwork in that household; more than a dozen in varied ages. I enjoyed going there even though I experienced extreme shyness. Everyone did their best to make me feel at home and the maid always gave me a snack. They were *de rich* family in my opinion.

I was captivated when I saw their maid moving an object over the clothes. The contraption was attached to a long cord and I didn't know what it was, but I figured it had to be an iron because it was flattening the clothes. We certainly did not have one of those. Our two irons were solid cast-iron. Some people used a *coal-pot* (an apparatus fuelled by coal) to heat their irons but we heated ours on the stove. We alternated between the two when ironing. Mummy was strict about ironing and would not allow us to wear *rough-dry* (unpressed) clothing. On ironing day all the starched clothes had to be *sprinkled* (dampened down) then tightly rolled up and left to soften in readiness for pressin'. My mother NEVER put her hand in water for the rest of the day after she pressed clothes. She said she would *ketch coal* (catch a cold) because her hand was hot for too long. I think that was a ploy to get me to do everything for the remainder of the day. When I started doing my own laundry she expected me to follow this rule. Her nagging fell on deaf ears, so she trotted out her famous "mark my words" speech. So far her words haven't come to pass because I can't remember ever *ketchin' a'coal* from immersing my hands in water after ironing.

I have fond memories of the Rodrigues clan from 80 Cowan Street in Kingston. I may not remember where we were living when Mummy had surgery but I know without a doubt the Rodrigues family left British Guiana on the 24th July 1963 while we were living at this address. I remember the beautiful dollies Pat, Cecelia and Geralyn were holding that day. I am missing from the farewell picture. I was sixteen and suffering from TRAP (Total Rebellion against Parents) syndrome. I did go with them to say goodbye, but was most likely hiding upstairs. I regret that now.

My parents, Uncle Deck, Aunty Hermina, Joel, Aunty Lin & Aunty Olga
Front Sharon, Donna, Anetta, Cecelia, Geralyn & Pat

### How Could Mummy Be Pregnant?

Further embarrassment was added when my mother fell pregnant at age forty. Come on! I was seventeen and didn't *t'ink dem ol' people were still doin' commonness.* This was one secret I was going to keep to the bitter end; especially from my friend Lita who came from a respectable family.

On her way to visit me, Lita passed Mummy who was now seven months pregnant. She noticed and questioned me but since it was my darkest secret I refused to admit the truth and pretended I had no knowledge of the pregnancy. Lita was appalled by my behaviour. She said it was nothing to be ashamed of and told me it was a beautiful blessing. [Lita dated Joel and Mummy wished she would become her daughter-in-law; she liked her *white* complexion].

I practically disowned my mother while she was pregnant. Our relationship remained strained right to the end of her pregnancy but I

315

relented and went to the hospital two days after my sister CeCe (Cecelia) was born. One look and I was besotted. Who do you think found a cradle for the new baby? Lita's Aunt was getting rid of theirs so I organised to get it home. It needed painting but I could not afford the paint. A friend heard of my plight and donated a stray can he had no use for. Have you ever seen a baby's cradle painted silver? *Ow meh goi*, the little angel had to *dodo* (sleep) in a cot riddled with lead. It's a wonder CeCe survived. She snacked continuously on the flaking paint; we saw the evidence in her silver coated lips but turned a blind eye.

My baby sister became my pride and joy. I attached a baby carrier to the handlebar of my bicycle and took her everywhere. Most Saturday afternoons I went *weddin' watchin'*, it was a popular pastime especially if I knew who the bride was. A big crowd of uninvited guests like me always stood outside the church to gawk and voice their opinion of the bride and guests; mostly to criticise or to guess whether the bride was 'up-de-duff'. Before I knew it, a rumour had circulated and people were saying the baby belonged to me. I knew the truth so I ignored what anyone said. I loved my sister to death, and to this day CeCe and I are closely bonded.

## Solex Envy

Every Guyanese from my era will remember the *Solex*, it was a motorised bicycle, ugly like sin but how I wanted one. Very few young people could afford a car; some had motorcycles which was what I would have liked, but that would have only happened *w'en fowl-cock get teet'* (never). A Solex was the most I could aspire—in about ten years on my wage. The young man who was *tacklin'* (courting) Jean next door had a Solex and I drooled over it every time he visited. The bike was parked close to our home when Lita came to visit one day. She had her camera so I sat on the bike pretending it was mine and asked her to *tek out ah pickcha*. Lil' Helen and Desiree can be seen in the background *skinnin' deh teet'*.

Me posing on a solex, Lil' Helen & Desiree looking on

Back Row-Me, Famena (Penny) & Ernesta Front-Peter,
Sharon, Lil' Helen & Donna

## The Fashion Police

Fashion conscious young women kept up with the latest trend, and some girls began wearing *hard-pants* (denim jeans) but I could not afford them. I had to stick to designing and having my t'ree fuh D dresses made by Miss Thelma. We were mostly ladylike in Guyana and would not be caught dead wearing trousers to a *fete* (party/dance); these were reserved for informal or casual wear. I never realised trousers were actually forbidden in some households and had to find that out the hard way. I paid the Martins a visit shortly after Johnny and I began dating. I was not yet acquainted with *de rules* in their family so I rocked up wearing a trendy pants suit. Mr Martin emerged from the bottom-'ouse and gave me a disapproving look before saying, "Good afta-noon yung man." Then he yelled, "Johnny, dere is a'fella 'ere to see yuh." I wondered if the man had lost his marbles, but Johnny later explained the reason. Needless to say, when I visited thereafter I never wore trousers.

The mini later came into fashion but my hemline had to be lowered to keep Mummy and the gossip mongers quiet. My reputation went down the drain when I was classed as a 'tramp' for flaunting myself on a float in a parade for the 1966 Independence celebrations. Mr Harrison who lived in our street (his daughters also attended Stella Maris) was the person responsible for me being on the float promoting a Toyota car. That astute man approached me because he recognised the figure of a super model. The float depicted a beach scene and he wanted sexy beach babes. Go ahead and laugh, but it is true! He supplied the funds and actually asked me to buy bikinis. I declined because I was much too modest. I bought two swimsuits instead. The black suit had risqué peepholes in the back and front. The other suit was brown with a yellow band around the hips and a simple scooped neckline. I will show you the picture in the black bathers so you can see what a 'tramp' I was back then.

## Attention Seeking

I was sadly lacking attention and found all sorts of ways to get it. Lita had become very clever at sewing and wore some lovely creations made from t'ree for D fabric. She should have gone into dress designing because she certainly had a flair for it. I loved every dress she made and wanted to copy it. I was like that; not an original idea in my head back then.

Valentines Day was approaching, another event we celebrated. It was a very special occasion for us young girls. We always went to a dance and had a new dress made in the red and white theme. Lita made a beautiful dress, and then Daphne and I got on the bandwagon and decided to make identical ones. I think it was a different fabric but the same style with red hearts all around the bottom of the wide shirt. We tried on the dresses when we got to my home and they fitted perfectly, then I said, "Le'we akse Gramuddah who looks nicer;" it was my inferiority complex speaking.

Gramuddah Philly was staying with us because she had an accident. [She had fallen off the ladder while picking coffee and had to come to town to have her broken wrist put in a cast]. I can't believe I had put that poor woman in such an awkward position, but she was very wise when she said, "Yuh both look very pretty." I could not accept that so I said, "But Gramuddah, who does de dress look nicer on?" She would not give a different answer so I persisted like a dripping tap until she said, "Yuh both look very pretty but Daphne is slimmer suh sh' looks nicer." Well it serves me right for pestering Grammuddah. I always thought I was a fat cow and now it was confirmed. I was devastated and never wore the dress when Daphne wore hers.

## The Amazing Miss Thelma

This wonderful lady will always be Miss Thelma to me; pure respect. She is a Portuguese woman with eight beautiful children and still found time to do dressmaking to make ends meet. She did not own a washing machine so the washing alone was a mammoth task. How she also found time to make bread for her brood is beyond me. I sometimes arrived for a fitting just as she was taking a batch out of the oven. She was a lady with a very big heart who always offered me one of her piping hot bread rolls.

Her generosity meant so much to me back then. Although my surname was the same as hers, we are not related. There is only one thing our families had in common. My last brother and her last daughter were both born on the same day, and both she and Mummy closed the maternity shop after that.

And now I am going to brag by telling you that I finally know someone who is famous. Pricilla Lopes Schliep is Miss Thelma's granddaughter. Just in case you have forgotten, she won the Bronze Medal in the hurdles in the Beijing Olympics in 2008. I am honoured to say I know Pricilla's family.

Miss Thelma always says, "'ow yuh doin' *chile* (child)?" whenever I call her in Toronto. Well *chile*, I would like to say you are a "very special" person, someone I will never forget. It is an enduring friendship after all these years. Miss Thelma still cooks me a Guyanese meal whenever I visit them in Toronto. Thanks so much for the wonderful memories.

Julian & Elizabeth stickin' their 1st birthday cake

## Enduring Friendships

My best friend Lita and her family moved to her grandfather's home in Regent Street. That house was big-big. It was two-storeys high, dark as a dungeon and had so many rooms you could easily get lost. I was there every chance I got and Lita was not my sole reason for visiting. They were the only people I ever knew who owned a Monopoly game.

Lita visited another friend of hers one day and found her doing something very interesting. Her imagination peaked after this friend told her of her plans to make a bedspread. There was no cost involved and all she needed was bits of scrap material, patience and time. Both Lita and her aunt Claudette sewed, so scraps were plentiful and since I just about lived there I offered to help. We sat for hours on the front verandah cutting out small circles of cloth from a cardboard pattern to make the tiny rosette. We basted around the edge of the circle then pulled the cotton tight before securing it with a knot; it was that simple. I lost track of how many rosettes we made but it must have been hundreds. The bedspread was never assembled because Lita and her family immigrated to Canada a month after CeCe was born in 1964. Eighteen years elapsed before I saw Lita again. In the meantime I had forgotten all about the bedspread.

When I visited Lita in Toronto in 1982 she invited me up to her bedroom saying she had something to show me. I gasped and had to choke back tears when I saw the bedspread that graced her bed. Our steadfast friendship was entwined in those simple bits of scraps. There were twenty-four squares and each one comprised of ninety-nine rosettes. In total it took two thousand, three hundred and seventy-six rosettes to make that amazing bedspread. It is truly a work of art that can be compared to Jacob's coat of many colours. And what did it cost? Simply time, patience and the companionship of true friends . . . well worth it!

Lita and I made hundreds of these rosettes to make a bedspread

Me, Lita, Ingrid & Daphne trampin' in the streets

## I Found a Second Name

Not having a second name has always been an issue, but I finally came up with one that suits me perfectly and I am sure you would agree. I actually have two to choose from, although I believe *Shame* wins over *Fas'*. I can honestly say not a week went by without an embarrassing episode.

Here is another anecdote that added to my shameful experiences. I was visiting a friend when my bicycle was stolen. This was a major catastrophe since it was quite a distance to Stella Maris in Kingston, where I worked. And if you think I was rich being a teacher, think again. The wage was only forty dollars a month at this time. Besize, I was a *big woman* so I had to pay board out of that *scrawly* amount.

Appearances were important at my age. I wanted a new dress among other things when I got paid which meant there wasn't much left to buy another bike. Duggie who lived over the road gave me *a drop* (a lift) some days until Daddy came to the rescue. He felt sorry for me so he scouted around and managed to get a frame, from god knows where. Every part of that bicycle was second-hand, but I was desperate. Thank goodness he got a straight bar because I would have been doubly embarrassed riding a *preggy* bicycle. I waited anxiously for him to finish putting it together.

I will never know what got into my father's head but he painted the bicycle the brightest blue without consulting me. Paint given to him at no cost I bet. No Pink Witch for me; I was *special* so I had a 'Blue Witch' that was a beacon. I couldn't go anywhere I did not want my parents to know about, because someone would spot the blue bike and report the sighting to them. I would no sooner get home and Mummy would say, "A'eard yuh were strayin' again, suh an' suh said deh saw yuh," and the interrogation would begin. Considering we had no telephone, the news travelled fast.

## Dr All-He-Saw Hospital

People in Guyana are really fas' I tell you. Not only fas', they also like to *waalk wid deh mout'* (carry news), and enjoyed minding *deh matty* business. My blue bicycle almost exposed a friend of mine one time. I went to visit her at a hospital, which was famous for performing abortions. I can't divulge the real name, but Dr All-He-Saw is as close as it sounds and boy did that man see plenty. Everybody went there to *t'row 'way baby* (abortion). It was a regular hospital, but the abortion rumors gave it a terrible reputation. If you told anyone you were In Dr All-He-Saw hospital they jumped to conclusions that you could have only been there for one *t'ing*. You know what I mean?

Someone's mother asked me to take some *unmentionables* to this hospital one day and I happily obliged. I had nothing to hide, and since I was only going to be there for a few minutes, I parked my bike at the front gate. As soon as I got home, Mummy attacked me saying, "Wha' yuh been doin' at Dr All-He-Saw hospital; who yuh know in deh?" Yes, some news carrier had seen my Blue Witch and made it their business to tell Mummy. I naturally wanted to know who told her and was so surprised I had to run to my bedroom so she couldn't see me laughing when she told me who the informant was. The sister of the person I visited had gone past the hospital and seen the bike then made it her business to stop and tell my mother. She was obviously trying to make *bassa-bassa*. Her mother had kept her sister's whereabouts a secret; they all assumed she was in the country for the weekend.

It was amazing how many young girls went to *de country* for the weekend but it wasn't to have fun. To this day I am sure she doesn't know what her sister did, but I will take that to my grave, along with something that happened to me when I was eleven years old. We all have a few secrets like that; don't tell me you haven't because I won't believe you.

I also knew a few girls from well-to-do families who told people they were going overseas to take up 'nursin', but the news always got out that it was *nursin'* with a different qualification. If that had happened to me I would have *cark duck* (had no hope) and had to bear the shame of having an illegitimate child.

My mother was forever warning me about jealous people who liked to *wash deh mout' on yuh* (to wish you the worse) and believe me, there were many jealous people waiting for an opportunity. I was lucky I had guardian angels.

## Infested With Vermin

A lot of people had to contend with a leaky roof but on top of that most homes were infested with vermin, it was an acceptable part of life then. The only thing I hated was finding a hole in the bread after a rat had taken a chunk. If that ever happened in Australia we would throw the entire loaf out, but we could not afford to do that when I was growing up. We cut out the surrounding area and happily ate the rest of the bread. This was not a daily occurrence; it only happened when we were careless. I complained to Aunty Olga once and regretted it. She pointed out something I had never thought of. She was laughing when she said, "Well Helena, yuh cyan see weh de rat 'ad 'e mout' but do yuh know weh 'e 'ad 'e batty (anus)?" I had never stopped to contemplate that equation. Needless to say I could never eat bread that was nibbled by a rat after that revelation.

We were also plagued by *cackaroach* (cockroach) and bed bugs. It's a miracle we were not all exterminated ourselves, because Mummy was forever crying out, "Helen, bring de flit-cyan," when she found the bed bugs. The fumes almost suffocated us. I can still smell the DDT (Damn Dangerous T'ing) spray we used to eradicate those pests. The smell was disgusting. Those bugs scurried so fast we had a job to catch them but Mummy was an expert at squashing them. I would like to say something in case you are thinking we must have lived in a pigsty.

That could not be further from the truth because my mother was one of the cleanest people around. She washed every day and hung the mattresses through the window to air them regularly, but those bugs always returned. The mystery of the bed bugs was solved when I read an article sent to me by a relative in Canada not so long ago. Scientists discovered fiber (coconut) used in mattresses contained a parasite which evolved into bugs. Fibers were banned after that discovery and I had an answer for the bug problem. All of our mattresses were made from coconut fiber, of course that was after we moved to town and *granulated* from banana leaves.

## Confessions for Stealing from de Safe

One of our prized possessions was an old food-safe that was used to store our foodstuff. The legs were immersed in discarded condensed milk tins filled with water to prevent ants from entering. The dome shaped top, covered in fine wire mesh had hinges that allowed one half to be lifted. We kept the perishables, or anything we did not want the insects to get at in that section. As a double precaution we sat the condensed milk tin in water. That condensed milk got everyone into trouble. There were four children in the house who could reach the top of that safe, but each of us thought they were the only one taking a suck from the can. We all denied the theft when Mummy discovered the deed.

The Klim was another thing I used to t'ief. I shoveled a mouthful in whenever I thought Mummy wasn't looking but she caught me one day. She asked me a question at the very moment the Klim entered my mouth. The dry milk powder choked me when I started to answer, giving the secret away. A few cuffs around the ears and she was happy. Daddy on the other hand had to keep his strength; god knows for what . . . maybe lifting his elbow to drink? He bought a big-big tin of Ovaltine and stupidly kept it in the *Safe*. How *safe* was that when I was around? It was *bung fuh* happen; he also caught me but Daddy was a softie. He tried to put on a serious face but all he said was, "Gyurl, yuh mekin' yuh eye pass meh, stap it yuh 'ear meh?" Okay Daddy, I will just make sure you are not home next time I take some.

I believe in the saying, "Everything happens for a reason." so all this stealing must be the reason I became a *Carta-lick*. How else could

I live with a guilty conscience? *Faddah* (priest) saw me every Saturday without fail because I always had something to confess. I wonder if he used to see me coming and say, "Shit, 'ere comes de Ovaltine or Klim t'ief" or "A'wanda if sh' 'ad a'wicked taut 'bout dat bhai nex' door again." I confessed everything; no one was holier than I was, other than our roof of course. How times have changed . . . you wouldn't *ketch* me anywhere near a confessional now. I have a direct line of communication with the good Lord these days and I am still confessing.

Who invented *fly-paper* (sticky trap for flies) I often wondered; it is the most revolting thing ever. The nasty black strip hung over our dining room table showing off its catch. I was fed up of looking at it one time and asked Daddy if he was going to buy a new one. After an extensive examination, the man looked at me seriously and said, "It still got sum landin' space gyurl, money doan grow 'pon trees."

## Lover Alert, Pickin' Fares and Cut-tail Lizard

There were some questionable characters living in this neighbourhood. We became friendly with the maid next door who told us her mistress was having an affair. Her husband worked away for long periods so she was having a bit of fun. Her lover actually came to the home but since the husband usually arrived home unannounced she worked out a signal. The maid said she hung a towel over the stick used to prop the jalousie window open. I was fas' so every time I went past that house I looked to see if a towel was hanging up. The poor woman could have just been drying her towel!

The relative Granny took-in was a beautiful young woman. She had a very handsome boyfriend but she was a *waabin* (prostitute) in his absence. She lived next door so naturally we saw the men coming and going; business was very brisk some days. That girl wore all the latest creations and Mummy called her a cut-tail *lizette* (female lizard). When this woman's boyfriend was in town she acted as if butter couldn't melt in her mouth, but one day all hell broke loose. Someone must have alerted him to this fact because he came home unexpected; caught her in the act and gave her a cut-ass. She ran naked from the house screaming blue murder! The soap opera *Desperate Housewives* probably originated in this neighbourhood.

I never realised we had a few *waabins* in our family until I ran into two of my mother's cousins. I was stunned to see these two ladies standing at the corner of Camp and Regent Streets at 4.30 in the afternoon dressed to kill. I said good afta-noon then asked where they were going. They looked at me like stunned mullets and muttered a feeble excuse. I later found out they were standing there *pickin' fares* (waiting for prospective clients), tut, tut!

We had a name for everything and everyone and most of the time I understood the reason for the name but a *cut-tail lizette* baffled me and it took a bit of figuring out. This was a term used to describe women who dressed and walked in a provocative manner. You did not have to be a *waabin* either to be called that. Let me give you the reason for the name. It is a known fact that a lizard will automatically release its tail when it is threatened; after letting go of its tail the lizard struts off shaking its rear end mimicking a walk similar to that of a sexy woman. Now, doesn't that name make sense? Take a break and go outside and try to catch a lizard by its tail and you will see for yourself. Go on a'gon wait fuh yuh.

We knew quite a few women that were referred to by that name. Who knows, someone could have even called me that behind my back because I enjoyed *dressin' up to de nines*; most of my dresses were backless. When I dressed to go out Daddy used to say, "Gyurl, yuh gon ketch a'fresh coal," but I never *voomps 'pon 'e*. A bare back is fine but I never showed cleavage; *besize* you can't show what you haven't got! That wasn't the real reason; I was just too modest and had some morals. No one can accuse me of doin' a Princess Diana because I wore a *half-slip* (petticoat) at all times.

Our Chinese neighbors across the street had a daughter that was a cut-tail lizette. Mummy stared in astonishment whenever she walked past our home wearing her *stretch-to-fit* (Lycra) pants and said they had to be pasted on because they were skin tight. Her long jet black hair swished against her *bee-tee* (backside) as she sashayed from side to side; she was a hot lizard!

## Using Joel as a Decoy

My mother was still very strict with me even though I was almost seventeen. She still hadn't told me the *real* facts of life but stuck to her no dating rule and kept reminding me that a girl could get herself into *serious trouble* if she was alone with a boy. Where there's a will, there's a way. Mummy preached that one herself. If she thought I was going to stay home and let grass grow under my feet, she had another thought coming. I was resolute in my bid for freedom so I enlisted the help of my brother and started partying big time. Mummy assumed Joel would be with me at all times but he was just a decoy. I frequented the popular nightclubs, Belvedere, Bamboo Gardens, Carib Hotel and Palm Court and danced the night away to the rhythm of the Telstars, Rhythmaires, the Ramblers and Combo Seven. On occasion the Merrymen, Byron Lee and the Dragonaires and Dave Martin's Tradewinds came to Guyana to entertain us.

By this time Delano was history; he had immigrated to Canada anyway. I was now madly in love with the lead guitarist Winston Duggin from the Telstars band. Duggie actually lived across the street from us so it was convenient to come home with him if I attended a dance where his band was playing. All this romance took place on a bicycle. Duggie *towed* (sitting on the crossbar) me up to the nearest corner where I hopped off and Joel towed me the rest of the way home, just in case the dragon was waiting up. I was such a devious wretch. It was an innocent relationship but try telling my mother that. Duggie was too busy playing in a band most weekends to take me out; *besize* he had women falling at his feet. My feet usually got cramped from hanging down on the bicycle so imagine my surprise when I got home one night (morning actually) to find one of my shoes was missing. We had to back track to find it.

## Cinderella

Having a boyfriend next door was not such a good idea. There were things I did not want him to see. No one in their right mind would want to be seen scrubbing steps like Cinderella. Not all of the homes we lived in had stairs, but this one did. Mummy said you were judged by the degree of cleanliness your stairs presented, so ours was done regularly. That chore fell to me every Saturday. I kept watch to make sure Duggie had left his home, then I got down to business armed with a bucket of water, a *scraper* (a sharp piece of metal) *salsoap* and a *floor-cloth*. God help the person who wanted to pass while I was scrubbing; they practically had to sprout wings. Ask Charlie how many times he copped a bucket of water. I must say it was a job well worth doing, even though I had better things to do with my time. To tell the truth, the front stairs in this house were the only part of the house in good condition and worth admiring. We might not have had religion in our life, but this house was so holy it made up for it; leaking like a sieve when it rained.

I was on the phone to my friend Norma recently who lives in Toronto and we were discussing the condition of our beds after a nights sleep. We both discovered no one would know we slept in a bed, because it was always so neat when we got out. I pondered the reason afterwards and came up with the answer. Nearly all of the homes we lived in leaked. We had to use buckets, pots and other utensils to catch the drips. I learnt to sleep without knocking over the pot of water that was often my bed companion. That has got to be the answer to my rigid sleeping pattern.

## Losing My Teeth at Seventeen

I had some bad luck with my teeth. No one in my family went to the dentist unless it was an emergency. We had homemade remedies for toothache but I have already told you about that.

My mother was an expert at extractions when I was little. She did not go to the trouble of using the door knob like some parents did. She tied a length of thread around the tooth and yanked until it came out. I stopped crying after she gave me the sweetie. The tooth fairy hadn't reached our shores back then but I'm sure she has made her way there by now. We had a ritual of slinging the extracted tooth onto the roof. We recited the incantation "Rata, rata, bring meh teet' back," while making a concentrated effort to hit the target. I lived in fear of the tooth falling to the ground because that meant the request would be denied. I told our children the *Rata* story and they said I made it up. No sir, it is *truh-truh*; *akse* any Guyanese.

Yuh see how quick a'fuget w'at a'was goin' tuh tell yuh? I started to tell you that I had some bad luck with my teeth. My front teeth looked perfectly healthy from the front, but were decaying from behind. Mummy finally took me to the dentist when I could no longer stand the pain. Since I was only fifteen the *quack* (dentist) confidently said he could save the teeth. His plan to partially cap them with gold appealed to me because Guyanese *luv gol'*; especially in their teeth. This method failed because the incompetent dentist neglected to fill the teeth before capping them with the gold. Air was allowed to enter and it caused rapid decay; the pain was excruciating. The damage was beyond repair and my only option was to have them extracted. This was devastating news.

The long school holiday was approaching so I asked the dentist (we could not afford a better dentist) if he would be able to get the entire job completed by the time school re-opened on the 30th September. I remember the date because it is my sister Anetta's birthday. He assured me it would be ready on the 29th September and I trusted that jackass. *Maan,* I had to start school without my teeth and I was so *shame.* I held my hand over my mouth the entire day so I would not *fryken de lil' chirren.*

Thank god it was ready the following day. Before I forget to tell you, there is more humiliation attached to this saga. I had to deal with the dentist son who was a well known *saga-bhai* around town. This Romeo was doing his apprenticeship so he decided to ask me for a date one day while my mouth was full of cottonwool. I politely declined, mumbling I would not be seen in public without teeth. Wait for it. He offered to lend me a denture for the date. Go figure!

My denture caused me to miss out on a few outings because I was always conscious of having to clean them in public. A certain duglah boy invited me to go camping for a weekend and I would have given anything to have gone with him, but I knew there would be no privacy at a campsite so I declined. I was damn *schupidee* back in those days. My vanity is such that my husband of forty-three years has never seen me without my false teet'. That will only ever happen over my dead body.

## Party Animal

My passion for dancing kicked in around this time; I could not get enough. A lot of people held fetes in their homes. These were called *sub-parties*; food and beverage were included in the entry fee. Some people gave the best fetes, like the Smalls in Cummings Street. That family had *nuff* (plenty) children; so many they could have held a party without inviting anyone. I was friendly with a few of the girls but Maureen was my real friend . . . and still is today. At one time she dated my big brother and I dated her twin brother; only for a short time. David married one of the girls who were in the GUYS with us. No, Maureen did not marry my brother; she married a guy from Barbados and even lived there for some time.

Georgetown is a very small place so we did not have to travel far to attend these parties. We rode our bikes or walked, however it was much more fun when a boy picked me up on a mota-bike. How I enjoyed hanging onto the back of those bikes. Mummy and I had many battles about a curfew; she wanted me home before midnight but I was only just warming up at that time. I stayed out late and faced her wrath the next day.

Old Year's Night was celebrated in grand style. By the way, that is the same night we now call New Year's Eve. Every nightclub and dance hall was fully booked. If you went with friends and did not have a date you prayed real hard that by midnight that handsome *bannah* you had your eye on all evening would want to kiss you; that was the whole point of the evening. But if you see a *phaglee* (undesirable) character coming your way, run like hell because I got caught once. A lot of *soorin'* (romancing) went on at those dances.

I cannot remember ever having to stay at home on Old Years Night. It was one night I took advantage of; the sun was usually coming up as I strolled home. I was *smellin' mehself* even more when I turned eighteen and could do as I pleased. It didn't matter what Mummy said, I wanted to dance and she wasn't going to stop me. Oops, I just woke up! Who am I fooling? Those times I got home in the wee hours I was staying at a friends place. That mother of mine never lost her power. I took her warning seriously when she said, "W'en yuh cyan lite yuh own fire an' turn yuh own key yuh cyan do as yuh please." I didn't even have a match to light the fire.

## British Soldiers in Town

Georgetown was overflowing with British soldiers who were always chatting up the local girls. The Red House which was the former residence of the Prime Minister Cheddi Jagan had become their headquarters. Stella Maris where I taught was next door so they had ample opportunity to chat up the teachers. I had an admirer who was called Jim; he tried to woo me with a pineapple. My superior got wind of this and called me 'de Pineapple Princess' after that. I dated Jim a few times. He decided I should be called 'Ellie' and gave me a gold ring with the name engraved. I lost it, along with Jim.

A few girls I knew married soldiers and followed them to their respective country. My cousin Ingrid was not quite seventeen when she married one from Austria. Her sister Vevica, Daphne and I were her bridesmaids. I know Mummy was secretly hoping I would marry one (because they were *white*) but none of them really swept me off my feet. I still had my eye on a duglah boy.

Aunty Olga invited me once or twice to attend the lavish fetes the troops laid on at *de Base* (Airport Base). She always kept an eye on me but I had fun dancing with all the *white* guys. The army served the most beautiful food I had ever eaten and it was worth going just for that treat. We were leaving after the dance one night when one of the soldiers who I had danced with came to the door to say goodnight. He took my hand, discreetly deposited something and squeezed my hand shut. The poor guy did not know he was dealing with a *packoo* (ignoramus) who did not know about notes being handed over that way. He had to suffer the embarrassment of me flinging it to the ground. He walked away in disgust while I tried to look for a hole to hide. I always wondered what that note said. It was most likely another narrow escape from someone after that *wan t'ing* Mummy says a man wants from a woman.

## The Very Special Aunt We Called 'Boer'

Let me explain the name . . . Aunty Olga married a Dutchman but never followed him to Holland. The last four letters of his surmane was 'Boer' which came in very handy as a false-name.

All of my aunts have played a special part in my life so this is not favouritism. I can honestly say that all the cousins feel this way about Aunty Olga and for good reason. She was a single parent who held down a full-time job to put a roof over her family and food on the table. Looking back on her life I can only now fully appreciate what an amazing person she was. There were numerous nieces and nephews in our family, but Aunty Olga made sure she had a gift for each of us on our birthday and at Christmas. It was always a pair of bloomers when I was *likkle*. She always laughed wickedly and said, "Cova yuh pum-pum from de boys." As I got older she gave me toiletries or a *dress lenk*.

Joel, Daphne and I were her eldest nephew and nieces and Boer was an aunt to whom we could talk so we all found ourselves at her home on the weekends when we became teenagers. She welcomed us and shared whatever she cooked with us. When Joel was old enough to drink she would have a *tooks* (a snap-glass of liquor) with him.

Boer had a unique way of greeting me. She gave my bubbie a squeeze, just because she was naughty! I adopted the same way of greeting her many years later when I visited her in Toronto where she lived with my cousin Donna and family. I always had a wonderful time in her company. She raised two beautiful daughters; unfortunately the one named Donna has no blasted respect. That woman hollers, "Hi Muddah Rat," whenever I call. Someone should remind her that I am her *big* cousin.

We lost our special aunty in March 2008 and she is sadly missed. Thank you Aunty Olga.

## Getting Too Big For My Boots

Aunty Olga had a special companion; this man was a family friend who visited at the weekend. He was a very nice man if you overlooked his lethargic demeanour. Making conversation seemed to be an effort for him. He lacked gumption and I thought he was *phaglee* (insipid). Mr Beck was ancient in my eyes but he had a much sought after commodity. His car could come in very handy for taking me and my friends to the creek for a swim but I never dared to ask. He was a confirmed *batchie* and I was afraid he might think I was interested in him. He must have been at a loose end one Sunday because out of the blue he asked Daphne and me if we were interested in going to Red Water Creek for a swim. He said there were some sand dunes nearby we could explore. Being a trusted family friend, I saw no need to go home to ask Mummy's permission; *besize*, I was a *big woman* anyway. That poor man waited as patiently as Job while we frolicked in the sand dunes. We even talked him into taking a few pictures of us. When we had our fill, we headed for the creek where we all took a dip, and then he said it was time to go home. It was beginning to get dark by the time we got back to town and I knew I would be in big trouble. I decided to act bravely and waltzed in, only to find Mummy waiting with her lemon-puff face. She demanded to know where I had been all day and was not amused when I told her the truth. She said, "J.B. yuh 'ave to teech dis gyurl a'lesson, sh' gettin' too big fuh sh' boots." Mummy actually expected him to belt me because I did not ask her permission. Daddy puffed himself up, squeezed my shoulders and in his sternest voice said, "Gyurl yuh mus' not do dis again, akse yuh muddah nex' time, yuh 'ear meh?" Mummy must have pressed clothes that day and was tired; why else would she ask Daddy who had a *rubber spine* to do what she usually did so well.

## Visiting Uncle Sonny at Blankendal

The end of the school year holidays were pretty long and being teachers Daphne and I had all that time to fill in. Money was short so when we ran out of ideas we visited her father for a few days. Uncle Sonny managed a rum-shop over on the West Coast at a place called Blankendal. It was a cheap trip and the shop was quite close to where the train stopped which was convenient. We didn't actually go to socialise with Uncle Sonny; we went to explore and pretty much strayed all over the countryside every day. We made friends with some children from the village who showed us the ropes and took us to the backdam. This was heaven because we were always looking for something to eat, and wild fruit called Monkey Apples grew in abundance. We ventured into muddy areas, poking in holes to dislodge *Sheriga* crabs. These small crabs were very tasty but we seldom caught any because they always scurried into their holes quickly.

Uncle Sonny was too busy working to cook so Daphne and I helped out. We especially enjoyed the huge living quarters upstairs of the shop. I enjoyed *lallin' off* in the hammock he had on the veranda upstairs.

## Discovering Sex at Cousin Nita in Pomeroon

We were getting too old for holidays in d'Riva so we only went for a week or two when I started working. My social life in town was much more exciting. I had outgrown swimming for hours but I still enjoyed going to see my grandparents and the relatives we had there in abundance. I especially enjoyed visiting Cousin Nita so I could sneak a read of the book I had discovered in my early teens; it was pure pornography in my opinion. A medical dictionary today will make that one look like Sesame Street. We never owned any books except for a *beat-up* (battered) bible so curiosity had gotten the better of me when I saw some books on a shelf. I thumbed through a few, but as soon as I opened that big book and saw a picture of a naked woman I knew it had to be juicy so I sneaked it out into the boat-house when no one was around. Devil (Cousin Eric) was a boat builder so there was always a half built boat lying idle; very handy for privacy. I was gone for hours but no one missed me, or so I thought. My eyes bulged when I read about how babies were born. I was never going to get a baby if that was how it happened. As for those pictures; I had never seen anything like it. I felt somewhat guilty for being gone so long and always tried to sneak the book back into the house. Then one day Cousin Nita bailed me up and said, "Ah see yuh readin'." Cringing inwardly with embarrassment I tried to cover up by saying, "Yes, a'was readin' 'bout de life cycle of a'fly, it suh intrestin'." She must have killed herself laughing. Looking back I realise she knew what I was up to but bless her; she never did let on . . . damn decent of her. This couple by the way were related to me on both sides. The first cousins belong to grandfather's brother Francis (Nita's father) and his sister Irene (Eric's mother). But to confuse matters more; Uncle Francis was married to Aunty Mary (Daddy's sister). The saying, *cousins make dozens* certainly applied in their case. Cousin Nita and Devil was a typical *Surra an' Durra* (inseperable) couple.

Cousin Nita told me a lovely story about Devil on our last visit to Guyana and I would like to share it with you. Pint size Devil enjoyed a tipple at Charity with his friends, and did so at every opportunity. Things got heated one night and he got involved in a brawl. He was lucky Dispenser Joseph was in their company because he patched him up. Cousin Nita was shocked when he arrived home with his head bandaged up. He had a tiny cut on the exposed side of his forehead but he told her that was "nutt'in'" compared to the one under the bandage. He did not want her to touch it and went into great detail about the size and the amount of blood he had lost. She was naturally concerned and insisted she had a look the next day. She took great care getting the bandage off, but to her utter surprise there was not a mark anywhere. You guessed it, the real cut was left unattended. That was some good rum.

Cousin Nita died on Daddy's birthday a few years ago and Devil followed her the following year. May God rest their souls; they were the best!

L to R Daddy, Devil (Cousin Eric) de Snail (Uncle Carlos)
& Uncle Mike enjoying a drink in Pomeroon

Aunt Phil, Uncle Mike, Me, Aunt Claudia, Aunt Mary & Uncle Carlos

## Near Drowning Experience

Holidays spent in d'Riva were always an enjoyable experience. The most dangerous thing my brothers and I had to contend with was a fake tiger. We never had any major mishap or injury but that changed for me in 1995. My husband, Daphne and I decided to make the trip to d'Riva before my two sisters and their families arrived in Guyana for a family reunion and Daddy's wedding. Shandrina's (the bride to be) fourteen year old grandson Trevoll had never been to Pomeroon so we offered to take him. My one ambition was to swim across d'Riva before I died and this was my chance. I almost accomplished both things in the same day. This adventure was going to be a secret from my aunts so I had to bide my time and Christmas baking gave me the opportunity. My aunts owned a *box-oven* (wood oven) which was rare so other family members were invited to bake their cakes. Cousin Ena had paddled down to join them so they were well and truly distracted; a perfect day to do the deed. We decked out in our bathers and told the *big people* (older generation) we were going to the waterside to swim.

My fifteen year old cousin Melissa is a very strong swimmer; she knew the workings of the tide on a daily basis so I enlisted her help. She said she would accompany me on the swim but suggested Daphne and Trevoll take the corial and wait for us on the other side. My husband said he would film the event. We had left it a bit late in the day and the tide was flowing a bit faster than expected when we started the swim, but I was determined to finish. I was so happy to see Daphne and Trevoll waiting to rescue me in the corial. Melissa assumed I was smart enough to know I should hold on to the corial until we got to the nearest stellin'. [I had gained a lot of weight travelling around the globe and was exhausted by the time I reached the sanctuary of the canoe]. In my haste to beach myself I started climbing in and the corial capsized sending the occupants into the river. That would have been perfectly acceptable and even hilarious but Trevoll could not swim. He disappeared and I panicked; he popped up and disappeared again until I managed to grab hold of his hair as he surfaced for the second time. He naturally grabbed onto me and sent me under. I was thankfully still holding onto to him when I came up for air. I cannot repeat the foul language used to get my message across to him. He then complied and held on to the upside down corial for dear life. All my concentration was on Trevoll when I heard a faint voice yelling, "Help! Help!" I suddenly realised it was Daphne, but where was she? Just then we saw cousin Ena coming to our rescue in her *ballahoo*. My husband who was recording the drama had alerted my aunts of the danger. As we were getting into Cousin Ena's boat we saw a corial coming in the distance. It was being paddled by an East Indian man and there was Daphne sitting at the bow looking like a mermaid in her skimpy bathers. *Ol' Witch* (his false-name) who was my cousin Dolly's brother-in-law must have thought he had hit the jackpot when he heard the cry for help and found Daphne clinging for dear life among the thorny bushes. Praise the Lord she only suffered minor scratches.

After we were all safely aboard the other boat, Melissa expertly righted the capsized corial and we all gave thanks for being alive.

My aunts gave us a tongue lashing for our stupidity and told us we should never under estimate the powers of *d'Riva*. That was one time I actually agreed with their philosophy.

# Chapter Twelve

*The grass is not always greener on the other side.—Proverb*

## 1964-65 NON PAREIL STREET

### Family Coming Out From the Woodwork

Alas a bigger and better place was offered and we were off again.

I was not happy with the location since it was back to the slums in Albouystown.

Our top storey dwelling gave us a bird's eye view of the neighbours living directly behind us in the tiny cottage and long range. Their shenanigans always provided some form of entertainment, although at times it was downright distressing. I witnessed a girl name Vesta being beaten almost daily by her mother; that poor girl ran for her life, but Mrs Smart always managed to *brakkle* (apprehend) her in a corner.

Our East Indian landlord built a huge arbour between our home and the little cottage. He planted *Nenwa* and *Jingie* (types of squash), *Bora* and *Sane* and all with their robust vines running freely, especially the squash. Some were as long as base ball bats. *Bora* is similar to a snake bean and *Sane* is a string bean, all very unpalatable to me. No amount of doctoring with meats and spices made any difference to me.

I needed a new loofah so I asked Vesta to steal a Nenwa for me from the vine entwined in the *Sijan* (drumstick) tree outside her bedroom window. The Nenwa was an edible gourd, but when fully matured and dry the husk was used for exfoliation.

A captive audience followed the intriguing saga of a catholic priest who regularly disappeared in one of the tiny units for hours. The clandestine meeting was regular as clockwork. I spied on Faddah as he diligently escorted the lady in question home. She walked alongside him as he pushed his bicycle with her shopping basket dangling on the handlebar. That lady must have had a lot of sins to confess because the priest spent hours locked up in her home. It was that sort of hypocrisy that caused me to become nonreligious; especially where confession was concerned.

The widow of Daddy's half-brother and her extended family lived in the house directly across the street from us. The household was relatively calm when Aunty Carmie moved in with her son Cleo (my godfather), his wife Thelma and their children Buster, Debbie and Maria, but that soon changed. It turned into a family affair when three of her other sons and Thelma's sister Hilda took up residence. Apart from the normal household, numerous relatives and friends from various parts of the country came to stay from time to time. Their household bulged at the seams with a mix of very interesting boarders; it sometimes looked like an Amerindian hostel with the many hammocks hanging from the rafters. The narrow street allowed us to conduct conversations from our sitting room windows; it was a lot of fun.

The household got even more complicated when the eldest son Simeon married his sister-in-law's sister Hilda. The bridegroom's brother Pope (Pius) and I were chosen to be their witnesses. It was the first time I had been asked to be a bridesmaid and I was a nervous wreck. I wore a slim fitting dress of blue satin with a lace overlay. My peepers were flirtatiously visible behind the matching lace fascinator which was held in place with a big bow; very swish. Pope fell in love with me around that time but he was my cousin, so the idea did not appeal to me.

Me & Pope (Pius) at Cousin Simeon & Hilda's wedding in 1965

## Daddy Expands His Coffee Business

There was no access to the backyard at this address for Daddy to parch the coffee, but Aunty Carmie had ample room in hers. This could have been a business arrangement because Daddy immediately began parching coffee in their yard. The derelict room under the bottom-'ouse was presentable enough after Daddy swept the cobwebs away and installed a few shelves. He ground and packaged the coffee in this *make-do* factory. It was during this time Daddy and I shared some special bonds.

We took turns at rotating the drum whenever I kept his company and we sometimes cooked a meal on the side of the fire. [Now that I live in Australia I can refer to those meals as bush tucker]. It was always split-pea cook-up. Since Mummy did not approve of us using her good pots we were assigned a discarded Klim tin. I also had to scavenge for the basic ingredients without her knowledge. She shopped on a strict budget and knew exactly what was in her cupboards. An onion, a piece of salfish, a handful of split-peas and the other ingredients were sneaked out bit by bit. The sneaking added to the adventure so it became a game. The meal inevitably got burnt on the bottom because we had no control over the temperature, *besize*, Guyanese always say, "W'en it bun it dun." That burnt bit is called *bun-bun*; it was most enjoyable.

No other meal ever tasted as good as our cook-up especially when eaten straight from the tin!

## A Trip to d'Riva for My 19th Birthday

Daddy and I seldom spent time together, but when we did, it was always wonderful. Just before my nineteenth birthday he called out, "Helen, yuh want to guh to d'Riva fuh yuh birt'day?" That was music to my ears! You bet I wanted to go to d'Riva to spend my birthday. We had already moved from this address when this event took place, but since it involves a neighbour at this address I will tell you that story now . . .

An East Indian family with two grown sons lived next door. They were Muslims and expected their sons to marry within the faith. The eldest son had only recently married my friend Jean who lived in Drysdale Street; Jean was Muslim so that made his parents proud. Their younger son had no such intentions; he was a *Saga-bhai*. A beautiful Brazilian woman came to stay with Aunty Carmie over the road and he fell head over heels in love as soon as he clapped eyes on *de t'ick bini* (curvaceous woman). All hell broke loose, especially since she was a divorcee with a young son in tow. The family disowned their rebel son and he became an outcast, but he didn't give a hoot. My mother always said, "If yuh cyan't stan' de 'eat get outa de kitchen." Their kitchen got so hot it almost burnt down; no hose could put out that fire! His lover fell pregnant so the disgraced duo fled to get away from the *backanal*. Why am I telling you all of this? To let you know Daddy and I broke our journey to spend a night on the coast with Romeo and Juliet.

We left the day before my birthday because the plan was for me to be in d'Riva on my actual birthday. The lustful pair lived at Adventure so we didn't have far to travel when we got off the M.V. Malali. The beautiful *bini* was heavy with child but the romance was still sizzling. It was so good to see them again. The atmosphere was laced with sexual tension; it was Peyton Place to my romantic nature. My eyes were synchronised to follow every move they made; in a sly way of course. They were living in a one bedroom hovel but it was wonderful to wake up on my nineteenth birthday in *de castle of love*. A delicious pepperpot was served up for breakfast and I noticed that Muslim boy enjoyed a hearty meal. His parents would have frowned on that *faux pas* since they only ate Halal meat as dictated by their religious belief. Well, he wasn't only eating meat, he was living *in sin,* but he was the happiest man on earth.

It wasn't long before the couple became parents to a beautiful baby girl but her complexion was a mystery and a few eyebrows were raised, including mine. A man in his position is called a *ku-nu mu-nu* (not very sharp); everyone made a mockery behind his back and said, *"Sh' gi' 'e blow"* (cheated on him).

I must have corresponded with them after I left Guyana because I have a time warp picture of the little girl that still makes me laugh. Guyanese like to *dress-up* their children (those who could afford it) and take them to a photo studio to get *deh pickcha-tek-out.* I never set foot in one of those photo studios, but I know that every one who did ended up looking like statues (just as I did in my sitting room) standing to attention.

This child's mother had obviously adopted the Guyanese custom; then again maybe the Brazilians did the same thing. The picture was taken to mark the occasion of the girl's third birthday.

I immediately recognised the studio because of the background; the décor never changed in all the years I lived there. There she was holding the customary basket of artificial flowers; one in each hand for good measure.

The many stiff cyan-cyans made her dress look as if it was a tutu. The fake mole on her cheek, combined with mascara and jet black eyebrows that extended to her temples gave her the appearance of a deer caught in the spotlight. It looked ridiculous on a child who was fair and blonde. The intended Lolita pout only serves to magnify the look of a circus clown. It is the funniest picture I have ever seen of a three year old child. I bet you want to see it. Sarry ah cyan't let yuh see sh' face, it's private. An' mek sure yuh keep dis story to yuhself, okay?

## Daddy Sings for My Birthday

Family started trickling in from d'Riva when word got out that Daddy and I were at Aunt Claudia at Charity. Pork Oil (Cousin Cecil) came armed with his guitar and Daddy had his harmonica. Devil (Cousin Eric) and Cousin Pelham accompanied them on a grater and some spoons. The XM came out and before long a jam session was in progress.

Straw Boss (Uncle Carlos) arrived looking *kass-kass* (dishevelled) as usual. He sat in a corner in his pissed trousers quietly knocking back the free likka. My private false-name for him was 'de Snail' because he carried everything he owned in a blue wooden *grip*. He must have had some hidden charisma because I lost track of the cousins he produced with a multitude of women. His last concubine was a young Amerindian woman. I was only a teenager when I met the odd couple. They were lodging at Aunt Maud with their five picknies at the time. My mother said he was a rolling stone who moved from pillar to post. Uncle Carlos had some weird ideas but this one stands out. He said it wasn't natural for humans to sleep through the night without food so he woke his family up at midnight and fed them.

No jam session was complete unless Sparrow's classics Sitara Girl or Jean and Dinah were sung. Daddy had a repertoire of songs that was his trademark. Some of the lyrics are sad but conveyed beautiful messages. That birthday was very *special* indeed.

I had to wait until 1982 for another of Daddy's performances.

We ventured on an extended overseas holiday in 1982 and invited Daddy to meet us in Toronto where he met his grandchildren for the first time. My cousins Daphne and Ernesta, along with their husbands Gilbert and Bill invited us to spend a few days at their lakeside cabins; a place called Green Bay. It was an idyllic spot for a holiday, made even more precious because we also have the legacy of Daddy singing on film; Bill accompanied him on the guitar. I believe that duo is singing above because Daddy and Bill departed this earth thirteen days apart in November 2008. You made sweet music guys.

I can't sing a note; it sounds like a distressed cat crying in agony, and on that revealing note I think it's time to tell you of the music of our culture.

Daddy and Bill (sitting) having a jam session in Green Bay, Toronto

## Calypso in My Blood

Music, like love is a universal language that speaks to us on different levels. The culture you were born into naturally plays a significant part in the preference of your music. For me, the music of my culture is embedded in the depths of my very being. It is a part of my identity. I can honestly tell you I was ignorant to the likes of Brahms, Beethoven or Strauss, until I came to Australia. My parents never mentioned these great composers. I can only assume they were never exposed to their symphonies. The radio was our only means of listening to music but the dial was always tuned to the station that played popular songs or our local brew of calypsos. No one in our family ventured to explore other musical aspects and thus, we had no chance to experience anything different. Schooling in Guyana could be classed as backward for not introducing music of this calibre. Then again there was the class system and it all depended on which scale you were relegated to. The upper crust of society would have had the privilege to access and attend concerts featuring this type of music. The class system in Guyana practically dictated one's destiny. I knew from an early age that we could never rub

345

shoulders with what we called *de Big Shots* and as such gave them a wide berth. It was as if we lived in two different worlds in my era. Sad to say I have no real appreciation for opera or any classical music but I enjoy a wide range of other music.

My siblings and I never had the opportunity to discover whether we had any musical ability since my family's financial situation could never afford the luxury of music lessons. However, we had family and friends who owned guitars and harmonicas. Our home had many impromptu concerts when a visitor brought a guitar. The spoons and grater were used as musical instruments while Daddy sang folk songs that moved me to tears. It was all good fun and rather enjoyable music, especially after they had a few drinks under their belt.

I have felt inadequate and out of my depth on numerous occasions when the topic of classical music arises. I also know a few hypocrites who proclaim their love simply to impress and prove just how knowledgeable they are in that arena.

With age comes wisdom, and I now realise that it doesn't mean I am ignorant because I do not embrace or appreciate classical music. We are all entitled to have our likes and dislikes and that goes for the choice of music. How many people have taken the time to really appreciate the music of my culture? Does everyone know what an art it is to make a musical instrument from a common forty-four-gallon drum? These are not drums just cut into sections and hit wily-nilly to provide music. No, it's a painstaking procedure that can only be crafted by skilled individuals because of the technique. The drum is divided into panels and a hammer is used to beat the steel into position until it emits the desired musical note, and that is just part of the process. It takes years to perfect the *groovin' and sinkin'* method that is necessary to fashion these drums with every musical note needed to form a complete orchestra. It is as complex as tuning a piano.

Guyana is a country in South America but we are more connected and in tune with the West Indies where Calypsos and Steel Bands originated. There is nothing more exhilarating than *trampin'* (gyrating to the rhythm of Steel Band music in a street procession). There were many bands in my era, but I can only remember Texacans, Troubadours, Invaders, Tripoli and Quo Vadis. No high tech studios for these musicians; most bands originated under a bottom-'ouse or in someone's backyard.

I was brought up with Lord Kitchener, King Cobra and the Mighty Sparrow who is the best calypsonian of all time. My blood pulsates with the rhythm of this music and inhibits the essence of my being. I am instantly transformed whenever I hear this music and cannot restrain myself from *wynin'* (gyrating) whenever I hear the intoxicating beat. I've been known to embarrass friends in department stores on many occasions.

My gullible father was taken for a ride when a well known calypsonian came to our home to purchase coffee. He was more of a con artist if you ask me. He asked for five pounds of coffee then had the cheek to tell my father he was going to *try it* before he paid for it. He never returned and still owes for the coffee.

## Adopting Furrin Ideas

Barbeques became very popular. The Veira family at Houston on the East Bank hosted most of them. Being on the bottom rung of a ladder climbing society did not earn me too many privileges, but my friends and I managed to get tickets to one of their gigs. I was not a drinker, so one too many made me loopy and I locked myself in the toilet. My dear friend Noreen banged and banged on the door telling me there was a queue; she was begging me to come out. I finally emerged and those ladies were not amused. They gave me some bad *cut-eye* (dirty looks) and *suck-teet'* as I sheepishly made my exit.

There was one thing wrong with those barbeques, they took too long to cook the chickens and then they always *bun-dem-up* (burnt them). They were trying to copy *furrin* ideas and knew nothing about barbequing from what I witnessed. That is a skill best left to the Australians. We, (yes, I am an Aussie now) are the experts.

Peter D'Aguiar (leader of a political party) hosted the best barbeques at his Bel Air Park residence. The property had ample grounds where lovers could stroll or get lost. I couldn't find the way out one night. Oh no, it's not what you're thinking. It was because it was too dark to find the exit. That's my excuse and I am sticking to it. That boy who got me lost may read this and remember.

In hindsight I realise this was the beginning of the introduction of Fast Food. This new phenomenon was pounced on like piranhas in a feeding frenzy. One time when the nuns had their stall at the St Joseph's school fair they decided we teachers were going to make French Fries. No one made them at home so it was a novelty. Our stall had the longest queue—an angry mob really. We nearly got lynched. How on earth did those nuns expect us to supply a crowd that size using a one burner stove. A batch took forever to cook. When we finally had some ready we looked for our *matty* in the crowd because they had *adge* over everyone else. What are friends for? Needless to say we chose something different to sell the following year.

## A Boyfriend Called 'Cow'

My cousins worked in the interior and enjoyed partying when they got back to town. Fedna came to pick me up one night and the buck boy he brought with him took a shine to me. His name was Alan, but since everyone had a false-name, he was called 'Cow'. Most people have a defining feature or habit that earns them the false-name, but I could not see the connection here; not like I can with Charlie. We used to call Charlie 'Sly Fox' for years, until Uncle Joe changed it to 'de clock'. I've talked about that brother for a long time now, so can you figure out why he got that name? Remember I told you Charlie lost his hand? Yes, he now has a long arm and a short arm hence *de clock*, simple as that.

I was telling you about the buck boy. He was trying to *tackle* me but having a boyfriend called Cow was not very flattering, and to tell the truth there was only one thing I was in awe of and that was his beautiful mota-bike. What the heck; you've heard of Shallow Hal, well this was Shallow Helena and it was enough to sway me. Yes, I know what you're saying but hey, a girl needs transportation to get to parties so I accepted a date. We mostly went out in groups which made it easy for me to escape the usual goodnight kiss. Cow finally pinned me down to attend a dance with him (alone) or so he thought. Unfortunately for him the dance was held at a popular venue and a lot of my friends were there. Nelson DeSouza was a great dancer and in no time I was on the floor with him. I became intoxicated with dancing and forgot all about poor Cow. His Terylene shirt was still dry when we left the party. I guess my antics did not amuse him because he almost got us both killed going home. He angrily revved the bike up and took off at high speed. The powerful machine vibrated under my ass and I could feel my *beehive* (hairdo) wobbling. He must have thought I was being romantic because I was hugging him real tight. No way, I was just petrified of crashing! Cow took the Seawall route, which was straight until it branched off in a steep bend. He banked so low I was almost hugging the asphalt. Words cannot describe my emotions; I was never so *fryken* in my life and lucky I've lived to tell the tale.

Cow worked in the gold fields and tried to impress me by giving me a huge gold ring. Sad to say, it did not earn him any favours and I ended the fake relationship. I disliked the ring and wanted no reminders so I had it melted down and made into a brooch and a pair of earrings. Please God I hope he doesn't read this. Oh, I forgot to tell you I found out how he got the false-name . . . it was because he constantly chewed gum.

## My Favourite Joint (hang out spot)

Everyone took a jaunt to their favourite place in Georgetown when the mood hit for something special. Ferage in Main Street gets top billing from me; especially since it was on the route to work. Ask any Guyanese and they will tell you they know Ferage. He made and bottled the extremely popular peanut flavoured beverage we called Peanut Punch. I stopped to indulge in one of these ice-cold treats at every opportunity. Ferage also sold the best *Crab-back* (crab meat seasoned and stuffed into the crab shell). The price was a bit steep; twenty-five cents if my memory is correct, so I couldn't lash out very often.

After a late night party, my brother and his friends would head to Huntes for a midnight feast of cook-up-rice with pig-tails and salt-beef. They arrived after closing time on one occasion and the tiny red ants had taken possession of the remains. Everyone was ravenous and quick thinking solved the problem. They asked Mr Hunte to turn off the lights. After all, if you can't see the ants then they aren't there. The ants might have even given the food extra flavour.

Rendezvous restaurant in Robb Street was another favourite place. This joint sold hamburgers which were a novelty in town; everyone wanted one. Barbeque chicken and chips had become popular around that time and it was all anyone could talk about. I seldom partonised Rendezvous because I simply could not afford it. I prayed my dates would take me there for a feed after the movie but I think some of them had even less money than me, especially since they had to pay for both tickets. A boy paid for everything if he took you out back then.

Mitzi who was to become my lovely sister-in-law invited me to join her and her friends for a meal at Rendezvous one evening. It was a very special treat, but I felt self conscious eating in front of her posh friends who worked with her at Royal Bank.

I've already sang the praises of Brown Betty; the most popular place in town.

Shantas' in Camp Street was, and I believe still the best place to get a good Dhal Puri, it melts in your mouth! [The last time I visited Guyana I indulged and it was still very good].

## Banks on de M.V. Malali

Travelling from the city of Georgetown to the Pomeroon River was quite an adventure. It entailed taking several modes of transport and many hours of laughing or crying depending on who you encountered on a given day. It ranged from buses that broke down and left you stranded, or men and women who had ample time to become *tanked-up* on the slow boat to China. These colourful characters certainly kept us entertained. It was a welcome relief to an otherwise boring ride on the M.V. Malali. Of course it wasn't that funny when the shoe was on the other foot. They say karma always catches up with you, and this certainly happened to me. God knows I had laughed at enough people on the Malali. I was seventeen when this embarrassing incident occurred. Banks (Aunt Agnes) decided to accompany me back to the city from Pomeroon. (My aunt earned this name for over indulging in *Banks* beer). On this occasion Banks polished off one too many beers and got into a solo act. I love my aunt and would normally find her behaviour hilarious and even encourage her. However, it was not funny, because a parent of one of my pupils from the upper crust was on board. The gentleman acknowledged me when we boarded and sat not far from us. I was not amused by my aunt's antics and almost jumped overboard from sheer embarrassment. I tried to distance myself from her but it was impossible because we were the only two *Putagee* people on the steamer. I could have killed her. In case you are wondering, Banks didn't strip, but her outrageous and uncontrollable laughter drew stares and snickers from everyone on board. [It's damn funny now!]

There are many nostalgic memories of times spent with Banks. The most memorable was the time she took me *yawkin'* in a nasty trench in the backdam. The word 'yawkin'' is not in the dictionary but it involves catching fish with your bare hands. Aunty Agnes barricaded a section of a trench that had an abundance of fish, then we got in stark naked to *ketch* them. She dove into the murky waters and grabbed a fish and asked me to do the same . . . easier said than done. The pitch black water scared me, and I was too timid to dive under so the only thing I was bringing up was mud. Aunty Agnes on the other hand was having a marvellous time. Her infectious laughter soon put me at ease and I found myself roaring with laugher too when one of the wriggling suckers escaped my inexperienced hands; nevertheless, we ended up with *a'good ketch.* The fish were threaded through their gills onto pom-pom weeds and proudly transported home. It was a hair raising but exhilarating experience I will never forget.

Aunty Agnes was married to a Mr Evans but it was a 'flash in the pan' from what I heard. Her income came from the crops she planted. She once lost a nice field of peppers due to flooding and was devastated because the trees were already budding. Flooding is a common occurrence for the farmers in Pomeroon and as such life was very difficult at times.

Age does not stop this adventurous lady, as proven when ex President Cheddi Jagan died. We were sent a tape with footage of his funeral and could not believe our eyes when we saw the white head in the distance; we knew it had to be her. Corentyne was the other end from Pomeroon where Aunty Agnes lived but we don't call her "pot-salt" for nothing . . . she was the only Putagee among the thousands of East Indian mourners. This agile lady is now in her nineties; she lives in Venezuela and is still as healthy as a horse as I write this. My husband adores her. I know it was another 'off the beaten track' story, but I had to tell you about Banks because she is one in a million.

Let's get back to the Malali . . . Livestock was another form of entertainment, and sometimes an annoyance, depending on the generosity of the family. When returning home after a holiday, everyone including myself was offered a live duck or chicken to take back to the city to make a special curry. It was considered rude to reject this generous offer. Cousin Dolly was so happy to see me after many absent years she proudly presented me with her prized duck. To make *duck curry* of course. I went to great lengths to get that duck to town but the poor thing never made it into the pot because it was found dead under the stairs the next morning from sheer exhaustion. Daphne was with me and she almost died laughing herself after the gruesome discovery was made. What a waste of a good duck.

Daddy, Aunty Olga, Aunty Agnes (holding a 'Banks' beer) Joel, Anne, Me, Daphne & my godfather Cousin Cleo. Celebrating Joel's 21st & engagement

The M.V. Malali steamer that travelled between Parika and Adventure

## Related To Everyone in Pomeroon

My husband is convinced that I am related to every living soul in the Pomeroon River because during our visit every second person calls out, "Hey, Cousin Helen yuh come to see we gyurl." Some I don't even remember but I acknowledge them, and in no time they tell me from which branch of the family tree they hang from.

My uncles and aunts lived on the dam at Charity. We stayed with Aunt Claudia and Agnes who shared a home when we visited in 2000. A funny thing happened when we were going home one day . . . just as we were about to pass the fresh fruit juice bar on the corner a man blacker than the ace of spades approached me and said, "'i gyurl, a'is yuh cousin, 'ow yuh doin'?" To say I was taken aback is putting it mildly, but the dear man soon sorted that out. He told me he was married to one of my mother's cousins. Don't let me tell you how distant she was; she must have been washed up with the tide. He said they had five children together then finished by saying, "Sh' leff meh fuh anaada man." I offered my sympathy and hurried away convulsed.

More relatives were found in 1995 while travelling to Pomeroon with my husband and Daphne on the Malali. The group of East Indian men I was observing from the upper deck caught me looking and invited me to join them for a'drink (rum). I was on holiday and figured there was no harm in that so I joined them. The men said they lived at Wakeanam; the next port of call. Like most nosey Guyanese, they wanted to know who my relations were, and before long one of them realised his niece was married to one of my distant cousins. I instantly became family and it was cause for more celebration. Those guys were having such a great time they decided to continue partying and followed me to the next port of call, Adventure. The guys reluctantly said goodbye and boarded the steamer for the return journey to Wakeanam. That was one of the best trips on the Malali.

## If Yuh Cyan't Beat Dem Join Dem

My late night partying days were the best times in my life, and if that was all my mother had to worry about she was damn lucky. Like most teenagers I wanted to be *cool,* so I smoked a *sigrit* or two when I went to fetes. Mummy only had to get a whiff and I was accused of smoking.

Well I did, and I didn't, but I could never convince her it wasn't habitual so I had to endure her *leckchas*. In all honesty I never smoked the way Mummy thought. I dabbled at parties to show off. I thought it was trendy to keep up with my peers but never once purchased a packet of cigarettes. I left Guyana a non-smoker and have remained one. This is leading to a story of course.

Charlie invited Mummy for a much deserved holiday while he was living in New York in 1979 and we decided it was the perfect opportunity to treat her to a holiday so she could meet her grandchildren. She was to visit Charlie first then come to Australia. My mother had reservations about the long journey but we managed to convince her. Let me tell you what happened when we met at the airport. We had not seen one another for eleven years and I was expecting some *luv-up* from Mummy, but the embrace was only lukewarm. I figured nothing had changed between us and left it at that. Johnny on the other hand got all the luv-up and I was a bit peeved as you can imagine. I introduced the children to their grandmother and we made our way to the car park. Johnny was putting her suitcase into the boot when she turned to me and asked, "Why Helen didn't come?" You could have knocked me down with a feather; my own mother did not recognise me. Do you want to know why? Apart from being *t'in-t'in*, I had baked myself in the sun and she thought I was an Aboriginal. It was priceless because she still wasn't convinced it was me when I said so. I wonder if Mummy thought Johnny was *gi'in' meh blow* (cheating on me) with an Aboriginal woman.

She certainly knew it was me when I started challenging her on certain touchy matters. I had flown the coop so she had no chance of clippin' my wings. I was going to *bray like a jackass* to my heart's content!

Another turn of events stunned me. Mummy pulled out a cigarette and began to smoke. I knew her views on the habit so had to ask what made her take it up at such an old age. She calmly replied, "If yuh cyan't beat dem join dem." The 'dem' she was referring to was my father. She said she was fed up of *tekkin' leff* when Daddy and his friends were drinking, and since she was never going to get him to change his habit, it was best to join in, and that was how it all started.

We helped her after she confided she wanted to break the habit. A 'Quit kit' offering results had just come out on the market so we got it for her. Mummy spent three months with us and by the time she left our shores she was weaned and very pleased with herself; we were very happy too. Hold on, it didn't end there... all was well until Mummy got flustered when she almost missed a connecting flight somewhere along the long journey home, and as you know I am still living behind god's back here in Australia. She told me she got herself into a terrible state and said, "Ah 'ad to akse a'man fuh a'sigrit to steady meh nerves." She was on the smoking bandwagon again.

My mother left Australia in May 1979. A few months later she wrote to say she had a hard boil in her groin and it was proving stubborn to treat. Mummy had always done the letter writing so I knew things were grim when I received a letter from Daddy saying, "I think this is it Helen." He didn't have to say the words; I knew my mother was gravely ill. The abscess had developed into full blown cancerous symptoms. Mummy sadly lost the battle to this insidious disease on the 2nd January 1981. She would have been fifty-seven years old on the 18th February. The legacy of her teachings lives on in all of her children. P.S: I love you Mummy.

Mummy divulged something when she visited that broke my heart and I would like to share it with you.

## A Search That Took Twenty Years

This story was the result of a search for my half-uncles and aunts who live in the jungle of South America. It will take pages to explain the entire saga. My grandfather had scandalised the family after I left Guyana when he took-up with a very young Amerindian woman and started another family. I had heard snippets on the family grapevine about an incident that took place at my grandfather's funeral involving my mother, but Mummy had never personally told me about it. Curiosity was killing me, and this was the perfect opportunity so I decided to broach the subject. My disgust grew as the story unfolded and I silently vowed to find those relatives for the sole purpose of apologising on my mother's behalf.

There is a monumental lack of empathy in today's society. Take poverty and injustice for instance . . . some individuals play on society by using poverty as a crutch for all their failures. I was brought up in poverty and on occasion I too have been guilty of that, but in my defence it was not to gain sympathy. I sometimes wondered what path my life would have taken academically had I been born into a financially secure family. Then I look at the other side of the coin and wonder whether I would have seen life in a superficial way. I have decided my birth was no accident and I have lived long enough to know the path chosen for me is perfectly aligned with the universe. The journey has not always been smooth, but what road doesn't have a few bumps along the way? Each obstacle in my view is another lesson, depending on which way you look at it. It was one such lesson that taught me all about faith, and seriously taught me compassion.

## My Search Is Finally Over

It took over twenty years to fulfill that vow but I finally found myself face to face with the family in question. I listened as my Aunt Salome (born the same year as my last child) gave the same account of the story. She finished by saying she thinks the sister responsible was named Carmen. The moment had arrived and I apologised on behalf of my mother and felt a weight lifted off my shoulders.

Adeline, the mother of the five children looked so much older than her actual age which was fifty-nine. She had suffered great hardship raising those children on her own. I cannot begin to describe the emotion that overcame us that day, but what really floored me was their faith. Through her tears, Adeline told me she knew in her heart that one of us would find them someday. The family desperately needed a motor to power their boat and enlisted my help to ask the extended family for financial help. Since this involved a substantial amount of money I could only promise to do my best. I was dumbfounded and heart broken with the hostility this request prompted from a few members of the family.

## Faith and Compassion Wins the Battle

It was sheer compassion that compelled me to take on the Herculean task of raising the money for the motor. Since *one hand cannot clap* I enlisted the help of my wonderful Aussie mate Pauline Hardidge with great faith and hope. Not only did she offer her home for the venue; she put her heart and soul into helping me fulfill the family's request. A fund raiser was organised with me relying on everyone's compassion. I planned on showing the video my husband had taken of the reunion, but for some reason we could not get sound that day. But here is where the motto I live by came into play. I've told you from the beginning that I believe everything happens for a reason. Showing the video without sound was perfect because it made a profound impact on those looking on with attentive eyes. No sound could have echoed louder than the emotion etched on the faces of my desperate family.

My dear friend Betty Jeffs said afterwards that the cricket bat leaning up against a tree beside their humble hut said it all. The simple words, 'Faith is action' was inscribed on the bat. Would you believe I had seen the video several times but had never seen the bat?

To this day I still believe there was a higher force at work. I was somehow chosen to be the instrument needed to orchestrate and fulfill a mission that stemmed from the profound faith of that family.

Yes, with a lot of faith and compassion we managed to raise the money for the motor.

I can attest to how a little help can make a monumental difference to someone's life. My family were able to get on their feet and are doing very well for themselves today.

P.S: It just dawned on me that I never did tell you what my mother did to cause the rift. This is an account of the story in a nutshell.

My mother travelled to d'Riva to attend my grandfather's funeral. As is customary, the mourners were all assembled at someone's home where the corpse was laid out for viewing. The mourners usually buried their grief with copious amounts of *likka* and from what I heard my mother was under the influence. She was enraged to find her father whiter (no make-up artist in d'Riva) than the sheet covering him and for some reason blamed his mistress for his ravaged appearance. She berated Adeline, accusing her of sucking my grandfather dry. [I bet he enjoyed every minute of it]. Grief stricken Adeline herded her children into a corial and fled, and that was the last anyone ever saw of the family until the day I found them.

And in case you are wondering what happened to my grandmother, my aunts encouraged her to divorce Ol' Joe after forty-seven years of marriage. She immigrated to Canada where she lived with Aunt Hermina and family until her death in December 1993. May God rest her weary soul and amen to the entire saga.

Me and Daphne reunited with some of our lost relatives at Red Hill

## Daddy Announces His Wedding Plans

Did you think for one minute I would deprive you of this next story?

The last thing I anticipated when I embarked on an overseas holiday in 1995 was my father getting re-married.

CeCe handed me the letter she was instructed to give to me on my arrival in Toronto. I opened the letter with delight and was expecting to find his usual request for Horlicks but that was never mentioned.

Daddy said since we would all be in Guyana for Christmas he had decided it was high time he made an honest woman out of Shandrina. He went on to say he did not want to continue living 'in sin'. What sin I wondered, the man was over eighty and the lady in question was in her late sixties. I joked with CeCe as to whether Shandrina could be pregnant . . . it could happen. My father had already set the wedding date for Boxing Day if you please. That was a presumption in itself because he did not have two cents to rub together to fund a wedding. Mind you, the matter of finance would never enter his head.

After the initial shock, I got to thinking I was very lucky to still have a father. I decided I would do my best to give him as nice a wedding as my budget could allow. Daddy on the other hand had confidently enclosed a list in his letter instructing me as to what was needed.

My husband and I were going to be in Toronto for a month which was ample time to make a cake.

In Guyana, 'Black Cake' is traditional for weddings and Christmas. Aunty Hermina kindly offered to help and we set about making one for the wedding. My cousin Mary Gomes who decorated cakes donated some iced figurines and I bought whatever else was necessary. My sister-in-law Anne (Joel's wife) also decorated cakes and I was confident she would do the honours when I got the cake to Guyana. Boxing Day was coincidently Joel and Anne's wedding anniversary so an extra cake was made for them, and I even got the Happy Anniversary banner to go with it.

Daddy knew his bossy big daughter would organise her two sisters and every detail would be taken care of, so I happily obliged and dished out the orders. Both of my sisters knew the bride because she and my mother had formed a close friendship after I left Guyana. On the other hand, I had never even seen a picture of the woman so had no idea of her build, looks or personality. Being the eldest daughter I naturally wanted to make a good impression. I decided I would befriend Shandrina by asking her to tell me what her preferences were for her wedding. What was she going to wear as a headdress I wondered? I decided to take an assortment of silk flowers and combs to fashion a headdress, that way she could direct me in her preference. I am very good at craft you know. I just wanted to blow my own horn, now you know something else about me.

All my good intentions went out the window when I met Shandrina and realised it would take a glue gun to hold a headdress into place. She had her hair permed for the wedding, but she must have gone to that woman who permed mine when I was nine because her *picky-picky* (little tufts) hair clung to her scalp in tight little balls resembling sheep droppings. I secretly put away my flowers and combs and tactfully asked what she intended wearing as a headdress. Shandrina shyly said, "A'wan' fuh wear ah 'at," and I secretly thought it was a damn wise choice. She asked if one of my sisters could bring one for her when they were coming.

Daddy's letter stated quite clearly, 'a blue dress for the bride', and I gave that task to Anetta. She and I had hunted for one while I was in Florida without success so I thought I better warn Shandrina that Anetta may have to choose another colour. My curiosity got the better of me and I asked, "Why does it have to be blue?" Shandrina dropped her head and coyly replied, "Yuh Daddy like blue, but a'wood tek any culla." Until then I had no clue Daddy's favourite colour was blue, but then again, how many hints were needed when everything we owned was painted blue, including my bicycle.

I was further dumbfounded when I asked Shandrina if she had bought shoes for the wedding. She just shrugged and said, "Meh dauttah seh, whoeva bring de dress does bring de shoes." They must have thought we were also mind readers. I called CeCe to ask her to get shoes, telling her Shandrina requested low heels, because she would not be able to walk in anything 'igh. I also advised CeCe about the head-dress dilemma and she was happy to lend Shandrina the hat she wore for her wedding a decade earlier so that took care of those issues.

## Bicycle Tube to the Rescue

Anetta finally arrived with the dress. It was indeed blue; covered in sequins, absolutely perfect, except for one thing. The sleeves were about ten inches too long when Shandrina tried it on. Again, it was left up to me to do the alterations. I am no seamstress, and try as I might I could not sew through the thick sequins to adjust the sleeves, so I abandoned that idea. Then inspiration came to me . . . remember I told you Guyanese are the masters of improvisation? Well here is my proof, I called Shandrina's grandson Trevoll and asked him to get me a discarded bicycle tube. He was puzzled until I explained the plan. I cut two, one inch sections from the tube and asked Shandrina to put the dress on. I slipped the circle of rubber onto her fat arms and adjusted the sleeves to the correct length. Walla! It was a perfect solution; she was happy and my work was done.

## Christmas Eve Dramas

I had instigated the reunion several months earlier with only one request; we must all sleep in one home on Christmas Eve, our father included. I am a sentimental fool and wanted us all to wake up on Christmas morning under the same roof.

This day stands out in my memory for many reasons. First and foremost I was going to be with all of my siblings for the first time in twenty-seven years and I wanted it to be *very special*. My husband and I were already staying with Charlie; the home chosen for the Christmas Eve gathering. The others were going to arrive later in the day.

*Let me put you in the picture with some back-up information.*

After living abroad for many years, the narrow roads were the first thing that caught my attention when I arrived in Guyana. Not so for my sister Anetta. She was the last to arrive with her family from Florida and what was her first observation? The beer bottles had gotten much smaller. To make up for this indiscretion she then had to drink twice as much to achieve the desired effect.

My sister-in-law Gale, Daphne and I were in the kitchen preparing some local cuisine for Christmas day and the men had gone to collect the hired chairs for the wedding. The rest of the clan was expected any time. Suddenly there was loud shouting from the street and this alarmed me. It was a known fact that bandits sought out overseas visitors and stormed homes to rob them. Heart pounding, I ran to the verandah to see what all the commotion was about. To my surprise, it was Anetta and her tribe. She was waving a beer bottle and shouting, "I'm here, where is everybody, MERRY CHRISTMAS!" The contents of those tiny bottles were certainly having a good effect as she was very merry. Someone got her into the house while I showed my disapproval (swell up like crappo). She hugged me and asked, "Who made you Mummy?" Then she told me to lighten up. The others arrived and the festivities continued while Gale, Daphne and I continued cooking.

Sometime after dinner Gale came to me and said, "A't'ink sumt'in' 'rong wid Anetta, sh' been in de toilet fuh a'very long time, yuh betta check on 'er." I was not amused and huffily replied, "If she's vomiting I won't be cleaning it." I headed to the toilet, knocked and asked Anetta if she was alright. She assured me everything was okay. More minutes elapsed before she emerged. I was curious and asked, "Are you sure you're okay Sis, you were in there for a very long time." Her priceless reply floored me. "It's dat damn toilet, the cistern is leakin' an' I t'ought I was still pissin'." Now you see why my family is unique and priceless? I wouldn't trade them for anything.

Joel, Anne and Daddy did not come because it was not safe to leave their homes unattended on Christmas Eve.

Around nine-thirty my two younger brothers got into a rip roaring quarrel. I was wondering if I should intervene when I heard the screeching sound of a motorcycle taking off. That was the last we saw of my youngest brother until late Boxing Day when the wedding was well and truly over. We could have been the paparazzi, because as *tourists* we had many cameras, but my brother is still sadly missing in all of the wedding pictures.

## Frogs in My Bed

Christmas Eve certainly had a lot of dramas. The tiny oven could not cope with too many dishes at once, therefore we had to be patient; not my best virtue. It was getting close to midnight and I figured the two chickens we had put in last should be ready by the time I had a shower. Everyone had gone to their various corners to sleep and it was just me, Daphne, Gale and Charlie waiting to finish off before retiring. I came into the kitchen wrapped in my towel and was just in time to see Gale drop the pan with the chickens. I almost dropped my towel when I jumped to avoid the spill. I took one look at the mess and was ready to cry, but Charlie came to the rescue in a flash. He grabbed the chickens, opened the back door and signalled the dogs with a whistle. I watched in amazement as two scrawly puppies cleaned the floor to a shine in seconds. Good thinking *bruddah!*

I was to share a mattress in the sitting room with my niece Sara and Shandrina's grandson Trevoll. Not wanting to disturb anyone, I gently lifted up the mosquito net and crawled in to take my place. I had no sooner settled when I felt something jumping on me. All hell broke loose. Those little buggers knew how much I hated frogs so they put a few in the bed to surprise me. I pulled down the net from the rafters in my haste to get out and my screams woke the entire houschold, maybe the neighbours too! Trevoll (should have let him drown eh!) the culprit was of course laughing hilariously. Everyone finally settled down around 2 a.m. that morning.

## Christmas Day Struggles

Christmas Day brought its own struggles. Everyone was up at the crack of dawn; all queuing for the only bathroom. I wisely waited until last knowing all the tiny water frogs would have departed by then. Just before breakfast we heard someone calling from the street. To our surprise it was Annie and her son Ryan. Annie was the girlfriend of a wayward nephew who had become a hobo and lived on the streets. This young East Indian girl had two children to Christopher; the eldest child had gone to live in America with her maternal grandparents. Annie must have heard on the grapevine that we were all going to be at Charlies and decided she would show up with Ryan. Not a problem, they were welcomed and a suitable gift was found for both of them.

The family relaxed and chatted after opening gifts and enjoying a traditional breakfast of garlic pork, pepperpot and other local delicacies.

Breakfast was not quite settled when the XM started flowing, and before long the gang decided to play cricket. They all departed into the garden and my Christmas spirit had abandoned me. I was fuming because there was still a lot to do for the wedding, and no one wanted to help.

We did not have enough crockery so I figured it was more economical to use disposable cardboard boxes to serve the wedding meal. These came flattened and had to be assembled. Since the others were enjoying themselves I decided to tackle the job. I took everything out on the verandah where I could *ketch breeze* and watch the locals passing as I worked. Halfway through putting the boxes together I heard a noise in the kitchen and went to investigate. I found Annie (Chris's girlfriend) squatting in front of the opened fridge door. She was stuffing grapes into her mouth as if it was the most natural thing in the world. The amazing thing was, she didn't *voomps 'pon meh*; she continued eating as I stood there speechless.

Charlie found abandoned sweet-drink bottles with only a few sips taken and blew his top so another quarrel erupted between him and the mother of the children concerned. The gang looked like they were going to drink themselves into oblivion and by lunch time a few of them were well on their way.

After lunch I pleaded with the guys to cut some coconut palm fronds because I wanted to make the traditional archway to frame the bridal table. They all just laughed, told me I was mad and asked why I wanted to go to that much trouble for two *ol' people*. More arguments over that, but I was determined and got my husband to comply. Charlie has a huge property with coconut palms growing in his backyard so he didn't have to go far. I trimmed the fronds and fashioned a beautiful archway. The paper wedding bells were assembled and hung in the middle. With streamers and *bladders* (balloons) in place my decorating was complete.

We decided it was best to have our outfits ready the night before the wedding, but another dilemma awaited me. That was when reality hit . . . my husband and I had embarked on a six month holiday and I had gone to great lengths to lose a lot of weight before leaving Perth in July. I weighed sixty one kilos the day we left but had eaten my way around the globe so by Christmas I was bursting at the seams like a stuffed turkey and nothing would fit! I was close to crying when my sister-in-law Gale without tact, snootily said, "Ah 'ave a'nice outfit from w'en a'was fat, yuh cyan try dat on." Just the words an overweight woman likes to hear. I had no choice, so swallowed humble pie and told her to get it out. Mercifully the skirt had an elastic waist and even then it barely fitted, but I was grateful to have something . . . so thank you Gale for saving the day.

## Daddy's Wedding Day

Boxing Day arrived with a hive of activity and great excitement. The wedding was scheduled for 9 a.m. and Daddy and Joel were already at the church when I arrived. Joel had his shirt buttoned up lopsided but no one had noticed. Daddy looked nervous but dapper in his suit and was proudly wearing the boutineer I made for him. After seeing Daddy safely into the church, CeCe and I decided to wait outside until the bride arrived. Shandrina got out of the car and held onto Jerome's (son) arm for dear life. She began taking tentative steps and appeared to be walking on hot coals. I wondered if the tight rubber bands on her arms had cut off the circulation to her feet! I quickly realised it was the tiny heels on her shoes causing her to *waalk like monkey 'pon iron*. It was hilarious to watch and naturally CeCe and I cracked up laughing at this spectacle. I'm sorry; we just can't help ourselves. I had never seen a bride so petrified. Shandrina walked down the aisle looking like a condemned woman in chains taking her final steps to the gallows.

The priest officiating was her nephew so that was a very proud moment for her. My husband and I were to be the witnesses and it was all going well until it was time to exchange rings, which by the way were gifts from my youngest brother who is in the gold mining business. Daddy attempted to put the ring on the wrong finger and silly me turned to the congregation and pantomimed to let them know what he had done. It wasn't until laughter broke out I realised my gesture appeared to be of a sexual nature. Thankfully, the priest did not notice.

Time for the family photos, but Julian still hadn't shown up. The entire family returned to the home but there was no sign of the bride and groom. Where could they be, we all wondered?

It is tradition in Guyana for the bride and bridegroom to arrive last with the car horn tooting loudly to signal their arrival, but in all honesty I did not expect this palaver seeing they were an older couple. We were all taken by surprise when we heard the horn blaring from a street away, signalling their arrival. The car came to a halt with the happy couple laughing like two teenagers and we couldn't help laughing ourselves. It was good to see them so happy! That is the way I would like to remember my father.

A wonderful day was had by all, except for one hiccup. I caught two little girls aged six and eight rifling through my suitcase with the intention to steal.

My father & Shandrina's wedding on Boxing Day 1995

## Meeting My Husband

It was at this address I officially met my husband, and we began dating. I say officially because I already had my eyes on him. There is a nice story I would like to share with you before telling you how we finally met.

Johnny worked at the Royal Bank of Canada. There were several branches but he worked at the Broad Street branch which happened to be on the same route I took each morning to work; intentionally of course. His desk was framed by a large window which gave him a perfect view of the road. I was conscious of him being there but always pretended not to see him as I rode past each morning. My sly glance always caught him smiling and he acknowledged me with a slow bowing gesture. I was over the moon for the rest of the day. That scenario went on for some time until I attended a dance at the Portuguese Club with Pokey Joe (uncle) and Joel. Johnny and I came face to face on the crowded dance floor and my heart sank. He was dancing with a girl I knew by sight from high school, and I naturally assumed she was his girlfriend. The only advantage I had over him was I knew his name. He kept steering his date as close to where I was dancing and he smiled to acknowledge me. He too must have assumed I already had a boyfriend but I just hoped he didn't notice my uncle's crazy antics. The lunatic had a mouthful of ice and was shaking his head from side to side wetting everyone who came within range. Uncle Joe is my mother's youngest brother and he enjoyed making a jackass of himself. I usually laughed along at his antics but it wasn't funny that night. Not when I was looking for a husband. I was convinced Johnny saw what Joe was doing because he and his date suddenly disappeared. I was so cross at Pokey Joe for showing me up.

I knew this boy's name because Mummy got wind that I was interested in the guy from the bank. He was considered *a'good ketch* so she decided to play cupid. She especially went to that bank to open an account just to find out his name. She told me she specifically joined the queue where Johnny was the teller. Looking back I wonder how much money she was actually banking; probably two dollars.

It was a well known fact that mothers and relatives started asking if *goat bite yuh*, if a girl was not married by her twenty-first birthday. No mother wants to think her daughter is going to be left on the shelf so it was in Mummy's best interest to embarrass me.

Back to how we finally met. Marilyn Nyguen who had only been teaching for a very short time with me at Stella Maris announced her departure for overseas. She invited me to the farewell party held at her home on the 23rd October 1964. How can I forget the date seeing it was on the night I met my husband. Joel was dating my best friend Noreen, who was also a teacher at Stella Maris so the three of us made our way to the party on foot. As we approached the intersection of Durban and Smyth Street, we stopped for an approaching car. To my surprise the driver was Johnny. I had no idea he owned a car. My heart sank when I realised there was a girl sitting next to him. I immediately assumed she was his girlfriend. The car stopped at the venue and the girl got out. My buoyed spirits deflated when I crossed the road and saw the car making its return journey in the direction it had come. Johnny saw me, bowed, smiled and he was gone. How strange I thought. Why would he drop a girl off at a party and not stay himself? Just as well I knew his name because I was able to ask Marilyn about the mystery girl he dropped off.

She said it was his sister and pointed Mitzi out in the crowd. To say I was disappointed is putting it mildly. However that did not last long; there were other fish to fry. I was a party animal and there were lots of nice looking guys to choose from *besize* no one wasted time when it came to dancing at a *fete*. Marilyn's brother, who I had never met, and whose name was also Johnny asked me to dance. Not my type, but I accepted to be polite. *Chiney* (Chinese) Johnny took a shine to me and would not *le'go*, he held on to me dance after dance. I was seriously thinking of a way to extract myself when the unexpected happened.

The Nyguens living quarters above their shop was accessed by an inner staircase which brought you directly into the sitting room. Well, here I was dancing with this other Johnny when I saw the guy from the bank suddenly appear at the top of the stairs. I could not believe my eyes or my luck. Johnny Nyguen wasn't letting go and I didn't want the guy who had just arrived to think he was my boyfriend. What a dilemma . . . I had to do something quick. I made a feeble excuse about being thirsty and escaped from captivity. I headed to the kitchen for some light refreshment then casually made my way back to the sitting room. It was time to position myself and look available. I sat there looking ever so innocent but I was praying Johnny would ask me to dance. I did not have to wait long because this man had come with one thing in mind and he was not missing an opportunity. Now it was his turn to keep me after every song but I did not mind one bit. Johnny asked me my name but I did not ask his in return (I was tounge tied in those days). Don't forget my mother had already done her homework on that score. Johnny told me much later in the relationship that this really upset him. He thought by not asking his name in return, it meant I was not interested. Was he *schupidee* or what?

We danced the night away to the Drifters singing tunes such as, Under the Boardwalk and Save the Last Dance for Me. When the party was over, John offered to take me home. I told him I came with my brother and girlfriend and was expected to go home with them. He kindly offered to take them home also. Since Johnny was also taking his sister home, I felt I had no right to be seated in front so headed for the back seat with Joel and Noreen. I thanked Johnny for the lift, said goodnight and wondered if I will ever see him again. NO, he did not kiss me; we had more manners in those days. I allowed him to hold me close, what more can he hope for on our first meeting?

I was not prepared for the sight that greeted me when I awoke the next morning. I always undressed in the dark after creeping in quietly hoping mummy would not see what time I got home. I was shocked to see my beautiful pink *peau de soir* (type of satin fabric) dress had turned yellow. I panicked thinking it was jaundice. I quickly consulted with my mother who assured me it was a stain. How could that be I wondered?

## Carlos Plays Cupid

The mystery did not take long to unravel. I was riding along Sussex Street two days later when our friend Collie (Carlos) passed me going in the opposite direction. He called out to say he would be coming to visit us around 7 p.m. that evening. I said that was fine and thought no more of it. Collie was Joel's best friend and visited often; he and I are also CeCe's godparents.

To my utter surprise I heard a car pull up outside our home at precisely the time I was expecting Collie. Before I could get to the window to see who it was Collie and Johnny were coming up the stairs. We had an inner staircase and our door was always open. After the formal introductions were over I plucked up the courage to tell Johnny about my dress. He knew right away his shirt had caused the problem and apologised. It appears his aunt (the same one who disliked me) had gone to Barbados on holiday and brought him the shirt as a gift. The inferior fabric and dye combined with our body heat (that man held me too close for too long) caused the discolouration of my dress. The damage was irreparable so that was the end of my beautiful dress. Who cares about a ruined dress when it looked as if *goat wasn't goin' to bite meh* after all?

I know you are fas' and want to know why Johnny came with Collie. Well let me end the suspense . . . Collie worked at a wholesale outlet called J.P. Santos where Johnny did the grocery shopping for his mother. Quite a few of my friends worked at this store and Johnny had gotten to know them. He paid the boys a visit on Monday morning to ask if any of them knew me. I guess Johnny was a bit wary of coming on his own for the very first time and needed some moral support. Parents were very strict in those days and I already told you Mummy did not want me going out with Tom, Dick and Harry, but Johnny passed the test. The romance blossomed from that evening. Okay, so I forgot to tell you why he ended up going to the party . . . what do you think? He was also invited to the party but declined because he did not have a date. Then he saw the girl he bowed to each morning and thought it was time to make his move. I hate to tell you this, but that man has forgotten how to bow after forty-three years of marriage.

Carlos & I at CeCe's christening in 1964

## A Guest on Teenagers Choice with Bertie Chancellor

Media access came via the cinema, newspapers and our lone radio station Radio Demerara. Our many distinguished announcers included Rafiq Khan, Hugh Cholomondeley, B.L. Crombie and Ayube Khan. Comedians Sam Chase, Jack Mello, Sam Dopie and Habeb Khan thrilled the airwaves with hilarious comedy, but the personality who stole our hearts was Olga Lopes-Seale, more affectionately known as

Aunty Olga. She had a heart of gold, working tirelessly to raise money for Radio Demerara Needy Children's Fund. She threw a big party for underprivileged children every Christmas and every child received a gift. She also hosted the Ovaltine Show and Birthday Request.

I will digress to relate this amusing anecdote. Guyanese from my era will remember B.L. Crombie for his distinctive voice. My mother was listening to him one day and turned the volume up when a gentleman who came to purchase coffee knocked loudly on the back door. The man peered into the house and in a serious voice said, "Sumbaddy shud tell dat man 'e does taalk too *hard* (loud)." I did not have the heart to enlighten him.

Christopher Deane, along with an upcoming DJ called Bertie Chancellor came on the scene in the sixties. Bertie ran two programmes for teenagers. Daphne and I met him at a party and he suggested we audition to become guests on his programme called Teenagers Choice . . . then again I could have begged him. He also gave us tickets to attend his other show called Teens-Ville which aired on Saturday morning and featured audience participation. Teenagers Choice featured two teenagers playing songs of their choice. The show was broadcast live on Saturday afternoons at 2.30 p.m. Some chatting had to be done between songs so I was a nervous wreck when the day finally arrived. There was no preparation before the show so I was stumped when Bertie asked me if I could recall any amusing incidents with my pupils. I could not think fast enough and ended up telling him one that was rather lame. We were allowed three songs each but I can only remember choosing, 'No Other Baby but You' because I dedicated it to Johnny. Unbeknown to me, his father tape recorded the entire segment. Imagine my surprise when I visited their home and heard my voice floating up from downstairs. Mr Martin wanted to surprise me but I was so embarrassed listening to my voice because I thought I sounded awful and downright corny. I was teased mercilessly for playing that song because of the title. I believe we still have that recording; I must dig it out for another good laugh.

I read the *love letters* I wrote Johnny recently and wondered who the hell that desperate woman was; no wonder he took pity on me . . . maybe Mummy greased his palm too. I hope you know that is a joke; she couldn't afford it anyway.

There was a Teenager of the Week segment in the Sunday papers and Daphne featured one week. I never was able to bribe anyone so never got the envious title.

Daphne, Norma and I were limin' on the Seawall one afternoon when a photographer from the newspaper spotted us. He approached us wanting to know if we could pose for him in bathing suits. We were flattered and more than happy to oblige. A date was set for us to meet him in the suitable attire. I wore the same black bathers I flaunted myself around town in because this also happened the same year. The picture was titled Bathing Beauties in the Sunday papers.

In 1963 I roped Daphne, Lita and Ingrid into dressing like idiots to go *trampin'*. A photographer spotted us in the street procession and took our picture for the papers. Those two pictures are my five minutes of fame.

Entertainment in our home was limited to a very old Grundig radio. We had to fiddle endlessly with the knobs to find the stations. The serials Portia Faces Life, Dr Paul and Aunt Mary were gospel in our home; no one was allowed to talk once the programme started.

We seldom bought the daily newspaper but my father always bought the Sunday Chronicle or Graphic and on occasion he splurged on the Evening Post. I can still hear the little boys at the street corners singing, "Eveeeenin' post, get yuh eveeenin' post." We all fought for the cartoon section whenever we got a paper. My mother and I enjoyed the antics of Blondie an' Dagwood; Mutt an' Jeff and Andy Capp an' Flo while my brothers devoured, Archie an' Jughead, the Phantom, Tarzan and Mandrake.

My parents took an interest in the news and Daddy was actually having the daily papers delivered when I visited in 1984. As you know my father likes to conserve energy. He rigged up a pulley system from the landin' for the newsboy. The money was thrown down and Daddy pulled the paper up.

Daphne and I catching up with Bertie Chancellor in 1995

Me, Daphne & Norma dubbed Bathing Beauties in the newspaper

# De Kissin' Bridge

There is a bridge in the Botanical Garden which the natives affectionately call 'de Kissin' Bridge'; it is symbolic for many Guyanese. The bridge holds many wonderful memories from my childhood and teenage years. Not sure of the origin of the name but it is most likely another folklore story; one I hope to find out one day. Even as a child I associated this bridge with romance and could not wait to be old enough to experience the intrigue and enticing mystery of de Kissin' Bridge. I especially like the way the bridge is constructed with its simple structure in the shape of a sweeping arch with about six steps leading up and down from the main platform. There is a small wooden ornamental feature that sits on the rail in the middle of the bridge. The sides are enclosed with a lattice feature that is painted white, while the supports and rails are painted green. These two colours blend perfectly among the many tropical palms and other foliage allowing the bridge to stand out majestically.

I question the size of the bridge built over such a narrow stream. A much smaller structure would have been adequate; therefore I believe it was intentionally planned and built simply for the purpose of creating the allure and legend we still know as *de Kissin' Bridge*. As you can imagine, this bridge is very popular with lovers. A young man was led to believe he had the right to take the liberty of kissing his partner if he succeeded in getting her on to this alluring structure.

Another major attraction lives in the murky waters beneath the bridge. No visit to the Botanic Garden is complete unless you are able to get a view of the lazy *Manatee* (Sea Cow). As children we would pick bits of grass or vegetation to lure the creature to the surface where it would float gracefully while nibbling on the treats. On occasion we saw two but that was a rare sight.

On my last visit to Guyana in 2000 my entire family paid a visit to the Botanical Garden. We naturally headed for de Kissin' Bridge to have our pictures taken once more just for sentimental reasons.

# Crossing a Metaphorical Bridge

After our marriage in Guyana on the 8th June 1968, my husband and I crossed another bridge when we migrated to Western Australia. Tentative steps had to be taken crossing this bridge since we were now in a foreign country where the culture was vastly different. The Cow and Girl butter we got at Christmas bearing the Australian trademark was all I knew about this vast and amazing country that gradually stole my heart. I would like to sincerely thank the Australians for making me feel like a true denizen. Australia is referred to as the Big Country and that goes for their generosity of sprit; they accepted me for who I am, accent and all. It took a while and many tears were shed while making the transition. Although it was heart wrenching leaving my family and friends behind, I am very thankful to be here. I fell in love with Australia, and was finally able to adapt completely to my new life. My navel string is buried in Guyana, but I am proud to call Australia *home*. I even wrote a Villanelle to prove it.

Farewell picture taken in 1965 on de Kissin' Bridge

## Homesick for Try-bes'–by Helena (DaSilva) Martin

A far off land has cured me of Try-bes'
On board that ship I might have been a stowaway
My soul found strength allowing me to pass the test

Sweet memories of home and Gramuddah I still caress
Not a happy bride; I cried most of the way
A far off land has cured me of Try-bes'

Australia my new home emerges over the crest
Drying tears I decide to embrace whatever comes my way
My soul found strength allowing me to pass the test

Homesick and lonely; nostalgic memories haunt me like a pest
But love for my homeland was not enough to make me stay
A far off land has cured me of Try-bes'

Pregnancy at last, now my aching heart may rest
Maternal instincts are growing every day
My soul found strength allowing me to pass the test

I never thought I could embrace another land with such zest
Taking care of my first baby kept nostalgia at bay
A far off land has cured me of Try-bes'
My soul found strength allowing me to pass the test

# Chapter Thirteen

*All good things come to those who wait.*—*Proverb*

## 1965-68—54 ALBOUYS STREET

**We Finally Own a Home**

My father had built up a good clientele and thought it was time to expand his business. A factory would be ideal, but where? Daddy probably figured he could do pretty much as he pleased if he owned his own property. His sole intention was to buy a house with potential to establish a factory; one with a bottom-'ouse would be ideal.

My bicycle was stolen once again and I was dreading having to walk past the gang of *kangalangs* who congregated at the street corner waiting to discharge an onslaught of vulgar insults. As I walked my thoughts drifted back to the day my parents announced we were moving to this notorious neighbourhood. I had no inkling they were even thinking of buying a home so it came as a big surprise. Could this really be happening to my family; it was a dream come true. I was very excited and dying to hear which suburb we were moving to.

## Living in Hell's Kitchen

We had always rented so my heart swelled with pride when I got home one day and Daddy said, "We 'ave good news Helen, we baut a't'ree bedroom 'ouse an' will be movin' soon." Did he really say, "t'ree bedrooms?" None of our other homes ever had three bedrooms; except for those we rented and shared with relatives. I looked at Mummy in disbelief, but she gave a nod to confirm my doubt. I thought Daddy must have finally cracked the Littlewoods Pools; god knows he sent in enough entries. It was high time I had a nice bedroom I thought to myself, as I mentally began decorating it. The wonderful news lasted about two minutes because it all went downhill from that point when Daddy, a man of few words divulged the location of the new home. My heart dropped and I wailed, "Why Albouystown?" Daddy who had no genuine ambition until now, said he needed a proper factory for his coffee business and this was the perfect place. What he really meant was, the rules and regulations were not as strict in this lower class area. I honestly thought it was high time my parents were able to afford a home in a better neighbourhood, but I was wrong.

I wondered how I could kill them to prevent suffering the humiliation. The thought of having to tell my friends the new address sent shivers down my spine because Hell's Kitchen was not for the fainthearted. Sure, a small majority of fair skinned people did live in this vicinity, but everyone scorned them knowing they did so mainly because of their financial situation. My blood boiled when I thought of Daddy spending endless amounts of money on *likka* to entertain and impress his freeloading friends. Why the hell didn't he put his money to better use, it was high time his family came first for a change. I knew my fate was sealed because the *magga* wage the nuns paid me to teach the kindergarten class would never allow me to choose a better option. Besides, no unmarried children I knew ever had the privilege of leaving home so that was wishful thinking.

Can the prestige of a *big t'ree bedroom* home be enough to take the edge off the stigma, I wondered. "How laang before we get de 'ouse?" I inquired in a softer and more humble tone. I detected a trace of pride when Daddy replied, "We gon get de keys nex' week."

The day dawned and for some reason it was only me and my parents who went to view the new home. The inspection took all of thirty seconds from the front door to the kitchen and I wondered where the rest of the house was. I missed the first bedroom because it was inconspicuous. The owner had used a sheet of *tentis* (Masonite) to convert a portion of the narrow gallery to make the room. What a rip off! The master bedroom was not that big either, but it was the dismal sight of the cubicle I was to share with my eleven year old sister Anetta that made me speechless. The saying, "Not big enough to swing a cat" certainly applied here; but then again we could not afford the luxury of a cat.

Moving day was always a grim occasion and *proud Helena* cringed at the thought of the neighbours gawking at their meagre household possessions. I was dreading the move but could not voice my feelings to anyone in the family, least of all to my mother. I was eighteen at the time of this move and good impressions certainly counted back then. There was no way I was going to be seen moving into the new home in broad daylight. You may find this a bit strange so let me explain the reason. It was common practice for the neighbours to blatantly peer out their windows to see what possessions their new neighbour owned. It was a perfect opportunity for them to access and judge your worth as a person before they met you. The quality of your furniture and personal belongings were used as the criteria for judgement; it determined the category you were placed in by the Guyanese society. Bluntly put, it was simply a measure of your social standing. [A lot of people moved house in the dead of night because of this reason]. I am not entirely certain whether this practice took place in the more affluent suburbs, because we never had the good fortune to experience living in the better part of town.

Back to moving day . . . The entire family was expected to contribute to the packing and cleaning of the home we were vacating. Once that was done it was time to leave. My mother and two sisters were going to hitch a ride in the removalist van and I was expected to follow the family to our new home, but I hatched a plan to deceive Mummy. I pretended to leave at the same time as the removal van but I waited until it was out of sight then did a detour to Daphne's home where I laid low until it was dark.

The home was built on stilts which left the bottom section empty. This was the bottom-'ouse the builders would enclose in due course to become the prestigious coffee factory. I saw the once solid wooden wardrobe which was intact only hours before now lying under the house in pieces. The clumsy removalists had dropped it into the gutter. I had already anticipated the dreadful mood Mummy would be in because of my disappearing act, and seeing the broken furniture added to my fear. I timidly made my way up the stairs and was barely through the door when my mother shrieked, "Suh yuh t'ink yuh too good to be seen movin' in wid us; wha' took yuh suh laang?" The tongue lashing went on and on until she ran out of breath.

Miss Carmen was not concerned over the deceased wardrobe. She said it would not have fitted in the house anyway. I should have known she would have said that because her motto was, 'Everything happens for a Reason', now you know where I learnt that. The universe sure knows how to even things out. Somehow I don't think she would have taken the same view if it had been her prized possession. She regularly sang the praises of her dressin'-table with the *bevelled edge* mirror. It was actually a rather neat piece of furniture. The adjustable mirrors on the side allowed you to see your profile from any angle.

## Characters from the Neighbourhood

I was deep in thought as I approached the corner and spotted the gang. I silently prayed *de clock* would ride up alongside me because I could depend on Charlie to protect me in a situation such as this. The hooligans would not dream of interfering with me if he was around.

A vulgar laugh from the *packoo* everyone called '*de Hyena*' interrupted my thoughts . . . I had a mental picture of him with a toothpick in his mouth and one hand on his crotch as he vulgarly said, "'ello sweet'art, come le'me show yuh a'lil' trick." I was well acquainted with the street lingo and knew exactly what the jackass meant. "Drop dead yuh dirty mongrel," I cursed him under my breath. Out of the corner of my left eye I saw the top of *Stumpy's* head with his nasty dreadlocks and trademark red bandana. *Cackaroach* was crouching next to him, snorting like a pig and running one hand over his brilliantine slicked down hair while fingering the heavy gold chains around his neck. His mother would skin him alive if she could move her voluptuous batty and big-foot fast enough to catch him. She was often heard bragging about her perfect son Nigel and his good looks. As I passed the gang, *Mousy* the skinny runt found courage and shouted, "Stuck up Putagee bitch." The others followed with more insults but I pretended to be deaf. I felt a stinging sensation in my back and realised they were firing sharp metal staples with their sling-shots. I was close to tears but would not allow those bastards the satisfaction. At no time did I look back to acknowledge their doings. I did my best not to flinch as each staple found its target. I held my head high and walked a little faster to get out of their range and to the safety of my home.

I was even more irritated as I climbed the stairs and heard voices and recognised one was *de Snail.* I walked in, and out of respect acidly said, "Good afta-noon Uncle Carlos." He grinned his Capstan stained teeth, put on his sweet-mout' and greasily said, "Eh-eeh Helen, yuh lookin' rosy gyurl, come an' gi' yuh uncle a'kiss nah." He and Daddy were drinking coffee while Mummy was putting down a plate of food not so gently for him. His dishevelled appearance sent out unhygienic vibes and I cringed anticipating the frowzy aroma as I hurriedly bent to give him the obligatory peck on his cheek.

Mummy used to say, *"Every molee biscuit got 'e vhum-vhum cheese* (there is someone for everyone);" and it was true because Uncle Carlos had relationships with several women. His beat-up wooden blue grip with all his worldly possessions was propped up against the safe in the kitchen, and I noticed Miss Carmen's face resembled a swollen crappo. Mummy was showing her displeasure for the unexpected and unwanted guest.

It was 5 p.m. so I expected his bed would be brought out from the grip after he finished freeloading. His hammock slung out from the rafters in the choked-up sitting room was becoming a much too familiar site, but there was no other space available. I had had enough for one day so I took a refreshing shower and retired to my rat hole until it was time to go dancing.

I was awakened by a loud voice in the yard. It was *de Mout'* from the house behind telling someone for the hundredth time, "Ah went to de

United States of Amerika yuh no." I shuddered, pulled the pillow over my head, and wished she would go back to America.

Our yard was a thoroughfare for the neighbours who lived directly behind us in the two-storey home and duplex range. The standpipe which was just beyond the boundary of our yard was used communally; also there was no other option for them to gain entry to their homes. It was a good thing we all got on so well.

Our neighbours were Africans and East Indians.

Naabah Daphne, our original neighbour still resides in that home. We communicate whenever she visits her son Ivor in Toronto.

## The Coffee Factory Is Built

Daddy was ready to start work on the factory as soon as the dust had settled, but he had overlooked a major problem. The house was much too low for such an elaborate scheme. Huge jacks were used to elevate the house while concrete blocks were put in place. The house looked as tipsy as Daddy did on occasion and we lived precariously for some time. It was dangerous but we had to grin and make the most of it because there was no other option. That was stage one of the conversion to a factory.

The bottom-'ouse was enclosed and the front steps were rebuilt and repositioned. The back and front steps now formed a Vee. No thought was given to putting a door between the two steps to gain entry into the factory. When the *faux pas* was discovered, an opening was cut into the wall to give access from halfway up the back steps. We stood on the steps and climbed into the factory through this opening . . . it was ridiculous. There was a double door at the front of the factory facing the road.

Purchasing and installation of the necessary factory equipment came next.

I was practically oblivious to what was taking place since my social life was far more important now that I had a steady boyfriend.

Daddy was well known for using the word "Chap" when he wanted to emphasise a point, and I noticed he was saying it more frequently since he established the factory. He was very proud of his achievement and wanted to tell everyone about the modern equipment. His good friend Mr Cutty came to visit and in the course of the conversation I heard him say, "Well chap, a'mus' tell yuh, a'baut a'bran' new secon' 'an' mota to do de parchin'." Daddy was not a boastful man so I knew he was only expressing his happiness and gratitude for the labour saving device. The motor might have been second-hand, but to him it was new. The second most important piece of equipment he bought was an electric mill. Life was perfect for the time being. D-day arrived and it was time to test the new equipment. It soon became apparent that Daddy had overlooked a very important factor. Apart from not providing an escape for the smoke, he had also put our lives in danger by having a fire in such close proximity to our living quarters. No building inspector would have passed such a hazardous situation and this leads me to believe no plans were ever submitted. The floors were not sealed and we almost suffocated when the smoke spiralled upstairs. Our home was redolent of freshly brewed coffee and most noticeable was the aroma on our clothes. This was especially embarrassing because it overrode the Topaz and Occur (Avon) perfume I wore. Potential suitors could not decide whether to brew me or kiss me.

The floors were eventually sealed with fire proof material but the smoke problem was only slightly alleviated. Daddy could not find a better solution and since it was our livelihood we learnt to live with it.

There was no need to go to church while living here because this house was holier than Brickdam Cathedral. We could have gone without taking a shower in the rainy season. My father half-heartedly attempted to seal the holes in our roof with tar but never succeeded. The poor man was mentally challenged where such matters were concerned.

Albouys Street home after the factory was converted into an apartment.
Daddy reading on the porch.

The rebuilt home where Julian and family reside

## Johnny Builds Me a Wardrobe

Did I promise to tell you about me and Anetta sharing a room? Oops!
I lied, it wasn't really a room. The double bed we shared occupied most
of the limited space. We practically landed in the kitchen when we got

out of bed. Lucky for me, I was dating a handyman. Johnny came to my rescue and kindly offered to solve the storage situation. He built a structure in the narrow space between the foot of the bed and the wall. A curtain made from fabric completed the wardrobe and I couldn't be prouder or happier. This social butterfly now had somewhere to hang her coffee scented outfits. I took control of the room being the *big sistah*, more of a *big bitch* Anetta would say because she was at my mercy. I grudgingly allowed her a very small portion of the hanging space, but that was the only privilege she had. Johnny also made me a dressin'-table. It was actually a shelf, with a mirror glued to the wall above, but it was perfect.

We eventually graduated to a double bunk which allowed us a smidgen of extra room.

Anetta has often told her version of us sharing a room. Some of the stories I honestly don't recall and some I am sure she invented because I can't imagine being that unkind. I truly hope she has forgiven me for all the horrible things I did to her. She was no angel herself, but I won't embarrass her as she is still alive.

## Daddy Buys a Cyar

Business must have been booming because Daddy bought a car, blue of course (his favourite colour). Mind you, I only found that out in 1995. We used Daddy's favourite saying, "Well dun chap" to tease him about the car at every opportunity. It took many attempts before he got his license but Daddy never gained enough confidence to drive solo. My mother always said Daddy's spine was made from *rubber* and I guess this was proof. Joel was a competent driver (without a license) so he agreed to accompany Daddy on deliveries.

I was hanging out of the sitting room window one afternoon when Daddy and Joel came home. Daddy got out of the car to give Joel directions as he reversed over the bridge into the factory. I *buss laff* when I heard Daddy say, "Yuh cyan back-back bhai, it safe fuh yuh to reverse back." Have you ever seen anyone reverse forward? Daddy was not amused and asked me what I was *skinin' meh teet'* at.

My father never mustered up the confidence to drive on his own, and Joel lost patience. The novelty of driving had lost its appeal and his social life was suffering so he put his foot down.

Daddy threw in the towel after he lost his chauffeur and that was the end of our car era. The car was sold and replaced with the 'blue birdcage' as I called it. This cumbersome contraption fashioned from iron was soldered onto the front of his bicycle. The carrier was somewhat awkward and it took awhile for Daddy to master balancing the bike . . . watching him provided some good laughs. A nasty accident occurred when his trouser leg got caught in the bicycle chain. He solved the problem with the purchase of bicycle clips. Daddy and his blue birdcage became quite an attraction around Georgetown and in record time the name 'Coffee Joe' was bestowed upon him.

The name suited him fine, but why did everyone refer to me as Coffee Joe Dauttah. It was a constant source of embarrassment. I know this is a lame excuse but I blame my prejudice on our social system. I wanted my father to have a more respectable job when he already had one, shame on me. In hindsight I realise I should have been proud that my father made an honest living. I now proudly acknowledge the fact that Coffee Joe was my father. He was still addressed as such by all who knew him (except for the neighbourhood thugs who called him Uncle Joe) when he died at the ripe old age of ninety-three on the 1st November 2008. My siblings and I actually christened him 'The Sheriff of Albouystown' because he was so well respected.

## How Could You Do That Mummy?

Complaining about being called Coffee Joe Dauttah was mild compared to the embarrassment of my mother exposing her *bubbies* in my boyfriend's presence. Now, don't go calling my mother a *waabin* because she had a legitimate reason. You will be relieved to know she wasn't exposing them to impress my date. She was actually breast-feeding my youngest brother. In Guyana most women don't see the need to conceal a normal function; although, some modesty and discretion should have been exercised to save my embarrassment. I joke about it now and ask my husband if that was one of the attractions that kept him spellbound.

My mother was well endowed so he probably thought he was going to get the same deal. What a disappointment I must have been.

My mother obligingly increased the population when we moved to this address. She would have had another baby before Julian in 1965, but a paroxysm of coughing (Ferrol did not work) led to a miscarriage. I wanted to slit my throat when I discovered she was pregnant.

It was difficult to conduct a 'love affair' under the watchful eyes of a bulging household. I had two options when a young man visited me, we could sit under the scrutiny of my mother or on the front steps in full view of the neighbours. Needless to say I did not bring my date home too often.

## Nicknames for Daddy and Julian

Julian was only eighteen months old when I left Guyana so I missed all of his growing up years. I heard Charlie and CeCe refer to him as Tunus a few times but never to his face. I did not delve further but can only assume he may have exhibited one of the traits from a street character from that era called Tunus. If that is the case I can understand why he objects to the name. Tunus was a Putagee man famous for more than one reason . . . his bad temper. It was said his bad temper led him to jail because he killed a policeman. He also had a reputation as a heavy drinker and frequented a popular rum-shop called the Red Coconut Tree. I would like to know how that rum-shop got its name; I have never seen a red coconut tree. Tunus was especially remembered because he played a mouth-organ with one hand and performed what we called *pumpin'* (masturbating) with the other hand. No one should broadcast a class act like that.

I can tell you how Julian got his proper name. Mummy went to an East Indian jeweller named Mr Singh in Alexander Village for many years when I was little. His son's name was Julian and I distinctly remember Mummy saying all those years ago that if she ever had another boy she would name him Julian. She finally got her wish at age forty-three. His second name is John and that was in honour of Mummy's favourite uncle and also my husband who Mummy thought the world of.

While I am exposing family secrets I might as well tell you about Daddy's false-name. The name 'Frame' was bestowed by my wicked cousin Fedna and for perfectly good reason. Daddy was always peckish and often had to have a snack, but that man did not have an ounce of fat on his body. He was not selfish though for he gave it all to me; I am forever dieting as a result!!!!

Fedna was always *mannish* and took the liberty to tease Daddy every chance he got. It was comical watching Daddy trying to assert himself when Fedna, Cyprian or the rest of his young nephews got on the bandwagon calling him "Frame." With right arm akimbo (his trademark pose) he pretended to take offence and would say, "Chap, yu'al proppa mek yuh eyes pass meh, stap it a'tell yuh or yuh guh feel meh 'an' on yuh behine." Daddy never meant one word; it was just an idle threat and they all knew it. My father was forever mimicking his old friend Sukra from Berbice who was famous for saying, "'old up, 'old up" if he wanted to slow down someone's speech (especially mine). He also liked to say, "Yuh mekin' sport chap" when anyone was telling him a story he thought was far fetched.

My mother got off so lightly not having a false-name, but then again I don't think anyone was game enough to give her one. Her mouth was a bit crooked when she smiled so I used to find fault and call her Twist Mout. She did not like me pointing this fact out so she used the pig proverb on me. She said, "Pig akse 'e muddah, why sh' snout suh long?" His mother answered, "Pig snout small now, but wait till 'e get big like 'e muddah." Geez, I bet you want me to explain that one too. It means, 'Do not criticize your family; you might end up looking like them when you grow up'. Shite, she was right because my kids tell me I also have a little twist to my mouth when I smile. It serves me right! But I think mine is sexy!

Come to think of it, I think CeCe must be the only one of my siblings who escaped a false-name, but then again I left home when she was four years old. I bet you any money she has one from her school days. Anetta got her name from the master of false-names . . . Charlie of course. The poor girl would have been around nine or ten when someone butchered her hair. She came home with *picky-picky* hair on her head and quick as a flash Charlie nicknamed her after a bird called 'Kiskadee'. Up to today if we are talking Charlie would say, "Gyurl like de Kiskadee fly away, a'ain't 'ear from sh' in a'laang time." That bird has migrated to

Florida where she now lives with her family. She has three children and she recently became a grandmother Kiskadee for the first time. She will no doubt give me hell after reading this.

## A Shocked Kiskadee

This little anecdote involves the Kiskadee so I might as well tell you now. It pertains to the negligee I had made for my honeymoon. It would have been nice to be able to afford some sexy lingerie from one of the stores but I had to make do with a home made version. Someone had given me a piece of sheer pink organdie (stiff as cardboard) so I thought I would ask Miss Thelma to make me a sexy negligee with shoestring straps. It was not lined so it left little to the imagination. I showed it to Anetta who was fourteen at the time. A huge gasp escaped before she could cover her mouth and with eyes opened wide she said, "Oh meh gawd Helen, yuh not gonna be shame to wear dat in front a'yuh 'usband?" I suppressed a laugh as I said, "A'will wear a'laang vest unda it yuh fool." She believed me of course . . . I bet she can teach me a thing or two about sex these days, isn't that right Kiskadee?

Anetta stickin' her birthday cake with Joel. I am behind Anetta

## Johnny Drops Migration Bombshell

Less than a year after I met Johnny he announced his departure to Australia. Why Australia, and did such a place really exist? I'm ashamed to say my knowledge of Australia rested on the Cow and Girl butter we imported, and I was told it was at the bottom of the world. I was even more taken aback when Johnny suggested we get engaged. I actually thought he was joking. Eighteen was old enough to be engaged, especially since I was willing to marry him but age was not the problem. It was the invisible shackles of society that prevented me from agreeing to this arrangement. My life would have been put on hold for an indefinite period because an engagement ring signifies a serious commitment. It also meant no socialising in public without my fiancé. The scandal and gossip would have been endless and I couldn't see myself sitting at home night after night with just a ring for company. I was a party animal and was not going to forfeit the good times for a ring that couldn't dance!

Johnny accepted my honest reason and we agreed to correspond and take it from there. He decided he wanted some special pictures to take with him to Australia as a memento. The famous Philippe was employed and we naturally went to the Botanical Garden to take a series of pictures on the famous Kissin' Bridge. I am only now wondering if anyone ever asked Johnny who the dalmation was when (if) he showed them the pictures. My outfit for the photo session was a white dress with black spots.

With pictures in his possession he left for a land that was only a figment of my imagination. The date those pictures were taken must have been an omen. It was the 7th June 1965 and we were married three years later on the 8th June 1968.

Johnny left a month before he celebrated his twenty-first birthday so I gave him his gift in advance . . . not what you are thinking folks, shame on you. It was a pair of gold cuff links and matching tie pin with his initials. I wondered whether he had intentions of impressing the Australian girls with my gift. To be honest, I never expected to see him again.

Sneaking a farewell kiss behind a Luxury Liner bus at Atkinson Airport

Johnny's farewell in 1965. L-R Mitzi, Gran, Louis (father) Johnny, Carmen (mother) me & Aunty Clarice. Front Aloysius, Maureen, Rose & Rowena

## Mummy Banned From Airport

The farewell was going to be a family affair and I was dreading it, especially since Johnny's grandmother and spinster aunt did not approve of the girl from the ghetto. The day started out badly because my mother and I had a major disagreement. She was adamant about wanting to go to the airport and I just as adamantly said, "NO!" I better explain my reason. Dating couples did not show affection in public, it was a big *no-no* (in my era anyway), especially in front of our parents. I naturally anticipated our final goodbye to end in an embrace and a kiss. It was bad enough having to deal with a disapproving grandmother, aunt, and his father who I feared without having to worry about the prying eyes of my mother. Don't think for a minute I voiced those fears to her. Oh no, I simply made excuses that would be more acceptable. I told her there was no room in the car and that ended the *wrowin'*.

The trip to the airport is a blur. I must have blocked it out because all I can remember is being extremely nervous and anxious. We stayed outside the terminal for a while so Johnny could pose for pictures with various members of his family. His grandmother's poker face made it quite clear she wanted nothing to do with me; she never once acknowledged my presence. Her grandson was going to Australia so she was quite confident he would marry an Australian girl and I would be history. [Look who got the last laugh]. The good-luck fairy must have been on our side because a bus load of East Indians had taken a Luxury Liner to the airport and we managed to duck behind it for a few minutes to steal a few farewell kisses. Then again it could have been an agreement because someone took pictures of us kissing behind that bus. Which member of the family took those pictures remains a mystery that has never been solved.

I cried so much on the journey home that Mr Martin said he would have to buy me another drink to replenish the liquid I lost. I was too sad to see the humour in his remark. The farewell was over but my mother did not forgive me, she gave me the cold shoulder for days.

Life went on and since I was still a free agent I started dating. Each beau came and went in a flash because I was very choosy and there was always someone who looked more promising. Dancing was my favourite pastime and I was fortunate to have a nice assortment of relatives and friends to hang out with. Some of the guys owned mota-bikes and I couldn't be happier when I was hanging off the back of one. How I am still alive is a mystery because I had a few narrow escapes.

## The Airport Saga

Going to *de Base* (Atkinson Airport) for the day was a highlight for most people. We planned and prepared weeks in advance. The excitement reached fever pitch by the time the day arrived. You may want to know what the fuss was all about; you could even be forgiven for thinking it was a very long distance from home, but it is nothing of the sort. The Base is situated twenty-five miles from Georgetown but not too many people had cars. It was a rare privilege to see someone off at the airport therefore it was considered a 'very special' outing. We did not have too many relatives coming or going in those days but we had another reason to go there. Red Water Creek was in the vicinity and it was a very popular picnic venue. I enjoyed going there to swim in the Coca-Cola coloured water. The water appeared to glow red in certain parts with the reflection of the sun. Daddy said the water looked "brackish;" another of his favourite words. I guess he likened it to the brackish cup of Red Rose tea he sometimes asked me to make for him.

I have been to airports in many parts of the globe but I have never witnessed farewells as dramatic as the ones in Guyana. It was a very big event when someone left the country. Relatives and friends made an effort to farewell the person because they believed they would never see them again. I was always devastated.

The East Indians hold the record for the best farewell. They hired one of the Luxury Liners buses so the entire village could go to the airport. The spectacle of this bus overflowing with relatives and friends on its arrival was an event in itself. The small airport was packed to capacity when an East Indian person was leaving Guyana. Their farewells were a form of entertainment. Their wailing was so loud anyone would think it was a funeral. I enjoyed eavesdropping, and for a while I believed it was the same group of people because I always heard them saying the same thing. Amidst tears and loud crying they imparted this message, *"Waalk good bhai, guh prospa an' come back to a'we."* [Go safely, be prosperous and come home to us]. It was mostly their sons who went overseas to further their education. That could have changed with women's liberation but I never ever saw a young woman leaving in my era.

No one would ever dream of going on *de plane* looking *kass-kass*. Everyone dressed-up for the grand occasion . . . and that it was for many, even a hat and gloves were worn by the more pretentious. I can still remember one of our *bouncious* (bumptious) neighbours who went to the USA for three weeks and came back playing *piass* (putting on airs) and sounding as if she had swallowed an English dictionary!! That was not all; she took to wearing a hat and gloves to go to La Penitence market to do her shopping. Everytime she met someone she said, "A'jus' come back from de United States of Amerika." I was so sick of hearing her say that. Anyway she got into a buezin' session with a neighbour a few weeks later and completely forgot she was an American. The hat and gloves were discarded and she went back to talking like a *blagyard* (black-guard) from Albouystown.

## Our Greatest Achievements

I lived here for three years before getting married and in that time saw a few changes for the better. Mummy bought a Singer sewing machine on *truss*; the neatly dressed agent came religiously on Saturday morning to collect the five dollars weekly payment until it was all paid off. Nothing amazing was ever made on that machine. Mummy mainly made straightforward items such as curtains and pillowcases. She attempted making dresses for herself but she never reached the heights of a professional dressmaker.

I used the Singer to hem and add a bright border of gingham to all the hand and tea towels I made for my wedding trousseau. I was very proud of my towels which featured embroidered bunches of fruit (I think it looked like fruit) and days of the week appropriately named. Every spare moment was spent on those towels in the months leading up to our marriage. I recall Sister Kostka saying one day, "Helen, is dat all yuh are goin' to 'ave in yuh 'ouse in Australia?"

Daddy purchased an old Olivetti typewriter in 1965 and I was able to practice my typing skills; changing the ribbon was a nightmare but I am happy I learnt to type properly.

Our ultimate ambition was to own a *chiffonier* (china cabinet); you had status with one of those, unfortunately we did not rise to such heights while I still lived at home.

I heard Charlie's cycling trophies graced the *chiffonier* when one eventually materialised. I laughed when I was told our esteemed visitors stole the trophies after my mother died. My sister-in-law Anne recently confessed to having one (it needed polishing she said) which she promises to return.

A *Berbice-chair* is another thing my parents never acquired, but we had one shipped to us in Australia. It was a conversation piece; some of my friends thought it was a birthing chair because of the unusual design. One of Daddy's friends wore baggy shorts and displayed his *crown jewels* whenever he reclined in his Berbice-chair. I am not sure how this chair got its name but can only assume it must have originated in Berbice, a well known region. The seat of the reclining frame was fitted with carpet. Chairs were either made with the arms permanently protruding or with hinges that allowed them to fold inwards for storage. The extended arm allowed you to comfortably *cock-yuh-leg-up*. A board across the arms was the perfect place for doing jig-saw puzzles or having a meal.

We made our neighbours envious one Christmas when we bought a hot pink three piece leatherette Chesterfield suite. Don't let me tell you how long it took Mummy to pay the instalments. We kept asking her when it was coming home as if it was a baby in an incubation ward. The plastic was intentionally left on for preservation but it made sitting on it quite difficult. It made us very sweaty! We eventually realised we were a pack of *neva-see cum-fuh-see* and got rid of the plastic. We had more urgent use for it anyway. The vinyl seats were just as slippery and uncomfortable without the plastic.

The biggest and best items we acquired in 1967 were the fridge and the SEVEN piece Formica dining room suite. Daddy was still using it when I visited him in 2000, although the chrome legs had rusted.

*Melmac* had found its way to our shores and we were ready to graduate, but not to the extent of throwing out the enamel dishes!!! Daddy must have purchased the set because the dishes were *blue*.

## We Can Make Jell-O!

Everyone can remember where they were when they heard the news of President Kennedy's death. Well can I say . . . I can remember where I was standing the day our fridge was delivered. That box in which it came, represented a badge of prosperity. It didn't matter that we had nothing to put in the fridge most of the time but WE HAD A FRIDGE! The first thing I wanted to make was *jell-O* (jelly) which my friend Lita had in her fridge when I first visited. It also meant we didn't have to buy ice from the neighbours anymore. Now we also started selling ice. The following anecdote reminds me of the proverb, *Penny wise, pound foolish.*

> A dispute between an ice vendor and a disgruntled customer ended up in the Law Courts. A man apparently always sent his son to purchase a penny ice, but when the boy returned one day, the bowl only had half the usual amount. The man complained to his neighbour who was the vendor, but she was adamant the boy was given the correct amount. This *schupidee* man decided to take the woman to court. He lost the case because he had never questioned the possibility of his son goofing off to play after he was given the ice, and so half had melted by the time he got home. He ended up paying a lot more than a penny for his foolish mistake.

We were happy to have ice but we could not afford *sweet-drink*. Soft drink companies Weiting and Richter, Coca Cola, Red Spot and D'Aguair, willingly delivered small orders to homes but we could only ever afford a case at Christmas time.

Whenever an unexpected visitor arrived we discreetly sent one of the younger children to the corner shop to get a Pepsi, and then pretended we had one in the fridge all along.

When Ol' Francesca came to town for my wedding, she stayed with us and did something I would like to share with you. I watched in amazement as Gramuddah draped a towel over her head whenever she had to open the fridge. Why? She said it prevented her from *ketchin' fresh coal* (cold), not to be confused with 'ead, ches' or *lynin' coal* (a lying-in period of nine days after giving birth). Isn't that priceless?

Johnny said he liked Lemon *Meringay* (Meringue) Pie and I had heard Mummy say, "A man's 'eart is true 'e stomak," so I set out to win him with a *Meringay Pie*. I bought the little box that made the filling. The recipe said, 'one cup of water'. I thought it was going to be easy, but I ended up making Lemon Meringay Soup instead. I guess you want to know why? I measured with the big enamel cups we had, after all it was a cup . . . he still married me so stop laughing.

## More Bicycle Drama

It was ironic that my bicycle was stolen (yet again) on Aunty Olga's birthday. She won it in a radio competition but agreed to sell it to me because her daughters were too young to use it and she already had one. Out went the Blue Witch! I was so proud of this bike, not only was it *bran' new*, it was a Raleigh so I cleaned and polished it every day. I was devastated when it was stolen. It happened before the house was raised. The original front steps had a platform at the halfway point so I used to lock the bike and leave it there at night for safe keeping. I was always the first one to arise in the mornings so imagine my surprise one morning when the front door opened and in walked Charlie. Before I could say anything, he said he had bad news for me. He used my bike after I had gone to bed without my permission, and left it under the house when he got home. He woke early that morning to check on the bike but it was gone. He had looked for it without success.

Bicycles were indentified by a license we purchased each year and also by the number stamped on the frame. It was serious business because bikes were stolen as soon as you left them unattended. Anyway I am happy to say the bicycle was found the next day. Naturally after that incident I lugged it upstairs so it could sleep in the sitting room.

## No Goobye from Muddy

Whenever I wanted to stay out late, I organised to stay at my friend Noreen who lived with her married sister Pauline. Her grandmother whom we called Muddy also lived with them. I recall Muddy coming to my home late one night to seek refuge; she said the married couple were *wrow'in* and she had to escape. I made room for her in my bed and in no time she was snoring. She awoke before *cock crowed* next morning, put on her head-tie, and was gone as silently as she came.

I was forever doing things behind my mother's back, so unbeknownst to Mummy I went on a double date with a *duglah* boy of whom she didn't approve. Some friends had borrowed a car so we could go to Red Water Creek for a midnight swim and to toast marshmallows; something I had never done before. I made plans to sleep at Noreen knowing we would not get home until the wee hours of the morning. The glow from the fire exuded romance in the pitch black surroundings of the creek. All too soon it was time to break the spell to go home. I was snuggled up to my date dozing in the back seat when the car lurched and a loud thud brought me back to earth. The car had come to a halt and had tilted on its side at the edge of a trench. In the pitch black the driver did not see the cow crossing the road. We were shaken but no one was hurt. The car was damaged so we had to make other arrangements to get home. I knocked on Noreen's window around three in the morning and she let me in. I slept until mid-day then enjoyed the lovely meal Muddy served before going home around 3 p.m. in the afternoon . . . life was good. I wasn't home ten minutes when Lincoln (Noreen's brother-in-law) came to tell me that Muddy had died. It was such a shock . . . that beautiful old lady had checked out without saying "goodbye."

## A Peeping Tom

Our bathroom and lavatory were situated in the kitchen. The shower recess did not allow much room for dressing so the custom was to wrap up as decently as possible with the towel then quickly head to our room where we dressed. Daddy lost his towel when he stepped out of the shower one day and I laughed. The towel was retrieved in a flash and I was admonished with this gem, "Gyurl doan eye-pass meh wid yuh eye."

I was repaid with karma. My ritual of opening the little window in my room every morning before heading to the shower led to a nasty experience with a voyeuristic neighbour. I was oblivious to the fact that the mirror over the little dresser on the wall provided this peeping tom with a perfect view from his sitting room window. I unknowingly stood in the same spot each morning to dress after showering. There I was in my birthday suit powdering the nether regions when *me an' de man eye mek four* (made eye contact) in the mirror. The neighbour (the two homes were very close together) was peeking at me from the other end of his home. I slammed the window shut and gave him a tongue lashing. That was the end of his good fortune because I never opened the window after that unnerving experience until I was fully dressed each morning.

## Guyana Gains Independence in 1966

Guyana gained Independence in May 1966 and many exciting things took place. The Queen and other members of the royal family visited. Buildings were painted, although it was only along the route of the motorcade; a facade to impress the royal family. This masquerade was reminiscent of the time Prince Charles visited. The YMCA building in Albouystown where he was due to appear happened to be on the same street where we lived. Daddy told me only half the block was given a face lift for the royal visit. All good, but I couldn't help wondering how they disguised the smell of the filthy street gutters.

The regatta on the Demerara River in which I was to play a part never materialised. You may recall me saying I was one of eight young women representing local flora. Our spirits wilted as we waited for the Duchess of Kent under the hot-hot tropical sun. Hours passed before we were told the event had been cancelled. We were all bitterly disappointed. Pictures taken on the barge is the only proof I have of being in the regatta.

The general public was treated to a spectacular street parade that ran for two days. This was the event where my reputation went down the drain. I was accused of flaunting myself half naked in public.

Me (centre) at the regatta on the Demerara River in 1966

Me on the float wearing the bathing suit that caused a scandal

The Merrymen (a popular band) also came to Guyana for the independence celebrations. Their music was superb but I was not impressed with the length of their hair, I was accustomed to seeing men with short hair.

That was the year I also dated a very handsome boy named Jayme Fernandes. He took me on a picnic to Bee Hive and to my first cricket match at Bourda. The Australian cricketers will never forget Bourda. It was that famous ground where they were almost bashed to death on a world tour some years ago. You can ask Maxi Walker, he was there. I am classed as a West Indian because we play cricket, but I have absolutely no interest in the game. The entertainment for me was watching the spectators who climbed to the top of the Saman trees around the perimeter of Bourda cricket ground. The freeloaders arrived hours before the match commenced to secure a perch. The unfeathered birds did not move from their position; they even relieved themselves at the peril of the spectators on the lower branches, and at times fought without leaving the tree.

## Guyanese Idioms

There are certain things said by a Guyanese that no one else may understand; it may not even make sense. I tried this one on my Australian friends and they could not even guess what it meant. You may even find this saying offensive but to us it was very normal. Everyone knew what *shittin' in 'igh grass* meant and I've already mentioned it previously, but this anecdote will allow you to grasp the true meaning. Some people can actually accomplish *shittin' in 'igh grass* without being embarrassed, but that was not my experience. It all began with the Merrymen, a famous band of musicians that hail from Barbados. They came to Guyana on occasion to perform gigs but I had never had the opportunity to attend a fete where they performed. I was determined not to miss out when they toured in 1966. The venue for the biggest gig was scheduled for the Carib Hotel. This was a well known night club a little way out of town on the East Coast. Luck was on my side because my friends and I managed to obtain tickets. *Maan*, that was all we talked about for weeks; we could not wait for the *jump-up* (dance). My friends were making new dresses for the occasion and I was not *tekkin' leff*, I made sure I had one too!

401

Time dragged by ever so slowly while waiting for the big event. With hair teased to the ceiling and smelling like a perfumery I was rearing to go! The place was already jam packed when we arrived, and the atmosphere of the star studded ceiling was electric. I looked around and noticed that Tom, Dick and Harry were there. Those three people got around a lot I tell you. My mother hated them and was forever accusing me of going out with them. A'know yuh dyin' to 'ear wha' 'appen suh a'betta tell yuh. I was more than surprised to see the leader of a well known political party at this venue. I had seen the man on several occasions from afar so this was an added bonus. It was not unusual for a gentleman to intrude on another party to request a dance, especially when that gentleman had status. I was dumbstruck and instantly got *Cumfa* (the shakes) when he came over to ask *moi* for a dance. The man in question was very tall and I am five-foot-two so my head was level with his crotch, and that alone was enough cause for shame. I am telling the truth here, that *mook* did not know how to dance. I know that because *a'mash 'e foot* (stepped on his foot) for the entire dance. I haven't finished yet, there's more! It was as if the man had two left foot; his knee kept bumping into my private parts, AND I was *flyin' de flag!* I was never so *shame* in my life and could not wait for the man to *put meh dung* (return me to my seat). Muddah Rat was looking for a hole to hide in that night.

As you can see, a person trying to *shit in 'igh grass* sometimes gets shit on themselves. That was the blunt definition, but in Guyanese society it simply means 'A person of low standing wanting to climb the ladder of high society'. That experience caught me off guard because until then I had never attempted to cross those social boundaries.

I know you are laughing at all the crosses I had to bear but I can laugh about it too—NOW!

## XM Sends Daddy to Hospital

It was shaping up to be a very exciting year until we found Daddy folded up like an umbrella at the bottom of our back steps; he was out cold. His faithful friend XM was to blame. He had one too many and almost paid the price with his life. Daddy suffered head injuries and spent three weeks in hospital, but that did not wean him of the destructive habit.

Not long after he was up to his old tricks, binge drinking with his buddy Bappo (Baptiste).

One thing I will say in Daddy's defence, he was a peaceful drunk. I had friends who had to flee their home in the wee hours of the morning whenever their drunken father came home. They were belted and had to seek refuge elsewhere for the night. We never experienced any of that. My father went quietly to bed to sleep off the effects. I never heard Daddy utter an expletive stronger than *cacahole, bleddy, shite* or *caramba*. He might have had a *rubber spine* but he was a gentleman and I loved him to death.

## My Father's Friends

My father had friends that were nice enough, but they were all leeches in my opinion. My mother despised them. She called them 'rum-suckas' or 'spungas' because they took advantage of my father's easy going nature.

My tolerance was calculated. I was the biggest *spunga*, I slyly helped myself to the *cuttas* (snacks eaten while drinking alcohol) whenever the gang bought any; especially when it was *plantin* (plantain) *chips*.

Bappo was considered to be Daddy's best friend. He was one of the 'blow-ins' I told you about. Cecil Baptiste hailed from the island of St Lucia. That was all the information he ever divulged in all the years we knew him. He had a long scar on his face but no amount of questioning allowed him to let his guard down and it remained a mystery.

Daddy met Bappo after he took-up with one of my mother's cousins. He never married her but they had four children. Bappo moved his family from the range in Charlestown to premises that backed onto a filthy *alleyway* (drainage area for sewage) not far from our home. No self respecting person ever ventured into any alleyway; especially the ones in Albouystown. They were notorious for filth and vermin. Bappo had an ingenious idea to remove a section of the fence in the alleyway to create a shortcut to his home but it had dire consequences and he smelt like a sewer at times.

His attempt of half tucked-in shirts gave him the *kass-kass* appearance of someone surfacing from a saloon brawl; wearing a tie if you please! Bappo took stabs at odd jobs but he was *cock-bran'* (unreliable). Once he was a watchman; one who carried a *flattie* (small bottle of rum) and slept soundly . . . that was a standing joke. Job offers dried up so he decided he was going into the coffee business. Daddy willingly outsourced his equipment to him with the agreement he would use the factory on certain days. That man was *sweet* (tipsy) most of the time. Some days he was too far gone to even get the job done.

Bappo was not overly concerned when he lost his dentures in the nasty gutter one day. He simply fished for it, gave it a shake and returned it to his mouth! Someone once asked him if he had ever been sober and I can still picture the expression on his face when he replied. His expressive eyes had opened wide and he smiled broadly to reveal a gold tooth before saying, "W'ah is de use, a'only 'ave to get drunk again;" it made perfect sense.

An East Indian man we called Cloak also hung around a lot; I never found out his proper name. I remember him paying me a compliment on my handwriting. I thought it was awful but he was illiterate so I guess any handwriting looked good to him. Cloak worked for a wealthy man who owned a boat. He sadly lost his life trying to swim (a non swimmer) after the boat when it lost its moorings in the Demerara River. He left a wife and seven young children.

Mr Cutty was black as the ace of spades; a real gentleman. I believe he and Daddy had a genuine friendship. They had long meaningful conversations and he was always very respectful to the family. Daddy became a recreant father during this period and this caused a lot of tension in our household. I turned a blind eye and escaped socially.

Daddy and his best friend Bappo (Baptiste)

Daddy with some of his drinking buddies.
Bappo is the one with the scar on his forehead

## Holiday in Trinidad and Barbados

My Aunt Clothil (Daddy's half sister) left Guyana donkey's years ago to live in Trinidad so I never had the opportunity to meet her. Her eldest son came to Guyana on business one time and paid us an unexpected visit. I was out *strayin'* as usual so missed meeting him. Mummy considered him *a'good ketch* and berated me for the missed opportunity. She completely overlooked the fact that we were cousins. Patrick had extended an invitation for members of our family to visit them in Trinidad so Daphne and I decided to save up for a holiday to check them out.

Our good friend Maureen Small was married and living in Barbados by this time so we planned to pop over to visit her for a few days.

The dream finally materialised and we were ready to travel during our long school holidays in 1967. This was the most exciting thing we had ever planned.

No respectable travel plans were made without a new outfit; not to mention playing *piass* (putting on airs and graces) because we were *goin' 'pon a'air-plane*. We had a good send off with the usual tears and I asked someone to pinch me to make sure I wasn't dreaming. We always did that when something was out of the ordinary or beyond our reach. I think I asked someone to pinch me on my wedding day because snagging a husband was HUGE in a girl's life. Especially since the man came back from *behind god's back* to get me.

Trinidad was rumoured to have television so I was really looking forward to this phenomenon; other than that I had no idea what to expect 'overseas' and the excitement was building. I was a bit sceptical about the flight after my childhood experience in *de duck* but it was vastly different. No crying or vomiting this time; just butterflies in the stomach and wobbly legs.

## My Overworked Guardian Angel

Looking back on my many near misses of being raped I wonder how I managed to escape. My guardian angel must have worked a lot of overtime because I got myself into so many scrapes.

My well intentioned *Trini* (Trinidadian) cousins had very slyly lined us up with escorts before our arrival. On the way home from the airport they stopped at a store with the pretence of getting supplies. Unbeknown to us, the two guys who owned the store were going to peek out the window to take a look at me and Daphne to decide on their preference. I drew the short straw, and I mean *short* although he was quite cute. The handsome Syrian guys were cousins.

We double dated safely for the first few times; although I was not too certain about the shady nightclub they took us to called The Crab Hole. That place had some sleazy crabs; their claws were all over the girls. Oh, I must tell you that my cousins had forgotten to warn us that these guys were well known playboys around town. An afternoon at the races made Daphne and I instant celebrities. A camera was thrust into our faces and we made the six o'clock news that evening. It was a surreal experience seeing myself on television. We were certainly *shittin' in 'igh grass!*

The guys wined and dined us and when they thought they had us eating out of the palm of their hands they wanted dessert!

The double dating plans changed after a few days. My date called to say he will pick me up to show me the sights of his wonderful country and I was more than happy to join him. He drove up a long winding road to a dark lookout so I could admire the view of the city. We had alighted from the car and I was leaning on the restraining rail enjoying the impressive sight when my date leaned over and whispered words that made my legs turn to jelly. I honestly cannot repeat them but you get the picture. I never knew anyone could be so crude. I caught my breath and said, "Please take me home." There was not another soul in sight on that dark lookout so I was lucky he complied.

That man had the gall to call for another date the following day but he didn't see me for dust for the duration of my stay. My cousins could not understand why I would not take his call and I was too embarrassed too tell them. [They will know what happened after forty odd years when they read about it].

P.S: I received a letter from this jackass proposing marriage after I returned home.

## Buying Life Insurance from a Peacock

I had another near miss when an older man tried to sell me some insurance. How very intuitive of him, my life was certainly in danger. I met this sleazebag at my cousin Ingrid's wedding. Daphne, the bride's sister Vevica and I were bridesmaids, he was Vevica's escort. That man wasted no time telling me he was an insurance salesman and tried to convince me of the benefits. I was too polite to say no, so he arranged a meeting at my home. I had misgivings and refused to sign on the dotted line on the appointed day. Mr Peacock preened his tail feathers assuming a drive in his car would be enough to sway me. He said he had a client to visit in *de country* and suggested I go along for a drive to discuss the insurance issue further. Come on, I didn't get to go for a drive too often and I was naive enough to think he was genuine. Don't let me tell you where he took me. In case you are wondering, *de country* was anywhere five miles out of the city. We weren't too long on the East Coast road when he took a right turn. Houses began to disappear and before long we were driving on a dam in the cane fields. He conveniently ran out of fuel just as I was beginning to question his motive. That was when the penny dropped. I praised god he was decent enough to accept the rejection. He drove me home and that was the end of my insurance policy. I didn't want to pay the premiums with my body, and later discovered he was a married man at that!

I had other boyfriends I would have willingly gone into a cane field with if I could have stopped the tape Mummy planted in my head about sex. Her constant mantra of, "If yuh mek yuh bed 'ard yuh will lie in it," was better than contraception; I enjoy a soft bed.

Daphne, Me and Vevica with our escorts at Ingrid's wedding in 1965

My gorgeous four-year-old sister Cecelia

## The First Time I Saw Television

My Trini cousins will read about this and no doubt have a good laugh; sorry guys, you had a country bumpkin for a cousin.

Television was something of a mystery to us; we only heard about it from relatives and friends who had gone overseas on holiday and returned with absurd stories. Most of the things they told us sounded like 'Nancy Story' and I never really took them seriously. What they told us about television was the most far fetched in my opinion, what imagination I thought. I honestly never believed this box with live people interacting actually existed. However, all that changed in 1967 when I visited Aunt Clothil in Trinidad. As soon as I saw the grand looking box with the screen in their sitting room I knew it had to be a television. My first thought was, they must be rich. The set was turned off when I arrived, but since it was my first meeting with these cousins I did not want to appear ignorant by asking them to turn it on. I wondered when next they were going to turn it on and the suspense almost killed me. It was getting dark when my cousin Monica finally said, "Let's go to de sittin' room to watch de news." I had to restrain myself from running in. It didn't matter that the pictures were black and white because it was magical; my eyes were glued to the screen. I was fascinated to see people walking, talking and laughing in that confined area; how was that possible I wondered. I could tell these cousins were highly educated, and was afraid they would discover my ignorance so resisted the temptation to go behind the television to see if I could figure out how those people had entered. You must think that is very foolish, but Guyana, in those times was still very primitive and at twenty I lived in a cocoon of ignorance.

Seeing a television set for the first time can be compared to an isolated tribe living in the jungle, they believe nothing exists besides them. Then one day they are confronted by a stranger; they stare in disbelief realising they are not the only life form on earth.

Now it was my turn to return home from holiday informing family and friends that not only was it true, I actually stayed in a home that had a television.

Little did I know I would be living in Australia the following year and have a television of my own.

I can still remember the day my husband brought it home. I treated it almost like a new born baby and could not wait to write the folks back home to tell them all about our prized possession. It wasn't long before I was an avid follower of General Hospital and Days of Our Lives, what bliss. Not only did I get involved in the lives of these characters; I actually cried when they got injured or became ill because I honestly thought they were *real people*, talk about being naïve.

My in laws immigrated in 1980, and thankfully by then I was no longer naive and knew the characters were only actors. However my dear mother-in-law was now the novice. One day while she was watching Coronation Street, I overheard her saying to my young sister-in-law, "Gosh, poor woman, she is really sick, look how pale she is." She was almost in tears over that character; it was hilarious! Yes, I was now laughing at my mother-in-law when I had done the very same thing years earlier. What a hypocrite I had become.

## Joseph's House of Many Colours
Coats were simply not thought of in Guyana in the same context as coats in Australia or other cold climates. They were certainly not an essential part of my wardrobe until I came to Australia. Guyana is well known

for its rainy season so naturally we talked about raincoats. You may be surprised to hear the most popular coat in Guyana was *a'coat a'paint;* especially at Christmas time. Every man and his dog scrounged for paint to brighten up their home or furniture.

A coat of paint caused embarrassment in my teenage years. You have all heard the story of 'Joseph's coat of many colours', haven't you? Well let me tell you the story of Joseph's house. Yes, Joseph was my Daddy's name; a quiet, likeable easygoing man. Actually it's best to be honest and say he had no real ambition; especially when it came to his home. My mother must have applied extreme pressure for him to take an interest in our shabby home one Christmas. Daddy proudly announced he would be painting the walls of our sitting room. Anyone who knew him would have thought he was going to climb Mount Everest from the announcement.

We were so excited and waited anxiously as Christmas grew closer. True to his word, Daddy finally brought the paint home but we were astonished to see so many cans. Why? We all wondered. Our postage stamp size sitting room would not require that much paint. The reason soon became crystal clear. My dear Daddy had started this heroic task by collecting any left over paint from family and friends who had finished their festive painting. You guessed it, the contents of each can were just enough to paint a few boards; in a different colour of course; but that was no real concern for Daddy. He simply opened another can and repeated the process until all the walls were painted. He then congratulated himself with his favourite phrase, "Well dun chap." And that was how our home became known as, 'Joseph's house of many colours'.

It might have been no bigger than a *chicken coop,* but I took great pride in our sitting room floor. It was my job to clean the house on Saturday and that meant polishing the floors manually! I applied the polish to the floor early in the morning then went about my other chores until Teenagers Choice came on at 2.30 p.m. in the afternoon. I danced with a piece of rag under both feet and had sparkling floors by the end of the programme.

## A Four Dallah Buezin'

My last Christmas in Guyana was very memorable. I copped a *bad buezin'* (severe tongue lashing) a fortnight before Christmas from two Coolie girls. I can't even remember how or where I met those two wretches, but it had to do with them selling vitamins or something of that nature. I believe it was a magic formula to make me into a *star-gyurl* (film star) and I was all for that because I thought I was the ugliest creature on the face of the earth. Whatever it was came in capsule form but I did not have the grand sum of four dollars so they gave them to me on *truss*. I obviously consumed the remedy, but guess what? I was still ugly, so I conveniently forgot to pay the witches. Why should I pay for something that didn't work? The girls must have been relatives of our next door neighbour, (also East Indians) because they positioned themselves in the bedroom which faced our sitting room and launched into *buezin'* me. The entire neighbourhood knew I owed them a lousy *four dallah* when they were done. Those girls called me every name you could think of and some I didn't even know. I was never so *shame* in my life. Needless to say I did not have the money to give them. Mummy got angry and got on the bandwagon. Oh no, she was not angry with the girls for abusing me. She asked me how I could be so *schupidee* to take something when I couldn't pay for it. I have a vague memory of my mother paying the girls to get rid of the disgrace I had brought on her.

## A Christmas Fright for Mummy

We were still friendly with Naabah Doris after that happened. She was not in agreement with the girls' behaviour.

It was tradition for the neighbours to invite one another into their homes for pre-Christmas drinks. It could be anything from a glass of Punch de Crème, *Coague* (also called egg-nog/flip) or Ginger Beer. I was considered old enough to partake in this custom so Naabah Doris invited me and Mummy over for drinks on Christmas Eve 1967. It was early afternoon so we took the two younger children. Anetta was old enough to be left at home alone; *besize* we were only next door. We were having a lovely time when we heard the loudest screams coming from our home. Mummy naturally thought a burglar had broken in and Anetta was in danger . . . I never saw a woman scale steps so fast. I staggered out onto the landin' just in time to see Mummy throwing our blue wicker chair over the rail of our verandah, barely missing Charlie as he made his escape.

Our home had sibling rivalry on a big scale. It was me and Joel, and Charlie and Anetta

Charlie came home unexpectedly and he and Anetta had gotten into a fight. The fright from my sister's screams riled my mother into top gear and Charlie's escape made her fume more. Her *passion* (temper) got the better of her that day and she gave Anetta a beating I will never forget.

Mummy showed no remorse when my father showed her the evidence a few days later. My mother's fists were lethal, but on occasion she called on the *belna* (rolling pin) to do the job.

It was not my best Christmas.

## Fedna's Mota-bike

My one wish was to ride the Honda mota-bike my cousin Fedna owned. I had no license and no experience, but I spent a lot of time on mota-bikes so assumed it was simple. Fedna came to visit one day and I kept badgering him until he relented. My intention was to ride around the block but I got no further than ten yards because I *lick dung* a black woman as soon as I took off. Thank goodness the woman was not injured. The bike fell to the left and I went with it. My right calf was unfortunately resting on the hot exhaust which resulted in a nasty burn. How was I going to face my mother; her wrath was going to be worse than the pain in my leg. Lucky for me, she was not witness to the incident because she would have punished me and curtailed my outing to the creek that afternoon. I pretended all was well and did not let on about the serious burn. Pain or no pain, I was not forfeiting my trip to the Red Water Creek to swim with my friends.

Infection set in a few days later and I needed help, but my mother had no sympathy and totally ignored me. She was so angry she refused to look at my leg but had this to say, "Yuh was schupid enuff to ride de bike suh now yuh cyan feel de pain."

Alas, Aunty Georgie came to my rescue. I have no doubt Mummy secretly called her because she came armed with a nasty smelling black potion called 'Carrion Oil'. I wouldn't have been surprised if it was made from rotten carrion crow. That darling woman came every day with a fresh feather to dab the stinking lotion on my burn. She treated my leg until it was better. To my utter surprise the scar formed the perfect shape of the map of Guyana after it healed. It was a reminder of my stupidity for many years to come, and it still hasn't faded completely.

P.S: Daddy said that woman I *licked dung* came looking for me a few months after I left Guyana, she was seeking compensation . . . she had a long way to travel to find me.

## Obeah Rituals in Our Home

Aunty Georgie was a very reserved person and also a devout Catholic. That is why I was so surprised to see her performing a suspicious ritual on my little sister who was supposed to possess an evil spirit. I had heard of *Jarrah* and *Curar* (spiritual cleansing) but had never witnessed anyone performing one of these ceremonies until that day. I stood at a distance to observe the ritual. Seven specifically chosen items were placed in a frying pan and cooked to a cinder. I cannot remember all of the items but Aunty Gee multiplied each one seven times. There were onion and garlic skins, red peppers, cloves, matchsticks and someone's hair (my sister's I think). The number seven must have had some significance because after the items were charred, my mother held CeCe while Aunty Gee who seemed to be in a trance swirled the smoking frying pan over her head as she repeated an incantation seven times. After the mantra was said, Aunty Gee placed her thumb into the charred items then pressed a black dot onto CeCe's forehead to ward off *bad-eye*. To my knowledge, it was only the East Indian babies who wore a Tikka/Bindi on their forehead. Many of them also wore a bracelet made from black beads solely for the purpose of warding off evil spirits.

Talking about babies reminds me of Carnation Babies. It was a competition to end all competitions in my era; one that mothers followed with envy. The fatter the baby, the better the chances were of winning. I think the prize was a case of Carnation milk and the prestigious title of *Carnation Baby*. The photograph in the papers showed the diaper clad winner wearing a sash, surrounded by a display of milk. The bragging was endless. I knew my sister was beautiful and wanted to enter the contest but we couldn't fatten her up enough. She is still a skinny runt today.

This home must have attracted a lot of evil spirits, because my mother accused one of my aunts of putting a spell on her. It was a known fact there was friction among my father's sisters and my mother. Mummy was convinced that Daddy's side of the family practiced witchcraft; although, I believe that came about after news reached her ears that two of the sisters *poun' 'er name* (spread gossip about her).

Not long before I got married I came home one day and found Mummy in a crotchety mood. She was ranting and raving about something despicable *W'ite-'ead* (Aunt Phil) had done. I had a date that evening so wasn't paying attention. She was still going on about it a few days later so curiosity got the better of me. I was dumbfounded when she said, "W'ite-'ead was *wukkin' obeah* (a voodoo spell) 'pon meh." I wanted to know what proof she had of this despicable deed. Mummy said she caught her burying *gangga eggs* (rotten eggs) in the yard. I could not believe my ears or her ignorance. We were forever buying gangga eggs in the market and had to throw them out. My aunt vehemently denied the accusation; but my mother never forgave her.

## Piercing Ears

Most of my friends had pierced ears and I was desperate to join them, but this practice was forbidden in our home owing to the traumatic experience my mother had in her school days. She had her ears pierced at a very young age but while playing at school someone pulled her earring and split her ear. She vowed that none of her daughters would have pierced ears.

The evidence of her split ear did not deter me, that was her sad experience; I was going to have mine pierced regardless. I coerced my friend Norma into taking the plunge with me. Yes, that same Norma who said we had "nuff guardian angels." She agreed to accompany me to consult the jeweller next to Channa Man on Camp Street. We were going to be partners in crime. This was all done without my mother's knowledge of course. My hair was shoulder length so I figured it would be easy to conceal the earrings while in her presence, but I had another thought coming.

The dreaded day arrived and we were both very nervous anticipating the pain. Norma and I watched as the jeweller sharpened the ends of the earrings. Yes, he was going to use the very earring as the instrument for the piercing. We gave each other quizzical looks because we were told the piercing was done with a sharp needle. We were too shy to question him, so we kept our traps shut. I decided to go first since it was my bright idea (always is). The man put a dab of mentholated spirits on a piece of cottonwool, gave my ear lobe a quick wipe and he was ready. It stung like hell when he pushed the sharp end of the earring in, but I held my composure as I didn't want Norma to chicken out. She squealed when it was her turn and wanted to know why I didn't tell her it hurt.

I guess the environment wasn't sterile because my ears became infected a few days later. I decided to remove the earrings to clean and disinfect the wound. Lo and behold I could not get them through the holes again. I got on my bike and went to Noreen to enlist her help. With a lot of pain and bleeding she got them in. A few days later, in an unguarded moment, my mother spotted the earrings and all hell broke loose. "So yuh t'ink yuh are a big woman now?" She went on and on about it. What was that Mummy? Did she forget I became a 'big woman' at fourteen when she told me I had to wash my own clothes? Make your mind up woman. I guess I was too old at nineteen for *licks* so her tongue did the job.

I had a second hole pierced in Australia because I am definitely a *big woman* now that I am married and able to *turn meh own key an' light meh own fire*. Tek dat Mummy! She will *turn in sh' grave* for that rudeness.

## Good Ol' Bappo Buys Beer

This was also the era of *teased hair* (back combed). All the girls looked as if they had a big load of *cow dung* (cow pat) on their head. It was fashion, and Miss Helena was not going to *tek leff*. A friend said that hair teased much better if beer was applied before putting in the rollers. I did not drink, but soon worked out a scam to get beer without spending a cent. Daddy's best friend and drinking partner Bappo always drank to excess. I waited until I knew he was well and truly *tanked-up* then asked him to treat me to a beer. He had no idea what I was going to do with the beer so he always handed over the twenty-five cents for the bottle of *Banks* . . . I had become a con artist. What a combination, I not only smelt like coffee, but beer as well. I guess I was too damn gorgeous because the boys never complained and I was never short of a date.

## Rescued By My Knight in Shining Armour

Johnny's unexpected arrival at my home took place at the end of January 1968. I cannot honestly tell you how we greeted each other. You may recall me saying at the very beginning that the moment of that meeting has been frozen in time. I hardly recognised him after three years. He was working as a bricklayer and the Australian sun had bleached his hair blonde. He was the same person otherwise so we took up where we left off in June 1965. A few weeks later he proposed to me. It was not the most romantic proposal, but I will never forget it because we were parked next to *de Seawall* (not where we were attacked), my all time favourite place. I did not expect the proposal, nor did I expect him to tell me we were going to live in Australia. My heart sank just at the thought of having to say *goodbye* to my loved ones, but that was the deal. It was a bittersweet moment, but I said YES!

## Daddy Starts a Farm

Farming is in my father's blood, so when the opportunity arose he got himself some land. I never knew whether it was purchased or leased. The farm was at a place called Linden up on the East Bank. I only ever went there once. Johnny had just returned from Australia so Daddy invited us to see the place. We travelled by car to Linden, but had to transfer to Uncle Joe's truck for the rest of the journey because there were no roads leading into the farm from the highway. It was a bumpy ride standing on the bed of the truck. Vines laden with Soo-moo-tu brushed our faces and we were able to pluck the fruit as we drove through.

My father had built a comfortable logee for shelter, but he slept in a hammock whenever he stayed there. Daddy cooked a huge pot of cook-up-rice in the fireside in the yard. It was a memorable day with the family, especially since Daphne was there too. I forgot what Daddy was growing at the time because I was too busy exploring the jungle. Johnny and I wanted to find the creek Daddy said was a little distance from the hut so we went in search of it. We found it and to my utter surprise Johnny decided to copy Uncle Naysh and took a skinny dip in broad daylight. We were alone but I refused to watch, ask him. I was too shy so I watched the monkeys jumping overhead instead.

## A Very Special 21st Birthday

Do you recall me saying my twenty-first birthday was very special? Well, not only was I celebrating my *comin'-of-age*, I was to become engaged. What could be more *special* than that? My birthday cake was made into the traditional key shape. It was a small affair at my home with a few close family and friends, but it was beautiful and memorable. Johnny's mother and sister Mitzi dropped by to congratulate us and to give me a gift. The white negligee set was beautiful, but what I will always cherish was the *extra* gift Mrs Martin gave me. Mops crushed a small envelope into my hand and whispered, "Open dis latah." Inside was a *crips* ten shilling note wrapped in a beautiful personal message. I still have both items as a memento.

Our wedding date was set for the 8th June because we had to board the Southern Cross in Trinidad on the 13th June to undertake the six week journey to Western Australia.

Key shaped cake for my 21st birthday and engagement

Guests Elizabeth, Ernesta, Claire, Norma, Sue, Jean and Lil' Helen
(standing) Mitzi, Anetta, Glenda, Me, Daphne & Donna at my bridal shower

## My Very Special In-laws

No one could be luckier than me when it came to in-laws; I had won
the jackpot. I was made to feel welcome from the very first time Johnny
took me to meet his beautiful mother. She was not just a mother-in-law;
she was my best friend and confidante. I was further blessed with five
sisters-in-law, Adele, Mitzi, Rose, Maureen and Rowena and brother-
in-law Aloysius, who we sadly lost at age fourteen in 1967. They have all
treated me as if I am another sister. I am even allowed to insult them,
just ask Mitzi. They are all loving and forgiving so I am truly blessed.
Thanks guys!

Mr Martin may have wished for someone more intelligent for his
son. (It was he who accused me of flaunting myself on the float and
relayed the 'tramp' news to Johnny in Australia). We did not always
see eye to eye and I was deeply offended when a relative told me he said
I was "schupidee" when she asked why I didn't drive. He came to live
in Australia after he said that, but I only heard about his remark after
his death. At least he had the good decency to keep that to himself. We
treated each other with respect and it was all I asked for.

P.S: I learnt to drive before he died in 1983 and proved him wrong.

## Tears To Sink the Titanic

Our wedding day is somewhat of a blur. I almost did not get my hair done because Baby (hairdresser) had repeated episodes of bad feelings and she had to keep lying down. I arrived home with half an hour to spare but my dear Aunt Claudia thankfully thought ahead and had a big tub of water ready for my bath.

Naabah Noor ran a *drop-cyar* service so Daddy and I went to the church in his car. The street was lined with nosey neighbours and other spectators. It was my turn to be judged as a bride . . . some cruel bitch said the bridesmaids looked better than me. That's karma for you.

I wouldn't argue too much with that because my wedding dress cost about twenty dollars. Cheap and nasty was all I could afford. Miss Thelma charged me five dollars to make it. She would have done it for *nutt'in*; but a token sum had to be paid because we have a superstition that says bad luck will follow you unless money crossed hands. Custom also said a bride should have sumt'in' old, sumt'in' new; sumt'in' borrowed and sumt'in' blue so I adhered to that rule. The veil was borrowed from Bernadette who had gotten married to one of Johnny's cousins a few months earlier. Ol' Francesca gave me her old hanky, the garter was blue and everything else was new. I had my heart set on blood red roses, but the lady who was making my wedding bouquet had an accident and *bruk sh' 'an'* on the morning of my wedding. Her daughter-in-law rustled up something that vaguely resembled what I ordered but I was too sad to care.

Johnny's grandmother and his spinster aunt were so disappointed with the match they refused to attend the wedding as guests. Curiosity must have gotten the better of them because the pair were seen crouching in the far corner behind one of the big pillars in the cathedral. Their hearts were set on him marrying a blonde, blue eyed Australian beauty. They could go and suck eggs for all I cared.

That same biggety aunty came to visit us in Australia and gave me instructions on how to make her drazees *white*. Oops! You bet they came out *blue*! If I wasn't good enough for her nephew, then I was not good enough to wash her drawers. She went back to Guyana six weeks later and gave a special tea party to show off her holiday snapshots. I was told her friends were appalled when they asked her to point me out in the pictures. There was not one picture of me. To add insult to injury she had the nerve to write and ask me to send one. I don't think so. She should have realised that when she was saying, "Helen, take one of me and Johnny," or "Helen take one of me and Andrew." On and on it went, but not once did she want one of me. I am sorry I stopped to vent but it saves me going to the shrink.

Let me get back to our wedding . . . The ceremony took place at the big Catholic Cathedral with Faddah 'Pain' officiating. The nuns had asked me to go to the convent after the ceremony so they could see me as a bride. The convent grounds had beautiful gardens so we took the opportunity to have our wedding pictures taken there.

The reception was held at the home of my friends Glenda and Gerry Fernandes. Glenda was also a teacher at Stella Maris. In the background of our wedding pictures you can see the entire neighbourhood gawking as we made our way up the stairs; those people *fas'* I tell you. I guess they were looking to see if I had a *big belly* so they could have something to gossip about.

Our first child was born thirteen months to the date of our marriage, hence the thirteen chapters in my memoir to show I am not superstitious. Number thirteen has been lucky for me many times.

## Our Wooden Wedding Cake

Tradition dictated the bride and groom were to be greeted by their mothers at the door of the reception with a glass of champagne. The mothers swap children and offer their new son/daughter a drink to welcome them into the family. Johnny is a non drinker and only took a sip out of respect. I drink on his behalf; what a good wife eh? I cannot begin to tell you the tears that were shed at our wedding reception. Charlie said we could have sunk the Titanic. I did not eat a thing for nerves and sadness.

Whenever I was envious of somebody or something Mummy would remind me that, "All that glitters is not gold," and as usual, she was right. Our absolutely impressive three tier wedding cake was a good example. Mummy was peeved that we did not agree to use our chicken coop of a house for the reception so she *swelled up like a crappo* and refused to help with the cake. We did not let that get in the way of our wedding plans.

We naturally wanted the traditional Black Cake for our wedding so Johnny and I rolled up our sleeves and got the job done ourselves. The batter was put in the hired pans and Johnny carefully carted them down to Dictator Bakery at the end of our street. Oh, I just remembered I lied to you (again)! It was actually two and a half tiers of *real cake* because we ran short of batter for the bottom tier. My quick thinking genius husband substituted a thick piece of wood which he carved to fit to make up the difference. No one except us and Johnny's Aunty Clarice knew the secret. Luck was on our side with the cake decorating because Johnny's aunt was the top cake decorator in Georgetown at the time, and she did ours as a gift and what a magnificent job!

The wedding cake is traditionally delivered to guests three days after the wedding. The miniscule piece of cake was only a token. You were supposed to rub it behind your ears for Good Luck. We were leaving on the third day after the wedding so we gave ours out a day early. Maybe that was the reason I cried all the way to Australia.

My relieved parents saying 'we are finally rid of her!' as I leave for the church

Wedding party Left to Right Antony, Mitzi, Carl, Daphne,
Johnny, Mc, Noreen & Rudolph

We are welcomed into the family by our respective
mothers-in-law with a glass of champagne

My Grandmothers Francesca (left) and Philomena

Cutting our wedding cake which was decorated by Clarice Evans

## Shameful Honeymoon Night

I was made to endure shame right to the very end of my life in Guyana. We could not afford to go to a hotel so a relative of Johnny offered us a bedroom for two nights. That was very kind of them, but did they have to leave the reception before us? You have to understand I was a very bashful and naive young woman, so imagine my horror when we got to the home and found a few of them waiting in the sitting room to welcome us. I wanted to go home to Mummy. I hope you are not waiting to hear how the man ravished me because I will tell you that *w'en fowl-cock get teet'*. I can't remember anyway, it was too long ago.

## My Humble and Sincere Tribute

Our walk is almost over but before I leave you I would like to pay tribute to a few people. This memoir was not only written for my family. It is a tribute to my birthplace Guyana and includes the diaspora at home and around the globe. Do not allow anyone to call you a 'mud-head'. We should be known as the three H (Hospitable Hilarious and Harmonious) people.

To you, the reader, I hope you have enjoyed *de waalk* and *de gyaff* with me. To all my many and wonderful friends from around the globe, I sincerely thank you for your love, support and encouragement, in not only writing this memoir but for being YOU. Each and every one of you has contributed to the making of the beautiful tapestry that is my life. I have collected a multi-cultural bouquet of friends along the way and consider myself blessed beyond words. THANK YOU ALL.

How can I ever thank or repay my unique and amazing family for the legacy of my beliefs and the unconditional love I was so fortunate to receive.

I will always cherish those twenty-one years in Guyana. I did not realise we lived in poverty because the love I felt from my parents, grandparents, aunts, uncles, cousins, friends and neighbours overcame all obstacles.

## P.S: I Forgot To Tell You . . .

This proverb was saved for last; I feel we can all learn a valuable lesson from it. It is easy to make an assumption on a person's outward appearance. I had a habit of doing that myself, but Mummy always said, "Never judge a book by its cover."

I believe Patrice and Sean Sawyer lived by that rule because I had the privilege of literally bumping into a total stranger when I met Patrice on her way to empty garbage. Bizarre is the only word to fit the description of what happened one Saturday afternoon in July 2009. I was out on a date with myself, as crazy as that may sound (an exercise from 'The Artist Way' by Julia Cameron) but that's another story. I was just out to enjoy a nice walk along the beach with an ice-cream treat in mind afterwards.

What happened here can only be described as *serendipity*. Halfway into my walk I got an urge *out of the blue* as happens in our family, to take a detour. Two minutes later I came across a campsite with cute little beach shacks and knew in an instant I had to have one because I was desperate for some solitude to work on my memoir. I first approached a group of people putting up a roof to ask if there were any available, but was told they were private and no one was allowed to rent out to strangers. After explaining my position the woman suggested I go to the office. On the way to the office I ran into Patrice and asked was I on the correct route. Which one, she inquired? Apparently there were two sections to this trailer park, unfortunately the same rule applied in her section. Without realising it, I had opened my mouth and found myself saying, "I am a writer and I really would love a place like this for a week so I can have peace and quiet to work on my manuscript." Don't forget, I had learnt from the best, so I knew when all else fails, use *bullshit* like Mummy. "I am a writer." Where the hell did that come from? Maybe I am a clairvoyant like Mummy too!

Patrice gave me a sympathetic look then asked which week I was looking at. I told her in two weeks time. She said her aunt and uncle from Canberra were scheduled to use the shack that same week, but her uncle had taken ill and had cancelled so it might be possible. She invited me to their shack to consult with her husband Sean. He listened while she relayed my story and to my surprise he said he couldn't see why not and invited me in.

Within five minutes the deal was done, although, Patrice did think to ask if I was running from the police. Well, wouldn't you be suspicious of a desperate deranged woman approaching you so suddenly?

How would I have had eight blissful days in a cozy beach side shack if Patrice and Sean had judged me by my appearance? I had to say I was a friend if the caretaker asked, but that was easy because after I collected the key I never saw another living soul in that section of the park for the duration of my stay. I have no doubt a higher force orchestrated the entire string of events that led to this amazing outcome. I would like to say a heartfelt "thank-you" to Patrice and Sean for their complete faith and trust in a total stranger. AMEN.

The waalk is ova suh guh 'long yuh way an' waalk good. Ah only want to seh one t'ing. It's truh-truh w'at deh seh . . . Typee conquers all!!

Sitting on the photographer's mota-bike to say farewell to Guyana

# GLOSSARY OF WORDS

### A

*Adge*—advantage
*Ah*—I/I'm/a
*Air-plane*—aeroplane
*Akse*—ask
*Al'yuh*—all of you
*Alleyway*—concrete drainage for sewage
*Angel-hair*—delicate gauze (gossamer) used to decorate Christmas trees
*Anti-man*—homosexual
*Atchee*—Amerindian stew made with fish, cassava juice and hot peppers

### B

*Backanal*—trouble
*Back-back*—*back-up*
*Backdam*—hinterland/fields a long way from home
*Backrah-pickney*—a child of half caste breed (dating back to slavery when children had master/mistress parentage
*Bad feelings*—nausea
*Bad-eye*—evil looks from envious spirit
*Baghee*—variety of spinach
*Bake*—girlfriend
*Bakes*—local substitute for bread/ dough made with flour and water

*Ballahoo*—boat

*Bam-bam*—bottom/backside

*Bambye*—saving food/item to eat/use later

*Bamsie*—bottom

*Banked low*—bearing towards the road when making a turn on a motorbike/bicycle

*Bannah*—a handsome boy

*Bassa-bassa*—stirring up trouble

*Batelle*—a pan used when prospecting for minerals

*Batty and Poe*—when two people have a very close relationship. [Associated with the closeness of anus and chamber pot]

*Batty*—backside/anus

*Beat-up*—battered

*Beddin'*—rags

*Bee-tee*—anus/bottom

*Behine*—behind/backside/bottom

*Belna*—rolling pin

*Besize*—besides

*Betroushe (Bête rouge)*—a mite that cause severe itching

*Bhai*—boy

*Big-comb*—wide tooth comb

*Big-eye*—a person expecting the lion share

*Big-foot*—Elephantiasis/swollen legs

*Big-people*—adults

*Big-shots*—wealthy people/upper class

*Big*—tall/grown up

*Bini*—a beautiful girl

*Black Cake*—rich fruit cake, made black in colour with burnt sugar

*Black Mariah*—police van used for rounding up criminals

*Bladder*—balloon

*Bla-gyard*—black-guard/low class person

*Blanko*—whitening agent for shoes

*Boo-boo*—gunk/residue found at the corner of eyes after sleep

*Botheration*—troublesome

*Bottom-'ouse*—vacant space below the house

*Bouncious*—bumptious

*Bowjie*—sister-in-law in the Hindu language

*Box-hand*—a contribution of savings within a group

*Box-oven*—oven fuelled by wood

*Brace-up*—leaning against an object

*Bradar*—a vulgar quarrelsome individual

*Brakkle*—apprehend/arrest

*Brekfus*—breakfast (which we called lunch)

*Brigah*—pretentious/feigning interest

*Bring dung*—lower temperature/object

*Broklax*—chocolate laxative

*Brown Betty*—the name of a popular ice-cream parlour

*Bruk*—broke

*Bruk-dung*—not working/dilapidated

*Bruk-up*—not feeling well/disrepair

*Bubbie*—breast

*Buck-sick*—fed up/had enough

*Buck*—slang for Amerindian

*Buckta*—briefs/underwear for men

*Buezin'*—verbal abuse

*Bun-bun*—burnt food scraped from the bottom of the pot

*Bung fuh*—bound to/guarantee

*Bung navel*—a protruding navel

*Buryin' groun'*—the grounds of a cemetery

*Bush hog*—a wild boar

*Bush meat*—wild game

*Buss cry*—burst out crying

*Buss laff*—burst out laughing

*Butt-up*—met up with/ran into someone

## C

*Cackaroach*—cockroach

*Caiman*—overgrown alligator

*Cake-shop*—patisserie

*Calabash*—dried shell of a gourd

*Canaree (Carahee)*—cast-iron type wok

*Candy fross*—fairy floss

*Cappadula*—local Viagra

*Cark duck*—no hope/out of luck

*Carta-lick*—Catholic

*Chanchie*—golden residue at the end of coconut oil making process

*Channa*—chick peas

*Charangi*—lustful love

*Chasie*—playing tag

*Chicken-in-de-ruff*—barbeque chicken served in a basket

*Chiffonier*—china cabinet

*Chigga (Chigger)*—a parasite

*Chile*—child

*Chiney brush*—a potion used to sustain an erection

*Chiney*—Chinese

*Chirren*—children

*Choke-an'-rob*—bandit/thief

*Choked-up*—cramped/crowded

*Chow-chow*—green mangoes chopped and seasoned with hot peppersauce and salt

*Chunkay*—to add fried ingredients to a dish after it has been cooked

*Cloak-up*—to sit/lie in a huddled up position

*Coal-pot*—an apparatus fuelled by coal

*Cocabey*—leprosy

*Cochore*—encourage/flatter

*Cock-bran'*—unreliable/con artist

*Cock-meh-leg-up*—put your feet up

*Commonness*—sexual activity

*Cook-up-rice*—peas and rice/pilaf

*Coomerish*—comical/like a clown/uncoordinated

*Cop-cop*—a species of ants that packed a mean sting

*Corial*—a dugout canoe

*Crappo*—crapaud/huge toad

*Crips*—crisp

*Cross across*—crossing over a street or obstacle

*Crosses to bear*—difficulties/woes

*Cuffum*—imitating traits of a fish by that name when swimming

*Cufuffle (kerfuffle)*—confusion/to confuse

*Cumpay*—a person's godfather

*Cungapump*—beverage made from locally grown tree and used for sexual enhancement

*Cu-nu mu-nu*—a person who is not very discerning/scapegoat

*Cuss*—curse

*Cut-ass*—a sound beating

*Cut-eye*—look of disgust/dirty looks

*Cutlass*—machete

*Cut-tail*—a whipping

*Cuttas*—snacks to accompany alcohol beverage

*Cutty*-cutty soup—soup cooked with a variety of vegetables coarsely chopped.

*Cyan*—can

*Cyan-cyan*—stiffly starched petticoats

*Cyar*—car

*Cyart*—cart

*Cyas'-net (cast-net)*—net used for catching fish

*Cyat*—cat

# D

*Da t'ing*—that thing/referring to an object

*Dan-dan*—dress/frock

*Dauttah*—daughter

*Dayclean*—daylight

*De base*—the airport base

*De odda day*—just recently

*Deh*—there

*Deh*—they/their

*Dem*—them

*Din-din*—dinner/a meal

*Dinnah*—dinner

*Dis time*—now

*Diya*—miniature mud/clay cup used for *Diwali* (lighting festival)

*Doan*—don't

*Dodo*—sleep
*Dolly-'ouse*—dolls house
*Don-kay-dam*—don't give a damn/not a care in the world
*Dotish*—doltish/senile
*Dova*—name brand of wood stove
*Draw bret'*—breathe
*Draw watah*—fetch/get water
*Drazee*—bloomers/underwear
*Dress dung*—move down a little
*Drop-cyar*—taxi service operated privately/ taxi
*Drugley*—an out house on wheels used for drying purposes
*Duff*—dumplings made with cornmeal
*Duglah*—a person with mixed parentage (African and East Indian)
*Dundapillah*—a brand of bedding called Dunder-pillow
*Dung town*—the heart of the city/town

E

*Eddicashun/eddicate*—education/educate
*Edge teet'*—sensitive teeth
*Enuff/nuff*—plenty
*Eye-full*—to obtain a good view
*Eye-pass*—disrespect
*Eye-turn*—dizziness

F

*Faddah C'ris'mus*—Santa Claus
*Faddah*—father/priest
*Faffey-eye*—rheumy eyes/a disfigurement
*Farina*—staple diet of the Amerindians
*Fas' (fast)*—inquisitive/curious/nosey
*Fawk-stick*—a forked stick used for gathering vines and vegetation
*Fete*—party or dance
*Finaral*—funeral
*Fine-fine*—an extremely thin person

*Finnie 'an' /leg*—a withered limb

*Fire-rass*—exaggeration of size/someone with an explosive nature/ flashy

*Fireside*—open fire place for cooking

*Fish-up*—to insult someone

*Flim-show*—film shown on a screen using a projector

*Flit-cyan*—a spray can

*Flutee*—flavoured ice confectionery

*Fly-paper*—sticky strip of paper that trap flies

*Fo'ce (force) ripe*—hasten maturity/children trying to become adults too soon

*Fo'day marnin'*—before daybreak

*Foo-foo*—boiled green plantain pounded in a mortar with a pestle to form a glutinous ball

*Fraffy*—frothy

*Fresh coal (cold)*—a sudden cold

*Freshie*—elderly men who are predators of young girls

*Front window*—a window in the sitting room facing the road

*Frukudy*—dilapidated/despicable

*Fry-ile*—cooking oil with the brand name of *Fryol*

*Fryken bad*—very scared

*Fryken*—scared

*Fuh*—for

*Full-mout'*—calling your peers by their first name is considered disrespectful

*Funkie*—unpleasant aroma of an unwashed body

*Furrin/furrinas*—foreign/foreigners

### G

*Gallery*—any area in the sitting room that gives a window view

*Gangga-egg*—rotten egg

*Gangga-sackie*—gecko

*Gas lamp*—Tilly lamp fuelled by kerosene

*Glamacherry*—berry that produces a sticky substance

*Goadee*—Hydrocele/Elephantiasis/swollen testicles

*Goat bite yuh*—spoilt/imperfect/have bad luck
*Good afta-noon*—good afternoon
*Good clothes*—dressy/your Sunday best
*Good marnin'*—good morning
*Good plates*—china crockery
*Gramuddah*—grandmother
*Granfaddah*—grandfather
*Grease a palm*—slyly passing money as a bribe
*Grip*—suitcase
*Groun' provision*—a referral to vegetable grown in the ground/ vegetables in general/tubers
*Groun's*—grounds/stale coffee sediment
*Guh*—go
*Gyaff/gyaffin'*—conversing
*Gyal*—girl in East Indian language
*Gyard*—guard
*Gyurl*—girl

## H

*Hairy worms*—caterpillars covered in harmful hairy substance
*Half-slip*—petticoat worn on waist
*Hard-pants*—denim jeans
*Head-tie*—a colourful head scarf
*Hi-fa-lootin*—people held in high esteem
*Hobble*—a pencil skirt
*Hungish*—greedy

## I

*Ice-apple*—apple
*Ice-watah*—water with ice

## J

*Jalousie*—a slatted window that is propped open with a stick

*Jargetung*—Georgetown
*Jell-O*—jelly
*Jheera*—cumin
*Jimmy jar*—container made from earthenware
*Jook*—to stab/poke/stick someone or an object
*Jumbie umbrella*—mushroom
*Jumbie*—evil spirit
*Jump-up*—dance/party
*Jutah*—germs from sharing food/drink

## K

*Kangalang*—hooligan/rascal/ruffian
*Kass-kass*—dishevelled/untidy in dress and appearance
*Kerry*—to carry
*Ketch breeze*—to keep cool
*Ketcha*—a game/ children chasing and catching each other
*Ketchin' swank*—showing off/flaunting yourself in public
*Ketchin'*—contagious
*Kinna*—scornful/an aversion
*Kiss-meh-ass*—no good/person/place/expletive
*Klim*—a brand of powdered milk
*Koka*—a sluice
*Konkee*—a sweet made with pumpkin corneal, coconut and raisins (wrapped in banana leaves and steamed)
*Konx*—a rap with a knuckle
*Kounce*—feces/defecate
*Ku-nu mu-nu*—a person who is not very discerning/taken advantage of

## L

*Laang handle broom*—broom with a long handle
*Laang-boots*—wellingtons/rubber /gum boots
*Lallin' off*—lolling/relaxing
*Landin'*—porch/platform/jetty/mooring for boats
*Lantin-post*—lantern/lamp post for street lighting

*Lap-cloth*—rags/cloth napkin used during menstrual cycle

*Lash out*—splurge

*Lawliss*—lawless/ person who is vulgar in their actions

*Le'go*—let go

*Leckcha*—lecture

*Lef-lef*—leftovers

*Lick dung*—knocked down

*Licks*—flogging

*Likka*—liquor

*Likkle*—little

*Limin'/lime*—hanging out with friends/ to socialise

*Linsey*—haircut with a fringe

*Littie*—a game played with stones instead of the little spikes (jacks)

*Logee*—a hut with a thatched roof

*Lolee/Lo-lo*—penis

*Loose-up*—unpick/take apart an object

*Loss away*—fainting

*Loss baby*—miscarriage

*Lynin'coal (lying-in cold)*—lying in bed for a period of nine days after giving birth

*Lysin*—license


## M


*Maan*—man

*Mac-may*—the mother of a person's godmother

*Mad-house*—asylum/chaos

*Magga*—meagre/thin

*Mannish*—a boy getting acting like an adult

*Marabunta*—a species of wasp

*Mash-mout'*—mouth caved in from lack of teeth

*Mash-up*—smash/destroy

*Matty*—friends in common/fellowmen

*Mauby*—local beverage made from a bitter bark

*Max*—brand of chewing gum (any other brand of gum was called Max)

*Maxkaraid*—masquerade
*Meche-meche*—residue of small food particles/odds and ends
*Metagee/Mettem*—vegetable dish cooked in coconut milk
*Modess*—brand of sanitary pads
*Mole-up*—to congregate/get together in a group/sitting down to relax
*Mook*—a silly/simple person
*Mota-bike*—motorcycle
*Muddah*—mother
*Muff*—a bouffant hair quiff for men
*MUM*—brand of deodorant

## N

*Naabah*—neighbour
*Nancy story*—fairytales
*Nara*—stomach ache
*Nennen*—godmother . . . used by the Portuguese
*Nenwa*—gourd . . . husk used for exfoliation
*Neva-see cum-fuh-see*—a person not accustomed to anything nice/
   expensive
*News carrier*—a person who carries gossip
*Nibee*—a local fiber used to make furniture and other household
   items
*Nutt'in'*—nothing

## O

*Obeah*—evil doings/Voodoo
*Oilskin*—plastic with an oiled appearance/waterproof
*Old year's night*—New Year's Eve
*Operation*—undergo surgery/diarrhoea
*Ow meh goi*—an echo of pity/sympathy for someone
*Own-way*—stubborn/determined

# P

*Packoo*—stupid/silly/dummy

*Pac-pac*—homemade/generic brand fruit wine

*Palin'*—wooden staves on a fence

*Palm a hand*—a bribe

*Pampazet*—to show off

*Passage*—paying a fare for transportation

*Pat-a-cake*—vagina

*Patty*—small meat pie

*Peau de soir*—type of satin fabric

*Pepperpot*—dish made with cassareep, meat and hot peppers

*Phaglee*—an insipid personality/undesirable character

*Piass*—putting on airs/showing off

*Pick meh*—pecked by a bird

*Pickcha*—photograph/movie

*Picked-up*—recovered

*Pickin' fares*—prostitution

*Pickney/picknies*—child/children

*Picky-picky*—tufts/little clumps/bits

*Pigin (pigeon) peas*—a variety of peas

*Pimpla*—thorns

*Pine*—pineapple

*Pip*—a poultry ailment

*Pit*—the cheapest and lowest seats in the cinema

*Plantin pap*—porridge made from plantains

*Plate-cloth*—dish cloth/tea towel

*Pointa (pointer) broom*—broom made with the spines from coconut frond

*Pokey*—vagina (very rude)

*Pork-knocker*—a person prospecting for minerals/a miner

*Posy/Poe*—chamber pot

*Powder Puff*—vagina

*Preggy bicycle*—bicycle with a rounded frame

*Prouge*—probed

*Pssssssst*—a call to attract females

*Pumpin'*—masturbating
*Punny/Pum-Pum*—vagina
*Punt Trench*—name of the canal where the punts travelled
*Pupil teacher*—trainee teacher
*Push teet'*—protruding teeth
*Push/drop-cyart*—small delivery cart operated manually
*Putagee*—slang for people of Portuguese descent
*Putta-putta*—mud/sludge
*Put-up*—store away
*Puzzlin' tin*—money boxes/piggy banks

## Q

*Quake*—basket with a small opening at the top/good for storing crabs

## R

*Raise*—an offer of money/asking for money
*Ranga-tangs*—unruly hooligans
*Rant*—mild version of the expletive 'rass'
*Rass*—expletive for backside/used as a profanity
*Reach*—to arrive at a destination
*Red-skin*—a person of mixed race with a light complexion
*Rice-eaters*—mongrel dogs
*Ropey*—extremely wrinkled
*Rough-dry clothes*—unpressed clothing
*Roun'-de-worl'*—haircut for boys . . . using a calabash
*Ruckshun*—quick tempered/ready to fight
*Rum-shop*—a drinking establishment/liquor parlour
*Rum-suckas*—friends who took advantage of their drinking buddies
*Run-dung*—feeling weak/to chase/hit by a vehicle/degrade

## S

*Saga-bhai*—a playboy personality

*Sakiwinki*—a species of monkey [belonging to squirrel monkey family]

*Salfish (salt-fish)*—salted cod

*Salipenta*—Salipenter lizard

*Salsoap*—used for laundry purposes

*Salt-goods*—salted food (pig-tails/beef/fish etc)

*Santapee*—centipede

*Scheupsin'*—sucking your teeth

*Schupidee*—not very smart/stupid

*Schupidness*—folly/foolishness

*Schupid*—stupid

*Scotch tape*—any adhesive tape

*Scraven*—extremely greedy/glutton person

*Scrawly*—puny/unkempt/undesirable/insignificant

*Seh*—say

*Sen-seh fowl*—a breed of chicken

*Shake-up*—convulse

*Shame*—local parlance for 'embarrassed' or 'ashamed'

*Shave-ice*—snow cone

*Short-time-place*—a house of ill repute

*Siddung*—sit down

*Sigrit*—cigarette

*Skin yuh teet'*—snickering/laughing

*Skunt*—expletive that can offend or humour the recipient

*Sliders*—boxer shorts/underwear

*Sling-shot*—a catapult

*Small bhai*—little boy

*Small fry*—a nobody/insignificant

*Snap-glass*—a glass that measures a single serving of alcohol

*Soft grease*—hot candle wax used for medicinal purposes

*Soorin'*—romantic overtures/close embraces

*Soti*—penis

*Sour*—chutney made with green mangoes or *souree* (bilimbi/kamaranga fruit)

*Souse*—pickled pig face

*Speed*—personal preference

*Spunga/spungin'*—someone who is a parasite/never contributes

*Standpipe*—a concrete trough with a tap/ used for washing and bathing

*Star-bhai*—star-boy/film star

*Star-gyurl*—star-girl/film star

*Stellin'*—a jetty

*Stickle*—hovering

*Stings/no stings*—agreeing or refusing to share a treat at school

*Stinkin'-toe*—loquat . . . named thus because of its foul odour.

*Stone crushers*—shoes with wide heels

*Strayin'*—going out without parents permission/gad about

*Strimps*—shrimp

*Sub-party*—monetary contribution

*Sugah bag*—burlap

*Sugah-bowl-cova*—panties/underwear

*Suh*—so

*Su moo tu* similar to a kiwi fruit

*Surra an' Durra*—a devoted couple

*Surwa*—gravy/liquid remains from a meal

*Swank*—local beverage made with fresh lime juice

*Sweet/ salt biscuit*—sugared/savoury crackers

*Sweet-bhai*—Romeo type personality

*Sweet-drink*—soft drinks such as carbonated beverages

*Sweetie*—candy/confectionery

*Sweet-maan*—lover

*Sweet-mout'*—tasty treats/words of endearment/flattery

*Sweet-soap*—soap used for toiletry

*Sweet*—tasty but not necessarily sweet/tipsy

*Sweet-woman*—mistress/lover

*Swellin'*—a wake or swell

*Swizzle stick*—a wooden implement used to puree/whisk


T


*T'eatah-'ouse*—theatre/cinema

*T'ick*—women/girls with a curvaceous body

*T'ief maan*—thief/burglar
*T'in-t'in*—very thin
*T'ree fuh D*—three yards of fabric sold for one dollar
*Tacklin'*—making overtures/courting
*Talk white*—speaking perfect English
*Tambrin*—tamarind
*Tanked-up*—inebriated/under the influence of liquor
*Tasso*—meat cured in the sun
*Tawa*—a flat baking grid
*Taw*—steel marbles/ball bearings can substitute
*Tea-cha*—teacher
*Tekkin' leff*—being left out
*Tek*—take
*Tengaleh*—the large tentacle on a crab
*Tennis roll*—small sweet bun
*Tentis*—Masonite/ply wood
*Tikka/Bindi*—red dot on forehead to ward off evil spirits
*Tizzick*—grief/annoyance
*Toops/tooks*—a snap-glass/ tot of liquor
*Tow*—giving someone a lift on your bicycle/motorbike
*Trampin'*—gyrating to the rhythm of Steel Band music in a street
    procession
*Truh-truh*—very true
*Truss*—credit/trust/bunch of fruit borne on a palm tree
*Typee*—passionate love

## V

*Vimto*—tart cherry flavoured soft drink
*Voomps*—to ignore/total lack of interest

## W

*W'at/wha'*—what
*Waabin*—a prostitute/loose woman
*Waalk wid/wit*—carried

*Wait*—move

*Wan-wan (One-one) time*—very seldom/now and again

*Wures*—crockery/dishes

*Warishee*—type of backpack used by Amerindians (supported by a band worn on their forehead)

*Waterside*—the edge of the river

*Weh*—where

*White people*—foreigners/European/fair skinned

*White-eye*—a sweet bun

*Wil'-cane*—bamboo cane used for corporal punishment in schools

*Wrowin'*—quarrelling

*Wutliss*—worthless

*Wynin'*—gyrating

## X

*XM*—a popular brand of rum

## Y

*Yaatin' boots*—yachting/canvas shoes

*Yawkin'*—catching fish in a confined space with your bare hands

*Yaws*—sores

*Yowarie*—small rodent/opossum

*Yu'al*—you all

# CREOLE SAYINGS

*A batchie*—bachelor

*A beatah*—short wooden bat used to beat the clothes when washing

*A constant bicycle*—bicycle with gears

*A curar*—spiritual cleansing ceremony to exorcise evil spirits

*A cut-ass*—a severe beating

*A dress lenk*—a dress length/three yards of fabric

*A flattie*—a pocket size bottle of rum

*A freck*—small amount of money/a pittance

*A good ketch*—a good prospect for marriage

*A good turn out*—good attendance at a funeral or function

*A grant*—an area of land (likened to a suburb)

*A jarrah*—spiritual cleansing ceremony to exorcise evil spirits

*A jil*—a penny

*A landin'*—a mooring for boats

*A lick an' a promise*—to execute a job inefficiently/hurried

*A luv-up*—hugs and kisses/show of affection

*A nail jook*—penetration by nail

*A pavement lot*—a measured allotment in a market

*A preggy bicycle*—bicycle with a rounded frame

*A safe*—a cabinet with meshed doors used for storing foodstuff

*A small piece*—small amount of cash

*A'gon buss yuh ass*—to threaten someone with a beating

*A'playin' white*—pretence at being a foreigner

*A'poun' a'beef*—one pound of meat

*A'see it wid meh own two eye*—witnessing for yourself

*A'wash meh 'an's of dat*—end of a situation/subject

*Bade yuh skin*—bathe/washing yourself

*Beatin' clothes*—using a wooden bat to do the washing

*Buck-up clothes*—soaping and rolling dirty laundry prior to laundering

*Cut-meh-eye*—turning a blind eye to a situation

*Cyat eat meh dinnah*—ran out of luck

*Doan 'ave two cents to rub together*—not very well off financially

*Doan pick yuh teet*—do not utter a word

*Eat till we belly buss*—eat to our heart's content

*Every molee biscuit got 'e vhum-vhum cheese*—there is someone for everyone

*Flyin' de flag*—menstruating

*Get on meh nerves*—irritated

*Gi' sh'/' e blow*—cheating on a spouse/lover

*Gon-up-in-de-worl'*—achieved success/risen above a situation

*Good fuh nutt'in'*—no good/worthless/a loser

*Got yuh wuk cut out*—have a big task ahead of you

*It set up*—rain clouds are forming

*Ketch case*—fell out/a disagreement

*Laff till we belly buss*—laugh until our stomach ache

*Me an' sh'/' e eye mek four*—to make eye contact

*Money in de hairy bank*—paying a prostitute/entertaining loose women

*Monkey waalkin' 'pon iron*—walking in a clumsy fashion

*Out-ah-dis-worl'*—grand/unbelievable

*Runnin' dung sumone*—gossip that degrades a person's good name

*Shittin' in 'igh grass*—circulate/mix with high society

*Shut 'e eye*—close his eye

*Skinnin' meh/yuh teet'*—smile/grin/snicker/laugh

*Smellin' mehself*—feeling of power/strength

*Stay back a class*—repeat the class

*Stay white*—remain fair skin

*Stick-de-cake*—cutting wedding/birthday cake

*Suckin' yuh teet'*—sucking air through your teeth.

*Swell up like crappo*—sulking/vex/showing your disapproval

*T'row 'way baby*—abortion

*Talkin' sumone's name*—to gossip about another person behind their back

***Tek-in-sick***—a sudden illness

***The GUYS***—Guyana United Youth Society

***To bad-talk someone***—speaking ill of another person

***To be 'rang and strang (wrong and strong)***—no reason needed to fight

***To be left 'igh an' dry***—stranded/abandoned

***To clap eyes on sumone***—laying eyes on someone

***To do chip-chip on a bicycle***—moving the bicycle along with one foot on the peddle while pushing with the other foot on the road

***To get a good cut-ass***—a severe beating

***To give sumone a dressin' dung***—to scold/reprimand

***To give sumone a'spung-dung***—administering a bed bath

***To grease sumone's palm***—money secretly passed as a bribe

***To have a finny 'an'/leg***—a person with a withered limb

***To ketch meh-self***—regain consciousness after fainting

***To ketch swank***—to attract attention/be noticed

***To let de cat out of de b***ag—exposing a secret

***To palm someone's hand***—to offer someone a bribe

***To poun' (pound) name***—gossip focused on a certain person

***To press hair***—straightening and styling the hair of Negro women

***To pull out***—to depart/leave

***To reach weh yuh goin'***—arriving at a destination

***To tek in sumone***—adopt/offer a place in your home

***To tek passage***—paying a fare on a vehicle

***To tow sumone***—giving someone a lift on your bicycle /motorbike

***To waalk wid/wit' sumt'in'***—to carry with you

***To wash yuh face an' 'an's***—washing face and hands to freshen up

***Up-de-duff***—pregnant

***Up-in-de-worl'***—achieved success

***W'en fowl-cock get teet'***—never

***Walk wid yuh mout'***—spreading gossip/carry news

***Wash deh mout' on yuh***—someone saying ill things against you

***Wash yuh 'ead***—shampoo your hair

***Washed 'e tail***—a severe beating

***Wukkin' obeah***—putting a voodoo spell on someone

***Yuh 'ard ears***—disobedient/not listening or paying attention

# AH REMEMBA

Ah rememba flyin' kites on de Seawall
Ah rememba w'en Granfaddah fryken meh wid the crappo
Ah rememba de smell of garlic pork on C'ristmus marnin'
Ah rememba buyin' sugah-cake from de lady on de street korna
Ah rememba drinkin' swank w'en it was hot
Ah rememba gettin' konx on meh head w'en ah was rude
Ah rememba drinkin' castor oil, cascara an' senna
Ah rememba gettin' a conc from Brown Betty
Ah rememba playin' on de punt trench
Ah rememba gettin' a good cut-ass fuh suckin' meh teet'
Ah rememba buyin' shave-ice wid syrup
Ah rememba usin' a slate an' slate pencil
Ah rememba meh muddah pickin' de lice from meh 'ead
Ah rememba meh muddah puttin' hot soft grease in a nail jook
Ah rememba meh brothers playin' bat an' ball on de road
Ah rememba lookin' out de front window in de gallery
Ah rememba drinkin' watah coconut an' cane juice
Ah rememba gettin' one present fuh C'ristmus
Ah rememba wearin' yaatin' boots w'en meh good shoes got wet
Ah rememba dancin' till marnin' on Ol' Year's night
Ah rememba drinkin' peanut punch at Ferage
Ah rememba laughin' at Kato an' de anti-men
Ah rememba swimmin' wid meh friends at Luckhoo pool
Ah rememba eatin' Labba an' Bush Hog
Ah rememba gettin' a pimpla in meh foot
Ah rememba fowl-cock crowin' at fo'day marnin'
Ah rememba de tea-chas beatin' me wid de wil'-cane

Ah rememba eatin' black cake at C'ristmus
Ah rememba eatin' green plantin an' salfish
Ah rememba Towa-towa birds whistling in cages
Ah rememba buyin' a jil bread wid salt butter at Dictator bakery
Ah rememba eatin' mangoes till meh belly buss
Ah rememba eatin' awarra, dunks, jamoon, sour-sop an' genip
Ah rememba Muddah Sally an' de Santapee band at C'ristmus
Ah rememba paddlin' in de corial in d'Riva
Ah rememba de boys doing Cuffum in the punt trench
Ah rememba eatin' tambrin and green mango till meh teet' edge
Ah rememba meh muddah tellin' meh about Ol' Higue an' Jumbie
Ah rememba buyin' de best Dhal Puri at Shantas'
Ah rememba jailbird cussin' meh from Camp Street prison
Ah rememba buyin' medicine from Mr Green drugstore
Ah rememba bawlin'w'en ah leff meh beautiful Guyana

Printed in Australia
AUOC010749050112
251126AU00001B/3/P

9 781452 503097